Troubadour's Song

Troubadour's Song

The Capture, Imprisonment and Ransom of Richard the Lionheart

DAVID BOYLE

Walker & Company
New York

First published in the United States of America in 2005 by
Walker Publishing Company, Inc. Originally published in
Great Britain in 2005 by Penguin.

For information about permission to reproduce selections from
this book, write to Permissions, Walker & Company,
104 Fifth Avenue, New York, New York 10011.

Library of Congress Cataloging-in-Publication Data is
available from the Library of Congress

ISBN 0-8027-1459-5
ISBN-13 978-0-8027-1459-6

Visit Walker & Company's Web site at www.walkerbooks.com

Printed in the United States of America

2 4 6 8 10 9 7 5 3 1

For Robin
born 15 July 2004

Contents

List of Illustrations

Section One

1. Three generations of English kings: (*clockwise from top left*) Henry II, Richard I, Henry III and John.
2. A French troubadour or possibly a jongleur.
3. Lancelot and Guinevere kiss for the first time.
4. Minstrels below the table.
5. A crusader knight.
6. The coronation of Richard I.
7. The king and his entourage set off on crusade.
8. Richard's neglected queen, Berengaria of Navarre.
9. Philip Augustus, Richard's former passionate friend.
10. Philip shocks the English by leaving Palestine before the end of the crusade.
11. *Richard I the Lionheart and Hugues III de Bourgogne claiming victory over Sultan Saladin and his army at the Battle of Arsuf, 14 September 1191.*
12. The engraver Gustave Doré's view of Richard's dramatic assault from the sea at Jaffa.
13. Richard's arrest in a kitchen outside Vienna.
14. Arrested in disguise by two soldiers, Richard kneels before the clean-shaven emperor.

Section Two

15. The scene of Blondel's song: Dürnstein and its castle as it was in 1650.
16. Ornate gloves played a key role in Richard's arrest.
17. *The Pedlar* by Charles Alston Collins, 1850.

Illustration Acknowledgements

1 British Library, London. MS Cotton Claudius D. VI, fol. 9v. Photograph AKG-images, London; 2 Bibliothèque Nationale, MS Fr 854, fol. 230; 3 Pierpont Morgan Library, New York/Art Resource; 4 British Library, London/The Art Archive; 5 British Library, London. MS Roy 2A XXII, fol. 220; 6 Chetham's Library, Manchester. Photograph Bridgeman Art Library; 7 Bibliothèque Nationale, Paris, MS NAL 1390, fol. 57v; 8 Giraudon Picture

Agency, Paris; 9 Conway Library, London; 10 British Library, London. MS Royal 16 G VI, fol. 350v. Photograph AKG-images, London; 11 Musée du Château de Versailles. Photograph © RMN/Gerard Blot; 12 Private Collection. Photograph Bridgeman Art Library/Ken Welsh; 13 Austrian National Library, Vienna; 14 Burgherbibliothek, Bern. Cod. 120 II, fol, 129r. Photograph AKG-images, London; 15 from *Dürnstein*, Edition Gottfried Rennhofer, Korneuburg, Austria; 16 Kunsthistorisches Museum, Vienna; 17 Manchester City Art Gallery; 18 Museum in Schotten-stift, Vienna; 19 British Library, London. Miscellaneous Chronicle, MS Cotton Vit. A XIII, fol. 5. Photograph AKG-images, London; 20 Archiv für Kunst und Geschichte; 21 From John Gillingham, *Richard 1* (Yale, 1999); 22 Bibliothèque Nationale, Paris. Nouv. Acq. Fr. 1050, fol. 77v; 23 British Museum, London. MS Royal 14C VIII; 24 Archivo Iconografico, SA/Corbis; 25 Photograph Museum of London/HIP; 26 Photograph by Stefan Drechsel/ AKG-images, London; 27 From Charles Knight, *Old England: A Museum of Popular Antiquities*, Vol. 1, c. 1860; 28 Photograph Amelot/AKG-images, London; 29 Illustration by Helen Stratton from Agnes Grozier Herbertson, *Heroic Legends* (London, 1911); 30 Nottingham City Museums and Galleries (Nottingham Castle). Photograph Bridgeman Art Library.

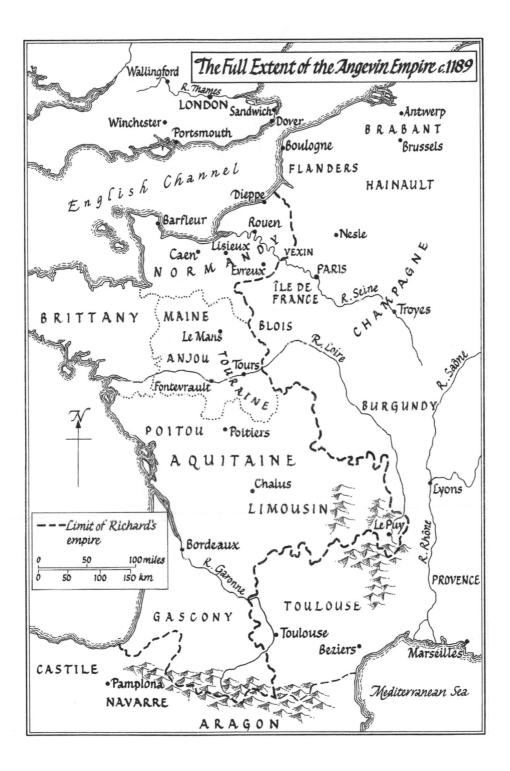

The Full Extent of the Angevin Empire c.1189

Wallingford
R. Thames
LONDON
Winchester
Sandwich
Dover
Portsmouth
Boulogne
Antwerp
BRABANT
Brussels
FLANDERS
HAINAULT

English Channel

Dieppe
Barfleur
Rouen
Lisieux
Nesle
Caen
N O R M A N D Y
VEXIN
Evreux
PARIS
ÎLE DE
FRANCE
R. Seine
CHAMPAGNE
Troyes

B R I T T A N Y
MAINE
BLOIS
Le Mans
R. Loire
ANJOU
TOURAINE
Tours
BURGUNDY
Fontevrault
R. Saône
POITOU
Poitiers
A Q U I T A I N E
Chalus
Lyons
LIMOUSIN
Le Puy
R. Rhône

Limit of Richard's
empire
0   50   100 miles
0   50   100   150 km
Bordeaux
R. Garonne
PROVENCE
TOULOUSE
GASCONY
Toulouse
Beziers
Marseilles
CASTILE
Pamplona
Mediterranean Sea
NAVARRE
A R A G O N

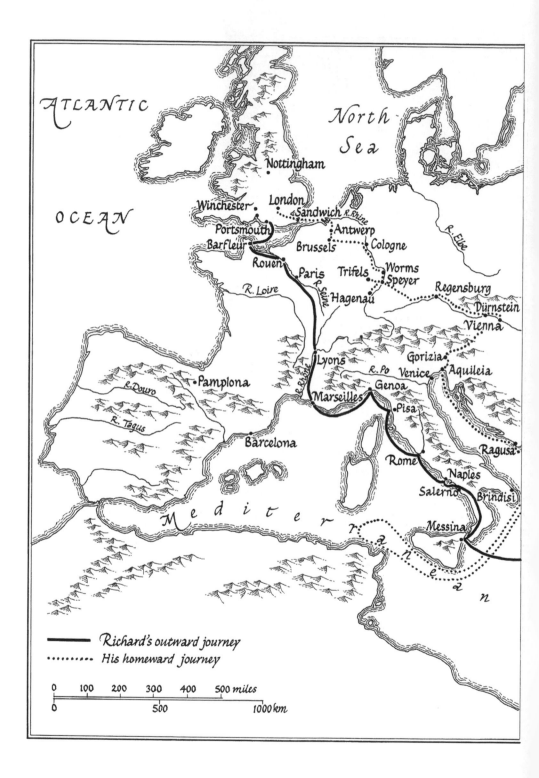

ATLANTIC

North
Sea

OCEAN

Nottingham

Winchester • London
Sandwich R. Rhine
Portsmouth Antwerp
Barfleur Brussels Cologne
Rouen Worms
Paris Trifels Speyer
R. Loire R. Seine Hagenau Regensburg
Dürnstein
Vienna

Lyons Gorizia
R. Po Venice Aquileia
Pamplona Genoa
R. Douro Marseilles Pisa
R. Tagus
Barcelona Ragusa
Rome
Naples
Salerno Brindisi
Mediterr Messina
a
n
e
a
n

———— Richard's outward journey
·········· His homeward journey

0   100   200   300   400   500 miles
0   500   1000 km

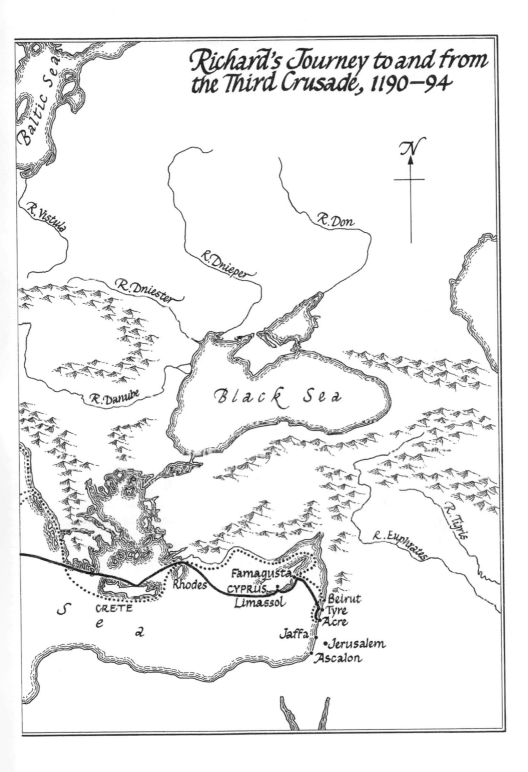

Richard's Journey to and from the Third Crusade, 1190–94

N

Baltic Sea

R. Vistula

R. Don

R. Dnieper

R. Dniester

R. Danube

Black Sea

R. Tigris

R. Euphrates

S e a

CRETE

Rhodes

Famagusta
CYPRUS
Limassol

Beirut
Tyre
Acre

Jaffa

Jerusalem
Ascalon

Dürnstein

Vienna

R. Danube

0 10 20 30 40 50 miles
0   50   100 km

AUSTRIA

Bruck
an der Mur

Judenburg   Knittelfeld

R. Mur

STYRIA

The Alps

Friesach

R. Mur

CARINTHIA

Villach

HUNGARY

Julian Alps

Pontebba
Pass

N

Udine

Via Julia
Augusta   Gorizia

Aquileia

Tagliamento

Adriatic Sea

Richard's Journey in Disguise
December 1192

Dramatis Personae

I have opted for anglicized versions of names in most cases.

Richard the Lionheart, King of England
  (1189–99), Duke of Normandy and
  Aquitaine, etc.

Eleanor, Duchess of Aquitaine Henry II, King of England (1154–89), Duke of Normandy, Count of Anjou, etc.	*his parents*
Berengaria of Navarre	*his wife*
Henry the Young King Geoffrey, Count of Brittany John 'Lackland'	*his legitimate brothers*
Geoffrey, Archbishop of York William Longspee, Earl of Salisbury	*his illegitimate brothers*
Marie of Champagne Alix of Blois Matilda of Saxony Eleanor of Castile Joanna of Sicily	*his sisters and half-sisters*
Henry the Liberal, Count of Champagne Henry the Lion, Duke of Saxony and Bavaria	*his brothers-in-law*

Henry of Champagne, crusader son of Henry the Liberal	*his nephews*
Henry of Brunswick, son of Henry the Lion	
Otto of Brunswick, younger son of Henry the Lion	
William of Winchester, Henry and Otto's younger brother	
Hubert Walter, Bishop of Salisbury	*his friends*
Robert, Earl of Leicester	
William de l'Étang	
Baldwin of Béthune	
Philip of Poitou	
Hugh, Bishop of Lincoln	*his self-appointed confessor*
Mercadier	*his mercenary captain*
Stephen and Robert de Turnham	*his admirals*
Savaric de Bohun, Bishop of Bath	*his helpers in Germany*
William de St Mary Église	
the abbots of Boxley and Robertsbridge	
Raymond V, Count of Toulouse	*his enemies*
Raymond of Saint-Gilles, later Raymond VI of Toulouse	
Walter of Coutances, Archbishop of Rouen	*his most reliable supporters*
William the Marshal, Earl of Pembroke	
William Longchamp, Bishop of Ely, chancellor of England	
Hugh de Puiset, Bishop of Durham	
John of Alençon, Archdeacon of Lisieux	
William Fitzhugh, Seneschal of Rouen	

Matthew of Clare, Castellan of Dover Richard, Bishop of London William, Earl of Arundel Hamelin, Earl Warenne	*Longchamp's party in* *England*
Hugh of Nonant, Bishop of Coventry Robert Brito Reginald, Bishop of Bath	*John's party in* *England*

Musicians and Writers

Blondel de Nesle Conon de Béthune Gace Brulé Chrétien de Troyes Chastelain de Coucy	*trouvères*
Bernart de Ventadorn Bertran de Bron Raimon de Miraval Giraut de Bornelh Raimon Vidal	*troubadours*
Reinmar of Hagenau Walther von Vogelweide	*minnesingers*
Andreas Capellanus Marie de France Wauchier de Denain	*romantic writers*

France

Philip Augustus, king of France (1180–1223)

Isabella of Hainault Ingeborg of Denmark Agnes of Méran	*his wives*

Margaret, briefly married to Henry the
    Young King   *his sisters*
Alys, betrothed to Richard

Palestine and the Mediterranean

Baldwin IV, king of Jerusalem (1161–85)

Baldwin V, king of Jerusalem (1185–6)   *his young nephew*

Sibylla and Isabella of Jerusalem   *their heirs*

Guy of Lusignan   *rivals for the throne*
Conrad of Montferrat

Tancred of Lecce, king of Sicily   *usurpers*
Isaac Comnenus, king of Cyprus

Baldwin, Archbishop of Canterbury   *other crusader leaders*
Leopold V of Babenberg, Duke of Austria   *outside Acre*
Philip, Count of Flanders
Hugh, Duke of Burgundy
Philip, Bishop of Beauvais

Saladin   *their opponents*
al-Adil, Saladin's brother

The Holy Roman Empire

Frederick I Barbarossa, Holy Roman
    Emperor (1152–90)

Henry of Hohenstaufen, later Emperor   *his sons*
    Henry VI
Frederick of Swabia
Philip of Swabia

Meinhard II and Engelbert III, joint
   counts of Gorz
Roger of Argentan
Frederick III of Pettau
Hadmar II von Kuenring

*Richard's pursuers
and captors*

Conrad of Wittelsbach, Archbishop
   of Mainz
Adolf de Altena, archbishop-elect of
   Cologne
Henry, Duke of Limburg
Henry, Duke of Brabant
Dietrich, Count of Holland

*Richard's supporters
in Germany*

Rome

Alexander III (1159–81)
Lucius III (1181–5)
Urban III (1185–7)
Gregory VIII (1187)
Clement III (1187–91)
Celestine III (1191–8)
Innocent III (1198–1216)

Popes

The Royal House of Jerusalem

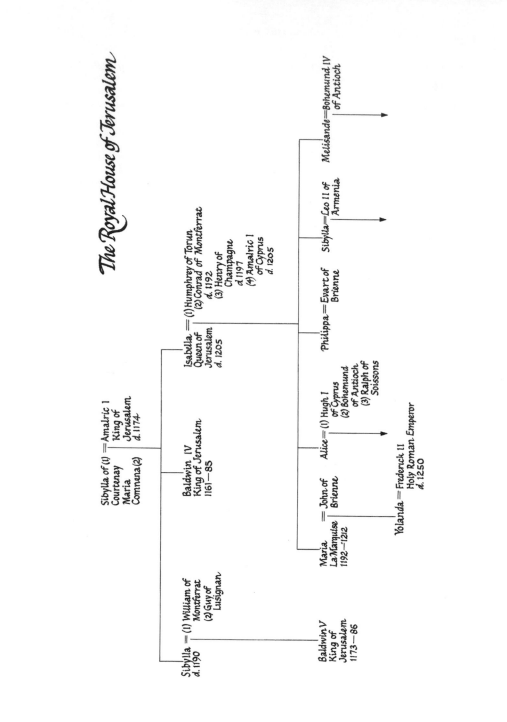

Relatives of Eleanor of Aquitaine
by Her First Marriage to Louis VII of France

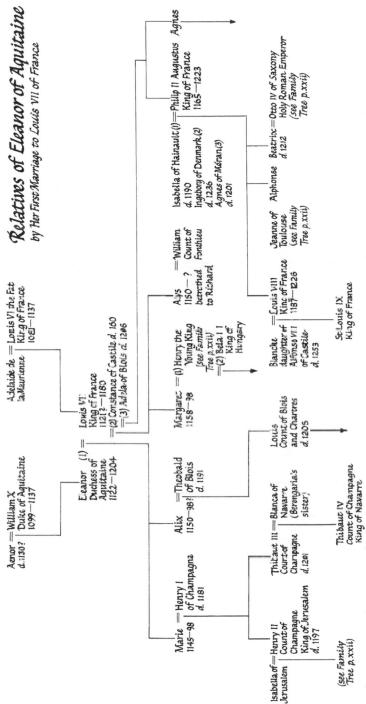

Relatives of Eleanor of Aquitaine
by Her Second Marriage to Henry III of England

Aenor = William X Duke of Aquitaine. 1099—1137

Matilda, daughter of Henry II of England and widow of the Emperor Henry V = Geoffrey Plantagenet Count of Anjou 1113—51

Eleanor = (2) Henry II King of England and Duke of Normandy 1122—1204 / 1133—89

(Illegitimate)

Geoffrey Archbishop of York. c.1159—1212 = Ela Devereux

William Longspee Earl of Salisbury c.1160—1226

John 1166—1216 King of England = Hawise of (1) Gloucester d. 1217 / Isabella of (2) Angoulême d. 1246

Joanna = (1) William of Sicily d. 1189 / (2) Raymond VI of Toulouse d. 1222 1165—99

Eleanor = Alfonso VIII of Castile 1161—1214

Constance = Geoffrey Duke of Brittany 1158—86 d. 1201

Berengaria = Richard I King of England of Navarre 1157—99 d. 1230

(Illegitimate)
Philip of Cognac d. 1221

Matilda = Henry the Lion of Saxony and Bavaria. 1156—89 d. 1195

Henry the Young King 1155—83 = Margaret, daughter of Louis VII of France (See Family Tree p. xxi)

William, Count of Poitiers 1153—6

Isabella = Emperor Frederick II d. 1241 / d. 1250

Eleanor d. 1275 = (1) William, Earl of Pembroke (son of William the Marshal) d. 1231 / (2) Simon de Montfort Earl of Leicester d. 1265

Richard = Isabella (2) Earl of Cornwall d. 1271 / daughter of William the Marshall

Henry III King of England 1207—72

Edward I King of England

Raymond VII Count of Toulouse d. 1249

Jeanne = Alphonse (son of Philip II) (see Family Tree p. xxi) d. 1271

Blanche = Lewis VIII King of France 1183—1253

(see Family Tree p. xxi)

Arthur Count of Brittany 1186—1203

Helena of = William, of Denmark Winchester d. 1213

Otto IV Emperor d. 1218 = Beatrice, (1) daughter of Philip II of France (see Family Tree p. xxi) / Mary of (2) Brabant

Agnes of = Henry, Count Hohenstaufen Palatine d. 1227

William, b. and d. 1177

Acknowledgements

Three encounters shaped the process of writing this book for me. The first was clambering up, on what seemed the hottest day of my life, to the ruins of Dürnstein Castle in Austria – the traditional spot for the legend of Blondel's song – and gazing down on the sloping vineyards and the Danube snaking along below. The second was sitting in candlelight during the atmospheric annual Advent service in Salisbury Cathedral, next to the tomb of William Longspee, the last of Richard the Lionheart's brothers to die, and imagining the scene of his funeral. And the third was in Vienna, while I was researching the book. I told one very helpful historian that I was writing about Richard's imprisonment. 'Ah!' he said. 'You are writing a children's book?' It was confirmation of what I had begun to suspect, that for some reason – and probably the legend of Blondel as much as anything else – the story of Richard's bizarre journey in disguise, his disappearance and his imprisonment has been relegated by serious historians to children's books and romantic novels. It made me all the more determined to write about it.

There is another reason for their reticence, of course. Although there is considerable evidence about Richard's ransom and home-coming, the chronicles give only the sketchiest details about his journey and arrest, and what evidence there is tends to be contra-dictary. But in the course of my research, I have found that, by retracing the critical parts of the journey, and sifting the local traditions that do not actually contradict each other, it is possible to build a convincing picture of what took place. It may not be definitive throughout and parts of it may not be absolutely certain – though little is certain in medieval history – but you have only to stand on the castle walls at Gorizia in Italy in winter and stare at the icy mountain wall that seems to block any progress to the east to have an overwhelming sense of which way Richard and his companions fled.

   This book is an attempt to weave together that sort of geographical evidence with local traditions from the route that Richard travelled in 1192 and information from the reliable chronicles – some of them based on eyewitness accounts – that we do possess. It is intended as a popular history, so I have tried not to interrupt the story too much with detailed argument about which legend or chronicle to believe, though some of the sources I have used are outlined in the notes at the back of the book. Throughout the process of researching the story, I have also found myself returning over and over again to the work of three medieval historians in particular. One is John Gillingham, whose dedication to the details of the life and world of King Richard has done so much to dust down his reputation, both as a king and as a military strategist. The second is Christopher Page, whose scholarship has managed to fill in so many gaps in the story of the development of twelfth-century music. The other is my godfather, Peter Spufford, whose pioneering work on medieval money – and in *Power and Profit* on the history of trade in Europe – has done so much to reveal the hidden forces behind historical change.

   So many other people have helped me along the way that they are too numerous to list. But I am particularly grateful to Dr Mark Philpott of the Centre for Medieval and Renaissance Studies at Keble College, Oxford, who read the whole book at a late stage, and whose detailed comments and incisive critique have made it so much better than it would otherwise have been. The remaining mistakes are where I failed to take his advice.

   I also want to mention and thank my father, who read most of the text and whose invaluable comments helped me enormously; my mother for all her encouragement and advice; Sandra Stokes, who read every chapter as it was written; Carol Cornish for all her help over the years, and for her support when I was first researching the story of Blondel; and all my other friends and relatives, who have been forced to talk to me at length about the Middle Ages. Other people I am enormously grateful to include my sister Louisa

Crispe for all her help, advice, translation and for making my trips to Paris and Picardy so much fun; Dennis Blandford for his effortless translation of Latin sources and for other invaluable pointers and book loans; Silvia Longo for all her help with the Italian sources and for her wisdom and good sense; Marion Genévray for her patience and enormous help with some of the French sources; G. Linker for his help translating German; Dr Reinhard Pohanka of Wien Museum for his time and generous advice at a busy time; Martin Mosser for all his help with the German and Austrian sources, and especially for his fascinating help with the early history of Erdberg; Esther Jakubowicz for all her help, support and companionship in Vienna; Bernard Lietaer for his invaluable insights into money and currencies; Linda Marini for her help at a weak moment in Gorizia; Pierre Le Roy for his time and unique expertise about the history of Nesle; Karen Ralls for all her advice about Templars; Jerry Blondel for his help about the Blondel family; and John Dillon from Wisconsin University for his help about the fate of Excalibur. I would not have been able to manage without them, though I am the only one responsible for the mistakes. I would also like to thank Claire Clam Martinic for her hospitality in an extraordinary Danube castle. Also the staff at the Warburg Institute and the British Library, both of them wonderful British institutions where resources are smoothly and efficiently put at the disposal of ordinary people like me. Also, mainly for being there, Crow on the Hill Bookshop and Renaissance Books in Crystal Palace.

My editor at Penguin, Eleo Gordon, has been so supportive and generous with her time from the start, and I could not have done this without her experience and her infinite patience. Nor could I have managed without my agent, Julian Alexander, and his assistant, Lucinda Cook, who believed in me and the project from the start, and to whom I owe a very great deal.

Last but not least, thank you from the bottom of my heart to my wife, Sarah, for putting up with the interminable medieval talk over the past two years, for coming with me to Vienna and on so many other shorter trips, for her advice and encouragement and much else besides.

There was one other more obscure reason I had for wanting to write this book. Many years ago, and just forty-eight hours before the unexpected death of Pope Paul VI, I was arrested as a disreputable-looking student in Rome, having hitchhiked along the route that Richard originally used to leave England on crusade. I was incarcerated in the former Gestapo prison called – as only Italians would dare call such a place – 'Queen of Heaven', and I was told I would probably be there for two years. I had been in the wrong place at the wrong time, as the notorious Roman police swooped on two female tourists, and they did not appreciate the fact that my friends and I had witnessed their behaviour. In fact I was imprisoned for only three days: the death of a pope triggers major prisoner releases. But three days locked in a cell for twenty-three hours a day with nine homosexual Egyptian pickpockets – and believing I would be there for years – was, on the whole, a formative experience. Before I finally took the train out of Rome, I spent those days leaning against the bars of my cell door, peering into the great well of the prison and whistling my school song as loudly as I could. This was not something I had ever expected to do, but I hoped that my friend from the same educational establishment, who had been arrested along with me, was somewhere in the same building. The clatter of prison life made it impossible to shout, because I would never have been heard, but I thought a whistle might just get through. When I heard the familiar tune echoed back to me, with a rush of relief quite out of proportion to the event, I promised myself that one day I would write about Blondel.

Prologue: The Legend of Blondel

'And when the first verse was finished, a voice within the tower took up the second, and sang it quaintly. And it was the voice of Richard.'

Agnes Grozier Herbertson, 'Richard and Blondel', in
Heroic Legends, 1911

The story of Blondel's song is one that everybody seems to know. In many different versions, and with a range of interpretations and subtle meanings, it tells how the faithful minstrel made his way through Germany and Austria in search of the missing King, Richard the Lionheart, singing hopefully under each castle wall. It culminates when, one quiet night under a tower, Blondel's song is taken up and echoed by a familiar voice inside.

The legend has seeped into our collective consciousness, even though it has been dismissed as serious history for more than a century. Maybe it is the story's whiff of romance, or its ideal version of faithful friendship, or its sheer mythic power, but somewhere deep inside, many of us can feel the cold, damp night air as Blondel fingers his lute and tentatively sings the verses he and the king had written together. There is a familiar echo, we sense, about the story, just as Blondel hears the unmistakable echo of his own verse wafting down and realizes that he has found the imprisoned king of England behind the great stone walls.

Some stories are like that. They have an element of universality about them that means they are repeated generation after generation, and a haunting quality that can't be pinned down by separating the elements and analysing what remains. You can find the story of Blondel in its classic version in dusty Victorian histories of England and Edwardian adventure tales for boys, but a century on the legend has been allowed to fade a little. The strange story of the arrest of one of the most celebrated kings of medieval England has been relegated by historians to the nursery, while modern publishers feel that the homosexual undertones – which their forebears seem not to have noticed but now appear obvious – make it unsuitable for children. So Blondel seems destined to join Cinderella, Snow White and Little Red Riding Hood in the realm of fairy tale, but without their mainstream appeal.

This book takes another look at one of the most romantic stories in the English tradition and makes a plea for its rehabilitation as serious history – not as it stands perhaps, but as a distant memory of the truth behind a bizarre, half-forgotten event in the Middle Ages. Because, unlike Snow White, both Richard and Blondel really existed and the events that provide the backdrop to this story really happened. On his return from the Holy Land, and just before Christmas 1192, Richard I – the king of England and joint leader of the Third Crusade – was arrested and flung into prison. He was threatened with death by his captor and effectively disappeared. He did not get home for nearly sixteen months, and not before his subjects had been forced to pay an unprecedented ransom.

Richard I – known to history as Richard Coeur de Lion – remains one of the most recognizable figures in English history, famous partly for his military prowess and partly for his failure to spend more than nine months of his reign in his own kingdom. He is the only king to have his statue outside the Houses of Parliament in London. As well as England's ruler, Richard was also Duke of Normandy, Duke of Aquitaine and Count of Anjou and Poitou, and he ruled over an empire that stretched from the Scottish border to the Pyrenees. His parents were Henry II, one of the most successful administrators ever to sit on the English throne, and Eleanor of Aquitaine, one of the most celebrated women of the age.

As for Blondel, though he remains shadowy and elusive, he was real too. The evidence for this can be found inside a beautiful classical building hidden away in the rue de Sully in Paris. The Bibliothèque de l'Arsenal is more like a gentleman's club than a library, though it is officially part of the Bibliothèque Nationale. Even so, having filled in the numerous forms that provide you with a day reader's pass, a short stay in its wood-panelled interior, with its long tables, numbered seats and leather-bound books from floor to ceiling, is enough to give you access to the microfilm which contains their manuscript No. 5198.

This is all that members of the public are allowed to see of an extraordinary thirteenth-century document, running to nearly 200 pages, with spidery nineteenth-century notes and index at the beginning. With its beautifully decorated initial letters and its immaculate black script and medieval music with square notes, this is one of the earliest song books in Western Europe. It contains more than a century of love songs by names who have passed into the history of poetry as the greatest troubadours of them all, and especially those who came from northern France and wrote in Old French – the so-called *trouvères*.

The Victorian editor has provided page numbers, and if you wind the microfilm reader on to page 88, you will find the following words written in red: 'Here ends the songs of the Chastelain de Couci and here begins the songs of Blondel de Nesle.' In other words, the mysterious minstrel who is supposed to have sung under Richard's tower was not completely legendary. He really existed, and he was a *trouvère* famous enough to have his words and music recorded a century after the events described in the legend are supposed to have taken place.

There are sixteen other manuscripts in existence in European cities like the one in the Bibliothèque de l'Arsenal. They can be found in the British Library in London, the Bodleian Library in Oxford and the Vatican Library in Rome; there are no fewer than nine elsewhere in the Bibliothèque Nationale in Paris, as well as others in Siena, Berne, Leiden and Modena. In total these manuscripts attribute thirty-four songs to Blondel, twenty-seven of which are believed by most modern scholars to have been correctly attributed. They are almost exclusively about love – passionate, hopeless love too – and there is some evidence that they were well known. Two generations later, a poet from Reims called Eustaches li Peintres mentioned someone called Bloundiaus in a list of great lovers alongside the Chastelain de Coucy – one of the most famous of the *trouvères* – and Tristan himself. It seems likely that the songs which have been so beautifully recorded in manuscript No. 5198 were sung widely in the Middle Ages.

The manuscripts spell the name of the man history knows as Blondel in a number of different ways: sometimes he is Blondiaux, sometimes Blondiels; sometimes he is Blondeaus or even Blondelz; sometimes he is just Blond. The place he is said to be from is sometimes Nesle, but just as often Neele or Noyelle. It seems clear, though, that this is not just the same person but the same person the legend refers to. In other words, while it may now be impossible to be absolutely sure who he was, and while the evidence for his origins and work may be contradictory and fragmentary, Blondel was real.

His story, as far as we know it, together with the bizarre tale of Richard's arrest, discovery, ransom and return, and the real meaning of the legend of the minstrel under the tower, is the subject of this book.

1. The Courts of Love

'To leap up on errands, to go through heat or cold, at the bidding of
one's lady, or even of any lady, would seem but honourable and
natural to a gentleman of the 13th or even of the 17th century, and
most of us have gone shopping in the 20th with ladies who showed no
sign of regarding the tradition as a dead letter.'

C. S. Lewis, *The Allegory of Love,* 1936

Were the whole world mine
From the Elbe to the Rhine,
I'd hardly value it at all
If only England's queen
Would lie my arms between.

Carmina Burana,
twelfth century German verse

A small plaque next to a slightly unkempt Georgian back garden
opposite Worcester College, Oxford, marks the site of Beaumont
Palace, birthplace of one of England's most celebrated and para-
doxical kings. There has been no trace of the massive wood and
stone structure since it crumbled away as a workhouse in the 1830s,
though in its heyday it was known for the beautiful murals of its
great hall. But on 8 September 1157 the private quarters of the
queen would have echoed with the cries of a new royal arrival –
a son to King Henry II and his glamorous, strong-minded consort,
Eleanor of Aquitaine. The new prince would be known in his
own lifetime as Richard the Lionhearted. He was second in line
to inherit his parents' joint empire, including not just England and

Normandy but duchies and other ancient fiefdoms stretching right down to the Spanish peninsula.

Richard was born almost a century after the Norman Conquest of England swept aside the Anglo-Saxon nobility. This had imposed a new layer of French-speaking aristocrats and institutions, enforced by a network of stone castles and intricate feudal relationships. This feudal combination of homage and tradition linked the new lords and ecclesiastical princes with the whole, overwhelmingly rural, social system. Richard was destined to spend little of his life in England, but a similar – though more informal and ambiguous – network of lords and vassals covered much of continental Europe too, so that everywhere he went the yeomen, serfs or *villeins* in every village, the shadowy inhabitants of the forests that covered so much of the countryside, and the monks and nuns in the religious orders were connected in chains of mutual responsibility all the way to the king.

The Norman invasion itself, ninety-one years before Richard's birth, was over the horizon of living memory, but not so long ago as to be irrelevant. The new prince was born in that period of English history when the divisions between Norman and Saxon were becoming more complicated than simply those between invader and vanquished. It was too early for each side to speak the other's language, but not too early for the first signs of a combined English language to begin to emerge. It had been a difficult few generations for the English. There may have been some in Beaumont Palace who remembered the death of the Conqueror's son William Rufus in a hunting accident in 1100. But many must have remembered all too well the hardships, chaos and descent into anarchy in the civil war that followed the death of Rufus's younger brother, Henry I, when 'it was openly said that Christ and his saints slept'. It was during those years that Richard's grandmother Matilda had stayed less comfortably in Oxford, escaping in 1141 from the castle there in the snow – the famous flight in which she was said to have worn her shoes backwards to disguise the direction in which she was heading.

But a new world was emerging too. When Richard was born,

his future opponent Saladin was a nineteen-year-old in service to the Syrian ruler Nur ed-Din. The Pope, Adrian IV, was from St Albans – the only Englishman ever to have achieved that position. The future archbishop and martyr Thomas Becket was the first chancellor of Saxon descent since the Conquest, and was filling the role with sumptuous hospitality and sartorial extravagance. On a visit he made to Paris when Richard was a few months old to negotiate marriages between the English and French royal houses, he took no fewer than twenty-four changes of magnificent clothes, plus a travelling chapel, twelve horses carrying table plate, plus hounds, falcons and a long-tailed monkey perched on the back of each horse. A new age of light and luxury was recognizably dawning. But the most obvious change was in architecture: the gloomy churches with their heavy stone arches and round Romanesque windows were giving way to soaring, pointed Gothic arches and magnificent windows that let in a flood of light to the new cathedrals and abbeys of the Continent.

Richard was born between these two worlds, perched at the beginning of a new era of learning, extravagance and light, as it must have seemed at the time. His wet nurse had a son born on the same day who became the great scholar Alexander Neckham. This ambiguity, in neither the old world nor the new, applies to almost every aspect of Richard's life and reputation – caught not just between darkness and light but between his mother's world and his father's.

His mother, Eleanor, was Duchess of Aquitaine in her own right and one of the most extraordinary women of the age. She had previously been married to Louis VII of France, a man given to disturbingly pious gestures: he had a habit of kissing lepers at moments of religious fervour.★ She contrived to have the marriage dissolved and – to the horror of the French – married the younger but highly eligible Henry of Anjou, heir to the Angevin empire,

---

★ 'I thought to have married a king,' Eleanor is supposed to have said about her first husband, 'but found I am wed to a monk.'

which controlled Normandy and most of western and southern France, and also a claimant to the throne of England.

Richard was their third son, and though the first, William, died as a baby, there was a prophecy of Merlin's – popularly supposed to apply to the Angevin dynasty – which said that 'the eagle shall rejoice in her third nesting'. Richard was certainly Eleanor's favourite. Her documents always described him as her 'very dear son', while her youngest son, John – his father's favourite – only managed a 'dear son' at best. Richard's parents had a stormy, bitter relationship, which ended in separation. This meant that he was to be brought up as a teenager in the colourful and cultured court of Poitiers, the very heart of the overlapping world of troubadour culture and courtly love.

We can only imagine the peculiar divisions that pulled him between the chivalric world of his mother and the brisk, administrative world of his father. Richard inherited both his temper and his generosity from his father. He was Henry's son in his military prowess, not just in feats of arms but in his strategic thinking too. He understood his father's world of devastated castles, of sore legs from being constantly in the saddle and of clerks working through the night as they agonized over the wording of the latest laws. Unlike his older brothers but again like his father, Richard was never interested in tournaments; he was fascinated by the noise, screams and excitement of real warfare. He proved his generalship while still a teenager in the bitter struggles to bring the uncontrollable vassals of Aquitaine to heel. But he was his mother's son in his love of show and his sophistication – she insisted that no men appear before her with uncombed hair – as well as his sense of humour, his poetry and his songs. Eleanor's palace had belonged to Duke William IX, her grandfather and the first troubadour, and it was decked out with tiled floors, silk hangings, glazed windows, linen tablecloths, sweet-scented rushes and carpets from the Orient, and Richard never lost that fascination for finery. He failed to master English, but he told Latin jokes, and wrote in both French and the language of southern France, Provençal or – as it is now known – Occitan. He also had a lifelong habit of impulsive chivalric gestures. Above all, he was Eleanor's boy in his love of music: as king, Richard would stand alongside the choir at the royal chapel, urging them with his hands to sing louder.

Perhaps he also inherited his sense of humour from his father, who was known to chuckle a great deal. Richard 'turned everything into a joke, and made his listeners laugh uncontrollably,' said the Yorkshire monk and chronicler William of Newburgh, and this was not written as approval. Richard's most famous joke was at the expense of the preacher Fulk of Neuilly, who accused him of having three evil daughters: pride, avarice and sensuality. Very well, said Richard, pointing neatly to the known weaknesses of the different arms of the Church, 'I give my pride to the Templars, my avarice to the Cistercians, and my sensuality to the Benedictines.' Neither the joke nor the sense of humour endeared him to the ecclesiastics who made up the majority of chroniclers at the time. Most were divided about him, as historians have been ever since. 'He was bad to all, worse to his friends, and worst of all to himself,' wrote one. 'Why do we need to expend labour extolling such a man?' wrote another. 'He needs no superfluous commendation. He was superior to all others.' Even a French chronicle the following century described him as 'the greatest of all Christian kings'.

It is hard now to pick a way through such a mass of contradictions. Richard could be cruel and arrogant, yet he twice suffered some kind of mental breakdown characterized by extreme self-loathing. He could and did cut a swathe through any battlefield, using his favourite mace with his long reach, scything down the opposition,★ yet he was actually slightly overweight, frequently sick and suffered from a continual shaking in his hands from some kind of malarial fever that nothing seemed to control. 'While thus almost continually trembling,' wrote the chronicler Giraldus Cambrensis (Gerald of Wales), 'he remained intrepid in his determination to make the whole world tremble before him.'

★ The mace was also the weapon favoured by bishops, because it allowed you to slaughter an enemy in battle without necessarily shedding his blood.

His great rival Philip Augustus of France – the longed-for 'Dieu-Donné' (given by God) of Louis VII – was born almost eight years later, to Louis' third wife, Adela of Blois. Giraldus Cambrensis, who was studying in Paris at the time, was awoken in the summer night when all the bells began to ring and he could see the flickering light of flames from bonfires. Poking his head out of his bedroom window, he was told, 'By the grace of God, there is born to us this night a king who shall be a hammer to the king of the English.' And he was. The uneasy relationship between the kings of England and France, dividing between them most of the provinces we now know as France, dominated Richard's life from his earliest years. It was complicated by the fact that the fathers of both Richard and Philip had, at one time or another, been married to Richard's mother. And as if that wasn't enough, there were the enormous problems faced by Henry when it came to providing for and occupying the time of his four surviving sons, Henry, Richard, Geoffrey and John.

What could occupy the young aristocratic men of Europe was one of the critical questions of the age. It worried the great thinkers like St Bernard of Clairvaux, gaunt and domineering – a leading figure in the Cistercian monastic order – and it clearly worried Richard's father. Henry tried alternating and equally disastrous strategies, but since he and Eleanor seemed to have bred the archetypal dysfunctional family – the so-called 'Devil's Brood' – it made it easier for Louis and then Philip Augustus to exploit the divisions between them.

At first Henry's solution was to provide his elder three surviving sons with land. That meant crowning Henry the 'Young King' as his heir, and watching with frustration as he seemed to fritter his life away with William the Marshal (later regent of England), storming the tournaments of Europe and demanding more responsibility from his father. Geoffrey was given Brittany to rule and Richard his mother's inheritance of Aquitaine. The problem of land for the youngest brother, the red-haired John, was never satisfactorily solved – hence his lifelong nickname, Lackland – and would prove just as disastrous as giving land to the others. Henry also planned to cement the uneasy relationship with France by marrying Louis' daughter Margaret to Henry the Young King and betrothing her sister Alys to Richard – the arrangement negotiated by Becket in Paris in 1158. Alys, who was then just a child, was sent to live in the English royal household, where she was duly seduced by Richard's father, and grew up to become a nagging source of irritation between the two kingdoms.

Aquitaine was considered ungovernable, but Richard learned to govern it at an early age, sometimes with the utmost brutality. When, in 1179, the rebellious Geoffrey de Rançon took refuge in fortified Taillebourg – believed to be impregnable – the 21-year-old Richard captured the castle in nine days. Nobody had even dared attack it before.

The old feudal tradition of owing your lord forty days a year in military service was no good to Richard. He needed a standing army to control a place like Aquitaine and so used the money his vassals paid in lieu of military service to employ a band of mercenaries. Through them, he learned the art of war. There was little actual fighting – pitched battles were so unpredictable they were avoided if at all possible – but Richard's life outside the court was an almost constant round of laying siege, plundering towns and destroying crops in the villages of his disobedient vassal lords. His life was then day after day of flashing steel and waving pennants, with smoke and flames billowing from some poor innocent farm, while cattle and horses were seized by the mercenaries. Although the system of peasant farming from one side of Europe to the other was stable and secure, it is hard to exaggerate the misery of getting in the way of princes and their warlords. 'When two nobles quarrel, the poor man's thatch goes up in flames,' went a contemporary saying.

It would have been a familiar experience for Richard: the mercenary camps with their whores and looted chalices, the villages left as smoking ruins, the burning crops and the raped women, their children left dead by the road, mouths stuffed with grass in a desperate attempt to find something to eat after the destruction of the crops. Richard's reputation as a hero has constantly to be balanced against this aggression, as well as his egotism, his delight in his own appearance and his friendship with wholly unredeemable warlords, like his loyal mercenary commander Mercadier. His dark and cruel side emerged with ferocity as Aquitaine rose in rebellion in the 1170s. In his own desperate and divided state of mind – his mother had just been imprisoned by his father – he ravaged the countryside of the rebels, putting out eyes and cutting off hands.

That was one side of Richard's life in adolescence, but it was only one. Because the Aquitaine court at Poitiers under Eleanor was not just where troubadours congregated, nor simply where chivalry became more than just a romantic dream. It was the centre of a multi-faceted movement that dominated the century and put women and the feminine spirit back at the heart of politics, culture and religion.

Europe at this time was still a continent of forests, monasteries and villages, where the social structure was rigidly tied to the seasons and to the duties owed by serfs on the lord's land or in military service. It was a period when coinage was still scarce and most payments were tied to these complex feudal traditions, and made in time or crops or service – with strange pre-modern measurements of acceptability. Peasants had the right to take home as much hay from the lord's land at the end of a day as they could carry on a scythe handle; a hen must be accepted as payment in tithes if it was healthy enough to be scared into jumping a garden fence.★

This was a Europe without meaningful unemployment, where serfs farmed about thirty acres each, but where all land and property was lent to them by their lord, who – theoretically at least – could marry them off to whomever he liked. It was a Europe teeming with wildlife and fish, where the forests belonged to royalty and were the subject of fearsome laws to protect the hunting in them. It also had a common culture of Christianity mixed with pagan

★ Similar rules included one that prevented millers from letting water rise so high behind a dam that a bee standing on top could not drink without wetting its wings.

superstition. There were about 13,000 monks in England alone, increasingly unpopular among the laity for their failure to keep to their own principles. It was a continent where travel was dangerous and unusual for anyone who was not wealthy, relying on the endlessly patched road infrastructure laid down a millennium before by the Romans, but also where the ruling classes could still travel freely and communicate in universal Latin.

This broad culture, with the beginnings of an explosion of trade, had ushered in a new kind of civilization, because Richard had also been born at a rare moment of some tolerance and humanism that seemed to challenge those rigid medieval certainties in favour of travel, pilgrimage and debate. This extraordinary combination of awakenings and innovations seven centuries after the fall of Rome – in sculpture, history, philosophy, scholarship and literature – is known as the Twelfth-century Renaissance, but it defies definition or explanation. 'Greece had the first renown in chivalry and learning,' wrote one of Blondel's fellow *trouvères*, Chrétien de Troyes. 'Then came chivalry to Rome, and the heyday of learning, which is now come to France.'

Why did some of the giants of European civilization – philosophers like John of Salisbury, churchmen like Abbot Suger (the originator of Gothic architecture) and Bernard of Clairvaux, writers like Geoffrey of Monmouth, historians like William of Malmesbury, architects like William of Sens, writers like Chrétien de Troyes – all emerge within a generation or so? Why did the trickle of wandering scholars at the beginning of the century, and the few pioneering traders, turn into a flood to the trading centres and universities by the end? Was the emergence of pilgrimages and widespread coinage the cause or the result of the slow decline of feudal power? It is impossible to know for certain, but it is clear that one of the key figures at the start of this revolution was the extraordinary theologian and teacher Peter Abelard.

Abelard was years – maybe centuries – ahead of his time. He was the inspiration for philosophies as diverse as Protestantism and existentialism. He was also enormously influential, especially to the generation who flocked to the new universities of Europe.

Small, dark-haired and sensitive, he came from Brittany, the eldest
son of a knight who gave up the chance of following in his father's
footsteps to be a scholar (as we will see, Blondel may have followed
the same route). But there was something about him that courted
controversy; he seemed quite unable to stop himself.

Abelard was a success from the moment he started teaching, in
1113, at the age of thirty-four at the monastery of Sainte-Geneviève
in Paris, one of the institutions that were merging together in
Richard's day as the University of Paris. Something about his
trenchant contempt for authority and his revolutionary approach
to theology – putting love, reason and conscience at the heart of
it, rather than the old authority and discipline – drew students
from all over Europe. They christened him the 'Indomitable
Rhinoceros'.

His classes attracted many hundreds, who squeezed into
crowded rooms to listen to him. But as a consequence other
teachers in the city, who were paid by their students in those days,
suffered and they conspired to drive him away. This was hardly
Abelard's fault, but he was still his own worst enemy. When he
went from Paris to Laon to study under the revered Anselm of
Canterbury, Abelard was damning about his teacher. 'If anybody
came knocking at his door in perplexity about some problem, he
would go away still more perplexed,' he said. On moving instead
to the monastery of Saint-Denis near Paris, home of the fearsome
Abbot Suger, he took the opportunity to question the truth of
their story of St Denis. When he returned to Paris a few years later
– once more attracting thousands of eager students into the city –
his crowd had to be accommodated on the Left Bank of the Seine,
thanks to the Abbot of Sainte-Geneviève, and that is where the
university remains to this day.* There he fell in love, married and
had a child with the niece of a powerful member of the cathedral
chapter, the famous Héloïse, and there, as a result, some paid thugs
cornered him one evening, beat and castrated him.

---

* This part of Paris is still known as the 'Latin Quarter', because that was the
language used by the university.

Abelard was not just a controversialist. There was something about his lightness of touch, his laughing contempt for pomposity, his wit and his prodigious memory – as well as that warm interest in human beings – that thrilled the generations of students who came after him. 'For by doubting we come to inquiry, and by inquiring we perceive the truth,' he said. This was a dramatically modern statement, and light of another kind. What made Abelard's thinking so revolutionary, and so contemporary for modern audiences, was his emphasis on what we *intend* to do: our intention is more important than whether we have broken God's law unwittingly. He refuted the idea that we have a bloodless, legal relationship with God. For Abelard, what counted was inner conviction and conscience, not feudal duties to heaven. So just as the children of serfs all over Western Europe were scraping together enough brand-new silver coins to buy their way out of feudal obligations and escaping to the newly enfranchised towns, Abelard was rejecting the old feudal relationship with God and starting again as an individual. This was not the medieval God of dread and fear, but the God of love and reason.

He even called his book about ethics *Sic et Non* (*Yes and No*), as if Christians or vassals had any such choice. The key lay in the subtitle, *Know Yourself*, which became the motto for the age. Abelard's teaching was like a breath of fresh air, but it was also dangerous. If conscience was important, after all, how could you tell heresy from truth? So it was hardly surprising that there was a reaction against him and his teaching. Abelard's great contemporary Bernard of Clairvaux – the main influence behind the Second Crusade – persuaded the canons to give him permission to preach at Notre-Dame in Paris. Tall, skeletally thin, with translucent skin and a shock of white hair, Bernard was a great subduer of his own and other people's flesh, and he preached a devastating sermon. There was no mention of Abelard by name, but everyone knew to whom he was referring, just as they later knew who his phrase 'hydra of wickedness' described.

The son of a Burgundian noble, Bernard was made Abbot of Clairvaux at the early age of twenty-four. His reputation was such that he could speak directly to the most powerful princes on earth, looking them straight in the eye. His only romantic encounter with women ended when he jumped into a pool of freezing water and waited for the excitement to die down. He really had no sympathy for a man like Abelard who allowed his name to become a byword for erotic love.★ 'I would that his poisonous pages were still lying hid in bookcases, and not read at the crossroads,' he said. 'His books fly abroad . . . over cities and castles, darkness is cast instead of light . . . his books have passed from nation to nation, and from one kingdom to another people.' Bernard was horrified that the young intellectuals of Europe were flocking to Paris to breathe the free air where Abelard taught, criticizing and questioning everything. And he was appalled that, thanks to Abelard, the city was filling with students who were snobbish and superior, lording it over peasants and monks alike, breaking every taboo they could, even going so far as to dissect pigs to find out how the body worked.

Abelard came face to face with his nemesis for the last time at Whitsun 1140 in Sens Cathedral. As he walked in, prepared for the challenge of an intellectual joust with Bernard, he could see the usual crowds of students waiting, but also the professors – many of whom were still furious with him for the loss of their fee-paying pupils. Alongside them were the senior dignitaries of the Church and – in pride of place – King Louis himself. It looked disturbingly like a court of inquisition. He may also have been told, as he prepared for his dramatic entry, that Bernard had taken the precaution of getting a condemnation of Abelard in advance from Pope Innocent II.

So Abelard lost his nerve, turned on his heel and fled. His appeal to the Pope fell on deaf ears: Innocent was just then lighting the fires in Rome that would burn Abelard's books. Abelard took refuge in the monastery of Cluny and died not long afterwards.

★There is a story that an innkeeper's wife attempted to seduce Bernard by slipping into his bed at dead of night. The future saint escaped by shouting, 'Thief!'

'By his coming, he enriched us with wealth beyond all gold,' said Cluny's abbot, Peter the Venerable. Peter was steeped in the true Renaissance spirit of the age: he had, for example, just commissioned scholars in Toledo to translate the Koran into Latin.

When Bernard turned next on Abelard's ally Gilbert de la Porrée, Gilbert was better prepared, arriving at the hearing with armed scholars and monks lined up behind him. This time, Rome reprimanded Bernard, who sent Gilbert a mollifying note suggesting that they might get together to discuss some points arising from the writings of St Hilary – and in the process laid himself open to an academic gibe. If you want a full understanding of the subject, said Gilbert, I suggest you give yourself a few years' exposure to a good liberal education. For the time being, the new academics had won.

What had divided the two great intellectual giants of the generation before Richard was partly Abelard's emphasis on the importance of God-given natural urges, such as to eat or to have sex. It might not always be right to follow those urges, he said, but it would be wrong to extinguish them altogether. Bernard, on the other hand, devoted his life to extinguishing his own urges completely, and as many of those he perceived in other people as possible. They were also divided by the key social issue of the age: what should young men aspire to? This is an issue for almost every generation, but it was especially pressing now that the practice of primogeniture – leaving the father's whole estate to the eldest son – left younger sons without a role or inheritance.

In fact, many of them spent their time carousing. Henry the Young King, for example, enraged his father in 1172 by refusing to join him for Christmas and instead inviting all the knights in Normandy called William for a feast.* They could devote their lives to tournaments, like William the Marshal and his friends – a brutal but potentially lucrative business, and forbidden by the Church. They could join the new intellectuals, the youths then flocking to universities, or they could take to the road as troubadours. None

---

*As many as 110 turned up.

of these were part of Bernard's plans. He criticized the scholars for
what he called their 'shameless curiosity', and urged them to flee
from Paris to save their souls. Instead, he devoted his life to
providing solutions that could occupy the young men of Europe
in his burgeoning network of monasteries or on crusade. It was
good for their souls, as he saw it, and it kept them out of trouble.
Abelard seemed to be undermining his great work.

Yet, despite their differences, Abelard and Bernard were people
of their own unique time, symptoms and causes of the spirit of the
age. Both agreed on the importance of tolerance to Jews, though
this was a controversial issue in the Church throughout the medieval period. Christ had Jewish blood, said Bernard. Both were
committed to the new cult of the Virgin Mary, another idea that
was reinforced by crusaders drifting home via Byzantium. Both
were convinced that the core of the individual was love – the first
medieval generation to think in those terms, just as the society
around them was filtering ideas of romance down from translations
of the Roman poet Ovid. Abelard's theology was based on the
effect of the crucifixion on the conscience of individuals – 'that
we may fulfil all things more by love of him than by fear'.

Both were also convinced of the importance of nature. 'You
will find more things in forests than in books; the trees, the stones
will teach you what the masters cannot,' said Bernard. 'Do you
think that you cannot suck honey from a stone, oil from the hardest
rock? Do the mountains not distil sweetness? Are the hills not
flowing with milk and honey? There is so much I could tell you
I can hardly stop myself.'

Bernard's vision of the crusades was to win Jerusalem for Christianity, but he also saw them as a way of occupying the energies of
rich, bored young men. Yet if they survived, these young men
stumbled back from the Holy Land with dangerous ideas. Maybe
they had experienced the luxuries of Byzantium at first hand, or
heard the ideas of the pagan Greek philosophers or Roman poets,
locked away in Arab translations for a millennium and suddenly
bursting into Western Europe again. Maybe they had been exposed
to Arab numerals – even the revolutionary symbol zero – which

were slowly filtering into Western Europe and would eventually allow merchants to throw away their abacuses, undertake complex business exchanges and carry out calculations on paper for all to see. Maybe they returned with their eyes opened to new ideas about love and women.

We should not try to interpret these ideas in a modern light. Women were not demanding rights or anything like them, and yet somehow the intractably male, brutal, heroic façade of European civilization was beginning to crack. This was a culture that had been based entirely on tales of warriors off to war, from Beowulf to Roland, and a religion based entirely on judgement, fatherhood and masculinity. But thanks partly to ideas from the East, and from Abelard, there was a softer spirit abroad. St Bernard had championed the cult of the Virgin; most of the delicate new Gothic cathedrals were dedicated to her in an age when – just a generation before – the only woman in the religious firmament had been Eve, complete with apple and serpent.

There were also the published love letters from Héloïse to Abelard, revealing a whole new female sexual and romantic power:

God knows that I never wanted anything from you, but you yourself; desiring, not what was yours, but you alone. I did not look for the bonds of marriage nor any dowry, nor did I even consider my wishes or desires, but I endeavoured to satisfy yours, as you well know . . . I call God to witness that if Augustus, the governor of the whole world, offered me the honour of marriage and granted me the entire earth to be mine for ever, I would esteem it dearer and more noble to be called your prostitute than his empress.

There were other new ideas emerging, such as the heresy based on purity known as Catharism, which was now taking hold across the south of France and regarded men and women as equal. There was even the heretical idea, borrowed from the Gnostics almost a thousand years before, that Jesus' women disciples were closer to him than the men; that it had been the women who found him first after the resurrection, only to be relegated later by the Church.

This was the root of secretive cults, not just of the Virgin Mary, but of the reformed prostitute Mary Magdalene. It was also the generation when the mysterious black madonnas began appearing in churches all over Western Europe, venerated as having special power, and it has been suggested that they were somehow linked to the Magdalene cult.

There are connections here between the feminine roots of Catharism, courtly love and the culture of the troubadours and *trouvères*, though these are now impossible to unravel (the black madonnas were known, and probably not by coincidence, as '*dames la trouver*'). But we do know that, at the heart of all these shifting ideas and moods about the female spirit, was Eleanor of Aquitaine and Poitiers, where Richard was growing up.

Something happened between Eleanor and her second husband in 1167, when Richard was ten, that was to make itself felt across Europe. It is more than eight centuries ago now, so we will never know exactly what lay behind it, but it may well have had something to do with Henry's mistress Rosamund Clifford. Rosamund was almost certainly the daughter of Walter de Clifford, who lived in Bredelais on the border between England and Wales and who joined Henry on his campaign there in 1165. Henry used to infuriate his entourage by his failure to keep to his plans and his habit of making unscheduled stops, and one of these was probably at the Clifford castle.

Rosamund was little more than a girl then, but beautiful and compliant enough to inspire an affair with the king that would last until her death a decade later in Godstow Priory, outside Oxford. 'Fair Rosamund', as she came to be called, provided potent material for poets and chroniclers in later centuries, including tales of a secret maze in Henry's park in Woodstock and the murderous machinations of a jealous wife.* Eleanor was then forty-five, and it may have been that her formidable self-belief and awareness of

---

* Woodstock in those days included a royal zoo with lions. Later, when he was king, Richard would keep a crocodile there.

her own charms had begun to unravel a little in the face of such a youthful rival. It is hard to believe that Eleanor reacted only to the infidelity. There had been other mistresses, and she had known all about infidelity in her own extraordinary past. Maybe there was just something about Rosamund.

At Christmas 1167, at the royal palace in Argentan in Normandy, Eleanor told her husband that she wanted to go home to Aquitaine, which was then on the brink of revolt over Henry's harsh rule. To avoid open scandal, Henry escorted her to Poitiers himself, together with her entourage of sixty aristocratic women. By the following Christmas, which she spent in what had been her troubadour grandfather's palace – together with Richard and her younger children – it was clear that she was not intending to return. The next six and a half years with his mother in Poitiers were enormously influential for Richard. Aquitaine was where his heart remained, and it was to secure the southern borders of Aquitaine that he eventually – nearly a quarter of a century later – married Berengaria of Navarre. At the age of fourteen, he was installed as Duke of Aquitaine in ceremonies in Poitiers and Limoges, wearing a silk tunic and gold coronet, and invested with the ring of Limoges' patron saint, St Valerie.

As soon as her escort had disappeared back to Normandy, at New Year 1168, Eleanor set about touring her all but ungovernable provinces, banishing Henry's mercenaries, who had kept down the revolt, and trying to disentangle some of the laws that had been passed there by her two husbands. And among the yellow-stone aqueducts and Roman amphitheatres she created something extraordinary that has had historians and critics arguing ever since. Eleanor was about to capture a movement and style that would give the troubadours, including Blondel and his northern colleagues, a narrative and a spirit for their songs in the generations to come.

Aquitaine and the small fiefdoms that made up what is now the south of France were always a source of disapproval for puritanical northerners, even without Eleanor. A contemporary guidebook for English pilgrims on the road to Santiago de Compostela despairs of the locals increasingly as it moves south. The author considers

Aquitaine elegant and generous, but warns that Gascons never use tables and share the same rotting straw as their servants. By the time he has reached the Basque country, he is describing locals who make noises like dogs, lift their kilts in front of the fire and are so keen on sex with animals that mares and mules have to be given chastity belts. Everyone knew that the women of Aquitaine painted their cheeks, lined their eyes with charcoal and wore exotic perfumes from the East. Worse, Aquitaine refused to punish women for adultery. It was a very shocking place. Eleanor was also a dramatically romantic personality, perhaps even the model for Queen Guinevere in the contemporary Arthurian romances that were pouring from the pens of her daughter's protégé Chrétien de Troyes and her sister-in-law Marie de France. In a period when women of all classes were sold by their overlords in marriage to the highest bidder, sometimes over and over again, Eleanor was the blueprint for a powerful, independent kind of woman.

She could not conjure Camelot out of the air, but she had turned her back on a second husband she considered boorish and brutal, and she seems to have been determined to create a different vision of the relationship between men and women. It was to be a creation of splendour, pomp, music and poetry that would capti- vate Europe and create a tradition that retains a mythic awe about it even today. The music and poetry came from the troubadours, and they in their turn were often expressing the emotions of what was then known in Occitan as *fin' amor*.

Nobody really knows where the ideas behind *fin' amor* came from – the term 'courtly love' was coined only in 1883 – but it turned traditional medieval values on their head. One source was the Roman poet Ovid, rediscovered as part of the revival of the classics that emerged as part of the Twelfth-century Renaissance. Another source may have been Arabic poetry brought home by returning crusaders or filtering up from Arab Spain. But wherever it came from, *fin' amor* was profoundly influential on the ruling classes. Women became the powerful object of love and longing, love not battle became the heart of romance, and the resulting ritual of seduction between the sexes was suddenly valued for its ability to refine and purify the seducer – so that 'for joy of her a sick man can be cured, and from her anger a healthy one may die'. The result was a complex game whereby young knights could woo aristocratic married women, whose role was to educate and refine their lovers by their distance and superiority. It was a whole new kind of literature, not exactly feminist but certainly a tribute to feminine power. It was also anti-monastic, anti-feudal, anti-Roman and anti all those ancient myths about Charlemagne and the Holy Roman Empire on which the kings of France based their authority. But songs of love were clearly not enough for Eleanor once she was mistress of her own duchy again. She wanted a cultural revolution.

The south of France was already a more equal place. Many small towns had local laws that forced men to get permission from their wives before they sold goods or property. Women and girls would also fight against the invaders alongside the men in the coming horrors of the Albigensian Crusade a generation ahead. But courtly love institutionalized this feminization as part of the European culture of chivalry. The new way of romance was rooted in two institutions, neither of which is absolutely secure as historical fact. One was a book called *The Art of Courtly Love*, written by Andreas Capellanus (Andrew the Chaplain), who was probably chaplain to Eleanor's daughter Marie of Champagne, who may even have commissioned him to write it. The other was the so-called Courts of Love, which Eleanor and her powerful women allies organized in Poitiers and other centres of the new movement, and which Andreas described in his book.

Courtly love as set out by Andreas was definitely naughty:

For when a man sees some woman fit for love and shaped according to his taste, he begins at once to lust after her in his heart. The more he thinks about her, the more he burns with love, until he comes to a fuller meditation. Presently he begins to think about the fashioning of the woman and to differentiate her limbs, to think about what she does, and to pry into the secrets of her body, and he desires to put each part of it to the fullest use.

It was also outrageously snobbish. Not only were men incapable of love after the age of sixty, wrote Andreas, but so were peasants – who were quite content to have sex 'naturally, like a horse or mule', and must not be taught about love in case they left their farms. If you happened to fall in love with a peasant women, you were allowed to use force, he wrote. It was an outrageous piece of advice, and taken very literally by Richard and his colleagues. Courtly love like this was also a challenge to the Church – a kind of parody of religion. 'The heart leaps when the beloved unexpectedly appears,' wrote Andreas, when once it had been supposed to be the soul leaping at the sight of the body and blood of Christ.

The famous Courts of Love were held in Poitiers, with aristocratic ladies sitting as judges on a dais deciding the questions of love brought to them by suitors, and presided over by Eleanor with Marie of Champagne, her niece Isabella, Countess of Flanders, and her sister-in-law Emma of Anjou, as well as Ermengarde, Countess of Narbonne.* Their rulings were set out in Capellanus's book as 'The Thirty-one Rules of Love', and woven through them all was the idea – which contradicted everything feudal society held dear – that love had to be mutual and freely given. It recognized that women might be sold into loveless marriages, but implied strongly that this need not be the end of passion for them. One of Ermengarde's rulings was about whether a woman had to forsake her love just because she got married. 'The fact that a new marital union has been entered into does not rightly exclude her former lover unless perchance the woman should altogether cease being devoted to her lover,' she decided. Infidelity wasn't necessarily infidelity, in other words. The key ruling was from Marie of Champagne, delivered by letter in 1174 – the only one with a date: that love cannot exist between husband and wife. Andreas did not accept this: he added also – as you would expect from a chaplain – that 'marriage is no barrier to love'.

Taken together, courtly love was as much a set of ideals about

*Ermengarde ruled her ancient city in her own right, even leading her own siege – of the city of Baux in 1162.

how to behave for women as it was for men. Andreas included a little story about a knight searching for his horse as three groups of ladies passed by. The first was beautifully dressed, each attended by a lover on foot. The second had such a clamour of competing suitors that you just wanted to escape from the cacophony. The third rode bareback, clothed in rags, unattended, covered with dust from those that went before. The first ladies loved wisely, explained Andreas. The second gave kindness to everyone that asked – always a mistake. The third group of ladies may have been beautiful, but they had also been deaf to the pleadings of every potential lover.

For Eleanor, love was not uncontrollable or indefinable. She was no romantic in the modern sense: she understood the realities of the world all too well. But like the *trouvères* around Blondel – whose lyrics were almost obsessively respectful to women, despite living in an age when rape and ransom were commonplace – she could imagine something different, beyond the whims of powerful men. It was as if she turned her back on her husband, took herself home to the place where she ruled in her own right – her favourite son at her side – and set about building a culture that would stand as a bulwark against everything she had come to despise.

Modern literary critics are hard on courtly love. The Marxists say that love was just a metaphor for money. The structuralists say that it was just a ritual, a game that rich young men played with each other to rise up the social hierarchy by making love to the wives of lords. Many modern critics say that *The Art of Courtly Love* was simply a parody, and that the Courts of Love were no more than a twelfth-century equivalent of satire. It is true there is little evidence outside the book that the courts were real, and even if they were, these peculiar events were in themselves a kind of satire – a playful comment on what was most important in the world. It is difficult to guess what really lay behind the phenomenon now, especially when we see everything as ironic in this postmodern era. But something was going on, and even if he was writing a parody, Andreas Capellanus must have had something out there to lampoon. If the troubadours and *trouvères* – in their various different incarnations – had just been clever, ironic social climbers, we can be pretty sure that at some point life would have begun to imitate art: we know that the troubadour Raimon de Miraval's wife took the whole game so literally that he threw her out.

Even Eleanor may well have been playing a sophisticated game, knowing all too well the limits of her new reality. The evidence is that Occitan culture rejoiced in aristocratic parlour games in which women submitted their love songs, or had them sung for them, to the judgement of an aristocratic woman, and Eleanor's Courts of Love may be an extension of these. These are controversial ideas now, as they were then. But I am inclined to believe that Eleanor of Aquitaine really held events of some kind – games as much as anything judicial – that could be caricatured as Courts of Love, not because she thought she could really turn the world upside down, but because she enjoyed it. But in doing so, she helped to mould the spirit of Blondel's generation that was just growing up.

'Fair Aiglentine, undo your dress, for I wish to look on your fair body underneath,' says a character in Jean Renart's *Roman de la Rose* early in the next century, suspicious that her daughter might be pregnant.

'I shall not do it, mother, for the cold can be fatal.'

That is the voice of the era – sensual, naughty and a little shocking. What came out of the south of France, and spread rapidly to the north, had that same sensual and disturbing spirit. It was a worry for the Church, a source of disapproval for puritans like Philip Augustus, but the troubadour spirit was also a creative powerhouse for Europe. This is the *tribairitz* (woman troubadour) the Comtessa de Dia: 'I would very much like to hold my knight some evening, naked between my arms . . . my lover, generous and kind, may I hold you in my power and sleep with you one night, and give you a loving kiss. Know also that I have a great desire to embrace you rather than my husband.'

That has the ring of authenticity about it, a fleeting glimpse of Richard's generation, though Blondel's songs would later emphasize the tragedy of love rather than the polite adultery enjoyed by the generation before. Both must have read Andreas Capellanus, and would have understood the idea of arguing about love in a court – one side versus the other – because that was the prevailing style of the Twelfth-century Renaissance. It was also the method of teaching used at the new universities. Disputes in class, public debates between Christians, Muslims and Jews, or even between orthodox Catholics and Cathar heretics, were the stuff of late-twelfth-century Europe. In the same way, the troubadour songs known as *jeux parties* were set out as arguments, and the troubadors who wrote them enthusiastically launched themselves into song contests with each other. Richard's generation loved debate, just as they loved paradoxes: it was in their songs and in their universities too. It implied equality in an age of hierarchy and tolerance in an age of authority. Above all, it implied conversation: it was the tolerant legacy of Abelard.

It is impossible now to know for sure exactly how much Eleanor created the culture of chivalry and how much she was influenced by it. She may have taken courtly love to new extremes and had an enormous influence on her son's generation, but it was also in the air all over Europe. The new culture emphasized spectacle and courtesy rather than brute force. It gloried in tales of King Arthur and the Round Table rather than Alexander and the Trojan Wars, and in the stories of Tristan and Iseult written by Marie de France.

Henry II may have been an obsessive administrator, but even he understood the power of chivalric generosity and spectacle. It was he who organized a massive festival at Beaucaire in 1174 in order to bring about a reconciliation between King Alfonso II of Aragon and Henry's rebellious neighbour Raymond V of Toulouse – though neither was actually present. As many as 10,000 knights were there, and thousands of minstrels and troubadours, witnessing the distribution of 100,000 sous to the crowd, and the extraordinary gesture of ploughing another 30,000 into the earth – presumably a symbolic way of making the land richer.

A decade later, the Holy Roman (German) Emperor Frederick Barbarossa organized an even bigger spectacle at Mainz over Whitsun 1184 to celebrate the knighting of his sons Henry (later the Emperor Henry VI) and Frederick. This attracted as many as 40,000 knights – 500 of them accompanied the young Duke Leopold V of Austria alone – as well as troubadours, *trouvères* and minnesingers from all over Europe. The imperial court was housed in a splendid palace made of wood outside the city, ringed by thousands of tents, but the festivities were brought to an abrupt end by a storm which blew down the wooden church, killing those inside.★

A generation after that, these spectacles had become even more bound up with courtly love. The festival at Treviso, near Venice, in 1214 included a 'Court of Solace and Mirth' and a castle filled with the ladies of the court and their maids, covered all over with the most precious silks, brocades and purple cloth from throughout the Mediterranean. This then had to be stormed by two teams of knights, from Venice and Padua, with the aid of apples, dates, pears, tarts, lilies, violets, rose water, cinnamon and much else in the way of flowers and spices. Unfortunately, the rivalry between the two cities turned into a violent brawl, the festival broke up and enmity between them lasted for generations.

Steeped in his mother's culture of feminine authority and basking in the light of her favour, Richard seems to have understood his own destiny in chivalric terms. If anyone in Europe could be said to embody the tradition and heritage of King Arthur and the age of chivalry – in a generation immersed in the Arthurian legends – it was Richard. He came to represent the very apotheosis of military skill, with his red-gold hair and beard and his height: Richard was taller than six foot. Later, through family tragedy, he would inherit King Arthur's throne and his nephew and chosen heir would be called Arthur. Even as Richard was growing up, Marie de France – probably his aunt – had won a place as the most successful romantic writer of Western Europe, and his half-sister Marie of Champagne had commissioned Chrétien de Troyes to write his legends of Lancelot and the Holy Grail.

★ The main talking point was actually the biggest chicken coop in the world, built to accommodate some of the menu for the gigantic banquets.

But it was more than that. Richard had been brought up like no other prince before him with the ideals of chivalry. He was the favourite son of the woman who might have been the original for the literary character of Guinevere, and whose court in Poitiers was filled with its culture. He had been brought up with the Round Table. When, just before his death, Henry II urged the monks of Glastonbury Abbey to start searching for King Arthur's tomb, we can be sure that Richard was paying attention.

But there was a confusion about Richard's own attitude to romance, and you have to wonder whether it might have its roots in the Courts of Love. He was fascinated by what was forbidden and was particularly attracted to the order of military monks known as the Templars. He may even have been a member of their brotherhood, initiated into their aura of mystery. He was fascinated by Saracen culture, a trait that was to lead partly to his arrest. But the tension between the idea of the absolute power of women over men – bestowing love where they wanted – and his father's brutal militarism seems to have muddled his sexuality. Historians have speculated since the eighteenth century whether Richard was homosexual or bisexual, fuelled by the peculiar accounts of his stay in Paris when he used to share a bed with Philip Augustus himself.

That in itself is evidence of nothing very much – people regularly shared beds in the twelfth century – but there are other hints. He was clearly in no hurry to get married, and when he was married, he had to promise under duress that he would start sleeping with his wife. He had no heir, so perhaps he failed to take the advice – or not enough. He was clearly not repulsed by women: his powerful sexual appetite certainly included them. He also had one illegitimate son, Philip Faulconbridge, lord of Cognac, and possibly an illegitimate daughter too – but when you think that the Bishop of Liège in the following century had sixty-two illegitimate children, that may not be testimony to enthusiastic heterosexuality.*

---

* The bishop managed fourteen of them in just twenty-two months: an amazing feat even for someone who had not taken a vow of celibacy.

Once again, Richard seems to have been torn in two violently different directions. In 1183 rebel barons from Aquitaine accused him of kidnapping their wives and daughters and, when he had raped them himself, handing them over to his soldiers. This is part of the undeniable dark side of Richard's career, yet there is also a message in existence from him to the wife of the Constable of Normandy, on a ribbon attached to his seal, which says, 'I am romance. Do not give me to the one who might separate our love.' It is almost as if his upbringing amidst the Courts of Love made him imbibe a little too much of the romantic powerlessness of men — as if he had to be brutal (with peasants) or hopelessly romantic (with aristocrats) or not love at all. The Blondel legend, of a troubadour searching for him across a continent with a love song, carries clear homosexual undertones, and it may be that Richard could only actually be passionate with men. Perhaps he learned this — as he learned much else — from the Arab civilization he so admired on crusade.

The evidence is very obscure. Victorian historians coyly compared him to his homosexual great-great-uncle William Rufus, but drew a veil over why. But there is some indication that his two nervous breakdowns had something to do with his sense of sinfulness. In 1195 one of these was brought on by a hermit who warned him to 'be thou mindful of the destruction of Sodom and abstain from what is unlawful; for if thou dost not, God's vengeance shall overtake thee'. Some historians say that the reference to Sodom could have meant anything at the end of the twelfth century, but that is not necessarily so. The curmudgeonly preacher Peter the Chanter at Notre-Dame had already identified the 'sin of Sodom' with homosexuality a generation before and this interpretation was being adopted by preachers across Western Europe. The words 'sodomite' and 'bulgarus' (bugger) came into the language in the twelfth century; so did some books of dubious Arabic poetry about boys, translated by Arabic scholars in Spain. There was no concept of 'homosexuality' as an inclination in the twelfth century, but it was known that people sometimes had sex with their own gender. Yet Sodom contributed to the zeitgeist in

Richard's lifetime, and although youthful sexual experimentation seems to have been part of the culture Richard may have taken that experimentation very much further.

Richard's nickname, thanks to the troubadour Bertran de Born, was *Oc e Non* – 'Yes and No' in the Occitan *langue d'oc* – and its meaning is obscure. It may be just that he blew hot and cold, or kept changing his mind. It is tempting to think there is some reference to one of the key books of the century, Peter Abelard's *Sic et Non*, by the man who famously loved according to his own conscience rather than the rules – though actually 'yes and no' is more likely to be an ironic reference to Richard's habit of swearing, because that is what the phrase refers to in the New Testament. Who knows, maybe it just meant he swung both ways. The truth is that Richard went through periods of predatory sexuality, that this may well have included his own sex and that he felt perpetually guilty about it.★

Richard's time with his mother in Poitiers, learning from her the skills that a ruler would need, was a golden period for him. But it was over all too soon. Two years after his investiture as Duke of Aquitaine, the sixteen-year-old prince was playing a major role in an extraordinary rebellion by his mother and brothers against his father's attempt to settle the succession. Henry finally marched into Poitiers on Whit Sunday 1174, dismissed Eleanor's servants and dismantled the court (perhaps this was the real meaning of the ruling of the Courts of Love that same year that love could not exist between husband and wife).

Richard carried on the battle alone for four months before coming face to face with his father in Tours on 29 September, weeping and falling at his feet to beg forgiveness. Henry raised him gently and gave him the kiss of peace, but had no such

★The Church seemed much less worried in those days about sins of the flesh. One set of rules stipulated five years of penance for a married man who committed adultery, or ten years for a priest and twelve for a bishop. If you were an unmarried man, that was reduced to two years, or one if it was with a servant girl.

forgiveness for his estranged wife. Eleanor was taken to England and locked inside the draughty castle at Old Sarum in Wiltshire for the next fifteen years and the Courts of Love – and the whole dream of chivalry and music she had created there – were scattered.

Within the decade, all Henry's plans for his inheritance, and his careful divisions of land between his elder sons, were also in ruins. Richard's younger brother Geoffrey was killed in an accident at a tournament, leaving behind a baby son called Arthur. Philip Augustus, his friend as well as his half-brother, was so distraught that he had to be physically prevented from leaping into the grave. Then in June 1183 Henry the Young King died of dysentery.* The inheritance question should have been simple, but Henry was haunted by the mistake he had made with his eldest son – crowning him as heir in the Angevin tradition and then giving him no responsibility – so he decided not to repeat his mistake with Richard. This time, he clearly told himself, he would hold back the reward of naming his successor. As a result, thanks to the clever whisperings of Philip Augustus, Richard came to believe his father was plotting to replace him with his youngest brother, John.

Every suggestion his father made seemed suspicious. Should John marry Alys instead of him? Should John take over Aquitaine? Richard urgently needed to strengthen his position and, in this mood in 1187, he travelled to Paris to enlist the French king's support. It was there in Paris, then the biggest and most magnificent city in Western Europe, that he may have encountered Blondel for the first time.

---

*His wife, Margaret of France, was also having an affair with his old tournament partner William the Marshal.

2. The Age of Light

'From just before its opening till a generation after its close, from the first conquests of the Normans to the reign of St Louis . . . from the first troubled raising of the round arch in tiers to the full revelation of Notre Dame – in that 120 years or more moved a process such as even our own time has not seen. It was an upheaval like that by which, in the beginnings of terrestrial life, the huge and dull sea-monsters first took to the keen air of the land. Everything was in the turmoil which the few historians who have seen the vision of this thing have called, some an anarchy, and others a brief interlude of liberty in the politics of Europe. It was neither one nor the other: it was the travail of a birth.'

Hilaire Belloc on the twelfth century, *The Old Road*, 1904

My lady is like water and fire;
And she can inflame me or extinguish me.

Blondel de Nesle,
'J'aim par coustume', *Chanson X*

As we have seen, something revolutionary was happening in the middle years of the twelfth century in Western Europe, as Richard was growing up, and its spirit suffused his life. After a long conva- lescence following the fall of the Roman Empire, Europe was finally beginning to stir and awaken.

The central motif of this new age was the sudden emergence of the first Gothic churches. The new style had been introduced by Abbot Suger of Saint-Denis, outside Paris, the resting place of the

French kings, and was now being copied all over northern France, at Chartres, Notre-Dame, Rouen, Amiens and Beauvais. In each cathedral the light poured in through the new stained glass, made by grinding up ancient mosaics for exactly the right colours, and in each one there was as much stone below ground level in the foundations as there was soaring above ground.★

The middle years of the twelfth century were an age of light in other ways too. It was a period where Europe suddenly opened itself up to ancient learning, with knowledge of mathematics and astronomy brought home from the East by returning crusaders, or bubbling up from the translators of Arab Spain, meeting together in the new universities, where suddenly everything could be discussed. This was an age tolerant enough for set-piece debates between Christians, Jews and Muslims, even Cathar heretics, though the results tended to be manipulated.† The Pope even had a Jewish adviser, and monasteries across Europe often employed Jewish financiers to manage their money.

Scholars were translating Aristotle and other classics in Toledo – the Spanish city where Jews, Arabs, Christians, Slavs, English and Germans all mixed freely in the search for secret knowledge – making them available in Western Europe for the first time, translated into Latin from Arabic. The Jewish zoologist Jacob ben Mahir ibn Tibbon was in Provence, translating lost scientific works from Arabic into Hebrew. Greek heretics were translating the Bible into Coptic, Armenian and even Chinese. The great Jewish mathematician Maimonides was calculating that every star was at least ninety times as big as the earth. It was a unique moment in history, when

---

★ The limestone quarries of Northern France produced more stone to build the Gothic cathedrals during 300 years in the Middle Ages than was used in all of ancient Egypt to build the pyramids.

† Emperor Frederick II in the following century shocked his contemporaries by holding debates and failing to fix the result. And although the debates themselves were symptoms of tolerance, it may still have been an uncomfortable experience for the Jewish, Muslim and Cathar debaters on the other side.

everything seemed to be coming together to break free of the old world of ignorance.★

This scholarship and the extraordinary awakening of the urge to travel were given added impetus by a series of discoveries of silver deposits in central Europe. These started around 1168, the first for well over a century, near the Saxony village of Christiansdorf, when Richard was eleven. Soon amateur miners were flooding there, and to the other new silver mines, from all over Europe. Fifteen years later, the silver was being transformed by the new mints into coins, and Christiansdorf had grown into a chartered town called Freiberg (Free Mountain). By Richard's twenties, these new, plentiful silver coins were appearing in northern France. By his thirties and forties, they had become a flood; there were even nine mints in the Middle East using the new silver to strike coins. Wherever European merchants traded – silk from China, precious stones from India, furs from Russia and wool from England – the silver coins were making their way. Nearer Blondel's home, Philip Augustus was producing *parisis* – silver pennies minted in Paris – and these were beginning to spread across northern Europe. They were being used by Henry the Liberal, the enterprising Count of Champagne, who was independent of the French monarchy, to invest in new mills, ovens and wine presses. His neighbours in Flanders were investing in the land-drainage schemes that would soon result in the new port towns of Calais, Dunkirk, Gravelines and Damme.

The coins made it possible for the first time for noble families to move from their dark and draughty castles into new homes in Paris, receiving rents in cash rather than in cattle or hens or crops. It was possible for them to pay mercenaries for their armies rather than relying on feudal obligations, and for the young clerks at the universities to pay their professors. The serfs could buy their way

★ Even Buddhism – or rumours of Buddhism – were filtering through Byzantium and into the West. Buddha himself finally emerged after various incarnations as St Josafat, with a church dedicated to him in Palermo.

out of their feudal duties with the same coins, earned by selling their surplus produce. The poor might welcome the ability to buy their way out of feudalism, but there were many others who mourned the passing of the feudal generosity and hospitality: suddenly travellers were expected to pay for their lodging, unless they happened to find a monastery – and even then, the monks often refused to take in hounds as well as horses. The coins made it possible for people to flock to the towns and get rich, but those who depended on generosity for their livelihood – like wandering scholars, troubadours and monks – mourned the side-effects of these changes. This was a period when the newly powerful cities began to flex their muscles and their hard-won freedoms, finding allies in kings and princes sometimes to protect them from their conservative feudal lords, and fighting sometimes for the right to set up the first rudiments of local self-government.★

It was a period of unprecedented prosperity across the 50 million population of Western Europe, driven, according to some economists, as much by the new silver coins as the more ubiquitous smaller denominations, produced in duller metals in local mints in great numbers and recalled and reminted every five to six years – after which you would tend to get three coins back for the four handed in. Where it took place, this *renovatio monetae* 'tax' system kept money in circulation or in productive investments – there was no point in hoarding it for too long if you were liable to lose it in a few years' time – and helped drive the dramatic prosperity of the so-called Twelfth-century Renaissance: 20,000 water-mills in France alone, thousands of sheep farmers in England or vineyards in France – the vast majority of them small, independent farmers, and even those still employed in feudal agriculture enjoying a life of unprecedented security with many more free days, when work for the lord was not required, than any employee has today. These small coin tokens, known sometimes as *méreaux*, meant that – even when the silver used for continental trade was scarce – there was still abundant local money in circulation, accepted locally

★ The Germans had a saying, '*Stadt luft macht frei*', town air makes free.

according to local laws, and spreading the prosperity of the age downwards through society. The *méreaux* would be used for local trade, and the silver coins for savings.

This dual-currency system, and the explosion of trade, may not have provided the spark that set the Twelfth-century Renaissance alight, but it certainly kept it running, providing the wealth for the great cathedrals and bridges that sprang up across Europe. It also provided the population with an excellent diet and almost unprecedented health. No wonder the skeletons of men and women excavated from twelfth-century London show that they were on average as tall as – and, in the case of women, slightly taller than – they are today. Of course there were famine, disease and poverty, but that was usually the direct result of the activities of warring aristocrats, with their habit of burning the crops and the villages that nominally belonged to their rivals. Generally speaking, the fledgling economic system seemed to work.

This was the world where Blondel and Richard grew up. Theirs was a generation that was tolerant and cosmopolitan by medieval standards, and thrilled by rather than fearful about the future. They belonged to a society that had finally burst out of dark medieval gloom and embraced a new architecture of light and ambition. Both must have been only too aware of the great changes around them, the luxuries pouring in from Byzantium, Damascus and Jerusalem, and the new coinage that was turning society upside down.

Blondel de Nesle, the *trouvère* and Richard's legendary rescuer, is a shadowy figure, but he belongs to this same age of light. His songs are his generation's deepest expressions of *fin' amor*, and although the music is difficult to interpret, his twenty-seven or more songs on the shelves of the Bibliothèque Nationale, the Bodleian and other great libraries are evidence of the world in which he and Richard grew up – romantic, tolerant and, above all, musical. One of the collections of songs in Paris is a document known as 'The Manuscript of the King', written in the 1240s, and it once included a portrait of Blondel, though this was torn out at some time in the past seven centuries or so. These songs and the legend – which is dismissed as serious history – would at first sight seem to be all we know about Blondel. But there are other clues to be found if you look more closely at the songs. In fact, two pieces of evidence then become very clear.

One of these concerns his rhymes. Consistently throughout the versions of his songs, there are linguistic peculiarities. Words that should end with '*ein*' are rhymed to end in '*ain*' as in '*painne*' or '*semaine*', and words that ought to end with an '*eur*' sound are rhymed to end in '*our*', as in '*valour*' and '*honour*'. These and other oddities pinpoint the author as originating from Picardy, the flat region of forests and wild boar to the north-east of Paris. The other points to a birth date, like Richard, some time in the 1150s. We know this because he dedicated two of his songs to the well-known *trouvère* Conon de Béthune, who left for the Fourth Crusade in 1204 and never came home, and he sent another one to the equally famous Gace Brulé, who was also one of the oldest generation of *trouvères* and was later exiled to Brittany. The evidence is that Blondel was a contemporary and probably a social equal of theirs.

Picardy was a region of brutal pursuits and superstitious habits, where cock-fighting survived into the twentieth century and priests were still exorcizing plagues of grasshoppers in the 1830s. The dialect that he spoke was described later by Jules Verne – who lived in Picardy and loved everything about the place – as 'clumsy, uncouth and doomed to disappear'. Like so many other agricultural regions, you could have sat in the town square and heard the usual bizarre tales of coincidence, quickness and cleverness (by locals) and astonishing stupidity (by strangers). But this was not a region divorced from the rest of the world. To the north and west lay England and Normandy, both part of the Angevin empire ruled by the Plantagenet kings. To the south was Paris, past the new Gothic abbey of Saint-Denis, the richest city in Christendom. To the east, past the five towers of Coucy-le-Château, lay the great trade routes and the independent principality of Champagne, the commercial centre of Europe. Merchants from all over the known world made their way to the annual Champagne fairs in Provins, Troyes, Lagny-sur-Marne and Bar-sur-Aube, their safety to and from the fairs, their 'justice, honesty and security', all guaranteed by Champagne's Count Henry.

As a native of Picardy, Blondel must have been aware of the polyglot bustle towards these centres. As he grew to adulthood and wandered down to Champagne, or stood on the banks of the Seine, he must also have seen the sugar heading for Paris from Spain, Syria and North Africa. Or watched the ivory from Africa, the pepper and spices from India, the furs from Russia, the pearls from Persia, the silk from China and the wealth of the world that was being unleashed in his generation, all unloaded at the Paris quays. He would have seen the wagons of grain – Champagne was known for its grain in those days, not its sparkling wine – trundling along the great road between Paris and Rome. Perhaps he visited the fairs himself, watching the foreigners and bankers crowding into the local inns, and marvelled at the sophisticated deals they could make there – cashing money orders at the fair taken out in England; spices bought and sold while they were still in harbour in Italy.

As he grew up, he met returning crusaders with tales of the fabulous Arab cities of the East, the public baths, the municipal water supplies and central heating.* Like others of his generation, he came across the wealthy mayors of local townships, with their long scarlet robes, and heard the whispers that – back home in their own village – they had actually been serfs who had escaped for a year and a day or simply bought their way out. He would have witnessed for himself the misery of the regular famines, the horror stories of Hansel and Gretel-style cannibalism, where peasants could waylay a passer-by – like the hapless Bishop of Trier at that time – and eat his horse before his very eyes. He must also have known from his own experience the rural, married priests whose job was both saving local souls and looking after the parish

---

* The twelfth-century aristocracy loved baths and used soap, invented in the East, made from mutton fat, wood ash and natural soda. It was not too effective.

bull and parish boar. They were part of the old world, like the
wolves in the forest, the drunken monks on the road – the butt of
jokes from Europe's growing intelligentsia.★

With so little surviving documentation, it is impossible to piece
much together about Blondel's life. One of the peculiarities in the
surviving manuscripts that include his songs is that, unlike his
contemporaries, Blondel never gets the title 'Messire' or 'Mon-
seigneur'. All the other *trouvères* were minor nobility, so it is still
likely that Blondel was that as well. It is even more difficult to
pinpoint the man himself because it is not clear whether 'Blondel'
was a surname or actually a nickname or pen-name – though this
was an era in which these tended to merge. If it was a nickname,
it might be that a title sounded inappropriate when it was written
down. More likely, he was the younger son of a junior branch of
a noble family.

The fact that he is remembered at all is thanks partly to the
efforts of an antiquarian from Champagne called Prosper Tarbé –
a great romantic himself – in the 1850s and 1860s. He rediscovered
Blondel's songs when he was asked to collect some regional poetry,
claiming that Blondel was one of those musicians who knew how
to take people 'from the miseries of the world and elevate the soul
to the highest skies, and slowly put them to sleep in the middle of
dreams of happiness'. Tarbé spent years researching everything that
remained about Blondel in an ultimately vain attempt to prove the
truth of the legend of his song under the castle walls. But it was
Tarbé who finally confirmed beyond argument that the Blondel
of the legend and Blondel de Nesle were one and the same person,
and who demolished the prevailing view that Richard the
Lionheart's companion was actually English. There had been an
idea that he was the William Blondel listed in the annals of the
Tower of London as having been granted land in Northampton-
shire after Richard's return from captivity.

★There were still wolves in Western Europe, even in the woods in England,
where Richard's brother John – after he became king in 1199 – used to pay a
levy of five shillings for every wolf's head.

Tarbé first published his collection of Blondel's songs in 1862, arguing that Blondel was the nickname of blond-haired Jean de Nesle, and that he was actually from Artois – which is where the oldest-existing description of the Blondel legend says he was from – from a small and now forgotten village called Noyelle, either outside Abbeville or the one near Boulogne. A generation later, in 1904, the German scholar Leo Wiese concentrated on the evidence of the dialect that Blondel was from Picardy to point instead towards the modern town of Nesle as his birthplace.

Having established that, historians have tried to pinpoint his identity more precisely. In 1942, the Finnish historian Holger Petersen Dyggve used a poem by the unfortunately named *trouvère* Audefroy le Bastart, who mentions another poet he describes as '*mon seigneur . . . qui de Neele est sire*'. He said this proved that Blondel was a nickname for the man who became Jehan II, Lord of Nesle and Chastelain of Bruges between 1202 and 1230, and who was well known as being stunningly attractive. But Jehan II was almost certainly too young to have written Blondel's songs, and in later life he became a fearsome crusader against heretics and troubadour culture in the south of France. It could have been the same man who wrote the gentle songs – other troubadours turned against the culture of Languedoc – but it seems unlikely. Even so, Dyggve's interpretation was widely accepted – you will find it in some of the modern music encyclopedias – and it was not until 1994 that the French philologist Yves Lepage attacked the theory, suggesting instead that Blondel was actually Jehan II's father, Jehan I, Lord of Nesle from 1180 to 1202. Jehan I was in Palestine with Richard on the Third Crusade, as legend suggests that Blondel was.

This is not impossible, but it is still unlikely. If Blondel, one of the most famous musicians of his generation, had been Lord of Nesle, you would expect the family genealogists to have recorded it, then or later. This silence and the lack of any kind of title in the manuscripts imply that, while he may have been from the same noble family – perhaps illegitimate – he was probably not himself either Jehan I or Jehan II. We will never know, because – very

conveniently for Blondel scholars, who might prefer not to expose
their theories to the cold light of fact – Nesle twice lost its town
archives, once when it was sacked by the Duke of Burgundy in
1472 and once when the town hall burned down in 1799. The
most likely explanation is that, in those days of shifting surnames,
the poet Jean de Nesle – a junior member of the noble house of
Nesle, and nicknamed Blondel because of his hair – founded a
dynasty that survives in the family name of Blondel in France and
Blundell in England and America today. As for his birthplace, there
are towns and villages called Nesle or Noyelle all over France, but
the Nesle of Jehan I and II – on the road north from Paris to the
Somme – is the only one with a tradition that Blondel was a local
hero. There is even a local story that assigns him a birth date in
1155, though few of these local traditions tend to predate the
nineteenth century. Even so, it is safe to assume that we know, at
least, where he came from – and that means that it is possible to
imagine a little about his childhood.

Nesle was almost completely flattened during the First World
War, so the only remaining features from the twelfth century are
a short stretch of moat and a short stretch of city wall – and the
very modern rue de Blondel de Nesle. But the river, which is now
little more than a ditch, was in Blondel's day 150 metres wide and
navigable, and it is here – or from the watch tower on the bend
of the river – that the young Blondel must have seen the barges of
goods on their way south towards Paris, or the carts trundling
south down the chemin des Boeufs, through the walls and into
the town, passing the castle of Yves III, Lord of Nesle – Jehan's
predecessor – on their right, and setting up in the town square on
market days. It was here, perched on the road between Paris and
the Channel ports – with the merchants of the world passing his
door – that Blondel would have grown up, before setting out on
the road himself.

For Blondel and Richard especially, this was also an age of music.
Their generation loved to sing. There was little else to do in the
long winter evenings when the candles and torches that lit dinner

had been extinguished and the hearth fire was the only light, but even in the summer in the towns you could see regular festival dances and singing in the open spaces and graveyards inside the new walls. Knights like William the Marshal would sing carols as they waited for tournaments to begin. Kings employed boys to sing them to sleep. When Thomas Becket visited Paris so spectacularly in 1158, he was preceded by 250 choristers singing English songs. Some of those hopeful travellers, setting out on the ancient potholed roads, were also minstrels or members of the still-mysterious camaraderie of the troubadours.

These were not the simple minstrels and jongleurs who were relatively common on the road, and who might look to the troubadours to provide them with material. The evidence is that these would use the songs that troubadours wrote, along with other accomplishments: a true minstrel, according to one thirteenth-century manuscript, could 'speak and rhyme well, know the story of Troy, balance apples on the point of knives, juggle, jump through hoops, play the citole, mandora, harp, fiddle and psaltery'. Many could also imitate birds and use performing dogs and puppets.*

The troubadours (from the south, the Languedoc, writing in Occitan) and *trouvères* (from the north, writing in Old French), or their German equivalent the minnesingers, were more than popular performers and remain something of an enigma. It is not clear whether they sang unaccompanied, played instruments or simply recited their poems, or whether they all had their own technique. We know the names of 460 troubadours, and that most of the early ones came from lands ruled by the Angevins, which anyway covered most of the area speaking Occitan. We know they wrote not just about love, but also about war and politics, and more than 2,600 of their songs survive, with rhyming lines for a new kind of music that had a regular number of syllables and music that matched the ends of the lines. But we barely understand what they sounded

---

*Henry II's minstrel Roland le Pettour was given land as a reward for his performance of 'a leap, a whistle and a fart'.

like, because their square boxes for musical notation carry no information about the rhythm, speed or metre.

The first troubadour was almost certainly William IX of Aquitaine, Richard's great-grandfather – a priapic old aristocrat who used to disguise himself as a deaf mute to seduce the wives of absent nobles in local inns. William seems to have been inspired by the romantic works of the Roman poet Ovid, but he himself managed to remain rather unromantic, and certainly avoided the high seriousness of Blondel and his colleagues two generations later. Most of his encounters with a woman ended – as he put it – with 'my hands beneath her cloak'.★

The names and characters of the early troubadours are more famous than those of the northern *trouvères*: Bernart de Ventadorn, who fell hopelessly in love with Eleanor herself and had to be exiled to England; Raimon de Miraval, who threw his wife out of the castle when she took his love poems too literally and encouraged her own suitors; Bertran de Born, who wrote songs praising war and execrating the Plantagenet family; Giraut de Borneil, said to be the greatest of them all, but whose 'wailing, thin, miserable songs' also irritated his fellow troubadours. Or Eleanor's own son, Richard himself, a troubadour, musician and poet in his own right.

They and their northern colleagues were generally high-born wanderers, entertaining their audiences with wit and sparkle, feeding networks of minstrels who were prepared to use their material and make them famous. Songs were messages – letters almost – that spread rapidly via their favourite performers: 'Little Hugh, my courtly messenger,' wrote Bernart de Ventadorn, in the middle of his unrequited love for Eleanor, 'sing my song eagerly to the Queen of the Normans.' But the troubadours were primarily entertainers in their own right. When the company in the castles and manors gathered round the great fire after dinner, when the table had been swept clear and put up against the wall – with the

---

★ William had watched in tears in 1101 as his crusading army was cut to pieces by the Turks, but lingered in Antioch and Jerusalem on his way home, thrilled by Arab culture and Arab translations of Greek and Roman classics.

valets running around with jugs of hot water to wash the food from people's fingers – they would begin to tell stories. Then, if they liked the audience and the woodsmoke was light enough, they would offer more. Then they would loosen their clothing, take off their belt, smooth down their hair – maybe put on a woollen cap – reach for their fiddle with its seven horsehair strings, lay it in their lap and sing.

We have one description by the troubadour Raimon Vidal of the journey he made south to Catalonia. 'And the night, as I saw,' he wrote, 'was very dark after dinner and next to the bright fire the company was large, knights and jongleurs, clever and accomplished and amiable, courtly and agreeable to courteous men . . . and the knights, without any reminder, went to bed when they were ready, for my lord wanted to remain with a companion near the fire.'

The lord he stayed awake talking to was a troubadour himself, Dalfi d'Alvernhe, Count of Clermont and Montferrand. Vidal was describing a journey to meet lords who are about to be ruined by the Albigensian Crusade against local heretics. It was an age that was about to disappear, and he knew it. But his hosts were still generous enough to justify the visit, which was how troubadours paid their way. 'God did not make this age so consistently bad that an ambitious, clever and frank man cannot get gifts out of it in order to rise and make himself noticed,' said Vidal, 'if he knows how to be clever, and has the right manner.'

They were generous with gifts because that was the chivalric spirit and because troubadours were the journalists of the age. Their songs spread tittle-tattle. They could praise or they could ridicule, just as Bertran de Born ridiculed Richard. Greasing the palm of a passing troubadour was a sensible insurance policy for keeping your faults well hidden – another reason why churchmen were enraged by the whole idea. Minstrels were denied the hope of salvation by the Church in the twelfth century, but even church-men knew that the times were changing, and began to make exceptions – as long as the songs avoided what they called 'wantonness'. 'The singing of love songs in the presence of men of eminence was once considered in bad taste,' wrote John of

Salisbury, the tolerant and enlightened scholar, around the time Blondel was born. 'But now it is considered praiseworthy for men of greater eminence to sing and play them.'

The *trouvères* of the north were more serious than the troubadours of the south. They were more high-minded than the lustful William IX or warlike Bertran de Born. They sang in a mixture of the related languages and dialects of Champagne, Picardy and Normandy, unlike the troubadours, who used Occitan, and – unlike the existing troubadour songs – the vast majority of *trouvère* songs that survive have music attached, though sometimes different melodies for the same song.

Trouvères were more unambiguously aristocratic, like Blondel's friend Conon de Béthune, later given the task of negotiating with Constantinople on behalf of the Fourth Crusade in 1203 on the grounds that he was the wisest and most eloquent. Like them, Blondel would have discovered his love of poetry and music at an early age, in those long winter nights. The basics of notation – the black squares and diamonds on little sticks that passed for music at the time – he would have learned by an early exposure to scales.★ Blondel may even, like Conon, have made his way to the Diet of Mainz in 1184, to the great meetings of minnesingers and *trouvères* at the festival there that year.

What we do know is that Blondel and the others were in constant touch in Paris or the great trading town of Troyes in Champagne, at the court of Richard's sister Marie de Champagne – patron of the pre-eminent *trouvère* Chrétien de Troyes – or the wool town of Arras in Artois, and that they developed a distinctive voice for themselves in keeping with the spirit of the age. It was deeply romantic, abjectly deferential to women and popular enough to be recited and remembered over a century later in the manuscripts now in Paris and the Vatican. If we read Old French, we can still now hear Gace Brulé complaining about the dawn driving him away from his lover's bed, or the mild masochism of

---

★In those days, scales were sung 'ut re mi fa so la', from the opening syllables of each line of the Latin hymn *Ut queant laxis/Resonare fibris*.

the Chastelain de Coucy in lines like 'joy rules in my heart while
I can stay/In her service, never to be free'. We can also see how
Blondel had a style very much his own, with slow rhythms and
short lines, and demonstrating the most cringing helplessness before
his beloved. This is classic Blondel:

> Remembering her face,
> So smooth and rosy-cheeked
> Has brought my heart to this:
> I cannot let it go.
> But since I asked for pain
> I must endure it now.
> And yet I missed the point:
> I should love it even more.

Even his faster-paced songs have a deep romantic melancholy at
the heart of them:

> Someone should sing the joy of *fin' amor*–
> But me, I find it difficult to sing,
> Because I lack the joy leaping inside
> Which lets you sing, and so I cannot sing . . .

Or:

> In the season of the wind,
> Thanks to the one who has me,
> But I still do not have,
> My heart grows black and grey.
> With a sincere, truthful love,
> I begged her with my heart,
> Though not inflamed like me,
> To grant me this request . . .

It is difficult so many centuries later to completely understand
what is meant by this joyful kind of misery, except that the respect

these songs are given twenty or more years after Blondel's death implies that his contemporaries loved it. They might not have treated women with quite such respect in practice. They might have flown into a rage if their wives or daughters had taken the lyrics too seriously, as Raimon de Miraval did. But something about the idea of an all-powerful lady – the *domna* in Occitan – seems to have thrilled Blondel's generation. In their imaginations, they rushed to abase themselves, loving 'pain the more'. It was an idea they had borrowed from their parents' generation but pushed to an extreme that was all their own, and it is hard now to read it as they must have done. But theirs was the first generation to take the new intellectual freedom and the wandering for granted. Like *fin' amor* and the Courts of Love, Blondel's songs belong in that same intersection between two worlds – the new world of global money, trading and freedom, and the old world of monasteries and feudal supplication – where briefly, and among a narrow elite, there was an unmistakable explosion of music, romance and chivalric love.

There is one other piece of evidence that dates Blondel and may also place him geographically in the earlier years of his career. This might also provide a clue about where he first met Richard, if we believe the underlying assumption of the legend that they were close friends. This is the coronation of Philip Augustus as the king of France in the traditional coronation place, Reims Cathedral.

In those days, it was the habit of the French monarchy to have the heir to the throne, the Dauphin, safely anointed and crowned well before the king expired. Philip was the spoilt, nervous and devious 'Dieu-Donné' of the pious Louis VII, and was fourteen in 1179, when he was crowned. Father and son were on their way together to Reims Cathedral when they stopped in Compiègne, and there Philip and his companions set off into the dark of the forest to hunt. Chasing a wild boar, the Dauphin suddenly found himself separated from the others, and it was some hours later when he stumbled weeping through the door of a charcoal burner's hut and collapsed with fever. The coronation was postponed and physicians despaired of his life. For three nights running, Louis dreamed of the murdered Archbishop of Canterbury Thomas Becket and, after the third night, he dressed as a pilgrim and crossed the English Channel – to the horror of his advisers – to pray for the life of his son. He was welcomed by Henry II and placed a cup full of gold on Becket's tomb. Back in France four days later, he found his son had recovered completely.

When Philip's coronation finally went ahead on All Saints' Day, Louis was dangerously ill with paralysis and would die the following year. But one of the songs sung in the cathedral during the ceremony was a setting of a poem by the archbishop's secretary and local poet, Walter of Châtillon, celebrating the occasion with a series of voices in harmony. It was called 'Ver pacis apperit': 'The springtime of peace/Opens the bosom of the earth.' The technical name for a song like this for more than one voice and set in Latin – the common language for educated classes and aristocracy across Europe – is a *conductus*. But the tune used for one of the voices exists separately and can be found attached to another song, ascribed to Blondel, and appearing in five of the manuscripts that include his work. This is 'Ma joie me semont', courtly, highly moral and very upright.

It is impossible to know which was written first, the coronation song or the verse about Blondel's '*joie*', whether Blondel borrowed the tune from some forgotten court composer because of its success in Reims, or whether Walter of Châtillon knew Blondel's tune already and adapted it for one of the parts of his royal anthem. Either way, it is evidence that Blondel was moving in court circles at the time, and at the age, if the tradition about his birth is correct, of about twenty-four. Blondel may not have actually been at the coronation himself though Richard and his brothers Henry and Geoffrey were there – but this implies that he was then based in Paris, somewhere between Philip's draughty palace and the scattered university emerging on the Left Bank of the Seine.

The coronation tune implies that he attracted attention in the highest circles in the French court, so it is likely that he was on the spot and that he learned his music there at the university and perhaps also that he met Richard there in the 1180s. His older contemporary troubadour Giraut de Borneil says in one song that he will give up singing and go back to being a scholar, and Giraut's biography says that he used to spend his summer moving from court to court with two singers to perform his songs, but his winters teaching rhetoric and poetic composition. The older troubadour Cercamon used to be called 'Maestro', which in those days was a reference to a university education. If Blondel was in Paris, he is likely to have had links with the university as well as the court.

Like other young men of aristocratic family, Blondel must have been able to play the harp and fiddle and to sing before he was grown up. By the age of nine, he would also know how to hunt, bet and wait at table – and to be a mild concern to his parents over what he should do, like so many other sons of minor branches of noble families. Probably he would have been taught to read by a chaplain or local priest, practising his letters on wax tablets or slates before being sent off to be a page at a nearby castle, perhaps at the castle of Nesle's lord – learning how to carve meat, how to kneel to present the wine cup, how to dance and play backgammon and chess, how to hawk and how to tilt. Those skills must have failed to catch his imagination, which is why, by his early twenties, Blondel almost certainly set aside the chance to be a knight – if indeed he was ever offered one – like the great teacher Peter Abelard before him, and made the day's journey from Nesle to the emerging university in Paris.

Arras, the cloth town with close links to Nesle, may also have been Blondel's home at some time during his youth or adulthood. Early manuscripts about his legend describe him as a 'Gentleman of Arras', and it was a place teeming with minstrels and *trouvères*: out of a population of 2,000, about 10 per cent claimed to be poets, organizing themselves into literary guilds, composing songs for each other, and attracting young people from all over Europe who wanted to learn. Arras was a truly international town, not fully subsumed under the authority of the French king until the seventeenth century. Its guilds and tapestries were the outward symbols of a place that was shaking itself free of feudalism, where free people could trade and be what they wanted to be, which is one reason it attracted poets. It is a leap of imagination to suggest that Blondel spent time there, but it is a reasonable one.

In both Paris and Arras, he was breathing in the spirit of the age, and in northern Europe there were no better places to do so. You can hear the authentic voice of the late twelfth century in the words of the song he wrote, 'Ma joie me semont', that uses the coronation tune:

> My happiness calls me
> To sing in the sweet season,
> And my heart replies
> That it is right for me to sing –
> And I dare not ignore
> The wishes of my heart.
> God, what times these are
> For those devoted to their talents!
>
> That is what joy is all about:
> To love sincerely,
> And, when the moment comes,
> To give generously;
> And one more thing as well:
> To speak courteously.
> Those who follow these three ways
> will never make their lives ugly.

Very briefly and simply, it sets out a way of life that seems to contradict so much of what we assume about brutal medieval life – love sincerely, give generously and speak courteously. It also captures some of the unique spirit of Blondel's generation: the idea of unprecedented times, the central importance of generosity, love and beauty – and the very modern thought that it is the poet's heart, not duty or religion, that he must listen to, and his heart tells him to sing. The song was part of a whole new literature that was a whole new departure from the old Franco-German idea of a holy empire that dominated heart and mind. No longer were monks, kings or emperors the custodians of our souls. The old literature celebrated great deeds of arms; the new celebrated King Arthur and his knights, and great deeds of love.

Blondel was clearly steeped in the world of courtly love, now in its second generation, its ideals spread by those like him all over Europe. This sense of the overwhelming power of love and beauty would have given him something in common with Richard when they met and when – by tradition – Richard asked him for song-writing and composition lessons. Troubadours were wanderers. The word comes from the Latin *trobare*, which means to find or invent, and their wanderings were not just to perform, they were to find material as well, though many of them also worked as teachers or diplomats. From Arras or Paris, Blondel probably wandered widely and could have encountered Richard in Poitiers or perhaps at his half-sister's court in Champagne. We know how Richard sought out musicians wherever he went. But equally, it was to Paris that Blondel probably came as a young man and it was to Paris, also, that Richard came in search of support against his father, and the chances are that – if they knew each other – they cemented the friendship there.

3. Paris and Jerusalem

The golden age comes round
The earth's salvation nigh
The rich man is thrown down
The poor man lifted high.

anthem sung at the
coronation of Richard I, 1189

'Now may God grant me that I may ascend to the high honour of holding the one who has my heart, and all my thoughts, naked once in my arms before I go overseas.'

Chastelain de Coucy

Students sometimes went to university in those days as young as thirteen, so Blondel would have gone to Paris by the early 1170s, when it was the biggest, richest and most exciting city in Western Europe. It had a population of 200,000 and the wealth of the world seemed to flow up the Seine to the docks and wharves along the banks. Louis VII and later Philip Augustus were also there, directly ruling the small expanse of land that was then the full extent of the kingdom of France, but claiming an uneasy overlordship over the surrounding counts, dukes and lords. After he succeeded, Philip's untidiness and fastidious fear of injury and disease obscured a reforming zeal and strategic determination. This emanated from one end of the Ile de la Cité from his dark and draughty palace, the open windows of which had been such a factor in the departure of his father's first wife, Eleanor of Aquitaine. This was a Paris that had already become the source of both the new Gothic design and the new learning a generation after Abelard's death – a city of debate, culture and intellectual excitement that had been described by one scholar as 'paradise on earth, the rose of the world, the balm of the universe'.

We know about Paris in Blondel's day because Alexander Neckham arrived there at the same time in the 1170s. Neckham – the son of Richard's wet nurse – was an exact contemporary of Richard's, and paid on arrival for cramped lodgings a year in advance, crammed with so many other new students into the rue Saint-Christofle. Blondel may well have lodged in the same street. Both must soon have come to know the mercantile centre on the Right Bank of the Seine as well as the students and intellectuals on the Left Bank. The dogs roaming the streets, the beggars, the famous hams hanging in the shops and the bridges covered with houses must have soon become familiar sights. Also the shepherds herding their flocks into the city, the revenue officers sampling the wine, the wandering apothecaries urging people to try their ointments and potions, and the paddle wheels grinding the grain underneath the Grand-Pont, the eighteen-foot-wide stone bridge where moneychangers and goldsmiths – the first bankers – piled their coins. New city walls and stone pavements were ordered by Philip Augustus, who was not yet on the throne when they arrived; before then, these were muddy streets – but still the thoroughfares of a city whose population was exploding, doubling in size every generation.

On the second Wednesday of every June, the prized possession of Notre-Dame – a piece of the true cross – was shown to the people. New students joined the crowds afterwards as they made off down the road to Saint-Denis, with the vineyards on either side, for the annual Lendit Fair. In their periods of leisure, they inspected the pillories and stocks in the town squares, the floor-shows in the taverns and the famous Paris gibbet, with space for twenty-four – with the oldest skeleton thrown into a pit to make way for the most recent malefactor. They must have brushed away the flies as they watched the butchers killing animals in their shop fronts and the fishmongers throwing the unsold fish into the street for the poor, and grown used to the smell of decomposing refuse behind the houses on the open land, and the daily business of avoiding the contents of chamber pots coming down into the gutters running along the middle of the street.★

Then there were the latest Paris fashions. In those days, this meant brightly coloured robes that fitted tightly around women's waists, with the edges of clothes cut into tongues, shoes with pointed toes, young men with long, curling hair and long, flowing sleeves in reds, violets and saffrons, and birds' plumage that – according to Peter the Chanter at Notre-Dame – would 'make a crow laugh'. Even the occasional beard was woven through with silver thread. Many fashionable women put white powder on their faces and had dyed hair, which was parted in the middle, with two long plaits hanging down their backs and a band across their forehead – still the fashion for nuns eight centuries later or just a crown of flowers. These luxuries would be beyond the pockets of scholars, who had to dodge the poppy oil, wax and paper sellers in the street, but watched the bakers selling leftover bread outside Notre-Dame on Sundays, or tasted the light pastries that were already such a Parisian speciality, or the pasties with chopped ham, chicken or eel that were carried around through the streets in little baskets covered by a white cloth.

At the heart of the city – at the other end of the Ile de la Cité from the palace, with its garden of pumpkins, roses, lilies and mandrakes – was the spectacular rebuilding of Notre-Dame in the new Gothic style, with the highest vault in the world taking shape before their eyes. It must have been an extraordinary sight, surrounded by merchants and stalls, with the new breed of crafts-men and engineers in their masons' lodges, wandering in and out of the site looking for work, while the marble pillars were dragged laboriously all the way by sea from Rome and up the Seine. Each soaring archway relied on the mathematical insights of Arab books,

★ Even the future king and saint Louis IX was caught in this way a generation later. He stormed upstairs, grabbed the student responsible and gave him a scholarship. That's the kind of behaviour that deserves canonization.

written in the East and translated into Latin in Spain. In an era when most churches were made out of wood and straw, Saint-Denis and Notre-Dame — filled with coloured light from the glass, and the green, ochre, blue and violet paint on the walls, hung with tapestries where there weren't paintings — were further signs of the emerging new age. Together with the new architecture, it was a new theological style that went hand in hand with Abelard's humane morality. Gone were the autocratic statues of Christ on a throne, lord over the world. In their place were the new Gothic carvings of Jesus suffering like a vulnerable man on the cross. It was a revelation of a human and tolerant God.

Blondel and Neckham will have understood these symbols in a way that we no longer can. They were hard at work, starting the day at five or six in the morning with the watchman's horn blowing from the Grand Chastelet tower the moment the upper rim of the sun appeared above the horizon. They would only have shaved once a week — as was the custom — and would have poured out on to the streets with fellow students on their way to lectures, via morning mass. Then they crossed the Petit-Pont to the Left Bank, with the houses of intellectuals giving way quickly to the vineyards and wheatfields that surrounded the abbey schools, still frequented by the occasional wolf in winter. There they sat on straw on the floor or benches, with their wax tablets at the ready, while the beadle patrolled outside to keep the streets quiet.

At 10 a.m., they adjourned for dinner, and there were another six or seven hours of lectures before they hurried to the banks of the Seine — or home to make notes on parchment while it was still light. We can imagine them working in their tiny rooms, with ink horn, goose quill and penknife to sharpen it next to them, and maybe a stick of lead to rule margins on the page, and a goat's tooth for polishing parchment — and a candle guttering in the draught as they fell asleep at the desk. Along with the other students, they retired to sleep between eight and nine at night, perhaps bringing home some hot food from the cookshop by the river, off the rue de la Huchette, and fell asleep or lay awake worrying about how to afford to rent more books from the stationers, listening to the night watchmen calling out the hours, timed by the rising stars.*

There was no choice about what subjects to take. Students in Paris had to study the trivium (grammar, rhetoric and logic), but Blondel would perhaps have found more interest in the subsequent quadrivium (arithmetic, geometry, astronomy and music). Music teaching had a particularly important place at the University of Paris, which was the centre of debate between those who wanted to develop the pious plainsong tradition – where no notes or solo vocalists pierced the constant holy rhythm – and those who wanted something more elaborate and exciting, and therefore shocking. Like other students, Blondel would also have had to find ways of managing his teachers – they sat on 'thrones' in gowns, rings and long gloves, the proudest of them demanding the status of knights and insisting their positions were hereditary – while constantly exhausted from the strain of speaking Latin all day long. Anyone caught speaking one of the hundreds of local languages and dialects was beaten.

It was no easy life, but we can imagine that Blondel excited interest on his rare visits home to Nesle, a young man of a noble family who gave it all up for the life of a scholar. Perhaps his father complained about the cost. Or perhaps, as in one contemporary story, he blinded his family with logic: a son, sent to university in Paris at great expense, persuades his father through logic that the six eggs on the table are in fact twelve; 'Well, you won't mind if I eat six,' says his father, gobbling them down and leaving the table bare.

It was in Paris that Blondel achieved enough fame as a musician to have his music performed at the coronation of the new French king in 1179 – or at least to borrow the music for himself – and

---

*In the days before printing, it took one man a year to produce a complete copy of the Bible.

here that it is most likely he and Richard met.★ There are other times and places where this was possible. Richard and his brothers were in Reims Cathedral for the coronation, and they may have crossed each other's paths in Arras or at the great meeting of troubadours organized by the emperor Frederick Barbarossa in Mainz. They may even have met in Poitiers. History does not tell us. We also know that troubadours and *trouvères* met and mixed at the courts of Richard's half-sister Marie of Champagne and his brother Geoffrey of Brittany. But if Blondel was still moving in court circles by 1187, when Richard came to Paris to seek Philip's support against his father, they may well have met to share their interest in music. Legend says that Richard asked Blondel to be his tutor. Everything we know about Richard suggests that, however tense the political situation, he would have had moments of luxury, amusement and music.

The French king was nearly eight years younger than Richard, but had inherited his throne nearly a decade before. Richard and Philip were also completely unalike. Where Richard was fearless, Philip was physically nervous, refusing to ride on all but the most placid of horses. Where Richard had genuinely poor health but good spirits, Philip was a hypochondriac with little or no sense of humour, and a puritanical streak. He once had some knights dunked in the river for swearing during a gambling game, while Richard liberally decorated his conversation with his favourite oath, 'By the legs of God!' Where Richard was resplendent, Philip was prematurely balding, his clothes were slightly out of shape and he never combed his hair. Where Richard was multilingual, Philip could not understand Latin – which made him almost illiterate, though he was himself clearly highly intelligent and surrounded himself with educated advisers. On the other hand, where Richard was impetuous, Philip was patient and never lost sight of his basic goal.

★ If he finished his seven-year course, Blondel would have finally achieved his master's degree, after which he gave his specimen lecture, took his oath of obedience to his school, had a ring put on his finger to symbolize learning and was solemnly kissed by his examiners, whom he had to invite to a banquet.

Philip would chew on hazel twigs at the Great Council of France, taking no part in the discussions, wondering whether it had been given to him to make France great again. During one of these reveries, he realized the solution: he had to destroy the Angevin empire. Through the early summer of 1187, there had been simmering tensions between the forces of Philip Augustus and Henry II, with Richard exhaustingly negotiating between them to avoid the dangers of a pitched battle. So when, shortly afterwards, the heir to that Angevin empire rode into Paris seeking his support, Philip must have regarded it as a heaven-sent opportunity. They quickly became extremely close friends. 'Philip so honoured him that every day they ate at the same table, shared the same dish and at night the bed did not separate them,' wrote the chronicler Roger of Howden. 'And the King of France loved him as his own soul; and they loved each other so much that the King of England was absolutely astonished at the passionate love between them and marvelled at it.'

So have people ever since. Many people shared beds in those days, so this kind of behaviour did not in itself carry any implications of sexual intimacy, but it has fuelled the controversy over the past generation about whether Richard was bisexual, and – as we have seen – there is other evidence that he may have been, though there is no similar evidence about Philip. What is more interesting is the chronicler's use of the word *vehementem* in his account. It implied passion beyond mere friendship, and it is this that Henry was unnerved by. Perhaps it also explains why the relationship, physical or not, turned within the decade into the most intense dislike. Either way, we can be certain that the two became extremely fond of each other during Richard's visit, though it is impossible to know how much this friendship was fuelled on Philip's side by its strategic advantages. We also know that, as Philip and Richard shared their bed in Paris, far-off events in Palestine were gathering force in a shape that would change all their lives.

★

Four months after Richard arrived in Paris, the news began filtering through of a catastrophic defeat for the Christian forces in Palestine. On 3 July 1187, at the Battle of the Horns of Hattin – the legendary site of the Sermon on the Mount – an army led by the brilliant Kurdish tactician Saladin completely routed the Christian army of King Guy of Jerusalem. The captured Knights Templar and Hospitaller (the soldier-monks who had taken oaths to protect the crusader states) were all beheaded, the surviving ordinary Christian soldiers sold into slavery and the city of Jerusalem fell once more into Muslim hands.★

The crusades have become a byword for medieval brutality. But at the time, the tiny outpost in the Middle East was the jewel in the crown of Christendom, and the crusaders had ruled over Jerusalem and the Christian holy places for the past century. Their leading figures had also been aware for some years that a crisis was approaching. There was a constant struggle to attract the kind of Christian population there that could defend their outpost effectively, rather than relying on the brief periods of official crusades. While Christian soldiers of all classes and conditions flocked to the Holy Land for the First and Second Crusades, they tended not to stay. Once their crusader oaths had been fulfilled – usually by a pilgrimage to the Holy Sepulchre in Jerusalem – most of the foot soldiers trudged back to their families.† They took with them tales of untold luxuries, of exotic fruits and perhaps the first stories of chivalric love, borrowed from the Arabs and then distilled into the songs of the troubadours. But few stayed to defend the conquests afterwards.

The land of Outremer, as they called it, was anyway an unhealthy place to live for Western Europeans. Few of the crusader kings of Jerusalem lived beyond the age of forty. King Baldwin IV of Jerusalem was no exception: he had leprosy and, by 1184, knew

---

★There had been omens as far away as London, where there was a total eclipse of the moon as Saladin massed his troops on the Golan Heights.

†The Second Crusade had not been a success. Eleanor of Aquitaine had been sent home in disgrace after rumours of an affair with her crusader uncle Raymond of Antioch.

he was dying. It was then that he sent a desperate appeal to Europe via Heraclius, the patriarch of Jerusalem, and the grand masters of the Templars and Hospitallers. The Master of the Temple died on the journey, but the other two met the Pope and the Holy Roman Emperor in Verona. They finally caught up with Richard's father, Henry II, at Reading, and on their knees they begged him to return with them to be the next king of Jerusalem. It was a tempting offer for an ageing king, and though his favourite son, John, begged to be allowed to go instead, Henry refused. But he promised that if he could sort out his relationship with Philip Augustus he would lead a crusade. They just needed to give him a little time.

But time was not on the side of the small crusader outpost. Baldwin died in 1186 at the age of only twenty-seven, and his young nephew, Baldwin V, died early the following year. At the same time, a brilliant Muslim leader was emerging who was, for the first time, able to unite the Arab world behind him against the crusaders. Al-Malik al-Nasir Saleh ed-Din Yusuf – known to history as Saladin – came from a family of Kurdish army officers in the household of Nur ed-Din, the dominant ruler in the Arab world. When he was still in his twenties, and because Nur ed-Din wanted a compliant vassal, Saladin succeeded his uncle as vizier of Egypt. When Nur ed-Din died in 1174, he married his widow and seized the empire. At the age of thirty-eight, he had power in both Damascus and Cairo, north and south of the crusader states. He was slight, modest and pious, holding on to his position by sheer strategic flair, generosity and honesty, believing that his great ambition – to drive the Christians from the East – demanded moral as well as military leadership.

The other factor in the coming Christian defeat was the hopelessly incompetent leadership of Baldwin's successor as king of Jerusalem, Guy of Lusignan. Guy was charming and devastatingly handsome, but tended to agree with whoever he had last listened to and, finally and fatally, agreed with the hawkish Templars and Hospitallers, who urged action at precisely the wrong moment. How did a man unrelated to the Jerusalem royal house – who had been exiled from his native Poitou by Eleanor of Aquitaine after an abortive youthful attempt to take her hostage – end up as king? The answer was that heat and disease had done for all the likely male heirs to the throne, which meant that – in practice – the crown would go to the husband of the next woman in line. When Princess Sibylla, Baldwin IV's widowed sister, seemed determined to marry Guy, there was futile horror among the Christian aristocrats at their marriage and his subsequent coronation.

So it was that, when it really mattered, the forces of Christian Outremer were led into a disastrous battle against the brilliant Saladin by a man who looked attractive but whom they dared not trust and could not like. The Battle of the Horns of Hattin destroyed the fighting strength of the crusader states and led directly to the surrender of most of Outremer, except Antioch, Tripoli and the coastal port of Tyre. This caused the most profound crisis for the beleaguered Christians, east and west, but especially in Christian Palestine. This was not simply because everything they had fought for was in jeopardy; it was also that thousands of fresh crusader zealots from Western Europe began arriving to help them. And while this was welcome to the desperate crusader leaders, they had developed a way of life very different from that of their relatives back home in France or England, learning to coexist with the Arabs, even breeding a new class of half-European descendants – the *poulains* or 'kids', as they called themselves. Often they saw themselves as Galilean or Palestinian, rather than European. They regarded the newcomers, with their beards and religious fervour – not to mention their Western smell – with some distaste. The new crusaders, on the other hand, took one look at the permanent inhabitants of the Outremer princedoms, with their turbans, long hair, clean-shaven chins, spiced baths, silks and soft slippers, and pronounced them corrupt.

Until Hattin, Outremer had provided a reasonable life. The crusaders who stayed on had summer retreats in the hills for the hottest weather. In Antioch, they even had a sewerage system and running water to their houses. They had borrowed liberally from Arab culture, which was far more advanced at this stage than that of Western Europe.★ But it was a way of life that depended on living alongside the Muslim world, making basic agreements with them and keeping them, and this was a shocking idea for the fanatical newcomers. Both the disaster of the battle and the shock of disapproving new crusaders challenged the century-old Christian colonies.

Immediately after Hattin, it was all the inhabitants of Outremer could do to survive. They remembered the 40,000 Muslims who had died when they stormed Jerusalem a century before. The city's Christian inhabitants now forced their daughters to shave their heads in penance. Some took cold baths on Calvary hill, but they could not stave off the inevitable. On 2 October, three months after the battle, Saladin marched into the city. However, to the intense relief of the Christian population, he refrained from massacring them. He took them into captivity instead and gave them the chance to buy their way out. The 30,000 bezants put into the treasuries of the Templars and Hospitallers by Henry II as part of his penance for the death of Thomas Becket were used to free 7,000 of them. Meanwhile, Josias, Archbishop of Tyre, set off in a black galley with black sails to carry the awful news to Rome, which he reached on 20 October. Urban III, Pope for under three years, died of grief when he heard. To him and those like him across Western Europe, the Christian hegemony over the Holy Land was a reward for righteousness, a blessing for which they seemed no longer to be worthy.

His successor, Gregory VIII, proclaimed a new crusade, urging Christians to redouble their fervour – fasting completely on Fridays for five years, and abstaining from meat on Wednesdays and Saturdays too. But the enormous effort – either of making the proclamations or of fasting – was too much for him as well and he died just fifty-seven days later. By then, Josias was crossing the Alps, on his way to see the kings of France and England.

★

★Richard's generation of crusaders took chess sets with them to Palestine, though actually chess had been learned from the Arabs; *shah mat* (checkmate) is Persian for 'the king is dead'.

The military disaster in Outremer would have been complete except for the efforts of a Western aristocrat on the run from his crimes. Conrad of Montferrat was accused of murder, carried out in Constantinople, as a result of which he had decided to disappear quietly on pilgrimage for a while. Completely unaware of the battle or its aftermath, this hard-bitten middle-aged warrior from northern Italy sailed innocently into the port at Acre a few days after its capture. He was familiar with its busy harbour, loaded with silks, dyes and spices bound for Europe, and was suspicious when the usual bell that heralded every ship's arrival failed to ring. When a Muslim official came alongside, he pretended to be a merchant and – horrified at the news – set sail at once for Tyre, a little up the coast. Saladin had been quietly negotiating the surrender of Tyre, which is why he had failed to press his siege of the city to a military conclusion. But Conrad's arrival there changed the situation completely, and he was asked to take over the defence of the city.

It happened that Saladin had Conrad's elderly father in custody – he had most of the leading aristocrats of Outremer under lock and key – and he now paraded him in front of the walls and threatened to kill him unless the city surrendered. The old Marquis shouted at his son to do no such thing and, just to make the point, Conrad fired at his father from the walls with a crossbow. Saladin withdrew in awe at such cold-heartedness, but – in a typical piece of humanity – he spared the father anyway.

Much to the horror of his own hawks, Saladin also chose this moment to release King Guy, shrewdly realizing that his presence would cause more dissension among his opponents than his continued detention. He was absolutely right. When Guy arrived at Tyre to take command, Conrad ushered him out, explaining, 'I am only the lieutenant of the kings beyond the seas, and they have not authorized me to give the city up to you.'

What could he do, this landless king denied access to his only remaining city and left outside on the porch? He had of course sworn to Saladin not to attack him as a condition of his release, but since this oath had been made under duress it was easy to find a senior churchman to release him from it. There was little choice before him, but he chose to make one of the few dramatically courageous gestures of his life and it actually worked. With his few followers, he marched south to the port of Acre and laid siege to it. In military terms, taking his small force through enemy territory looked insane. His first attempt to scale the walls failed and it was clear that he could not seriously take the city by himself, but by occupying the narrow strip that connected Acre with the mainland – known as the hill of Toron, three-quarters of a mile to the east – he could divide the Muslim garrison from its sources of supply. He could then starve them into submission, supported by a sea blockade organized by the Pisan fleet, while he waited for the help from the West that he knew was bound to come if he could just hold on.

It was a desperate gamble, but it paid off. Saladin's failure to capture Tyre – which seemed such a small mistake at the time – now proved crucial. And try as they might, the Muslim troops could not dislodge Guy's men. Slowly, small parties of reinforcements began arriving, among them groups of enthusiasts too impatient for the Western monarchs to organize a rescuing crusade. One of these was Baldwin, Archbishop of Canterbury, leading a small contingent from England. He followed a group of French counts and other aristocrats who had arrived in the summer of 1190, under the leadership of one of Europe's most eligible bachelors, Henry of Champagne, the son of Marie of Champagne, Eleanor of Aquitaine's daughter and co-conspirator in the Courts of Love.

Even so, perched on his narrow promontory, all was not going well for Guy of Lusignan. For one thing, food was beginning to run short in his crusader encampment. Eggs now cost a silver penny each, and a sack of corn fetched 100 gold pieces. Each day there was the unedifying spectacle of his troops fighting over pieces of bread. There was a serious danger that the besiegers might starve before the besieged. This was all the more likely since it was clear that Muslim ships were managing to run the crusader blockade, slipping through by shaving off their beards and wearing Western clothes — some of them even putting pigs on deck to disguise themselves — and bringing the desperately needed supplies quietly into Acre harbour in the early hours of the morning.

Worse, Guy's wife, Sibylla — whose claim to the throne under-pinned his own — died in the summer of 1190 in one of the endless epidemics that swept through his camp, together with their two daughters. There were already open discussions about whether he was fit to be king. Worse still, in the relative safety of Tyre, Conrad was buttressing his own claim. The next in line after Sibylla was the attractive eighteen-year-old Isabella, the younger daughter of Baldwin's predecessor, King Amalric I. There was a slight impedi-ment here in that Isabella was already married — to the scholastic, beautiful and clean-shaven Humphrey of Toron, one of the few leading Outremer aristocrats who could also speak fluent Arabic. Humphrey was regarded as slightly effeminate, but he was also one of the only people who had ever been kind to her and she loved him.

But these were desperate times and many of the leading figures of the kingdom were determined to appoint a leader they had more faith in than Guy. It was also dawning on a horrified Humph-rey that there was a chance he was next in line to the throne, a post for which he felt himself ill-suited. To the rage of his wife, he escaped Tyre with her and made his way south to join Guy's party outside the gates of Acre. From there, Isabella was abducted from her tent by Conrad's supporters and dragged in front of her mother, who set about persuading her that her marriage was invalid.

The most senior Church figure available was the Archbishop of Canterbury, and he angrily denied the petition to dissolve Isabella and Humphrey's marriage. But there were others who recognized the urgency of the military situation, and Conrad turned next to the Archbishop of Pisa (a number of senior European churchmen felt it was their duty to be on the spot). Brushing aside rumours that Conrad had at least one wife still alive, he gave the necessary permission in return for a series of trade concessions for Pisa — and handed over the desperate couple for marriage to the king of

France's cousin Philip, Bishop of Beauvais. Baldwin furiously excommunicated everyone involved, to little effect. Five days before the grizzled old warrior Conrad of Montferrat married Isabella – on 24 November 1190 – the Archbishop of Canterbury died of rage.

Already the rival parties that would lead directly to Richard's future imprisonment were beginning to emerge. One camp was in Tyre under the leadership of Conrad; one was perched outside the city of Acre. Relations between the two were disintegrating, but they had agreed on one thing at least – by themselves, they could not stand up against the combined forces of the Arab world. All they could do was to hold out and wait for help from the West.

Within months of the loss of Jerusalem, the campaign to raise an army to recapture it was in full swing. Troubadours were writing songs about crusading, preachers were setting up in market places all over Europe, carrying with them a widely distributed poster of the Church of the Holy Sepulchre in Jerusalem, with a Saracen knight on a horse that was urinating on it from above. Those who conspicuously refused to go were sent a distaff and wool, the equivalent of white feathers. 'I can offer you a splendid bargain,' St Bernard had said a generation before, urging on the Second Crusade, and the same message was adapted for the Third. 'Do not miss this opportunity. Take the sign of the cross. At once you will have indulgence for all the sins which you confess with a contrite heart. It does not cost you much to buy and if you wear it with humility you will find that it is worth the kingdom of heaven.'

'Taking the cross' was the promise to go on crusade, and it must have seemed for some people a bargain commitment. Not only would you get to see the Holy City, but your debts would be postponed until your return and your property would be under the protection of the Church while you were away.

When the disastrous news of the Battle of the Horns of Hattin arrived in Paris in November 1187, Richard had taken the cross from the Archbishop of Tours and sewn it on to his surcoat, even before asking his father's permission. When Henry heard, he was so shocked that he shut himself up and refused to see anyone for days. Richard said he would go as long as his father promised him the succession, and this Henry calculatingly refused to do – twisting a little further the cycle of suspicion that would finally divide father and son. Henry and Philip met for a conference on the Normandy border on 21 January the following year – hearing a sermon by the Archbishop of Tyre himself – and both felt moved to take the cross as well. Chroniclers reported that they could see the shape of another cross in the sky above their heads as they did so.

Their agreement was that French soldiers were to wear red crosses, English soldiers white crosses and Flemish soldiers green crosses. There would be special rules forbidding swearing or gambling among the troops, and this time there would be no women, except what they called 'washerwomen of good character'. The whole project was to be paid for with a serious tax across the whole of both kingdoms, known as the Saladin Tithe – one-tenth of everyone's income for three years. Those who refused to pay would be excommunicated; those who took the cross were exempt.

Impatience to see the heroic armies set off forced Henry and Philip together for a peace conference a year later, early in 1189, in Bonmoulins. Henry's first shock was to see Richard arrive with Philip hand in hand. His second was their joint ultimatum – including the demand that Richard should be allowed immediately to marry Philip's sister Alys (still Henry's lover) and that Henry should acknowledge Richard as his heir. Philip had been playing on Richard's fears – why hadn't his father's favourite son, John, taken the cross? Was it because he was grooming him to replace Richard? But Henry refused to be forced into any commitment that might relieve his fears. 'Now at last I must believe what I had always thought was impossible,' said Richard bitterly, and he knelt and gave homage to Philip for all Angevin lands on the Continent. It was a kind of declaration of war against his father.

Having done so, Richard stormed out of the meeting. Henry sent his illegitimate son Geoffrey – his legitimate son Geoffrey of

Brittany had already died – and William the Marshal after him, but when they reached the place he had stayed the night before, they found he had sent out 200 letters that evening. There was clearly little chance of persuading him to return and an open rift between father and son seemed inevitable. The Pope's legate failed to bring the sides together and, in June 1189, Richard and Philip jointly invaded the Angevin county of Maine, bringing Richard face to face again unexpectedly with William the Marshal in an ambush.

'By God's legs, do not kill me,' shouted Richard in the mêlée. 'I am unarmed.'

'No, let the devil kill you, for I won't,' said William, chivalrous as always, spearing his horse instead, and leaving Richard in tears on the ground, surrounded by his knights.

But Henry was ill and tired, and for once the rebellion was too much for him. He limped exhausted back to the safety of his own castle of Chinon. From his sickbed he agreed to an amnesty for everyone who had conspired against him, and on 5 July he was brought a list of their names. And there on the top he saw his own favourite son, John. 'Is it true that John, my heart, John, whom I loved more than all my sons, and for whose gain I suffered all these evils, has forsaken me?' asked Henry in despair. When it was clear that the list was accurate, he turned to the wall and lapsed into a delirium. He died the following day, leaving instructions that his brain should be buried in Charroux in Poitou, his heart in Rouen in Normandy, and his embalmed body next to his father in Fontevrault Abbey. His last words had been, 'Shame, shame on a conquered king.'

As soon as he was dead and Geoffrey, the only one of his children who was still with him, had left the room, his servants stole all his personal effects and fled. When Richard reached Chinon and stared at the corpse, it was said that blood flowed suddenly out of its nose as an accusation of murder. When the news reached Salisbury, Eleanor's jailors set her free after nearly sixteen years' imprisonment, and – in the name of her son – she started issuing edicts, relaxing the forest laws and emptying the prisons. She also had poor Alys – her husband's mistress, whom Richard had now failed to marry for nearly two decades – confined to her apartments in Winchester.

Richard was now king, and his first acts were – rather perversely, it seemed to his closest followers – to reward those who had stayed loyal to his father. There was a scene of chivalric reconciliation with William the Marshal, who had nearly killed him less than a week before. 'Thank you, sire. Thank you, fair sweet sire,' said William, rewarded with a marriage to a considerable heiress. 'I did by no means desire your death.'

On 13 August, Richard sailed from Barfleur and was welcomed with enthusiasm in Portsmouth. Two days later he was received in Winchester, was reunited with his mother and, to his great relief, secured the royal treasury. On 1 September, mother and son rode through the streets of London, which were hung with tapestries and garlands, the roads spread with fresh rushes all the way to St Paul's Cathedral. From there, a procession escorted them across the River Fleet, up what is now the Strand and to the royal palace at Westminster. Two days later, he was crowned in Westminster Abbey, the traditional place of coronation of English kings and already more than a century old. He was determined that his coronation should be the most sumptuous. You would expect nothing less from the first king of England since the Norman Conquest to have succeeded to the throne without question or opposition, and from a romantic determined to wrap himself in the spirit of Arthurian chivalry – and, what's more, as a Christian prince embarking on a voyage to seize Jerusalem back for Christendom.

He processed along a path of woollen cloth from his chamber in the palace right up to the Abbey's high altar. At the head of the procession was a group of priests carrying crosses and sprinkling holy water. Ahead of him came four senior barons carrying golden candelabra and the crown jewels – including the great golden crown of precious stones looted from the German treasury two generations before by his grandmother the Empress Matilda. Barechested at the altar, he was anointed with holy oil. Then he handed the crown to Baldwin, Archbishop of Canterbury – about to leave for the Holy Land – who in turn placed it on his head. It was so heavy that it required two earls to reach over and take part of the weight. A bat fluttered around the throne as Richard sat there. It was considered a bad omen.

The coronation banquet was a sumptuous affair, including 5,050 dishes, 1,700 pitchers of wine and 900 cups. But at the height of the meal, a disaster took place outside which was to cast a dark shadow over Richard's reputation. In line with the holiness of the ceremony – a coronation for a departing crusader – no women had been allowed to the coronation, and the wealthy Jewish moneylenders had also been asked to stay away. This was to be a male, Christian affair. But a group of Jewish leaders decided it would be politic to arrive anyway, bringing gifts for the new king. Not only were they barred from the banquet, but they found themselves attacked by the crowd outside. Many of them were killed, including Jacob of Orléans, one of the most learned men in Europe, who happened to be visiting London at the time. The riots then spread quickly across the city and Jewish families shut themselves up in the Tower of London for safety.

When he heard about the disaster, Richard ordered that the ringleaders should be executed, and sent letters around the country demanding that Jews should be left in peace. But thanks to crusade fever, some new spirit was abroad that was demonstrating the shadow side of the twelfth century's tolerance. The anti-Semitic crusading spirit spread quickly across the country to Bishop's (now King's) Lynn, Norwich, Stamford and Lincoln. In March the following year, a hideous massacre took place in York, where 150 Jews took refuge from the mob in the castle. Many of them killed their own wives and children and committed suicide rather than surrender. The rest were promised safe conduct if they would accept Christian baptism, but when they came out they were murdered anyway.

It was a crime that was repeated in other parts of Europe in the grip of crusading insanity, and it tainted the reign of the new king. But by then Richard was already back on the Continent and on his way to the Holy Land and destiny. Among his entourage, by tradition anyway, were his other illegitimate brother, William

Longspee, Jehan I of Nesle and the *trouvères* Gace Brulé and
Blondel.

It would take more than eighteen months from the coronation for
Richard to arrive outside the walls of Acre as joint leader of the
Anglo-French Third Crusade. The first few months of his reign
were a period of frenetic organization and fund-raising, partly by
collecting the Saladin Tithe, but also by any other means that
emerged. The English court was in for an unpleasant surprise.
They knew, of course, that their splendid new king was intending
to leave as soon as he could for Palestine, just as they knew
that the German emperor Frederick Barbarossa was preparing an
enormous army with the same purpose. But they were unprepared
for his sweeping series of new appointments and his vigorous
fund-raising methods.

The biggest shock was the appointment of William Longchamp,
the Bishop of Ely – Richard's former chancellor in Aquitaine – as
Chancellor of England, in charge of all the finances of the kingdom.
Longchamp was short and limping and he had a stammer – he was
like a 'hairy deformed ape', according to the chronicler Giraldus
Cambrensis – and was rumoured to be the grandson of a runaway
serf. He was unswervingly loyal to Richard, but also worryingly
confident and ambitious. He spoke no English and not only
disliked the English but made the mistake of saying so. He was
also widely accused of paedophilia.

Crusades were staggeringly expensive, and Richard and Longchamp together were a fund-raising duo of frightening determination, selling off manors and sheriffdoms all over the empire.
Richard 'would fight for anything whatever, but would sell everything that was worth fighting for,' said the Victorian historian
Bishop Stubbs. He was, in short, an enthusiastic privatizer. Even
existing office holders were expected to pay for their continued
employment. Longchamp himself set an example by paying £3,000
for his own position as chancellor, though someone called
Reginald the Italian had actually put in a higher bid. Ranulf de
Glanville, John's former tutor and the keeper of Henry's prisoners

– not a popular man with the new king, since one of the prisoners had been Eleanor – was ruined by the effort of buying back his own titles and had to leave for Palestine himself to postpone settling his debts. The new Pope, Clement III, also allowed Richard to excuse his vassals from their crusading pledge on payment of a hefty fee.

Thanks to the efficient Angevin administration of England, Longchamp was able to levy high taxes on what was an increasingly prosperous country, with a population of somewhere between 2 and 3 million. For Richard, England was not just the jewel in the crown of his inheritance but the equivalent of a giant bank. 'I would sell London itself if I could find a buyer,' he said.

His need for money and the demand of towns for self-government happened to coincide neatly. He and his brother John later were great providers of charters to towns, setting up new links with the town 'communes' against the staunch opposition of the local aristocrats. Other rulers across Europe were brutally suppressing these early communes, the self-appointed corporations of local townspeople. But when they received petitions from towns and cities asking for the right to form a commune, to run their own affairs rather than live with the continued despotism of the local lord, Richard and Eleanor's instinct was to agree. And with Richard, it helped that he could also charge a reasonable fee. London took the opportunity of a break for self-government, and in 1190 they appointed the first Mayor of London, Henry FitzAilwin. He stayed mayor for life.

Richard prepared the country for his departure at breakneck speed. The Scots were reassured and released from treaty obligations in return for another large payment. The feuding monks of Canterbury were successfully brought together. Richard's illegitimate brother Geoffrey was neutralized as a claimant to the throne by forcing him to take holy orders – priests could not inherit – and making him Archbishop of York. In the position of justiciar – the prime minister's role – Richard appointed Longchamp south of the Humber and, to keep him in check, Bishop Hugh de Puiset of Durham north of it. To Eleanor's grandson Otto of Brunswick, the son of Henry the Lion of Saxony, was delegated the task of ruling Aquitaine, and the untrustworthy John was loaded with lands in the West Country to make him a little less hungry for taking over his brother's.

There were two routes to Palestine in those days: the hot, exhausting overland route and the fast, cool but unpredictable way by sea. The Third Crusade was the first to plan a sea voyage and Philip had contracted with the Genoese republic to take his own men down the Mediterranean. Richard commandeered every seaworthy ship on the English coast from Hull to Bristol and ordered them to Dover, agreeing to pay two-thirds of the cost. He also placed orders for arms and armour all over his domains, including 50,000 horseshoes from one ironworks in the Forest of Dean. Some were too impatient to wait for the king, like Baldwin, Archbishop of Canterbury, and a flotilla from London sailed through the Straits of Gibraltar on Michaelmas Day 1189. Ye Olde Trip to Jerusalem Inn, underneath Nottingham Castle, dates from this momentous point in English history when the whole nation was impatient for the army's departure on a holy enterprise for which so many of them had contributed with extra taxes.

Richard divided his treasury among the fleet and decided to leave behind the mummified hand of St James from Reading Abbey. This was another of the priceless items looted by Richard's grandmother from the Germans in Cologne, and a festering sore in his relations with the Holy Roman Emperor, Frederick Barbarossa, that would prove important on his journey home. Richard contented himself with stripping the hand of its gold covering. But as both kings prepared for their armies to meet in France, ready to set sail, there was a series of disconcerting pieces of news. First there was the unexpected death in childbirth of Philip's wife (she became the first French queen to be buried in Notre-Dame). As she died it was reported that Frederick Barbarossa had crossed the Bosphorus and into Asia Minor at the head of a gigantic army, following the route of Alexander the Great fifteen centuries before. But by the time the French and English armies met outside Lyons in July 1190 – probably around 10,000 of them rather than the chroniclers'

100,000 – the news was filtering through that Barbarossa had been thrown by his horse crossing the Calycadnus River and had died after suffering a heart attack from the shock of the cold water.

It was a devastating blow. Barbarossa's body was kept in vinegar for the rest of the long, hot march, but this turned out not to be an adequate preservative. All that remained of him was buried quickly in Antioch Cathedral, with a few bones secretly taken with what remained of his army under the command of his younger son, Frederick of Swabia.

Meanwhile, the English fleet set sail from Dartmouth at Easter 1190, complete with a set of fearsome regulations about proper conduct, which were entirely ignored when the soldiers went on the rampage after putting in at Lisbon. Gathered on either side of the Rhône, with the banners of Richard (golden lions on a red background) and Philip (golden fleurs-de-lis against blue) fluttering over them, the main body of French, English and Flemish troops finally set off southwards on 4 July 1190 by the light of flares. Women brought jugs of water to the roadside for them, people cheered and sang hymns as they went by, and there were tearful final embraces and babies lifted up high to see them pass by. The peasants fled, taking their livestock as far from the army as possible – medieval armies had to fend for themselves and could have the same effect as locusts on the surrounding countryside.

When Richard arrived in Marseilles there was still no sign of the English fleet, which was still trying to extricate itself from Lisbon. But he set off anyway in his own galley, *Piombone*, along the Riviera coast, hoping that the rest would overtake him by sailing directly between Corsica and Sardinia. He went briefly ashore again at Genoa, past the famous lighthouse, with the townspeople hanging carpets out of their windows above the port to welcome him. He had meetings with the local lord Grimaldo Grimaldi, whose family still rules Monaco to this day.* Then a quick visit to the Bank of St George, which was handling his

---

* Grimaldi's younger son, Frederick, joined the crusade as master of Richard's crossbowmen.

money, and it was back on the voyage down the Italian coast towards Sicily, putting in at Pisa, but refusing to see the Pope, whom Richard disliked, and in Salerno to see the famous doctors about his recurrent shaking.

It was a triumphal progress by a supremely confident monarch revelling in his own status as the hero of Christendom and the romantic successor of King Arthur. Perhaps it was to celebrate this apotheosis of Christian chivalry, perhaps it was to assuage the deprivations of the Saladin Tithe, but it was at this moment that the news filtered out that the monks of Glastonbury Abbey in Somerset had discovered the grave of King Arthur and Queen Guinevere.

The story went back to the months of Richard's final showdown with his father, when a new abbot arrived at Glastonbury, which was then struggling to recover from a disastrous fire that had burned down their buildings five years earlier. He suggested that they act on royal advice given some years before to find out if the stories of the Welsh bards were true and that Arthur was really buried there. So as Richard was sailing down the Italian coast, they dug at the legendary spot between two ancient stone pyramids, and behind screens to keep out the public. Some way down they found an unusual cross with the inscription 'Here lies buried the renowned King Arthur, with Guenevere his second wife, in the Isle of Avalon'. By the time they had got sixteen feet down, they found an enormous hollowed oak coffin. At one end were the bones of a woman with her golden hair still attached. A monk grabbed at the tresses and they fell to dust in his hand. At the other end of the coffin was the skeleton of a gigantic man. The skull was so big that the eye sockets were almost the size of a palm. There were the marks of wounds all over the bones.★ The news spread across Europe that the bones of King Arthur had been discovered. It was a tremendous omen: the very epitome of chivalry seemed to have risen from the dead to bless his heroic successor.

★

★ The bones have been missing since the Reformation and the lead cross since the seventeenth century.

Richard's preliminary objective was Sicily and here he ran into difficulty in a typical fashion. Having landed quietly by himself and set off with just one knight towards the town of Gioja, he heard the cry of a hawk. Following it to the house of its owner, he found – to his great irritation – that the man was unwilling to part with the beautiful bird, despite (as Richard saw it) not being of sufficient rank to deserve it. Matters quickly got out of hand. Richard lost his temper, grabbed the hawk and prepared to leave the house. Having no idea who he was, the family refused to let him go. In the mêlée, one of them drew a knife and attacked. Richard responded by hitting him with the flat of his sword, and at this crucial moment it became clear that there was a flaw in the steel and the blade broke in half. He escaped by the skin of his teeth.

Safely back on board his own ship the next morning, he arrived in the Straits of Messina to find that they were filled as far as the eye could see with French and English ships. But when Richard reached them, he found that the inevitable underlying tensions between the two armies were being exacerbated by the new ruler of the island. Tancred of Lecce had allowed Philip to find comfortable lodgings in the city, but – following trouble with the townspeople – was refusing to let the English soldiers land.

Sicily was always going to be a problem. For one thing, Richard knew that his formidable mother was on her way to meet him there, having travelled – at the age of sixty-nine – all the way to Navarre, in the north of what is now Spain, to fetch his bride, Berengaria. It was a marriage alliance negotiated in the utmost secrecy, but before any arrangements had been made to extricate himself from his original engagement to Philip's sister Alys. For another, Richard's sister Joanna had married William II of Sicily when she was eleven, but he had died without leaving an heir the previous year.* The Pope had been horrified by the prospect of the next in line, Constance of Sicily – married to Barbarossa's eldest son, Henry – uniting Sicily with the Holy Roman Empire

* William's main claim to fame was his salacious habits with slave girls from the Barbary coast.

on either side of his lands. He had therefore intrigued to hand the throne instead to Tancred, an illegitimate cousin of William's and also widely considered by contemporaries to look like a monkey. Richard was determined to retrieve his sister, now under house arrest, as well as her dowry.

Growing tensions with the locals, and Tancred's failure to comply with his immediate demands – plus the discovery of a secret passage into the city – led to Richard's snap decision to take Messina. It was accomplished 'in the time it takes to say Matins', watched uncomfortably by Philip from his lodgings inside the walls. Tancred duly responded with apologies for their treatment, and handed over 40,000 ounces of gold from Joanna's original dowry. She herself followed a little later. She had been away since she was a child and was now twenty-five, beautiful and brilliant. Philip met her as well and was clearly taken with her, especially as he was now searching for an eligible new bride.

Richard and Philip's agreement was that they would split the proceeds of the crusade between them equally. An embarrassed Philip now demanded half the city which had been taken under his very nose, but Richard gave it to the Templars and Hospitallers, and instead organized the building of a massive fortified wooden tower overlooking the city walls, known as Mategriffon ('curb the Greeks').

It had always been their plan to spend the winter in Sicily, making final preparations for sailing to Palestine. It was not considered safe to cross the Mediterranean after the end of September. But it was a long, irritable autumn, culminating in Christmas dinner in Mategriffon, to which Richard invited Philip. It was almost their last friendly meeting. After Christmas, the matter of Alys and Richard's marriage would simply wait no longer. In the early spring, he asked Philip, Count of Flanders – well known as intelligent and articulate – if he would mediate with the king of France.

In the end, Philip Augustus had no choice but to accept what he was told. He had no reason to suppose that Richard was lying when he said that Alys had been his father's mistress, and in those circumstances it was impossible to insist that the marriage go ahead. But stiff conditions were attached (10,000 pounds of silver) and, with great irritation, Philip gathered his ships and set off towards Acre, smarting at what had been a humiliating rebuff. Carefully timed to avoid him, Eleanor of Aquitaine's galley then slipped into Reggio harbour in Sicily. She carried with her Berengaria of Navarre – said to be 'sensible rather than attractive' – whom Richard had chosen after meeting her at a tournament in Pamplona, and wooing her exhaustingly according to the rules of courtly love, possibly since the age of twenty. As such, she was the chivalric choice; but she was also the choice of a southern prince – the alliance with Navarre would secure the southern borders of Aquitaine.

It was Lent and weddings were banned under ecclesiastical law, so Eleanor left immediately on the long journey home overland via Rome. While they were dismantling Mategriffon, packing it in sections into the ships, Tancred took Richard to see Mount Etna and on an impulse showed him letters from Philip promising help if he rejected Richard's demands. Moved by this unexpected display of friendship, Richard experienced one of his episodes of impulsive generosity. He sealed a comprehensive alliance with Tancred there and then and agreed to marry Tancred's baby daughter to his own heir, Geoffrey of Brittany's son Arthur. To seal their understanding, Richard presented Tancred with a sword he said was Excalibur, with the strong implication that it had been found in King Arthur's tomb in Glastonbury.

The medieval intrigues of European diplomats were always complex. Richard probably congratulated himself that he had negotiated the potential pitfalls very skilfully, and in some ways he had. But in twenty short months or so, he would have cause to realize that the seeds of his disastrous arrest had been sown in Sicily. It was clear, for one thing, that his relationship with Philip, and therefore the French, was firmly on a downward spiral – as Tancred's letters would have reminded him – just four years since they had been sharing a bed in Paris. But he should also have been concerned that he had allied himself with the illegitimate usurper

of the throne of Sicily, when the rightful heirs – Barbarossa's son
Henry of Hohenstaufen and his wife, Constance – were even then
marching south to take it back.

But as the English fleet finally set sail, in Easter week 1191, these
concerns were probably disappearing from Richard's mind on the
sea breeze. His high admiral Robert de Turnham, whose brother
Stephen was also commanding ships, eased the 203 ships into six
lines of galleys, with the big transports known as busses at the rear,
and sailed them out of the straits and into the Adriatic. As darkness
fell, a light from the mast of the king's ship guided the others
through the night. But the very day they sailed, the diplomatic
situation was twisting further. Pope Clement III died in Rome –
another short-lived papal reign – and four days later the cardinals
elected in his place the 85-year-old diplomat Giacinto Bobo, who
actually had to be ordained in order to take up the position. In his
younger days, the new Pope, Celestine III, had been a brilliant
thinker, a defender of the great Abelard himself and a vigorous
negotiator on behalf of the papacy. But the thrusting Bobo was
now the frail and timid Celestine, and the papacy – the only means
of controlling recalcitrant kings and princelings – was suddenly in
weak hands.

His first act was to crown Barbarossa's heir, Henry of Hohenstaufen – who had arrived with his army in Rome on the way
south to invade Sicily – as the Holy Roman Emperor Henry VI.
In a final demonstration of his own superiority to temporal power,
the Pope horrified onlookers at the coronation by kicking the
crown off the new emperor's head: it was his last burst of resistance
against Henry's domination. Making her way through Rome at
the same time going north, Eleanor also met the new Pope –
whom she had trusted as a go-between with her husband and
Thomas Becket – but studiously avoided the imperial couple. She
needed papal support if she was going to control the different
factions back in England. She would not have guessed that, in two
years' time, she was going to need Celestine very badly indeed.

4. Acre

'Blondel de Nesle!' he exclaimed joyfully – 'welcome from Cyprus,
my king of minstrels! – welcome to the King of England, who rates
not his own dignity more highly than he does thine. I have been sick,
man, and, by my soul, I believe it was for lack of thee; for, were I half
way to the gate of heaven, methinks thy strains could call me back.'

Richard greeting Blondel in Sir Walter Scott's novel,
The Talisman, 1825

'Hope deferred maketh the heart sick.'

Psalm 13

Richard's Mediterranean voyage with his enormous fleet did not
go according to plan. The ships were hit by an exceptional storm
on their way east which sank twenty-four of them and scattered
the others. The drowned body of the bearer of the Great Seal of
England, Roger Malcael, was washed ashore on the coast of
Cyprus, with the seal still safely around his neck. When the remains
of the fleet took shelter in Rhodes harbour, it became clear that
the galley carrying Berengaria and Joanna was missing. It had taken
twenty years for Richard to finally find himself a wife, and – as
well as the concerns he would have had for them – he undoubtedly
cursed the thought that he was going to have to start all over again.
But their ship turned out to be sheltering outside Limassol harbour,
on the coast of Cyprus, an island that had been for five years under
the iron grip of a junior member of the Byzantine royal house,
Isaac Comnenus, who had tricked his way into controlling it as an
independent state. Worse, he had also negotiated an agreement

with Saladin which, it was widely believed, involved drinking each other's blood.*

Isaac knew precisely who was on board the ship. He refused them fresh water and prevented them from landing in preparation for taking them hostage. But he had reckoned without Richard, who descended on the island with a fury, stormed up the beach at Limassol and – in a daring night attack – narrowly missed capturing him. Isaac rapidly came to terms and then, just as rapidly, tore up the agreement. Once ashore, Richard also discovered a high-ranking delegation waiting for him from Acre, including Guy of Lusignan – the hapless king of Jerusalem – as well as Guy's brother and the now divorced Humphrey of Toron. They told him that Philip had arrived there three weeks before and was plotting to replace Guy as king with Conrad of Montferrat. Richard unwisely gave them his support.

Then, lending part of the army to Guy to track down and capture Isaac, he finally married Berengaria on 12 May 1191, in the Chapel of St George in Limassol. She was crowned queen of England there by the Bishop of Evreux. Richard had no plans to invade Cyprus, but now he had successfully done so, it seemed a strategic masterstroke for the embattled crusaders. From the eastern shores of the island, you could see the mountains of Lebanon. This was at last an effective island base from which to keep the Christian outpost supplied.†

Binding him in silver chains – in order to keep a promise not to clap him in irons – Richard put Isaac and his family aboard the fleet and set sail on the fast galley *Trenchmere* for the Holy Land. It was 5 June. Nearly a year had gone by since the joint army had set off from Lyons. Conrad refused to let them drop anchor at Tyre – an ominous sign – and on 8 June they finally landed outside

---

*Five years before, Isaac Comnenus had arrived in Cyprus with forged documents declaring him the new governor from Constantinople. Once he had taken over the key fortresses, he claimed the island as its independent ruler.

†The Cypriots were not necessarily better off. Richard imposed a 50 per cent levy on the population and confirmed the traditional laws of the islands, but forced the Greeks on the island to shave off their beards.

Acre. Having led the way to Tyre, Richard was almost the last to arrive. But the embarrassing moment of the arrival of his new queen was generously glossed over by Philip (still nursing a grievance on behalf of his rejected sister), who embraced her and lifted her down from the boat himself.

As he arrived, Richard would have seen tens of thousands of people spread before him – the besieged city and 'the flower of the world camped around it' – from Saladin's command in the distance on the Hill of the Carob Trees to the hundreds of crusader tents and the 300 catapults and siege engines surrounding the city walls. These had challenging names like the Bad Neighbour and God's Own Sling, and were soon to be joined by Mategriffon and the others. With the constant thudding as the engines dispatched their loads, and the screams of the wounded, it was hard to sleep at night.* There also were the miners tunnelling under the foundations of the city walls. In the coloured banners around him, Richard would have recognized representatives of almost every aristocratic family in Western Europe, as well as those of bishops from all over the known world, and Templars under their great black and white *Beau-Séant* flag.

What he could not have seen was the intricate web of rivalries that were tearing the crusader camp apart. The Pisans had tried and failed in a bold assault on the Tower of Flies, the stone sentinel at the harbour mouth, and were bitter about it and declared themselves for Richard. The Genoese had already declared allegiance to Philip and the French, and therefore Conrad. When he heard rumours that Philip was offering three gold pieces for any non-aligned soldiers to join him, Richard could not resist offering four.

Richard himself was a magnificent sight, appearing dressed as he had been at his wedding, on a Spanish charger with golden spurs, a silver scabbard and a scarlet bonnet with birds and animals

---

* Such was the passion of the besiegers that one woman, mortally wounded in the fighting, offered her body as part of the stones and rubbish being used to fill in the moat.

sewn on to it. 'When Richard came, the king of the French was extinguished and made nameless, even as the moon loses its light at sunrise,' wrote one chronicler. Philip clearly felt the same.

Either through courtesy or lack of military confidence, Philip had delayed the final assault on Acre until Richard's arrival. But having once arrived at the objective, both kings fell ill from some kind of scurvy that made their hair and nails fall out. This was a peculiar torture for a hypochondriac like Philip Augustus, who stayed suffering in his tent. Richard had his sickbed carried near the city walls and occupied his time picking off Saracens with a crossbow, offering four gold pieces for any piece of city wall that could be removed. The extraordinary courage of the Muslim garrison, manning the walls night and day without sleep, was increasingly impressing the crusaders, but it was clear that the city must now fall. Saladin's faithful eunuch Karakush, commanding the garrison, was able to negotiate a surrender that would mean safe conduct for the garrison for a ransom of 200,000 gold pieces, the release of 1,500 Christian prisoners and the restoration of the Holy Cross. When a Muslim swimmer managed to leave the harbour and get through the Christian lines to tell Saladin what had been agreed, he was horrified and sat in front of his tent composing a message that forbade the garrison to submit on those terms.★ But as he did so, he could see the crusader banners being unfurled on the city walls. It was too late. The treaty had been made in his name and he was a man of honour, so he would honour it if he could.

'Pen cannot fully describe, nor tongue tell, the people's rapture at his arrival,' wrote Canon Richard of Holy Trinity in London about Richard's arrival in Acre. 'Horns resounded, trumpets rang out, while pipers added their shrill notes. To show the gladness of their hearts, they burst into popular songs.' Richard, with his wife, Berengaria, his sister Joanna and their entourage – and according

---

★ Saladin had to rely on swimmers and birds to keep in touch with the garrison; a large house for homing pigeons was kept next to his pavilion.

to Sir Walter Scott this included Blondel – moved into the royal
palace on the middle of the north wall. Philip Augustus moved
into the former Templar headquarters by the harbour. All would
then have experienced for themselves a city that made crusaders
of previous generations gasp with astonishment. This was the port
where the gold and silver coins of Western Europe poured through
the docks and customs, in exchange for cargoes of pharmaceuticals,
herbs, spices, jewels and pearls – not to mention the luxurious
fabrics of the Middle East: damask (Damascus), gauze (Gaza) and
muslin (Mossul).

What is now the dilapidated walled Israeli city of Akko, eight
miles from the modern port of Haifa, was a former Phoenician
trading city as important as Constantinople. Even then, it was a
meeting place between two worlds, and for the newly arrived
crusaders it was a glimpse into another universe. The new arrivals
wandered through the captured city. Its famous wine shops and
brothels, pulled down by the Muslims, had been replaced with
7,000 new cookshops and 1,000 baths to serve Saladin's army.
They must have watched the heavy iron chain raised and lowered to
let in the ships that began to flock once again to the inner harbour,
and heard the church bells ringing for their arrival, heralded by the
sentinels in the Tower of Flies. Like everyone else, they will have
joined in the Acre habit of watching to see what flag was flying from
the mast of the galleys as they arrived – whether it was St Mark
(Venetians), St Peter (Pisans) or St Lawrence (Genoese). Or if it was
a whole convoy – and sometimes 100 ships arrived at once, the bigger
ones carrying anything up to 1,000 packed pilgrims each or 500 tons
of cargo – they watched the forests of masts and sails squeeze into
the docks, and experienced the enormous injection into the local
economy from the passengers and crew. The new arrivals docked
first at the wharf of the inner harbour. Straight ahead of them they
would have seen the Court of the Chain – the customs – the round
tower and the coffee house. They would then have glimpsed the
great iron gates into the city on the left, and on their right the
Church of San Marco, dominating the Venetian sector of the city,
facing out into the bay.

There, ranged before them, were the taverns, dice games and prostitutes, and they would have experienced the strange sensation of watching the whole world pass by in the narrow streets. Acre was also a divided city. There were Jews, rabbis and synagogues from rival sects all over the Mediterranean. The bitter trading rivalries of Italy had also transferred themselves there, to such an extent that the different nationalities had their own city walls and squares, even their own officials and police inside the city – and their own clutch of customs officers at the dockside making sure their own nationals got their respective privileges. As well as the Venetian quarter, there was the Genoese quarter, around the church of St Lawrence, with its covered shopping street and its famous soap-makers. Both the Templars and the Hospitallers had their own cities within the city, and their own rival systems of weights and measures. There were enclaves for Pisans, Amalfitans, Provençals, Germans and Bretons. There was even an English street, dedicated to poor pilgrims, with a hospice named after St Thomas Becket. There was also the magnificent Hospitaller headquarters, with its underground chambers and beds for 2,000 patients. The new arrivals took all this in as the city sprang back to life around them, sipping the spiced tea with sugar and lemon like the locals, tasting the dates and the sugar cane – Acre had its own refinery – as well as the gingerbread from Alexandria and the oranges from Lebanon. It was also for many of them their first sight of bananas – the crusaders called them apples of paradise – grown on the left bank of the Jordan.

It is possible to imagine Blondel and his compatriots wandering down the main rue de la Boucherie, running from the outer wall to the harbour, holding their noses at the stench of the slaughterhouses and tanneries down by the docks, and watching Acre's notorious sex trade rapidly re-establishing itself through the bazaars. Not to mention the smell of camels mixed in with the pepper, cinnamon, nutmeg, cloves, ginger, figs and pomegranates, all set out on stalls under canopies to keep off the sun. Around them, the mosques were being converted quickly back into churches and minarets into bell towers, and pigs were arriving back on to the streets to eat the garbage. And the banks were re-establishing their branches so that crusaders could cash a money draft rather than carry gold all the way across the known world. This was a city of remittance men, spies, heretics and assassins, of plots and skulduggery, where poisons were openly on sale in the street and where even the priests rented their houses out as brothels because it was just so lucrative. It was a place of misunderstandings, with a multiplicity of races and languages – Saladin's secretary complained about the appalling translation problems they had interrogating prisoners – and of uncategorizable mixtures of races too. And here from his palace high on the walls, Richard planned the next stage of his advance.

Richard's first few weeks in this wonder city included two of the most important events of his life. The first, barely remarkable at the time, would be a major cause of his eventual arrest; the second would leave a stain on his reputation that history has never quite washed out.

Two days before Richard moved into the royal palace, the non-aligned barons – some of whom had been outside Acre for two years, waiting for the booty that would make the trip worthwhile – held a protest meeting. Richard and Philip met them and promised they would be rewarded, though absolutely nothing happened, and many of them just sold their arms so that they could go home. The German army was led by Barbarossa's younger son, Frederick of Swabia, but he had died of disease earlier in the year and, in the spring, Duke Leopold V of Austria arrived from Venice to take command of the remaining Germans. He was a nephew of Barbarossa but also – and here was yet another diplomatic twist – the son of Theodora Comnena, a relative of the Cyprus tyrant Isaac, still in his silver chains and therefore a source of continued friction between the two families. It was even said that Richard had conceived a passion for Isaac's daughter. Leopold came to represent those remaining barons who owed allegiance to neither the French nor the English.

To make matters worse, once the crusaders had moved into the city, Leopold ordered a small protest on their behalf. He ordered his flag to be flown next to Richard's lions and Philip's fleurs-de-lis. This was more than just a gesture – it was a claim to share the city's booty from a junior party in the crusade. The banner was removed by English soldiers and thrown into the moat. Whether or not Richard had actually ordered this, Leopold firmly believed that he had. Modern scholarship suggests that Richard might have ordered the disposal of the flag as a gesture of solidarity with his brother-in-law and Leopold's enemy, Henry the Lion of Saxony. 'From what lord do you hold your land?' Richard asked him when Leopold challenged him over the flag, with the strong implication that Leopold was a mere princeling among kings. Leopold stormed back to Austria, and in little over a year Richard would have reason to look back on this contretemps with serious regret.★

The other incident was never forgiven. Negotiations with Saladin to fulfil the surrender agreement were delayed and constantly broke down, partly because Saladin was in no position to meet their strict terms so quickly. Meanwhile, the remaining hostages Richard and Philip were holding from the Muslim garrison were a serious drain on their resources. They had to be fed and guarded and there was no way that the crusaders could march on until they had been handed over. Richard finally came to believe this was a deliberate policy to delay him and, giving in to the advice he was getting, he ordered their execution. On 20 August they were slaughtered outside the city walls in full view of Saladin's army; it was a bloody business and it took all day.

'The time limit expired,' explained Richard in a letter to the Abbot of Clairvaux. 'And as the treaty to which Saladin had agreed was entirely made void, we quite properly had the Saracens we had in custody – about 2,600 of them – put to death.' Their stomachs were cut open in case they had swallowed precious

---

★The modern Austrian flag, with its two red stripes, is said to be derived from Leopold's time outside Acre, and from the wounds he received mounting the city wall. His shirt was stained red with blood, except for a white strip around the waist, which had been protected by his belt. The red, white and red motif is a reference to Leopold's bravery.

stones, and their bodies were burned and the ashes sifted through to widen the search. This outrage was approved by most of the Christian chroniclers, but the Muslim world never quite forgot it.

More complications followed. Richard and the army council hammered out an agreement between the rivals for the throne of Jerusalem: Guy would stay king for life and would be succeeded by Conrad, and both claimants would share the revenues in the meantime. But the disease-ridden crusaders were not good company for a serious hypochondriac like Philip Augustus, especially one who was continually being upstaged by his partner and former friend. In the heat and worry, Philip demanded half of Cyprus – according to their agreement – and when this was refused, he came to believe that Richard was plotting against his life. With the death of Philip of Flanders without an heir in a mêlée outside the walls a few weeks before, Philip also realized that he could be overlord of the whole of Artois if he was on the spot to claim it. Add to that his growing sense of being unneeded in Acre and going home seemed increasingly tempting.

Three tearful French nobles came to see Richard and he guessed immediately what it was they were telling him. Although he begged Philip to stay, all he could extract was a solemn promise – sworn on the holy disciples – not to harm Richard's lands until forty days after Richard had returned home himself. On 31 July 1191 Philip sailed with Conrad of Montferrat – still intriguing for the throne of Jerusalem – as far as Tyre, and three days later he set off on the voyage home. Back in Paris some months later, he went straight to Saint-Denis to give thanks for his survival, and publicized his continuing fear of Richard by going around the city with armed guards, letting it be known that he carried a bludgeon with him at all times. Richard was left in sole command in Palestine. 'Never have we had to face a subtler or a bolder opponent,' wrote the Arab historian Baha ad-Din. Philip left behind most of his army and some treasure to pay them, under the command of Hugh, Duke of Burgundy. The treasure ran short within weeks and Richard was soon having to advance them money. When his reserves ran short in turn, Hugh refused to serve under him.

Conrad, meanwhile, was still disaffected because of Richard's support for Guy, and remained fuming in Tyre.

So it was a difficult alliance – now also without Leopold and the Austrians – that marched south down the coast towards the port of Jaffa. But it was disciplined, without the usual military hangers-on – the only women allowed were what the eyewitness chronicler Ambroise called 'elderly laundresses, who washed clothes and got rid of lice'.* Richard's tactics were to march close to the shore, supplied by the fleet who sailed along beside them – all the surrounding crops had been destroyed under Saladin's orders – with the foot soldiers marching alternately on the right and then the left to give them a break from the constant harassing attacks. At the front, the great Templar battle flag, *Beau-Séant*, was carried on a cart of its own, drawn by four horses. As the soldiers marched, they chanted, '*Sanctum sepulcrum adjuva*' (Help us, Holy Sepulchre), fighting off wave after wave of attacks from Arab archers on horseback and lightly armed African and Bedouin foot soldiers. The arrows did not pierce the crusaders' chain mail, but stuck out awkwardly, and after some hours the knights began to take on the appearance of hedgehogs. It was an exhausting march in the searing heat with little or nothing to drink – undiluted wine in the sun was believed to cause insanity and death – and it soon became clear that Saladin was determined to force a battle on the plain to the north of Arsuf. In the middle of the morning of 5 September, Saladin's men moved forward with the beating of drums and the clashing of cymbals.

Strangely enough, like his father before him, Richard had never fought a pitched battle before. They were just too dangerous in Europe for most military leaders to risk unless they absolutely had to. But there was no doubt what the tactics should be: the overwhelming advantage the crusaders possessed would be a heavy

---

* The verse chronicle of the Norman minstrel Ambroise has a fascinating history. Lost for centuries in the Vatican Library, it was finally discovered and published by the medievalist Gaston Paris in 1897. The laundresses he mentions were 'as clever as monkeys when it came to getting rid of lice,' Ambroise wrote.

cavalry charge by the knights, but timing was absolutely crucial. If it came too early, Saladin's men would simply get out of the way and then cut the knights off from the main body. If it came too late, the battle could be over already. It was a hair's-breadth military decision.

As the morning wore on, Richard began to receive increasingly urgent messages from the Hospitallers in the rear, who were taking the brunt of the fighting, begging for permission to charge. Richard consistently said no, but by late afternoon two of them – the Marshal of the Hospital and Baldwin of Carew – lost their nerve and went ahead anyway, scattering the Christian infantry in front of them. Making the best of it and dashing to the front, Richard was able to get into a position to lead the charge – hundreds of knights with streamers flying, holding their reins and shield in their left hand, their lance under their right arm, as their heavy war horses plunged into Saladin's lines in clouds of dust. Right at the front, Richard was able to regroup and charge a second time – and the battle was won. It was a serious blow to Saladin's reputation. Richard had been wounded slightly in the side but was described at the height of the battle as 'carving a wide path for himself, cutting them down like a reaper with a sickle'.

Three days later, they arrived in the port of Jaffa to find its fortifications razed to the ground. Jerusalem was just twenty-five miles away, but they were inhospitable desert miles. 'With God's grace,' Richard wrote in the army's bulletin in October, 'we hope to recover the city of Jerusalem and the Holy Sepulchre within 20 days after Christmas, and then return to our own dominions.'

It took three months after Arsuf for the fortifications to be rebuilt and the castles along the road from Jaffa to be repaired. But Richard kept stolidly to the timetable he had drawn up. Just before Christmas 1191, the army was finally camped at Beit Nuba, just twelve miles from Jerusalem. But once they had got there, it became increasingly clear that their situation was not good: they were too far from the sea and the supply fleet to lay siege safely. In January the army council agreed and Richard gave the order to march back to Jaffa. It was a bitter blow to the soldiers and pilgrims, who returned in heavy rain and thunderstorms, while the disaffected French went all the way back to Acre. Soon there were rumours from there of orgiastic drinking sessions in the streets. The crusade was no longer going according to plan, because the planning had taken them no further than the start of the siege. Any military strategist peering any further ahead had serious questions to ask.

As agreed with the army, Richard led the main body to the next port down to the south: Ascalon. This was well known for its olive and sycamore trees, its towers and its silkworms. Its significance depended on who you were: Richard believed it was the key to the road south to Egypt along the coast; the French saw it as an irrelevant and distant southern outpost. Once again, the fortifications had been dismantled by Saladin some months earlier, and – aware of the need for the army to be kept busy – Richard spent the next four months rebuilding the walls and turning it into one of the strongest cities on the coast.

Time was passing and on 15 April 1192 news arrived that Richard had been dreading. Only seven and a half months since Philip had left for home, he was threatening the borders of Normandy. Added to the regular and worrying reports about the factional disagreements in England, it meant that Richard badly needed to go back to England – but if he left now, the feuding crusaders would tear the precarious kingdom apart. The issue simply had to be decided, so the following day he called a meeting of the army council and gave them a choice of kings. They voted unanimously for Conrad.

Richard can't have been surprised. He apologized to Guy and, as a consolation prize, made him Lord of Cyprus. The Lusignan family ruled the island for the next two and a half centuries. Meanwhile, he sent his dashing nephew Henry of Champagne north to give Conrad the good news. When he arrived in Tyre, Conrad fell on his knees, asking God not to let him be crowned if he was unworthy to be king. A hasty coronation was arranged in Acre a few days later. But on 28 April, God intervened.

Conrad had intended to have supper at home with his young wife, Isabella. But she took so long in one of those scented crusader baths that he gave up waiting and went to see Philip, Bishop of Beauvais, the friend who had married them eighteen months before. When he got there, the bishop had just finished eating, so he wandered back through the streets of Tyre. On the way, he met two monks, one of whom indicated that he had a letter for him. But when Conrad went over to collect it, the monk drew out a knife and stabbed him. Carried back to his palace as he died, he begged Isabella to give the keys to Tyre to nobody but Richard or the elected king of Jerusalem.

Before their execution, one of the monks admitted that they were actually followers of the shadowy leader of a heretical Muslim sect that followed Rashid el-Dun Sinan, known as the Old Man of the Mountains. Sinan lived secure and secluded in the mountain fortress of Alamut, and specialized in sending his fervent followers on suicide missions, promising them they would live for ever, dreaming dreams, if they died carrying out his commands. They were known as Assassins, from the Arabic '*hashish*', which they were widely rumoured to use to put them into a state of ecstasy. The Old Man of the Mountains may have had a particular disagreement with Conrad, but the reasons for his shocking dispatch were never clear, and there were those who remembered Richard's previous opposition to Conrad and pointed the finger at him. It was another omen for the future.*

Henry of Champagne hurried back to Tyre and with difficulty persuaded Isabella to surrender the keys of the city to him. The townspeople then took the initiative themselves. Henry was a bachelor; he was good-looking and brave and he had an air of command. Whoever married Isabella would be king, so it seemed

---

*Saladin had one terrifying encounter with the Assassins. A messenger arrived and demanded to see him alone. Saladin refused to dismiss his most trusted bodyguards, and was disconcerted when the messenger spoke to them himself, asking them if they would murder Saladin if ordered in the name of the Old Man of the Mountains. 'Command us as you wish,' they said. That was, in fact, the message.

to them a marriage made in heaven. Yielding to public opinion, on 5 May Isabella married for the third time at the age of just twenty-one – making no secret how relieved she was to trade the brutish Conrad for the dashing Henry. The couple fell passionately in love and couldn't bear to be out of each other's sight. The Muslims were less impressed. There had been only a week of mourning and Isabella was pregnant. When Saladin's secretary asked a crusader courtier during a negotiating session who would have paternity, he was told it would be the 'queen's child'. 'You see the licentiousness of these foul unbelievers,' he wrote.

Richard was a pragmatic diplomat – endlessly good-humoured with his enemies – and was sensible enough to realize that keeping open lines of communication could also tell him a good deal about their morale. But he also admired what he saw of the Saracens, of Islam and of advanced Arab culture, with its detailed knowledge of astronomy and mathematics and its romantic literature that must have reminded him of the days of the Courts of Love. Whatever the reason, he was soon attracting further controversy by building as close a link with Saladin as he could. 'It is the custom of kings when they happen to be near one another to send each other mutual presents and gifts,' he wrote to Saladin. 'Now I have in my possession a gift worthy of the sultan's acceptance, and I ask permission to send it to him.'

The two great leaders of the age never actually met. Saladin refused at first and, when he finally agreed, the Christian barons resisted the idea so passionately that Richard promised not to go. Relations broke down after the killing of the Acre garrison, but Richard was determined not to let anything like that happen again. The two exchanged presents throughout the conflict, much to the horror of fundamentalists on both sides. And when Richard was ill – as he continued to be – he sent a message to Saladin asking for snow from the mountains. Saladin often sent presents of peaches and pears. They negotiated generally through Saladin's brother al-Adil, who the crusaders called Safadin, and whom Richard became increasingly close to. Each tried to outdo the other by providing the very best cuisine and entertainment that his culture had to offer.

It was becoming increasingly clear to Richard – though not to many of his colleagues – that simply taking Jerusalem was not the solution to the Outremer problem. The crusaders would cheer, make a pilgrimage to the holy places and then go home; the city would simply fall straight back into Muslim hands. There were really only two options. First, they could ignore Jerusalem altogether, carrying on marching with the safety of the sea on their right and invade Egypt, dividing Saladin from his main supplies. But that would require resources that were seriously dwindling, and it would need some kind of unanimity in the army. Second, they could negotiate a peace that provided them with some of what they wanted, and a breathing space that would allow the tiny Christian kingdom to survive until Richard returned with an even bigger army. That meant flying in the face of all the fundamentalist assumptions – yet what was his choice, given the problems back home?

As Jaffa's walls began to rise again – before the first advance on Jerusalem – Richard intensified his meetings with al-Adil. Both Christians and Muslims were bleeding to death and lives were being sacrificed, he told Saladin's brother. 'The time has come to stop this.' His first proposal was that al-Adil should be given Palestine to rule and could marry Joanna. Saladin accepted immediately, assuming it was a joke: he had already become used to Richard's bantering style. But when al-Adil returned, Richard told him with disarming honesty that Joanna had flown into a rage when he suggested she should marry an infidel. Was there any chance, perhaps, of his becoming Christian?

There wasn't. But on 8 November 1191 al Adil returned the hospitality, entertaining Richard in his own tent with the finest Turkish dishes. At the height of the meal, Richard asked if he could hear some Arabic singing, and a woman with a guitar was hastily brought before them. As the soft strumming wafted over the Saracen camp in the moonlight, Richard was absolutely delighted. In Walter Scott's *The Talisman*, he imagines Blondel at the scene, entertaining the Arab negotiators in return with his own style of music. It was just the kind of relaxed contact between the two religions that most horrified the Christian fanatics and would add to Richard's problems when he came to return home.

As the news began to filter through of trouble in England, Richard intensified the negotiations again, once more to the horror of the hardliners. After the débâcle outside Jerusalem, and as the army got down to the long business of rebuilding Ascalon, the Prior of Hereford arrived in Palestine, sent by Longchamp from England to warn Richard that his brother John was attempting to take over the government. Richard was now in a peculiarly difficult position. If he waited to capture Jerusalem, he would be able to dictate his own terms throughout Europe. But if he failed and reached home too late, the chances were that Philip and John would have carved up his penniless empire between them. It was hardly surprising that this was the moment he fell victim to one of his periodic nervous collapses.

Richard spent days alone in his tent, refusing to see anyone. He was finally rescued by one of his own chaplains, who managed to talk to him about his triumphs in the past. 'You are the father, the champion and defender of Christendom,' he said. 'If you desert God's people now, they will be destroyed by the enemy.' It was obviously the right thing to have said. Within hours Richard was his usual self, announcing that he would stay until Easter 1193 and that it was time to prepare for the siege of Jerusalem. As a result, the army was soon back in Beit Nuba, from where Richard and his companions were led to a number of pieces of the True Cross that had been hidden during the Saracen advance. One of them came with a messenger from a local hermit, who turned out to be naked except for the unshaved hair which covered his body. He took them to a small hidden cross, said to be made from wood of the original, and predicted that Richard would fail to win Jerusalem this time no matter how hard he tried. He even foretold his own death in seven days. Richard kept him in camp to check out the veracity of this prediction at least. Sure enough, in a week the hairy hermit was dead.

Saladin did not have access to this foresight. He knew that Jerusalem could not be held and ordered that all the cisterns be poisoned and the wells destroyed within a two-mile cordon round the city. He performed Friday prayers there on 3 July with tears rolling down his cheeks.

But the hermit was right. The situation was no different from when they had been at Beit Nuba six months before, and Richard knew it. The army council talked the impasse through and delegated the decision to a committee of twenty, including five Templars, five Hospitallers, five Syrian Christians and five crusader nobles. By the end, only the French – who had returned to the army now that Henry of Champagne was king – were determined to carry on. Richard offered to go to Jerusalem with the army, but not as their commander, refusing to lead them into a trap. Later, they agreed, the Christian forces would advance on Cairo and cut Saladin off from Egypt and the Nile valley, and force him to let Jerusalem go. But not now. In the meantime, Richard had to contend with an insulting song about him composed by the Duke of Burgundy, and spent his time composing his own in reply. A few days later, riding in the hills, he suddenly caught sight of the walls of Jerusalem itself and quickly covered his face with his shield, determined not to see the city until he could overwhelm it himself.

So once again, the day after Saladin's prayers, the army turned round and trudged back to the coast. 'Do not be deceived by my withdrawal,' Richard wrote to al Adil. 'The ram backs away in order to butt.' But he added, more revealingly, 'You and I can go on no longer', reminding Saladin that he had sometimes accommodated the requests of Christian holy orders. 'On many occasions monks who have been turned out have petitioned you for churches, and you have never shown yourself niggardly,' he wrote. 'Now I beg you to give me the Church of the Holy Sepulchre . . . will you not, then, give me a barren spot, and the ruin of its shrine?'

Saladin responded generously: 'Count Henry shall be as a son to me, and the Basilica of the Resurrection shall be given to you. The rest we will divide . . .'

The outline agreement gave the coastal strip to the crusaders and allowed their pilgrims to visit Jerusalem. The only part Richard could not stomach was Saladin's demand that he demolish Ascalon, after so many months of rebuilding its walls. He was still negotiating when he got back to Acre. But he had been there only one day when the most dramatic sequence of events of the whole crusade suddenly began to unfold.

On 29 July he heard the news that Saladin's army had surrounded the city of Jaffa. In a few hurried hours, he had dispatched Henry of Champagne south with the army. Then, with a small band of hand-picked knights and crossbowmen, he set sail in the galleys and reached Jaffa against the wind two days later. The small Christian garrison there was led by Alberi of Reims, who had ignominiously tried to escape by boat and been brought back by his comrades. He took command of the city's defence really because 'it was the only thing that remained for him to do'. In fact, the garrison had surrendered after three days, and Saladin – ever the humanitarian – had promised to let them leave with their goods. But his mutinous army immediately began killing and looting, and he advised the Christians to lock themselves up in the citadel until he had regained control.

So, on the sixth day of the siege, when Richard's thirty-five galleys arrived outside the city – his own galley, *Trenchmere*, painted with a red hull and a red sail – it seemed clear to him that he was too late. But a priest managed to climb down the walls of the citadel and reach the beach, from where he swam out towards his ship to explain that situation. 'Are any of them still living?' shouted Richard from the deck. 'Where are they?' Then he saw the small banner still flying from the tower.

What followed was a dramatic assault from the sea. Richard brought the ships close to the shore and, tearing off some of his leg and waist armour so he could move faster, plunged into the shallow water with a sword in one hand and a crossbow in the other, shouting, 'God sent us here to die if need be; shame on anyone who holds back now.' His men followed close behind. Perhaps it was his fearsome reputation, perhaps it was genuine force of arms, but Richard's small force beat back the invaders. 'In every deed at arms he is without rival, first to advance, last to retreat,' wrote one emir who witnessed the scene. 'We did our best to seize him, but in vain, for no one can escape his sword. His attack is dreadful. To engage with him is fatal. His deeds are not human.'

Saladin's negotiators arrived at Richard's camp after the battle at his request, to be subjected to his usual teasing. 'This sultan is mighty and there is none mightier than him in the land of Islam,' Richard joked. 'Why then did he run away as soon as I appeared? By God, I was not even properly armed for a fight. See, I am still wearing my sea boots.'

On 4 August Saladin tried again against Richard's tiny band of eighty knights and 400 archers – camped outside the city because there were too few of them to defend the walls – sending the Muslim cavalry forward in the early hours of the morning. The defenders were protected by a thin line of men with lances, with crossbowmen working in pairs behind them. Half dressed, Richard's knights managed to hold them off again. Filled with admiration for his defence – despite Richard's loss of a horse at the height of the battle – Saladin watched from the hill above and sent down two fresh horses as a present for his enemy. It was Richard's supreme military achievement. 'What of the king, one man surrounded by many thousands?' wrote the English chronicler Richard de Templo. 'The fingers stiffen to write of it and the mind is amazed to think of it.'

As the high summer wore on in stalemate, there was more sickness in the crusader ranks. Richard had been the first to fall ill, and he was followed by many of the other leading members of the expedition. He had also never really recovered from his scurvy attack during the original siege. He had suffered from diarrhoea since his arrival, and by now was almost too weak to carry on negotiations. 'My only object is to retain the position I hold amongst the Franks,' he wrote in an exhausted message to Saladin. 'If the sultan will not forgo his pretension to Ascalon, then let al-Adil procure for me the indemnity for the sums I have laid out repairing the fortifications.' That was the hint that Saladin was waiting for and he called off further attacks. Finally, on 2 September, both sides agreed a three-year truce. Many of the crusaders set off to see Jerusalem – which was, after all, what they had promised to do. Richard did not join them. He was determined that he would enter the city only as its conqueror.

For all his faults, and despite that basic failure, Richard had secured the survival of what was now the Kingdom of Acre. He could have taken Jerusalem, been hailed as a hero and then abandoned it to its inevitable fate. Instead he had been honest enough to be strategic. The capture of Cyprus had guaranteed the kingdom's supplies, and time had been bought to consolidate and bring in fresh troops. But that was not the way that many of his contemporaries saw it. Philip Augustus had now been home for eight months, and the French propaganda machine was busily justifying his return: Richard had plotted to kill him and – worst of all – he had made peace with the despoiler of Jerusalem. The previous summer, Philip had landed in Otranto and made the rest of the journey home by land. In Rome, Pope Celestine had freed him from his crusader oath because the remains of his sickness were all too apparent. On the journey north he found that Henry of Hohenstaufen – the new Emperor Henry VI – was still in Italy.

Henry's march on Sicily had been a miserable failure. He lost half his force, became ill himself and finally abandoned a hopeless siege of Naples in the face of dysentery and the overwhelming heat of summer. At one stage, the Empress Constance was even captured by Italian allies of Tancred. Henry was now burning with rage at the way Richard had allied himself with the other side. So when the two European leaders met, Richard was top of their agenda. He really was a serious threat to Christian idealism and peace, they agreed. If Richard happened to come back home through Germany, Henry promised to arrest him.

5. Setting Sail

Treacherous people have hurt me,
but let them; them I never loved.
Their gossip and their accusations
Made others fear I was the same as them.
Then all my joy in life just ebbed away –
I knew of no escape from pain and from betrayal.

Gace Brulé, 'In the Sweetness of the New Season'

O Jerusalem, now art thou indeed helpless. Who will protect thee
when Richard is away?

Ambroise, *L'Estoire de la Guerre Sainte,* eyewitness epic account
of the Third Crusade by a Norman minstrel

A legend grew up over the next few years around the Chastelain de Coucy, Blondel's friend and fellow *trouvère.* The story identified him with a man named Regnault, who fell in love and was encouraged to join Richard on crusade by his lover's jealous husband. On the way to the Holy Land, he was wounded by a poisoned arrow, but managed to write one last song and a letter to his lover before he died. These were dispatched home to her, together with his embalmed heart and a lock of her hair, in a small box. Unfortunately, when it arrived, the box was intercepted by the husband, who had the great minstrel's heart cooked and served to his wife. In the moment of revenge as she swallowed her meal, he turned to her with relish and told her what she had just eaten. 'After such noble food,' the lady replied, 'I will never eat again.'

The legend was written early the following century, and nobody suggests this was what actually happened to the Chastelain, who died in 1203. But there was something about the Third Crusade – the crusade of Richard and Philip – that encouraged stories with that tone of betrayal and noble failure. There remains an atmosphere behind the narrative, created partly by its attitude to Richard's chivalric ideals of principled adultery, but also partly by its romantic hopelessness. The new King Arthur had failed to take back Jerusalem for Christendom. The crusade had been the culmination of Richard's life so far, and it was the first time since his teenage years that he had come so close to outright failure. The experience must have shaken his beliefs, just as it shook those of his contemporaries.

Historians confirm that Richard's strategic skills probably preserved the tottering Christian regime of Outremer for another century, securing Cyprus and the Palestinian coastal strip as a guarantee of its survival. But Christendom had hoped for the big prize, and had put its faith in Richard as its champion, and he had longed for it just as much, but it had eluded him. He knew very well that he could have captured Jerusalem – the temptation took him and the army all the way to Beit Nuba a second time – but he realized that, though it would have made him a hero to the whole of his world, it also would have been a kind of lie. The city would inevitably have fallen to Saladin again once the crusaders had drifted home. There needed to be a more permanent solution, and there is every indication that Richard was planning to return to provide exactly that. But it was too late to stamp his authority on the way the story of the campaign was being told back home. To the English, the hint of heroic failure arose in retrospect as a courageous dream. But the English – those of them who had survived – were still in Palestine, preparing to take advantage of the agreement with Saladin and pay their respects to the Holy City. Their French and German colleagues were already back home, telling the story without the heroic gloss.

'We who were there, who saw it and knew it at first hand, we who suffered there, we dare not lie about those who, as we saw with our own eyes, suffered for the love of God,' wrote the English minstrel Ambroise, explaining that those who had died there 'will be at the right hand of God in the heavenly city of Jerusalem, for people such as they conquered that other Jerusalem'. You can hear the note of hurt justification. Ambroise was hitting back specifically at tales that hinted at a very different story, spread by disaffected soldiers in the crusader camp and broadcast to the world by Philip Augustus: that the crusade had ended in failure because of Richard's plotting and his greed, and because he had insisted on negotiating with the infidels. Philip's early departure from the struggle was explained because he was a victim of this overweening ambition: his life had been threatened by Richard, and was still under threat. He had been forced to leave and, because of this, the crusade had been doomed.

Many of those in the combined army that had set out from Lyons in July 1190 would not return. Historians have never been able to agree how many there were to start with, but contemporary chroniclers claim that as few as one in twelve were left on the quayside in Acre, staring out towards the harbour at the Tower of Flies, getting ready to sail home. It was a very stormy autumn, and many of those who remained were destined to drown on the return voyage. Those who did manage to survive the disease, the battles and the journey home, found themselves not returning heroes, as they had naively expected, but the objects of ridicule because of how little had been achieved.

Though he never spoke their language and spent little time there, Richard seems to have been a hero to the English. Elsewhere, his reputation was a victim of his pragmatism, and his clear admiration not just of Saladin but of Islamic civilization as a whole. He had chosen the worst option – he had stayed in Palestine long enough to make sure that his enemies were first with the news in the great cities of Western Europe, but not long enough to outface them by actually capturing the city. Worse, despite the expectations of the Pope and Saladin alike, no attempt had even been made to lay siege to Jerusalem. Richard loved pomp and spectacle – especially if he was the heart of it – but he believed in his destiny as a crusader, and wanted the achievements of his crusade to be real.

It was true that he had overwhelmed the Muslims militarily.
The fearsome name of Melec Ric – the Saracen name for King
Richard – was used for centuries later to silence children or chivvy
horses. 'What's the matter?' the Muslim rider would whisper in
their horse's ear. 'Is England in front of us?' But as well as the
stories told in Paris and Cologne of treasonous dealings with the
enemy and a betrayal of the crusader ideals, there were other
rumours circulating in the courts of Europe too. It seems likely
that these included rumours about his exotic sex life in the East –
separated from his new wife by miles of desert, possibly even
tempted into new experiences at the hands of al-Adil. They certainly included allegations that he had planned to have Philip
Augustus killed in the camp outside Acre. Worst of all, Conrad of
Montferrat's old friend and supporter, the Bishop of Beauvais –
the man he had wandered round to dinner with on the night of
his murder – had taken the boat home some months before,
convinced that it was his duty to spread the word that Richard
had been the architect of his friend's assassination. 'At every stage
of his journey he spread the word that that traitor, the king of
England, had arranged to betray his lord, the king of the French,
to Saladin,' wrote the Winchester monk and chronicler Richard
of Devizes, 'that he had the marquis' throat cut, that he poisoned
the duke of Burgundy; that he was an extraordinarily savage man,
thoroughly unpleasant and as hard as iron, adept at deceit, a master
of dissimulation.'

Richard had set out as the hero of a Europe united in faith and
determination; he was about to return to a very different en-
vironment. He was only just becoming aware of the potential
dangers of his complete failure to publish his version of the story
first. It was a danger that could, he realized, make his journey home
inconvenient at the very least. He did not know then the extent of
Philip's efforts to denigrate his name, nor did he know about the
crucial meeting between Philip and the new Holy Roman Emperor,
Henry VI, outside Milan, but he knew enough to be concerned.

When news reached the West of the peace agreement with
Saladin, it arrived as confirmation of all the worst rumours. But

the truth was that it was signed only just in time. When Richard gave his final assent on 2 September 1192, unable to move from his sickbed or even read the text of the agreement in detail, he was almost penniless. He had spent the entire war chest that had been raised so mercilessly by William Longchamp and borrowed from the Lombardy bankers. He even spent his sister Joanna's dowry, which he had gone to the trouble of seizing from Tancred in Sicily on the journey out. And the urgent messages asking for more money to be arranged that he had sent home to the Abbot of Clairvaux – his main conduit for communications with broader opinion back home – had not resulted in any new funds arriving in Palestine.

He was aware that the political situation in England was precarious. He had known that English political life was likely to be dominated by power struggles between John and Longchamp. He had set up contingency plans to deal with this if it became uncontrollable, but he now knew that not even these were enough to guarantee his lands – hence the increasingly desperate messages from his mother as 1192 progressed. Most worrying was the arrival in April of a personal envoy sent by Eleanor to report the most dangerous threat yet to emerge to his rule and to urge his return. But most pressingly of all, he was very ill – too sick to walk, suffering from hallucinations and under the care of the Knights Hospitaller.

The Hospitallers were then in the forefront of medical knowledge, skilled at operations for hernia, gallstones and Caesarean births and at setting broken bones – they used herbs from the East as anaesthetics for operations and battlefield pain relief. This was an age when modern scourges like cancer and VD were rare, and there was also no distilled liquor, so little serious alcoholism, but they struggled with diseases caused by bad diet, poor hygiene and clothes that irritated the skin. In this case, it seems to have been hygiene that undermined Richard's health so disastrously, as a result of the hundreds of unburied bodies left in the ruins of Jaffa. Even camping outside the city had not prevented disease spreading through the crusader camp.

It is difficult to catch disease directly from bodies. But decomposing matter can mingle with dust and get into the human system through inhalation or open cuts. There can be a surge in the local rat population, bringing a whole range of other diseases. It is possible, therefore, that Richard was suffering from a form of typhoid fever, dysentery or possibly malaria, or a form of malaria like relapsing fever, all of which bring a debilitating combination of high temperature, headaches and stomach cramps which made him send messages to Saladin begging for peaches and mountain snow. The illness was almost certainly exacerbated by his despair at what he saw as the failure of all his hopes. The Hospitallers feared it might be tertian fever, a form of malaria that recurs every other day, and treated him with leeches.

On 9 September, he handed over command of the army to Henry of Champagne, the new king of Jerusalem, and left him in charge of dismantling the defences of Ascalon, as agreed so reluctantly with Saladin. He was then carried on a litter along the coast road that he had marched down so dramatically the previous year in the days before the Battle of Arsuf. A few days later, he arrived at Haifa, across the bay from Acre, then a quiet and pleasant retreat at the foot of Mount Carmel, and stayed there to recover his strength. It was here that he heard the news of the death in Acre of Hugh, Duke of Burgundy, Philip's remaining representative on the crusade, whom he had come to detest cordially. The news cheered him up and he began to recover. Unfortunately this only added to the whisperings that the duke might have been one of Richard's victims.

Richard and Henry of Champagne had been concerned that there should be no rush by all their troops to visit Jerusalem, in case they simply decided to wander home afterwards, their pilgrims' vow fulfilled. They stipulated that nobody should be allowed through the Saracen lines without a letter signed by one or other of the two kings, and that pilgrims must visit the city in one of four organized parties – one of which was led by Richard's friend Hubert Walter, Bishop of Salisbury, tall, elegant and good-looking and about to play a major role in Richard's future. With exactly the opposite object in mind, Saladin made strenuous efforts to allow as many Christians to visit the holy sites as he could.

Saladin also invited Hubert Walter to see him, the first time he had come face to face with a leading figure from the crusade on equal terms. They were not alone, and the main points of the conversation were noted down. It was clear that not only did they find each other congenial company but they also trusted each other enough to move the discussion on to the character of Richard himself. Saladin said he admired his opponent, but was also aware of his weakness. 'I have long been aware that your king is a man of honour and very brave, but he is also imprudent, indeed absurdly so, in the way he plunges into the midst of danger and his reckless indifference to his own safety,' Saladin told the bishop. 'I would like to have wisdom and moderation rather than excessive wildness.'

The long-awaited meeting between Richard and Saladin never took place. Richard was happy for his soldiers and commanders finally to wander the streets of Jerusalem, to pray at the Church of the Holy Sepulchre and to fulfil the pilgrims' vows they made when they took the cross, but he was not prepared to go there himself. He did not intend to discharge his crusader vows yet.

Towards the end of September, Richard was well enough to move back into the royal apartments in Acre, to be cared for by Berengaria, Joanna and maybe also Blondel. His admiral Stephen de Turnham, Robert's brother, had prepared a seagoing galley, and on September 29 Turnham set sail with Berengaria and Joanna aboard, together with Isaac Comnenus (still in silver chains) and his daughter, whom, rumour insisted, Richard was infatuated with. They had an uneventful voyage to Sicily, where Tancred – Joanna's former gaoler – entertained them with lavish hospitality. From there they sailed to Naples and then travelled by road to Rome, where they remained. There were stories that Berengaria wanted to consult the Pope about the difficulties she was already experiencing with her marriage. But they were also returning crusaders, and entitled to the protection of the Church, and Richard must have calculated that – of all the cities in Europe – they would have been safest there.

The ten days after they had sailed were taken up with Richard's hurried and increasingly secret preparations for his own departure. He seems to have realized the danger posed by the rumours about his conduct, and he did what he could in the time available to him to tackle the problem of his reputation. Acre's town crier was soon announcing, on Richard's behalf, that all debts owed to the king would be cancelled. He also made strenuous efforts to ransom the gallant William of Préaux, who had saved him the previous year when he was nearly captured in woods near Lydda. Saladin eventually agreed to swap him for the ten most valuable Saracens in Richard's captivity.

It was all rather too late. His fiercest critics had long since left for home, to paint his leadership in the worst possible light. And as the days before departure went by, it was dawning on Richard – the start of a long process – just how dangerous his situation was. He was receiving a series of warnings that specific princes and pirates were lying in wait for him on the way home. Although theoretically he had the protection that the Church extended to returning crusaders, it was clear that there was a diplomatic hue and cry emanating from Paris, and that he was the heart of it. There would be a number of ambitious men prepared to take advantage of his vulnerability on the road or the high seas and to sell him to the highest bidder. And if his luck was out, that bidder might just be the king of France.

He chose a large buss rather than a galley, precisely because royalty habitually preferred the comfort and speed of a galley. He also chose a few companions to join him on the voyage: there would be no accompanying fleet and no escort. They would rely on secrecy and good navigation. The date and time of departure were closely guarded secrets, though the French chronicler Bernard le Trésorier reported that at least one spy slipped aboard in these few days. Richard's last effects were taken in small boats out to the eastern section of the harbour, because the ship was too large to come right up to the wharf at Acre. The realization that he really was leaving was greeted with a dismal sense of gloom in the city. People prayed openly in the street, convinced that his presence was all that lay between them and complete Saracen victory.

Once night had fallen on Thursday 9 October – after the last date that it was believed to be safe to sail from one end of the Mediterranean to the other – he and his companions strode quietly down the rue de la Boucherie to the harbour and were rowed out to the ship that bobbed gently on the swell. The normally bustling quays of Acre were silent as they slipped past the Tower of Flies without an answering tolling of the bell. The king of England, joint leader of the most powerful army ever to set sail from Western Europe, was skulking home in very different circumstances from those he must have imagined even a few months before.

It was a clear night as the crew took bearings from the stars, and the ship turned north to hug the coast towards Tyre. Wrapped in a cloak at the stern and watching the shapes of Acre's towers disappear into the night, counting the days no doubt until Christmas, when he believed he would reach home, Richard was overheard making a very personal vow: 'O, Holy Land, I commend you to God,' he said, only partly to himself. 'In his loving grace, may he grant me such length of life that I may give you help as he wills. I certainly hope some time in the future to bring you the aid that I intend.'

Leaning against the rail of his ship, the triangular mainsail filling with wind above him as he headed for home, Richard had time to review the extraordinary events of the past three years – the culmination of his life so far – and wonder whether he might have acted differently. He knew he would have the time to do this: voyages were notoriously unpredictable, and this was dangerously late in a stormy autumn. A generation later, the French king Louis IX had his fleet scattered across the whole Mediterranean from a storm near Cyprus. When he was king in later years, Richard's brother John once spent eleven days just sailing across the English Channel. Richard also, no doubt, spent time thinking through his tactics for his return to England. He was at least two months out of date in his news of the upheavals among his ruling

elite, and the imminent threat of an alliance between his brother
John and Philip Augustus, and he knew his mother would not
urge him home without good reason.

In fact, his arrangements for governing Aquitaine had survived
well under the control of his nephew Otto of Brunswick, son of
Frederick Barbarossa's great rival Henry the Lion of Saxony. His
most difficult neighbour, Raymond V of Toulouse, had attempted
to foment a rebellion, but had been frustrated by a dramatic intervention from the south led by Berengaria's brother, Sancho the
Strong of Navarre. But England was deeply nervous, made worse
by the appearance on a number of occasions through the year of a
mysterious redness in the sky. This was the Northern Lights, seen
as far south as London and described by one contemporary as
'twinkling with a kind of blood-stained light'. It was widely
regarded as the harbinger of tragedy for the king.

Richard's arrangements for England had been designed to hold
in check all the most ambitious figures in the land. He knew his first
minister, William Longchamp, Bishop of Ely, was overwhelmingly
ambitious but also wholly loyal. He had been Chancellor when
Richard first set sail, but since appointing Longchamp as co-
justiciar, he had managed to gather into his hands the positions not
just of chief justiciar – which made him head of the royal finances
and courts, as well as the government's administrative machinery
– but also of papal legate. This final title gave him authority
over the Church. Richard's decision to let his illegitimate brother
Geoffrey go ahead with his consecration as Archbishop of York
had been designed as a small check on Longchamp's ecclesiastical
authority. There was also an arrangement if everything else failed.
When she had been in Rome, Eleanor had taken the precaution
of getting agreement from the Pope that – if it ever became
necessary – Longchamp could be overruled as papal legate by the
widely trusted Archbishop of Rouen in Normandy, Walter of
Coutances – actually a Cornishman – who was given letters of
authority if Longchamp was to overreach himself.

Richard had been far-sighted enough to anticipate most of the
obvious crises that might arise. He knew what his brother John

was like, and had intended to ban him from England while he was away until his mother begged him to reconsider. Eleanor had seen each of her sons in turn lured to Paris by the king of France and turned against their family: the last thing she wanted was to have her youngest wandering aimlessly around the Continent. There were bound to be tensions between John and Longchamp, but these could be managed. It had been predictable that, as doubts grew about whether Richard would ever come home alive, the influence of John would begin to rise as barons shuffled to position themselves favourably in case he became king. It was also predict-able that the pompous and demanding Longchamp would appoint his own family to as many positions as he could, and be deeply resented by many of those who found themselves subject to his power. It must also have been clear that rival parties would grow up around the two of them, a party loyal to Richard around Longchamp and a party that believed he would never return around John, and that they would loathe each other. Richard was a strategic thinker and must have expected all these trends.

Sure enough, Longchamp was a deeply unpopular figurehead. His limping gait and sexual habits made him a figure of fun among those who knew, but his money-raising tenacity – trying to recoup the hole in England's finances left by the crusade – made him anything but. He was arrogant and intolerant in his defence of Richard. 'Planting vines, Marshal?' said Longchamp to his sparring partner William the Marshal, accusing him of insinuating himself into the good opinion of John, who might – after all – succeed all too soon to the throne. 'The laity found him more than a king, the clergy found him more than a Pope,' wrote the contemporary historian William of Newburgh. 'And both an intolerable tyrant.'

Chroniclers describe him dashing around the country 'like a flash of lightning' with a thousand armed soldiers, humiliating anyone whom he perceived as undermining his power or that of the king. He was particularly brutal in his dismissal of his fellow justiciar, Hugh, Bishop of Durham. 'You have had your say at our last meeting, now I shall have mine,' said Longchamp, once the bishop had been ushered into his presence. 'As my lord the king liveth, you shall not quit this place till you have given me hostages for the surrender of all your castles. No protest – I am not a bishop arresting another bishop. I am the Chancellor, arresting his supplanter.'

But if the rivalry between Longchamp's party and John's party was inevitable, it would have been harder to predict the effect of Richard's visit to Sicily in 1190. His spur-of-the-moment alliance with Tancred was a shock to senior barons in England. They never expected it, did not understand it – given the resulting tensions with the Holy Roman Empire – and it made them more careful about protecting their own positions. And when Richard named his nephew Arthur as heir at the same time, in order to betroth him to Tancred's daughter, the news came as a particularly unpleasant shock to John. John had been travelling around England, distributing funds generously, endowing hospitals and encouraging the idea that his brother might never return. Now there seemed no reason to stay patiently loyal, waiting for Richard to disappear; he would have to entrench his own position to fight for the succession even if Richard failed to survive. Handing over the succession to the child Arthur, at the same time as he handed over Excalibur to Tancred, seemed to John a gross act of disloyalty. The other unpredictable event was the death outside Acre of the Archbishop of Canterbury, filled with rage at the hasty marriage between eighteen-year-old Isabella and Conrad of Montferrat in November 1190. The most powerful position in the kingdom under the king himself was therefore vacant. Longchamp was inevitably going to intrigue to secure it for himself, and his opponents were inevitably going to try and stop him.

These tensions had come to a head in autumn 1191 – a year before Richard sailed home – with the news that Geoffrey had been consecrated in Tours and now wanted to come home to take up his position of Archbishop of York. Longchamp regarded him as a potential ally for his opponents and a rival for the Canterbury position, and warned him that he had promised Richard to stay abroad for three years.

The scene was set for a national scandal. On 13 September 1191

Geoffrey landed at Dover, where it so happened that the castle was in the hands of Longchamp's brother-in-law Matthew of Clare, who was married to his formidable sister Richeut. When Longchamp heard of Geoffrey's arrival, he ordered his immediate arrest, and it was Richeut who dispatched two knights and fifteen armed men to St Martin's Priory, where Geoffrey had sought sanctuary. After a brief siege of four days, they found him at the altar – just as Thomas Becket had been found at the altar at Canterbury by four knights a generation before – and, deliberately manipulating this symbolism, Geoffrey grasped the processional cross and refused to leave. The knights removed their cloaks to reveal chain mail underneath, genuflected in front of the altar, struck their breasts three times and seized him. They dragged Geoffrey, still clutching his cross, all the way to Dover Castle, his head bumping on the priory steps.

He was hauled before Matthew, the castle's constable, who – aware of the symbolism just as everyone else was – entirely lost his nerve. He burst into tears and fell on his knees before Geoffrey, begging forgiveness, much to the rage of his wife. Geoffrey refused to eat, having his own food sent up from the town. It was an uncomfortable few days for the constable as well.

Confusingly, Henry II had two sons called Geoffrey. But the illegitimate Geoffrey was already a national hero, partly because of his role fighting the Scots in his youth, and partly because he was the only one of Henry's sons to stay loyally by his father until the very end. There was outrage at the thought of his being bumped on the steps, in this worrying echo of the murder of Becket. It was also precisely the kind of event Longchamp's opponents had been waiting for. Sure enough, eight days after Geoffrey's arrest, the Bishop of London pleaded with Longchamp to let him go, offering his own diocese as surety, and the new Archbishop of York made his way triumphantly to London, where he was received by the bishop on the steps of St Paul's Cathedral.

The leader of John's party was the calculating propagandist Hugh of Nonant, who was in his spare time – as one historian puts it – also Bishop of Coventry. He had suffered a particularly bruising encounter with Longchamp over whether it was fitting for a bishop to hold sheriffdoms.* Now he calculated that Richard was never coming home and was devoting his considerable talents to putting John's case against Longchamp effectively. Hugh and John then seized the initiative, bringing together all the senior justices at Marlborough – including William the Marshal, who had risen fast after he spared Richard's life a few days before he became king – and urged the bishops and barons on the Great Council of England to meet them in Reading. Together, they issued Longchamp with an ultimatum: to meet them at Loddon Bridge over the Thames, outside the town.

On the morning arranged for the meeting – Monday 7 October – Longchamp set out from Staines with the Earl of Norfolk and the Bishop of London. After four miles, the news reached him that John was there, accompanied by a band of Welsh soldiers, and he nervously turned round again, sending a message ahead that he had been taken ill. Back in Staines, he discovered that John's soldiers were accompanying a baggage train that had been sent on ahead to London. Longchamp misunderstood this, concluding that his greatest fear was being realized and the king's brother was trying to seize the city, and he set off there himself as fast as he could.

When the news that Longchamp was not on his way to meet them after all reached the other barons on the road, they stopped. 'What shall we do now?' asked Reginald, Bishop of Bath. 'Shall we go back to Reading?'

'Certainly not,' said Hugh of Nonant, according to the chroniclers. 'Let's go to London and buy some winter clothes.'†

---

* Hugh of Nonant was already notorious for sending troops in against his own monks. 'What did I tell you about monks?' he said to Richard 1189. 'If you would follow my advice, in a short time not one monk would be left in England. To the devil with all monks.'

† Reginald was about to be one of the shortest-serving archbishops of Canterbury, dying later in the year before he could even be consecrated. His place at Bath was taken over by the fearsome Savaric de Bohun, who later used military force to annex Glastonbury Abbey into his diocese.

Where the two roads converged outside London, Longchamp's escort ran into John's baggage train and there was a brief mêlée during which one of Longchamp's knights wounded John's chief official, who died later in the month. But Longchamp's company had the worst of the fighting and fled down the road towards London, sending messages ahead to his supporters to summon London's leading citizens to Guildhall. When he reached there himself at the end of the day, he urged them to shut the city's gates. Arguments broke out immediately about whether that was a wise thing to do in the face of the man who might soon be king. Members of John's party in the assembly found themselves on the winning side of the argument and accused Longchamp of treason, but by then the argument had spilled out into the streets around Ludgate. It was dark, and people came out with lamps to find out what was happening, as the gatekeepers argued with John's messengers. Again, the cautious merchants of London decided the risk of offending him was too great and the great gates swung open. Longchamp and his staff fled to the Tower.

The following day, the bells of St Paul's rang out as the leading citizens of the city, together with the barons and bishops of the Great Council, met in the cathedral chapterhouse to decide what to do. Geoffrey read out a letter from Richard giving him permission to land in England, and this was conveniently translated into French by Hugh of Nonant, for the benefit of those who did not understand Latin. The discussion continued at the so-called folkmoot, the gathering of London citizens around the wooden cross outside the cathedral, where the crimes of Longchamp were recited again. After that, the decision seemed clear. The Great Council would depose Longchamp as chief justiciar and replace him with Walter of Coutances. John was given the meaningless title 'Governor of the Whole Realm', which, in effect, recognized him as Richard's heir, and in return he confirmed that Londoners should have their own municipal government and their own mayor. The ancient office of Lord Mayor of London officially dates from this moment.

It was a uniquely dangerous moment for Longchamp, who –

for all his considerable faults – believed he was loyally defending
the throne of England against John's machinations. He knew it
was too late to lay in provisions for a siege, and there really was
no alternative but to come to some kind of terms. Hugh of Nonant
made sure he was one of the four bishops who came to the Tower
to inform his great rival of the Great Council's decision, and
particularly enjoyed the moment because Longchamp fainted at
the news and had to be revived with a bucket of cold water.

He came round for a final show of defiance, but the die was
cast. Early on Thursday morning, Longchamp emerged to find an
enormous, noisy and hostile crowd waiting for him on a field to
the east of the Tower, near what is now St Katharine's Dock. 'He
was as pale as one who treads upon a snake in his bare feet,' wrote
one chronicler. Alone against the crowd and his enemies on the
Great Council, he bravely warned the barons that John was determined to steal the crown from his brother. 'Let all of you know,'
he told those assembled, 'that I do not lay aside any of the offices
that the king entrusted to me. You, being many, have overcome
me because you are stronger than I.'

The short, broken figure of Longchamp was escorted to Dover
Castle, which he was allowed to keep. He was not completely
alone. The elderly conservative barons of England and the earls of
Warenne and Arundel had stayed loyal to him as the man appointed
by the king, but there were few of them, and the completeness of
his fall from power hung heavy on him. He still had further to go.

What happened next was never explained – except by Hugh of
Nonant, and it may not be sensible to take his word for it entirely.
Maybe Longchamp believed his life was in danger. More likely he
believed he would be prevented from leaving the country. Either
way, by the time he reached Dover on 17 October, he had decided
not only to escape abroad, but to do so in disguise. This proved a
serious mistake, because, most unwisely, the Chancellor – this was
Longchamp's remaining office of state – decided he would be most
inconspicuous dressed as a woman. Even more unwisely, he chose
an attractive green gown that was too long for him.

Limping characteristically, he made his way dressed in this from the castle down to the beach to find some means of conveying himself across the English Channel. There he attracted the attention of a bare-chested fisherman who had just landed his catch. After a brief and disturbing flirtatious discussion, the fisherman put one arm round Longchamp's neck while the other felt down towards the groin. There was a sudden intake of breath, and – most unexpectedly – the fisherman let out a raucous, leering guffaw, pulling the gown up over Longchamp's head and shouting to the rest of his crew to come and see what he had caught. At this point, a couple of Longchamp's servants, who had been keeping an eye on him, intervened to rescue the Chancellor of England from further molestation.

The second incident was fatal. A woman passer-by admired his dress, fingered the cloth on his arm and asked how much it had cost. There was no reply – Longchamp spoke no English – and the woman became suspicious. She called over her friends and pulled back the green hood to reveal a small, frightened man. The mob descended and Longchamp – now beyond the reach of his servants – was dragged off to a cellar in Dover. A week later, when the news reached London, the new 'Governor of the Whole Realm' ordered his release, and Longchamp finally took a boat to Flanders. Far away in Palestine, Richard was repairing Jaffa and planning his first advance on Jerusalem, little suspecting the fate of his most loyal supporter.

Hugh of Nonant enthusiastically passed on the details of Longchamp's humiliation to anyone who was prepared to listen. But astonishingly Longchamp did not stay humiliated. His feisty determination returned almost as soon as he had set foot in Normandy. He was, after all, a papal legate. His first task as he saw it, therefore, was to inform the Pope of at least some of the details of his dismissal. It took about twenty days for a messenger to make the journey from Normandy to Rome, down through Champagne and across the Alps. And on 2 December the normally mild-mannered Celestine dispatched a furious letter of complaint to the Great Council of England, which was sent to Longchamp in

Normandy to deliver in person. Celestine was outraged at the treatment of his legate. 'All applauded him when prosperous; all murmur against him when fallen,' he said. The letter was sent along with two cardinals, Jordan and Octavian, who met Longchamp in Paris and renewed his position as papal legate – while the agents of Richard's mother kept him under observation to make sure he never strayed too close to the palace of Philip Augustus.

The presence of the two cardinals worried Eleanor of Aquitaine. She was suspicious of them, and she particularly wanted to prevent them from crossing the Channel and upsetting the delicate and unpredictable balance of power in England under Walter of Coutances. There was little she could do to prevent this, but there was something. The cardinals should strictly have asked for letters of safe conduct across Normandy in order to get to England, and this they failed to do. So when they arrived in the capital of Normandy on their way north, asking to see her, the drawbridge of Rouen was raised against them. Acting under strict instructions from Eleanor, William Fitzhugh – Rouen's seneschal and the senior officer there – explained to the cardinals that their failure to ask for safe conduct was a breach of Richard's rights as a crusader to have protection against foreign agents. The cardinals protested that they had something better than letters of safe conduct from Richard: they had one from the Pope himself. An angry exchange took place outside the gates, and the furious cardinals withdrew, smugly claiming, 'It is meet for the servants of the Lord to suffer contumely from his adversaries.' Unable to involve Eleanor, they stayed away from England.

As a papal legate, Longchamp then issued a flurry of excommunications against the people most responsible for his dismissal – though he stopped short of excommunicating the king's brother – with a special execration for Hugh of Nonant, demanding that he should be strictly avoided by everyone.* In return, the new

---

*The phrase 'sent to Coventry' is supposed to have originated in the English Civil War, but this example of the Bishop of Coventry being 'sent to Coventry' may imply an earlier explanation.

government in England laid an interdict – a mass excommunication – on Longchamp's own diocese in Ely, which meant they could siphon off the revenues from there into the treasury. It was a fearsome ecclesiastical sanction, which meant that no services could be performed, no masses said, no funerals or burials carried out. It meant that bodies were left unburied on village greens across affected dioceses. The two cardinals, now back in Paris, then excommunicated William Fitzhugh for their treatment outside the Rouen drawbridge, together with the entire garrison, and laid an interdict on the whole of Normandy. Archbishop Geoffrey also excommunicated his own suffragan bishop of Durham, the man Richard had originally placed in charge of the north of England. Longchamp had himself already been excommunicated by the bishops who met at Reading, urged on by Hugh of Nonant, which gave Eleanor an excellent excuse for not seeing him. It was against ecclesiastical law to eat or drink with people who had been excommunicated and she was able to avoid being drawn into the power struggle by refusing to meet an excommunicate.

So far, the emergency arrangements set out by Richard and his mother seemed to have worked. Longchamp had overreached himself, but his place had been taken peacefully by Walter of Coutances. The new chief justiciar was having to deal with increasingly angry letters from Rome, but that was to be expected. What happened next had not been planned for at all – and it was the reason for Eleanor's desperate letter to Richard that arrived in Palestine on 15 April 1192. It was this letter, and those that followed, that must have been uppermost in his mind as his ship slipped its moorings in Acre and sailed north under the Mediterranean stars. On 20 January 1192 – just as Richard had been entering Ascalon – Philip Augustus met William Fitzhugh with a copy of the agreement he had made with Richard in Messina, complete with royal seals, and demanded that he hand over his sister Alys, together with the disputed Norman territories of Gisors, Aumale and Eu. Suspecting correctly that the document before him was a forgery, Fitzhugh refused.

Philip stormed back to Paris and began raising an armed force.

The whispering campaign, which claimed that Richard was never coming home, was stepped up. Philip also wrote to John, inviting him to cross the Channel and promising him that, if he did so, he would be made lord of all the Angevin lands in France – including Normandy and Aquitaine – and that he could marry Alys, strengthening his claim to the English throne. The fact that John was already married was apparently beside the point. Worse, it became clear that John was prepared to act on the invitation. He had gathered a force of mercenaries and was in Southampton, preparing to sail to join Philip.

When the news reached Eleanor in Rouen in the first week of February, she realized that everything now depended on her. She could no longer avoid the situation simply by avoiding Longchamp. Setting off immediately, she landed in Southampton on 11 February, before John had left. But instead of remonstrating with him, she ignored him completely, heading straight for Winchester and the treasury. Once there, she sent out letters to the barons who were capable of shutting off John's access to money, and convened a series of councils in Windsor, Oxford, London and Winchester. In each of these, her rhetoric provided the members of the Great Council with enough courage to stand up to John – and just in time. He abandoned his plans and withdrew to his castle in Wallingford, from where he emanated ill-will.

To complicate matters further, a messenger arrived from Longchamp during the London meeting to say that he had arrived in Dover and was staying in the castle. He considered himself not only still Chancellor of England but also an emissary from Rome. This was an unnecessary complication, because to summon up enough nerve to withstand the Pope, the barons felt they needed John's support. Reluctantly, they sent a delegation to see him in Wallingford. John used the opportunity for a threatening reminder that he now had no access to funds. 'The Chancellor fears the threats of none of you, nor all of you together. Nor will he beg your suffrance if only he may succeed to have me as his friend,' said John, according to the chronicler Richard of Devizes, reminding them of their powerlessness if he was to choose to back

Longchamp after all. 'He has promised to give me £700 of silver within a week, if I shall interpose between you and him. You see, I am in want of money. To the wise, a word is sufficient.'

Faced with this blackmail, the Great Council had little choice, and they agreed to outbid Longchamp. They also wrote a joint letter with Eleanor, advising Longchamp to return across the Channel, 'unless he has a mind to take his meals under the custody of an armed guard'.

Having successfully held England together, Eleanor embarked on a flurry of tidying other outstanding issues. She brokered an agreement between the two northern bishops at a meeting in the Temple Church in London.★ She successfully appealed to the Pope to lift the interdict on Normandy, and a tour around the diocese of Ely – 'wherever she passed, men, women and children, a piteous company, their feet bare, their clothes unwashed, their hair unshorn' – convinced her to lean on the new administration to lift the interdict there too.

Eleanor of Aquitaine retained her ferocious political talents and she had briefly succeeded in preventing John from creating a rift with his brother that would have torn the Angevin empire apart. The news had reached her that, in fact, Philip's most important barons had refused to take up arms against a crusader. But the situation was still extremely unpredictable. By personal reputation and willpower alone, Eleanor was holding the kingdom together. But for almost a year now she had been urging Richard to come home. If he could just have taken Jerusalem, not even the king of France would have dared stand against him. As it was, the factions inside the crusade, as well as those inside the crusader kingdom, seemed to be conspiring to make sure he never reached home at all.

★

★ The round Templar church, which is still in existence, had been consecrated by the Patriarch of Jerusalem only seven years before. It was considered a neutral place for negotiation. John was challenged by his barons here before the signing of the Magna Carta in 1215.

For medieval sailors, dependent on a clear sky to fix their position, the Mediterranean was unpredictable at the best of times. It may have been the most navigated ocean in the world, but even the biggest three-masted ships clung to the coastline when they could, and resigned themselves to extraordinary detours at the hands of the mysterious currents and winds – the sirocco, the ghibli, the mistral and the bora. Roman military writers used to advise nobody to sail beyond 14 September, but it was the practice by the twelfth century to allow ships on to the Mediterranean until 10 November before closing the ports for the winter. Richard would be cutting his journey very fine to reach the French coast in that time.

He had chosen an inconspicuous buss that was for many years believed to have been called *Franchenef*, though that is now thought to have been a misunderstanding of the original chronicle. But even if its name has been forgotten, Richard chose this ship because it was ordinary, so we can picture it with some confidence: just over 100 feet long and maybe 40 feet wide, with space for maybe 1,000 passengers or 100 horses and their attendants squeezed together below.* It probably had two masts, with a large triangular cotton sail on the mainmast, and a spare sail of canvas for stiff winds, but none of the usual colourful pennants and ensigns to show who was aboard. There was a platform at the bows – the forecastle, where a few trusted men at arms were posted – and another at the stern, from where the two heavy rudders on either side eased the ship through the narrow channels between the rocks along the southern coast of Asia Minor, dodging between islands to evade potential pursuers.

Also at the stern were stored up to twenty spare anchors, probably made in Venice and leased from the big anchor store in Acre, strapped to the ship because anchors were notoriously easy to lose. Underneath the stern platform was Richard's cabin, a small room with windows looking out behind. We know that similar ships half a century later had their chambers for nobles panelled and

---

* This was big, though the Saracens had ships capable of carrying 1,500. Three centuries later, Columbus's *Santa Maria* was only 75 feet long.

there is no reason to suppose this one would have been any different. There was probably no latrine on board, so everyone would have been expected to use a bucket, emptying it over the side after making very sure which direction the wind was blowing. There must have been cargo, some equipment belonging to the king and maybe others – possibly a closely guarded secret. It may have been a small, wide ship by modern standards, but it had a large, highly experienced crew of seventy-five, including a ship's scribe, a cross between an accountant and a lawyer, who kept a record of everything coming on or leaving the ship.★

The only way Richard's master could judge their position was with an astrolabe to measure the altitude of the sun. At midday, by the master's pocket sundial, they could then work out how many degrees they were from the Equator. That gave them latitude; a method of judging longitude was still some centuries away. Alexander Neckham, the son of Richard's wet nurse, described a compass back in the 1180s, but these were not yet reliable and were reserved for when the ship was fog-bound – and even then probably consisted of no more than a magnetic needle in a bowl of water. Masters put their faith in lookouts in the crow's nest above the mainsail; they could see for up to eight nautical miles, or an hour and a half's journey time, around them. But there was also the position of the pole star, and the lamps that were lit at night outside chapels on promontories dedicated to St Nicholas and to Mary the Virgin all along the northern Mediterranean coast – often in converted temples to Poseidon and Artemis – put there specifically to guide shipping in the dark. The behaviour of seabirds and clouds could also tell the crew about the nearest land. Along particularly dangerous coasts, the master used local pilots who knew the channels. This was a vital and responsible job: under Catalan laws, incompetent pilots were beheaded. Otherwise it was

---

★Not only would the masters normally have insisted on inspecting the cargo, they would also have to show whoever was hiring the ship any ropes needed for hoisting cargo on board – the origin of the expression 'showing the ropes'.

a matter of relying on the experience of the navigator and the will of God.

Sailing was an uncomfortable business as well as dangerous, listening to the waves crashing against the hull and the groaning of the ship's timbers, and trying to ignore the inevitable seasickness and the stench of rat urine. The poorest pilgrims normally stayed below deck, next to the horses and the pump, existing on a diet of bread, salt and water. These would not have been on Richard's ship. His small party – by tradition this included Blondel – would have brought their own warm clothes and mattresses, and bedded down in a corner of the deck near the capstan, or the big hatches, or the permanent altar on the quarterdeck. They would have heeded the advice to sea travellers of the day to bring with them their own ginger, figs, pepper, cheese and salted meat, because ships' food was notoriously maggot-ridden. Most voyagers between Western Europe and Palestine – and there were already regular sailings from Venice – ate on land every night, because that was where the fresh food and the firewood were, and it reduced the chances of the braziers setting fire to the ship. But Richard was in a hurry, and they were sailing by night as well as by day, stopping regularly to take on water and check their position with the locals. Their meals were otherwise taken on board, heralded by a trumpet – first for the travellers to bring them to the small tables on deck, and then again for the crew. Richard ate alone, but in full view: by tradition, kings had to eat in public. Then there were chess, cards and dice on deck, and communal singing – perhaps some of Blondel's better-known compositions – military voices carrying over the dark ocean.

The process of gathering together the fleet from England and sailing with it from France to Palestine had fascinated Richard. So had the experience of working with the Pisan fleet to keep his army supplied, and he had come to know a great deal about maritime fighting and sea power. In later years, he would use this knowledge to found the Royal Navy and its historic base at Portsmouth. His character and temperament being what they were,

Richard would not have left the master to himself as they felt their way between the islands; he would have been by his side, urging him on to greater speed and greater risk.

The midnight sailing had given Richard a head start. It was important to land before the informers who hung around the alleys of Acre could get their messages to his enemies that he had sailed. They continued up the coast past Tyre until they could see Beirut on the starboard bow, then Richard's ship turned west and, within three days of their departure, anchored in the harbour of Limassol in Cyprus.

It has never been clear exactly why Richard needed to stop there, potentially giving his journey and schedule away to the spies who clustered in these outposts where the different religions and races of the region mixed freely and anonymously. It was probably to secure the administration for the hapless Guy of Lusignan. Although he had been given the island by Richard under the agreement to hand over the throne of Jerusalem to Conrad, Guy might well have needed Richard's presence and authority to make it quite clear to the remaining Templars there that he was now in charge. Richard probably also needed money, and Guy had taken on the commitment to pay for the island, something the Templars had failed to do.

From Cyprus the ship probably set sail at night again – striking north along the coast of Asia Minor at a best speed of six knots, heading for Rhodes. The rising swell made it clear that the weather was already closing in. This was no simple voyage even in summertime, and Richard was sailing against the wind. In 1103 the early pilgrim Saewulf had arrived in Rhodes sailing the other way, and finally managed to reach the Sea of Marmora and Constantinople more than three months later. 'The voyage from Rhodes to Chios is dangerous,' wrote one mariner two centuries after Richard's voyage. 'As the land of Turkey is very close on the right hand; and there are many islands, both inhabited and deserted on the other side, so that it is dangerous to sail over this route at night, or in bad weather.' Richard was doing both, picking up local pilots where possible, pressing on when not, with the currents behind him pushing them north.

At Rhodes, the ship sailed into Emborikos harbour, avoiding the sandbank by the entrance of the main commercial port and passing the site of the famous Colossus, one of the seven wonders of the ancient world. Leaving Rhodes through the Dodecanese islands – each one with its own particular hazards of shoals and rocks – they sailed south-west, leaving Karpathos to the starboard, heading for Crete. Then, avoiding the ports on the safer northern shore – in Byzantine hands – they took the fast route along the southern side of the island, which meant risking the sudden squalls and the reefs of Gavdos Island. Then north again up the western coast of Greece.

Richard passed safely through the area of limbo that his mother had told him about when he was a child, where she had been briefly seized along with all her baggage by Byzantine corsairs on her way home from the Second Crusade, and under the very gaze of her first husband, Louis VII.★ Richard no doubt breathed a sigh of relief having avoided his mother's Mediterranean fate, and set course for Corfu, passing between Odysseus' island of Ithaca and the Greek coast. The approach was especially dangerous, and it was customary to arrive and leave from the south to avoid the Erikoussa islets. This meant that Richard's ship would have hugged the coast through the Zakynthos Channel between Corfu and the mainland, avoiding the Strofades Islands and their reefs, including the notorious rock Arpia, which gave its name to the Harpies.

Philip had also stopped in Corfu – then ruled from Constantinople – on his way home, and it is possible that Richard risked coming ashore here in connection with Philip's visit. Corfu was another meeting place between three worlds, the Byzantine, the

---

★ Eleanor had been rescued, only to be blown across the Mediterranean throughout the summer of 1148 by a vicious wind known as the gregale, which took her all the way to the North African coast before her ship was able to limp back to Palermo.

Muslim and the Western, with its rival Italian traders. It was a place where secrets were known and for sale, and Richard needed information: which was the safest way home and who were now the most dangerous intriguers against him? It was almost certainly here that he met agents sent from Sicily by Tancred, who told him about the crucial meeting between Philip and Emperor Henry VI, at which Henry had promised to arrest Richard if he ventured into his territory. Even if the possibility was still in his mind, this information would have decided Richard firmly against travelling back through Italy. It seems to have been in Corfu that Hubert, Bishop of Salisbury, left ship to make his own way home through Italy, now that Richard could not.

Richard sailed from Corfu on 11 November, past the great citadel towering over the town and the Venetian ships hauled on to the shore for the winter. It was near the deadline beyond which no ship should be at sea for fear of the winter storms as they set out into the Ionian Sea – rough even in the summer months. It was here that Odysseus had been washed ashore at the end of his wanderings around the Mediterranean.

A few days later, Richard's ship was seen by some pilgrims off the coast of Italy, heading for Brindisi. It was the last sighting before his disappearance – evidence for the doubters back home that he was on his way. Even so, it was almost certainly a piece of disinformation, as it had never been his intention to land at Brindisi. At best, that would have meant an enforced stay in Rome, as happened to his wife, his sister and the Cypriot princess; at worst, arrest by the emperor's men. It is possible that he deliberately allowed the ship to be recognized heading in that direction, before turning away again the moment the useful pilgrims were out of sight. In fact, Richard and the crew went round Cape St Maria di Leuca, across the Gulf of Taranto and probably not through the Straits of Messina, where he had sailed at the head of his fleet just eighteen months before – and where he was too liable to be seen – but down the southern coast of Sicily. The objective now was the south of France, and from Sicily it was generally advised that the quickest way there – given that Richard did not want to hug the Italian coast all the way to France, giving advance warning of his arrival – was to cross direct with the currents that flowed towards Cape Spartivento and the North African coast. It was wise to avoid running too close to the dangerous west coasts of Corsica and Sardinia, with their treacherous rocks.* Equally, sailing too close to the North African coast risked wandering into the territories of the Barbary pirates and Muslim corsairs who hunted in those waters.

Keeping a sharp lookout, it was here – off the North African coast near Tunis, and only three days' sailing from Marseilles – that the full seriousness of his position came home to Richard, and he opted for an even more uncertain alternative. There are still many mysterious aspects to his decision to turn round, and why it was taken here. It is possible that he put into Sicily as he sailed down its southern coast and met agents sent by Tancred to warn him. Or had he been mulling over the new risk revealed to him in Corfu all the way across the Adriatic? Or did he simply hail a ship passing in the other direction? Whatever it was, Richard was given information about a plot to seize him and take him hostage the moment he stepped ashore in the self-governing port of Marseilles. Worse, the eldest son of Raymond of Toulouse, Raymond, Count of St Gilles, had bands of trusted men at all the ports in southern France. Given his character, Richard's first reaction would have been to accept the risk and fight it out. But the prospect of being at the mercy of his most troublesome vassal was extremely worrying, especially as he was almost certainly in league with Philip. If Richard was captured by that combination, it would seal the fate of England and probably Aquitaine too. His advisers on board were led by William de l'Étang, one of the handful of trusted knights who had held off the Saracen attack outside Jaffa in August. There were only a few of them with him on the ship and they must have urged him not to even consider that option. The moment Richard stepped ashore in Marseilles or any of the

*It was a fearsome crossing: a century later, half the Sicilian fleet would be wrecked on exactly this journey.

southern French ports, he would have been recognized. There really was no alternative. He had to land somewhere else.

But where? He could have landed along the east coast of Spain and made his way home to Aquitaine through territory controlled by his new allies in Navarre, but that would have required first landing in Barcelona, in what was now the combined kingdom of Aragon and Catalonia, which was on bad terms with its neighbours – including Navarre – and had quite likely been offered a considerable bribe by Philip to arrest Richard if he came ashore there. Aragon also then controlled most of the coastline of Provence. Richard must by then have heard about the invasion of Toulouse by his brother-in-law Sancho of Navarre, and knew that sailing to Barcelona risked interception by patrols from Toulouse, Pisa or Genoa. It would also have involved getting dangerously close to the island of Majorca, then still in Muslim hands and the base for corsairs who were patrolling the approaches. He could have landed in northern Italy, but the risks there would have been even greater for the journey home. Genoa was now a close ally of Philip's and the French, and the territory north of there around Piedmont belonged to the relatives of Conrad of Montferrat, whose pride that Conrad had been chosen as king of Jerusalem was now tempered by their conviction that he had been murdered on Richard's orders. Even his former allies in Pisa had signed a treaty with the emperor for his forthcoming attack on Sicily, as Richard must by now have been aware, and this could well have involved his arrest.

The obvious option – to press on through the Straits of Gibraltar – was also impossible because of the strong currents in the opposite direction, faster than the speed of the fastest vessel then afloat. Before the fourteenth century, all the seagoing traffic through the Pillars of Hercules went eastwards; none of Richard's original fleet of English ships would ever have returned home. Making the attempt would also have risked landing in Muslim territory on either side of the straits. No, there was really only one option, and by the time their ship had reached North Africa, it was clear to Richard what that was. In the light of what happened next, the idea of turning round, sailing up the Adriatic in winter, landing near Hungary and making the long overland journey to Saxony to link up with his brother-in-law Henry the Lion seems outrageously foolhardy – if this was Richard's decision, and even that is imposs- ible to know for certain. But it was definitely bold and, in his predicament – the whole Mediterranean world united against him and only six weeks to Christmas – Richard required boldness.

Still, it must have been a controversial decision among his loyal group of companions, and there must have been at least some secret forebodings of looming disaster as the ship's two rudders were heaved over, the great triangular sail was tacked and they headed back to Corfu.

6. Disguise

'In a very short time the wind had filled the sail and blown us out of sight of the land of our birth. And I tell you now that anyone who sets out on such a dangerous course is foolhardy. For at night you fall asleep without knowing whether you will find yourself the next morning at the bottom of the sea.'

Jean de Joinville, on leaving for the Seventh Crusade by sea

'O lord, heavenly father, let the angels watch over thy servants, that they may reach their destination in safety . . . that no enemy may attack them on the road, nor evil overcome them. Protect them from the periods of fast rivers, thieves or wild beasts.'

medieval blessing for pilgrims

Richard and his colleagues were now under no illusion about the peril of their situation. The whole of the north coast of the Mediterranean had been transformed, in a frighteningly short time, from a series of friendly ports ready to welcome and cheer the hero of Christendom to a border bristling with hidden menace where he might be seized and condemned as a murderer, compromiser and traitor. The fact that this sudden shift in European opinion had been so quick that it had to have been coordinated – by either Henry VI or Philip Augustus – was really no comfort. Every inlet and haven now held dangers for Richard and his companions.

Their chosen solution was also dangerous. Sailing back across the Mediterranean in winter was difficult enough, especially when it was illegal to be at sea, according to the laws of most of the local maritime powers. Travelling across Europe from south to north, without proper maps or languages, carried its own pitfalls and threats. But the real worry for Richard was not so much the risk of physical harm — a fear he was unusually immune to — as the danger to himself as king. England lay on the brink of civil war; Normandy faced invasion from a powerful neighbour. His disappearance at this critical time might be enough to guarantee disaster. But capture could have been far worse: the chances were that he would then be handed over to the king of France in return for a generous payment, with untold implications for England and the empire. There would be a show trial, and mischievous and destructive proclamations would be made in his name that he would be powerless to prevent, followed by either a humiliating treaty involving the loss of Normandy and other French possessions or worse. England and France teetered for centuries on the edge of merger into one kingdom under one or other royal line — even in 1940 the idea of merger was debated by the French cabinet as an alternative to defeat by the Nazis — and Richard's capture by a clever monarch like Philip might easily have decided the matter France's way.

When he set out from Acre, still under something of a misapprehension about the welcome that awaited him in Europe, Richard could have expected to reach Venice or Brindisi by November and be home in early January. It was clearly going to be a long and difficult period before that was now possible. As he and his companions were turning the ship around from the coast of North Africa, his wife and sister and the Cypriot princess had arrived in Naples with the English admiral Stephen de Turnham, who immediately set off with them on the road north towards Rome — their home for the next six months, under the protection of the Pope. Retracing his steps meant for Richard once more braving the unpredictable currents around Sicily, hugging the Italian coast and sailing due east towards Corfu — this time on an almost empty and far more lethal ocean. Navigated by Stephen de Turnham's brother Robert, the ship passed again through the unpredictable eastern Adriatic islands that harboured the pirates who had briefly seized his mother more than half a century before. But this time, they would not be allowed to pass through unmolested.

Mediterranean trade in those days was seriously threatened by pirates, but the dividing line was blurred between corsairs, who were praised for preying on Muslim shipping, and those who were execrated for preying on Christian shipping. There were pirates who might be financed legitimately as investments in Venice or Genoa to haunt the sea lanes between Corsica and the Barbary coast, spreading fear among the Muslim traders plying their trade between North Africa and Spain. Seizing Muslim cargoes could be a lucrative business venture. But if for some reason that trade seemed sparse, they might in practice swoop on a shipload of Christian pilgrims and sell them into slavery at the nearest Muslim port.

As it became clear that the two galleys with high prows approaching them were intending to attack and board their ship, Richard and his companions would have unpacked what they were still carrying of their armour. Chain mail rusted easily and was always packed away carefully for the voyage, so there may not have been time to find it. If there had been, it meant slipping an undershirt on first – a special guild of linen armourers made clothing to wear underneath chain mail to stop the links being embedded in the flesh following a sword swipe – then pulling the heavy chain tunic over their heads, down to their calves and over their hands. Their helmets were probably nearer to hand as the pirate ships approached, with their fearsome crews poised to leap over the side, and they would have had their swords and shields ready to receive them.

Before medieval sea battles, it was traditional for minstrels to play while the grappling irons were laid out and the crossbows were being armed at either end of the ship. Most sea battles involved throwing what was known as Greek fire from the height of the prow: a mixture of pitch, resin, sulphur, naphtha, saltpetre and charcoal that could be extinguished only by a mixture of vinegar and urine. Ships sailed into battle protected by felt soaked in vinegar – but there was no time to prepare anything of the kind now. In any case, pirates would not normally risk setting light to the ships they wanted to seize.

As the galleys approached, Richard's companions could see the marines and armed boarders gathering on the platforms at the bows, next to the bronze catapult used for throwing Greek fire. Pirates could not board over the side because even making a galley list a little would make rowing impossible. What happened then defies explanation or description. Somehow, just as the ships clashed, Richard was able to summon up the reserves of authority that made him such a successful military commander and prevent the battle from taking place. It is not clear how he achieved this, but it may have involved him making himself completely recognizable and trusting to his fame. According to one story, the pirates surrendered to him as soon as they realized who he was – his reputation as a military miracle worker was clearly still intact. According to another, Richard was somehow able to deflect their attack into a negotiation about hiring their ships. Either way, with relief from his companions, an agreement was quickly reached that the ships and crews were his for hire for 200 silver marks. In order to sail in early December secretly up the tortuous narrows of the coast of Dalmatia he would require a crew with a wealth of local knowledge; there was no point in defeating them and taking the ship from them.

There are alternative accounts of Richard's encounter with the pirates. The English historian Roger of Howden had him sighting the galleys from Corfu, moored towards the mainland, and taking a boat out to them directly to open negotiations, but, as with many aspects of Richard's abortive journey home, it is impossible to know exactly which account is correct. Most detailed sources say that his final leg by sea was conducted in either a pair or a trio of galleys. Either way, for the second time in a month, they anchored under the great citadel that towered above the town and harbour of Corfu – for centuries a haven from the fierce winds of the Adriatic for sailors, for Venetian traders on their way to Byzantium and for returning pilgrims from the Holy Land. Most of those had now disappeared for the winter, and it must have been a conspicuous royal party that set foot there this time. Their presence must have been noted by those who kept the emperor informed.

Roger of Howden was very precise about the number of companions Richard kept by him – he says there were twenty of them – and perhaps this is a clue as to why he needed two boats. In the first of many similar manoeuvres on his secret journey north, Richard divided his companions to make it ambiguous which group he was with. The group that stayed with him included William de l'Étang, the lawyer Baldwin of Béthune, Richard's clerk, Philip of Poitou (later Bishop of Durham), his admiral Robert de Turnham, his chaplain, Anselm – who would eventually be the source of the most reliable account of the journey – plus four Templar knights. Apart from Hubert Walter, who made his own way back through Italy after their first visit to Corfu, the others who had set out with him from Acre drop out of the pages of history. But there is one exception – at least perhaps in the pages of mythology – and that is the dramatic, legendary encounter between Richard and one of them, Blondel de Nesle, as they sang to each other through the walls of Dürnstein Castle.

If Richard's buss was barely seaworthy after mid-November, this was nothing to the problems faced by sailing anywhere by galley a few weeks later.* Galleys were smooth coastal craft designed for naval actions, or for transporting royalty swiftly from port to port. They were not easy to manage even in mild ocean conditions, and the Mediterranean could be anything but mild. Naval historians believe that medieval galleys probably reached their limits, with their low seaboards, in a Force 4 or 5 gale – and weather of that magnitude was almost certain at some time on the short voyage north. But Richard and his advisers must have calculated that – especially after their deliberate ruse outside Brindisi – his ship was now too well known and expected imminently

---

*Galleys required considerable stocks of salt and water (one writer estimates seventy-six gallons a day) just for the crew. With the oarsmen stuck behind their oars and no latrines on board, you could probably smell the approach of a medieval galley before it came into view.

all over the southern coast of Europe. It made sense to shift into something less predictable.

The only description that survives of the galleys Richard hired was that they were 'high-necked' and 'Rumanian'. They had rams, and he may have felt these were necessary because he feared some kind of arrest from seagoing Venetian patrols. They had not been used in the original attack on Richard's previous ship, presumably because it was so valuable. If this was anything like the average galley at the time, and there is no reason to think otherwise, Richard would have become temporary master of a sizeable crew, with two decks of over 100 oarsmen under a large triangular sail, plus four helmsmen – two on duty at any one time – an assortment of marines to board their prey and handle the rockets and catapults, and a few boys. But galleys were also fast and at this point Richard needed speed as well as anonymity. They could probably manage a cruising speed that would allow progress of up to 100 miles a day, and at this speed Richard could begin to accelerate his frustratingly slow progress northwards.

But nothing was going according to plan. At some time early in the second week of December, as the king's galley snaked its way between the green islands scattered off the Dalmatian coast, the fearsome Adriatic wind known as the bora intervened. A storm battered the galley and forced a decision to put in at the nearest port, Ragusa.

Richard's galley never made it into Ragusa harbour – modern Dubrovnik – the safe haven under the walls of one of the great Adriatic trading ports. He was forced ashore within sight of his goal on the island of Lokrum, about half a mile out to sea and at the very entrance to the harbour. He and his companions, as well as the galley's crew, struggled ashore across the large rocks that cover the island's beaches in all directions at the height of the storm and must have sheltered under the trees. As the weather began to lift, they may have walked to the top of the hill to work out where they had come ashore, mindful of Richard's promise as the ship veered towards the rocks that he would spend 100,000 ducats (gold coins from Venice) building a church if and wherever he had the good fortune to land. Or perhaps they had by then discovered the door to the small Benedictine priory there, where the monks prepared a meal for him and his companions, and heard about Richard's typically spendthrift vow.

It is possible that Richard was intending to disguise himself as a Templar when he landed. That would have been an obvious first thought. He was with four trusted Templar knights and it was the self-appointed task of Templars to protect crusaders on their way to and from the Holy Land. It was also their special role to look after holy relics and Richard was probably carrying some of these, perhaps even one of the pieces of the True Cross that he had stumbled upon outside Jerusalem six months before. This might also have been a particularly appropriate disguise, because legend has it that Richard considered himself to be a Templar. Before setting sail, Richard seemed to describe himself to the Master of the Temple as a 'brother Templar'. It was an ambiguous phrase, which may simply have meant that he was asking for the privileges of a fellow Templar, but it would have been very much in character for him to be secretly initiated into the order as some legends say he was – and the Templars would have been only too happy to oblige.

The story of Richard's journey and his arrest contains so many mysterious elements that are now impossible to make sense of. It seems extraordinary, given the circumstances, that he should have arrived within a couple of miles of Duke Leopold of Austria, one of the few men in Europe with a seriously personal motive for arresting him, after the humiliating rebuff when his Austrian banner was thrown into the moat at Acre. Perhaps the continuing mystery might be explained by a secondary mission on behalf of the secret-ive order of soldier-monks, which might explain the presence of the four unnamed Templar knights. But if there was one, it is now beyond recovery.

It may be that, as Richard was rowed from Lokrum across to Ragusa harbour, he was still intending to stick to the Templar story. But there seems to have been no attempt to do so once he arrived among the masts and sails and the ships pulled up on the beach for the winter. Perhaps the pirate crew, who discovered his identity as they tried to storm his ship, were unable to keep the secret. Perhaps he knew they would be unable to. Either way, he was welcomed to Ragusa by the leading figures of the city under his own name. Richard appeared to have chanced upon one of the few ports where he was not in danger of arrest. Rumours of his munificent offer to build a church on Lokrum reached the city before he did and a delegation of the leading inhabitants came to him and begged him instead to help them rebuild the dilapidated cathedral, which was in need of repairs having been there since the seventh century. Richard agreed, on two conditions – that the Pope would allow him to change the terms of his vow and that some of the money would be spent rebuilding the monastery on Lokrum.

This was the kind of spending that required a loan. Richard had not set sail equipped to build cathedrals. Luckily, as a port that was soon to rival Venice, Ragusa was well endowed with banks prepared to lend him the ducats he needed. Perhaps this is also where he met a man simply described as Pisan who sold him three extremely expensive jewelled rings that he took a liking to, but it could perfectly well have been in one of the other ports on the return journey – Rhodes or Corfu or even back in Cyprus. But it was in Ragusa that Richard once again had access to money, and he may have felt he would need jewellery somewhere on the way home. Like many kings at the time, he believed that almost every local princeling could be seduced by jewels.

When the medieval cathedral of Dubrovnik was excavated recently, its foundations predated Richard's arrival by decades, which casts some doubt on the story. It is anyway far more likely that he was asked to contribute towards it, and he did so as much to help recover his lost reputation as to fulfil his vow. Richard may by now have been so obsessed with defending himself, or so excited about having ready money again, that he did not stop to consider that endowing cathedrals did not sit easily with slipping secretly across Europe. Ragusa's Romanesque cathedral church –

supposedly built with the help of Richard's money – survived for nearly five centuries, until a disastrous earthquake hit Dubrovnik in 1667. The present Baroque cathedral is built on the same foundations.★

Even if there was a secondary and mysterious purpose behind Richard's enforced voyage up the Adriatic in winter, the objective seems clear. He was making for Saxony and the safety of his brother-in-law. Henry the Lion was one of the great figures of shifting German power at the end of the twelfth century. In 1192 he was sixty-three and past the peak of his influence but he had been a focus of resistance against the imperial rule of Frederick Barbarossa. A formidable duke, he had successfully cleared the Baltic of pirates and extended his lands towards the pagan east, even finding time to found the city of Munich in his Bavarian lands. But in 1182 he had been defeated and exiled for a period of three years that he spent in England, where he had built up even closer relations with the Plantagenets – he had in fact married Richard's older sister, Matilda, in 1169 and his son Otto was ruling Aquitaine in Richard's absence.† Once Frederick had left on the Third Crusade, on the way to his fatal encounter with the river crossing, Henry had returned to Saxony, gathered his old vassals around him and once more become a thorn in the side of the emperor – by now Frederick's son Henry VI, who took his own claims for overlordship over the whole world extremely seriously. Henry the Lion's alliance with England was of increasing concern to the Emperor. He was an absolutely reliable haven for Richard and, even more importantly, he controlled the Baltic ports of

---

★ The monastery on Lokrum survived until Napoleonic times.
† When Henry the Lion and his wife were in exile, and spending Christmas at Henry II's court in Argentan in 1182, they encountered the troubadour Bertran de Born, who fell for Matilda: 'A court where no one laughs or jokes is never complete; a court without gifts is just a paddock full of barons,' he sang. 'And the boredom and vulgarity of Argentan nearly killed me, but the lovable, noble person, the sweet, kind face, the good companionship and conversation of the Saxon lady protected me.'

Hamburg and Lübeck, from where it would be a relatively short sea voyage to England.

Even so, it was no simple matter to cross Europe from the Adriatic to the Baltic without falling into the hands of the Holy Roman Emperor or his vassals. Richard was probably heading for what is now Pula or Zadar – now Croatian ports, and formerly the Italian naval strongholds of Pola and Zara, but in 1192 in Hungarian hands. Hungary meant the cosmopolitan rule of King Bela III, one of the wealthiest sovereigns in Europe because of the mineral riches of upper Hungary and the salt mines of Transylvania, with lands that stretched down to the Adriatic in the south. Bela was married to Margaret of France, the widow of Richard's older brother, Henry the Young King, and former mistress of William the Marshal, so he would have been among old friends. Perched between the rule of Western Christianity under the Pope and Eastern Christianity under the Byzantine patriarchs, the Arpad dynasty of Hungary had asserted its right to be Catholics but without the inconvenience of papal authority. They resisted demands to suppress the Bogomil heresy, with its emphasis on purity and poverty, versions of which were now powerful in the south of France. They only very reluctantly allowed Western crusaders free passage on their way to Palestine. And it was this truculence in the face of Western authority that paradoxically gave Richard a hunch that he might be safe there.

Bela was on friendly terms with the French – he was, after all, married to Philip's half-sister – which must have added an extra unpredictability about travelling through Hungary. But only six years before there had been considerable discussion about the possibility of a marriage between Bela and Richard's niece, and that must have reassured him that he would be welcomed. He was also known to be involved in a long-running dispute with Duke Leopold of Austria.

But again, it was not to be. Richard had only rested in Ragusa for a day or so. Given that it was now December, the Adriatic would have been almost completely clear of shipping, but his boat – no doubt hired from the grateful city fathers – was soon off, hugging the shore past the island of Hvar and Diocletian's old palace at Split. Yet once more he found himself in the grip of the notorious bora. For a second time, Richard and his exhausted companions despaired of ever reaching home as the wind plunged them out to sea into an unfamiliar part of the ocean, and drove them helplessly past the longed-for coast of Hungary, before depositing them and all that remained of their belongings somewhere not far off the coast of Istria, when the boat finally began to sink. They struggled ashore somewhere in the Gulf of Trieste, a little to the west of the Roman city of Aquileia – not in Hungary, but in territory under the indirect control of the Holy Roman Empire.

They probably had little or no idea exactly where they were, but suspected they had overshot their objective and may have strayed – as they had in fact – into territory disputed then and almost ever since between the power of Venice in the south and Salzburg and Austria in the north. There is a tradition in the area that says that Richard was arrested here rather than in Austria, which means it may not be very reliable. But it also suggests that he landed in an almost deserted area of swamps and forests, and had to be led with his friends to safety by hermits through the mists and sodden undergrowth. If this part of the legend is based on fact, he may have landed somewhere in the estuary of the Tagliamento, with its swampy beaches.

By the time he emerged from the forest and on to the road to Aquileia, the Templar identity was not sufficient. Richard's hair and beard were long, as were those of his companions. The implication in the chronicles is that long hair and beards were the local style and this was appropriate, though it was not the Templar clean-shaven style. But once they had recovered from the ordeal of picking their way through the marshes and their exhausting second struggle ashore – the crash of surf on rocks still echoing in their ears – they set about finding clothes that made them look a little more like the locals, and reconsidering the story they would tell about themselves. This was an age when you were expected to reveal your name and destination outside the gates of every town. The decision was taken that they would be pilgrims returning from Palestine in the company not of a Templar knight or our errant king, but of a wealthy merchant called Hugo.

Aquileia had once been one of the largest cities in the world, before it was sacked by Attila the Hun. A monastery survived, and the palace of the powerful patriarch, but that was almost all when Richard surveyed the ruins of six centuries. It was 10 December 1192, or thereabouts. It was decided between them, once they had bought horses for the journey, that the right direction was north-east, towards where they imagined Hungary to be. This was also the direction of the castle of the local count, and the plan was to ask him for directions and safe conduct. It is not clear from the conflicting accounts where this castle was, whether it was simply a large house in Aquileia or the castle that still dominates the town now known as Gorizia further to the north-east. The most reliable source, the chronicler Ralph of Coggeshall – who had the story from Richard's chaplain, Anselm – says that they landed 'in Slavonia' and headed to a town he calls Gazara. The evidence is that this is Gorizia, and that Richard and his companions were still determinedly heading towards the safety of King Bela's court.

It is unlikely, in that atmosphere of quiet watching and whispering in ports around the Mediterranean, that donating Venetian gold to endow a cathedral only 300 miles away in Ragusa would have gone unnoticed. Richard's presence would have been bound to be reported further north, as he must have realized as he prepared his disguise outside Aquileia. As his advisers would no doubt have told each other wryly, you can't both cross the Continent in disguise and repair your reputation at the same time.

His gesture may not have done much to repair his good name in Western Europe, but it was remembered for centuries in the Balkans – a region where memories are particularly lengthy. More than seven centuries later in January 1916, at the height of the First World War, the Serbian ambassador to Paris reminded his audience of Richard's munificence, claiming, 'It is not Great Britain who will fail in keeping her promises.' 'Great Britain has known us ever since Richard received our hospitality,' he said, 'and built for us a most beautiful church on the spot where our ancestors had saved him from a shipwreck on his way back from the crusade.'

The story of Richard's arrest has been passed over by historians through the years. It is the stuff of children's stories, and that is often the only place you will find much account of it. And the journey he made across central Europe is normally portrayed – if at all – as a brief and rather vague meander, during which he happened to stumble upon the Duke of Austria. The truth is that Richard's journey home, or as far as he reached, was an achievement of courage and determination in the face of serious obstacles. It was difficult, gruelling, dangerous and confusing, and he and his companions knew it would be the moment he turned the ship around off the North African coast.

It was not so much that the endeavour itself was extraordinary. Richard's generation, and his parents and grandparents, were those who rediscovered travel. For the first time since the Dark Ages, Europe was awakening to itself, driven to travel by conviction or education – and enabled to spend time away from home by the sudden abundance of silver coinage, which meant that wealth was no longer bound up in land and produce and could take to the roads. What had begun so tentatively in Abelard's lifetime with the first wandering scholars and monks had become a flood: crusaders on their way to Palestine, pilgrims heading towards the tombs of saints, masons in search of the next great Gothic construction, lawyers heading for the cities, the first students heading for the first universities, the merchants on their way to market. These people sharing Europe's dilapidated roads had a common European culture, presided over by the Church, and often a common language too – educated Latin – and between them they were building a new Gothic Europe. There they were, those early travellers, moving slowly in small groups for safety, from court to court, from inn to monastery to hostel. They travelled by barge, by horse or on foot if they were poor, at the speed of the slowest oxen.

As the ruler of an empire that stretched from Hadrian's Wall to the Pyrenees, Richard was used to travel. But he was not used to travel like this – setting aside his identity as king and hero of Christendom, and becoming just an ordinary merchant, on roads he did not know, through towns and villages he had never heard of, past people who spoke a language that he could not understand. It was simply too risky to seek out the local clerks and aristocracy and converse in Latin. And even in those days, journeys across Europe were so dangerous that the Church included travellers in prayers along with prisoners and the sick. Crosses were erected on lonely roads, lanterns kept burning in churches at night, and pilgrims would gather together – along with minstrels, bears, jugglers and herbalists – to venture along the old Roman roads. Conventional advice to travellers at the time was to give alms, make a will, put someone in charge of your house, settle all your differences with people, ask for people's prayers for you, your home and your family, and then put yourself in God's hands. Travelling was so insecure that it required the services of no fewer than three patron saints.

Richard's journey was also in mid-December: the snow lay ahead of them and the vast majority of travellers – except for those with urgent or nefarious reasons for being out – were home for Christmas, or resting until the spring. He was also still suffering from the effects of the fever that had made him so ill in Jaffa. Nor was it possible to derive much in the way of help and advice from the few fellow travellers who remained. When they greeted him on the road in the traditional way, asking who he was and where he was going, neither Richard nor his companions could answer truthfully. Worse, the last five centuries or so had seen almost no road and bridge building; instead, people relied the infrastructure that the Romans had left behind until it collapsed or wore out. Villages or local lords were occasionally given specific responsibilities for keeping some bridges repaired, but this period marked – as the historian Peter Spufford puts it – the 'nadir of the European road system', when the Roman legacy of 3,000 miles of military roads had been fixed temporarily for centuries with little more than earth to fill the potholes caused by a thousand years of frost. The twelfth century had woken up to the importance of bridges – for example, there was the new bridge at Avignon, and the

Steinerne Brücke was built across the Danube at Regensburg, which Richard was shortly to see for himself — and those who built them were honoured as saints.

Richard and his companions would have to expect broken roads covered in mud or ice, avalanches and wild animals — wolves or mountain lions — along the way. Europe might have awoken to the possibilities of travel, but nature was still a hostile force, able to sling at travellers deadly heat, cold or floods, as well as mists and snow, drought and disease and the most terrifying storms. Darkness and lightning were believed to send people mad. Even wading across a river included all the necessary ingredients for a fatal chill. Travelling by road was the stuff of the darkest European fairy stories, and ahead of them lay forests and craggy ranges of unknown extent. There would come a moment in winter when any road in this region became impassably frozen, and they would have to struggle to stay ahead of the weather.

But even worse than the prospect of negotiating a crumbling road system as the temperature dropped was the prospect of crossing the Alps. This normally required some local knowledge of the passes, but crossing them in winter must have seemed foolhardy in the extreme.* If they had been travelling openly — without fear that their guides might guess Hugo's real identity — they might have made it to Verona and gone from there across the Brenner Pass and home along the Rhine, but the central Alps were completely impassable in December. They would not have known what to expect in the eastern Alps, but would have known the terrifying medieval tales of Alpine crossings in winter, with desperate monks or saints crawling on their knees across sheets of ice, suffering terribly from frostbite and exposure. The century before, the Emperor Henry IV had tried to cross the Alps in winter, attempting to take the horses and ladies of the court on ox skins, crawling on hands and knees over the ice, and was lucky to escape with his life.

So if Richard and his companions, heading off towards the

---

*Most of the Alpine passes were opened in the following century. The St Gotthard Pass, for example, was open from the 1220s.

north-east and the nearest town, made a mistake in making contact with the local count at this point, you can see why. They needed support and protection on the road, but above all they needed guidance. Sometimes in these border areas, where unpredictable bands of returning crusaders made use of their positive balance in the spiritual bank to steal from anyone they met, an armed escort was compulsory for travellers – and had to be paid for too. The region of Aquileia was known to be infested with robbers. But there were also vital questions to ask. Which way was it safe to cross the mountains? Were there any roads that were passable at Christmas? They must have calculated that if they could convince the local lord of their identities, then no rumours about the presence of a king in disguise creeping through the countryside would make any difference.

So the argument for going to the local castle was a good one, except they almost certainly did not know they were in Gorizia – and even if they did, they would have had no idea of its significance. Because Richard had actually landed in potentially one of the most dangerous regions for him, the territory of the counts of Gorz (the German name for Gorizia). The counts were unusual in that they ruled no specific territory but had a hereditary position as Advocates of Aquileia, and at this time the role was shared between Engelbert III and his brother-in-law Meinhard II – later described by the emperor as a 'loyal subject of ours'. Meinhard was also a nephew of Conrad of Montferrat. Again, it is impossible to know for sure whether the castle they approached was in Aquileia or the much more substantial castle in Gorizia itself. Either is possible, because both are on the road to the north-east, towards northern Hungary, where Richard had been planning to go before the storm. But a strong local tradition in Gorizia suggests that he was there, and no equivalent stories exist about Aquileia, so it seems likely – even though it was almost a day's journey further on – that it was Gorizia castle they headed for.

Gorizia is in that unusual region of central Europe, now the far eastern corner of Italy, where Italian, German and Slovenian cultures have interacted for a thousand years or more. The three languages are so enmeshed that every place name has its equivalent in the other two. It is a confusing area even today, but then it was the border lands between Venice to the west, Austria and the Holy Roman Empire to the north and Hungary to the east, and on the other side of the mountain ranges that mark the border between Italy and Austria to this day.

Having arrived in the town at the end of their first day on the road, barely recovered from wading ashore with what remained of their belongings, they would have found an inn in Gorizia and, exhausted from their ordeal, settled down for the evening. Richard sent a messenger to the castle that – even to this day – dominates the town, asking for safe passage and a guide, and evoking the truce of God – the universal protection that was supposed to be given to crusaders. And here he made his great mistake. As a token of peace, he sent the messenger with one of the ruby rings he had bought from the Pisan – worth, says the chronicler, at least 900 bezants or Byzantine gold pieces. In the castle above the town as darkness gathered and torches were lit in the great hall, Engelbert received the messenger and took the ring. Who is it that wants safe conduct, he asked, and was told they were pilgrims on their way home from Jerusalem. What are their names?

'One of them is called Baldwin of Béthune,' said the messenger – presumably the name William de l'Étang would have been too recognizable. 'The other is called Hugo, a merchant, who also sent you this ring.'

But this reply did not satisfy the count. He stared thoughtfully at the ring in his hand, weighing up the extraordinary generosity of the gift against the rumours he had presumably heard from Corfu and Ragusa, as well as the instructions from the emperor to all his vassals along the coast. 'He is not called Hugo, but King Richard,' he said to the frightened messenger, adding, 'Although I have sworn that I would arrest all the pilgrims coming from those parts and would not accept any gift from them, nevertheless, because of the worth of the gift and of the lord who sent it who honoured me – an unknown man – I send back the gift he sent and I give him free licence to go away.'

Shocked and disturbed, the messenger made his way quickly
through the town to the inn, where the others were by now
bedded down for the night. He told Richard the story, and both
were equally suspicious. There really was no alternative but to
pack again, collect the horses from the stables and set off through
the night before Count Engelbert could change his mind.

Richard's party set off at speed to leave the town as soon as they
could. It was clear now that Hungary was out of reach and the
direction would have to be Bohemia. Either in Corfu or Ragusa,
Richard and his companions would have heard that Ottakar, the
Duke of Bohemia – the hereditary cupbearer to the Holy Roman
Emperor, or so he claimed – was in bitter dispute with the emperor
and might therefore provide him with safe passage. That meant a
journey north, across the mountains towards Vienna, where the
Duke of Austria – who, Richard must now assume, was among
his most determined enemies – would be preparing for Christmas.
But once Vienna was passed and the Danube successfully crossed,
it would be only a few days' travel to safety in Moravia, ruled by
Ottakar's brother Ladislaw, and from Bohemia it was an easy
journey to Saxony and home.

There has been some speculation among historians about which
direction they took – whether towards the Pontebba Pass through
the Alps or the Predil Pass further to the east, near what is now
the border between Italy and Slovenia. But nobody who stands in
the town square at Gorizia – and especially not on the walls of the
castle, the very same walls Richard would have seen from the inn
– can have much doubt which way they went. Gorizia is surrounded on three sides by mountains. To the north and east, the
range looks like a great snow-capped wall, and it would have
looked the same to Richard and his companions as they tried to
puzzle out the best way to go. Without guides, even a hopeless
optimist like Richard would almost certainly have shunned the
freezing, mountainous northern route. The local Slavs were known
to be particularly hospitable, but they could not risk any of them
guessing their identity. They would have set off in the only direction that seemed possible, north-west towards Udine or Cividale.

The English chronicler Ralph of Coggeshall, who had the story from Richard's chaplain, who was there at the time, reports another reason for believing this was the direction they went. Count Engelbert may have reassured them that they could go peacefully on their way – though they distrusted him – but he also sent a messenger to his brother-in-law to warn him that Richard and his group were heading in his direction and urging him to arrest them. In other words, Engelbert was able to predict exactly which direction they left in, and he was right. It was the obvious way.

Wherever Meinhard was, the message must have arrived at the next town at much the same time as Richard and his companions, early the next morning. Meinhard summoned one of his most faithful assistants and relatives, Roger of Argentan, the husband of his niece, and urged him to search some of the inns where pilgrims were staying in the town to see if he could recognize the king – promising him half the city if he could apprehend him. Which city this was is not clear. The counts had possessions in Cividale, but the most obvious place to head for – the nearest route to the main road north – was Udine, and this is probably where Richard's group and the forces searching for them converged, under the castle mound that still dominates the city.

The choice of Roger was not completely random. He had been in the service of Meinhard and his family for twenty years, but his homeland was Normandy – Argentan was the town where Richard's parents often spent Christmas. He may not have been able to recognize Richard because it was two decades since he last saw him as a teenager, if indeed he had ever seen him, but he might recognize something. Yet this was also the very reason why Roger of Argentan was the wrong choice for Meinhard. He searched assiduously through the lodgings of the town the next day and eventually came upon a tall, unkempt figure who did not look like the merchant he claimed to be. But as a Norman, Roger's loyalties were seriously divided. He confronted Richard and there followed a long discussion throughout which Richard initially stuck to the identity of Hugo. Roger became more animated and impassioned and, having assured Richard of his loyalty to the

Angevins, very emotional. In the face of this blackmail, Richard could not sustain his story. As Ralph of Coggeshall put it, 'Eventually he was compelled by the tears of his pious inquisitor to confess who he was.'

Richard was in luck. Still in tears, Roger of Argentan urged him to leave town secretly and gave him his own horse to expedite matters. Returning to Meinhard, he then said that the reports about Richard had just been a rumour. He had found Baldwin of Béthune and his companions returning from a pilgrimage to the Holy Land; there had been no Richard. Meinhard refused to believe him. In a fury, he ordered the arrest of the whole party, but it was too late. Without sleep now for some nights, the royal bird had once again flown.

Many of the towns in the region have half-forgotten legends about Richard's arrival and most of them involve some kind of bloody confrontation. Gorizia has a story about capturing him there and so does Trieste (although there is no evidence that he went to Trieste, a Roman arch is named in his honour there). But the story told later by the emperor suggests that in Udine at least the story was true. The Bavarian chronicler Magnus of Reichersberg claims that some of Richard's party were killed by local nobles in a mêlée. Either because Richard divided the company in two to confuse Meinhard's pursuers or because he was genuinely caught and had to fight his way out, eight of his attendant knights seem to have been captured there. Richard had slipped through the net again, but it was at a cost.

The mistake with Engelbert was to become a theme, because showing off was Richard's Achilles heel. By tradition, kings are not good at disguise. Traditional stories make it possible to recognize royalty in the most subtle ways – even princesses who are so sensitive that they can feel a pea through piles of mattresses – and Richard was no exception to this rule. He was tall and distinctive. Anyone who had been outside Acre or Jaffa with him would have known him immediately. But more fundamentally, he had no sense of what were appropriate levels of spending and giving in his new identity. His lavish behaviour seems to have given him away constantly, right up to his final arrest outside Vienna.

Richard seems to have reverted to his Templar disguise; it was too late for Hugo. His main strategy now and later appears to have been to stay with the dwindling numbers of travellers on the main roads, to go to the places where he was most likely to be able to disappear into the crowd. Maybe this was another reason why he took the road north from Udine rather than risking some of the tiny mountain passes to the north-east, and he joined the old Roman way from Aquileia to the Alps known as the Via Julia Augusta. There, on the twenty-two-foot-wide stone highway, he would have melted in with other travellers braving the road north in the wintry weather. From them, he and his companions would have learned of at least a possible way through the Alps, which were looming ahead of them out of the flat plain on the horizon, with snow-capped peaks which looked as forbidding as they looked frozen.

The twelfth century was warmer than subsequent centuries, so snow would not yet have been certain as the small group crept past the fortified town of Venzone and found themselves turning eastwards into the extraordinary valley inside the eastern Alps known in Italian as the Val Canale, with the mountains sheer on either side and the vast river bed awaiting the great thaw in the spring stretching into the distance like the mouth of an ocean.

It was now two or three days since the shipwreck near Aquileia and Richard and his companions had been on the move without sleep almost the whole time. Richard's fever also seemed to be returning with the exhaustion and the stress; he had never fully recovered in Palestine. They must have searched desperately for somewhere to rest as night fell on the second day, and probably waited until they had entered the Val Canale, with a sense perhaps of security, before they slept. The evidence suggests that industries along the Roman road through the Val Canale had only recently been revived, and the road may have been in particularly poor shape – most passes through the Alps were gruelling journeys from boulder to boulder without the aid of roads at all. So when they saw the monastery of Moggio towering above them on the rocks, the temptation to stop there must have been overwhelming. They may well have done so, taking the winding track up to the summit. The valley ahead of them looked a bleak prospect, and if they had taken turns to watch through the night, they would have had good warning of anyone following behind.

So far on their secretive journey north, Richard had twice attempted to stay in inns – each time forced back on to the road – and these would normally have provided rest for the night, if not a particularly comfortable one. Not even nobles got a room to themselves in those days, and sometimes not even a bed to themselves. In one inn in Arezzo two centuries later four beds were provided for fifteen travellers, and the innkeeper's family would probably have had to share them too. Often there was no heating or latrines; guests were usually expected to relieve themselves in the stables. There were also risks from the other guests. Or from the innkeepers: there were medieval stories about landlords who stole from the pockets of guests at night, and even murdered and ate them.

A monastery might not have been any more comfortable, but it would have provided them with some intelligent conversation and useful local knowledge, as well as hot meals, and monks might be more likely to keep to the Truce of God. It would have been worth the risk of sleeping at Moggio. Maybe this was where they added to their party the nameless boy who spoke German, who was soon to play such a crucial role. And as the dawn rose the next day – working backwards from the date of Richard's arrest, it was probably 13 December – they set off back down the hill, a little rested, for the cold and difficult journey through the Val Canale, past the great ravines carved out of the mountainsides by glaciers, the pine and fir forests stretching above them, and the old abandoned Roman resting stations that dotted the road.

The Val Canale is not strictly a pass across the Alps, it is a valley that runs along between the mountains from west to east, before finally emerging after forty miles on the Austrian side approaching the town of Villach (the Roman city of Santicum). The old road was used by the Romans, and again in Richard's time – and in our own – for transporting metals mined in the valley. For the Romans it was also a military road to the Alpine province of Noricum, but it was always border country, and one where the mountains and forests had been almost untouched by Roman civilization. The south-western villages owed their allegiance to the patriarch of Aquileia, the north-eastern ones to the bishop of Bamberg. It had been the route that Roman legions took to subdue the German tribes, just as it was the route that Italian and Austrian armies fought over in the First World War. As Richard and his companions passed the church of San Giovanni in Pontebba (Pontafel in German) deep in the valley, they may not have realized, but they were passing the ancient border between two cultures.

It would have been a nerve-racking journey, the snow poised to fall and halt their progress maybe for months, and the strange mountain people around them in the lonely corners of the pass. Perhaps they even saw evidence of the previous week's Krampus festival – a folk festival known only in the Val Canale – a celebration of St Nicholas involving horned masks and ringing cow bells. Perhaps they had been warned to watch out for the local demon, an ugly old woman known as the Mari de la Gnot (Mother of the Night). It was a relief to pass Tarvisio and see the way opening up beyond the Alps.

Even so, the mountainous region of Carinthia, where they were emerging, was itself a peculiar corner of Europe with little cultivation, cut off from the areas round about, where Slavs and Europeans intermarried and created a small, powerful culture and folklore of their own. Even in the nineteenth century, half the births there were illegitimate. The Roman writer Tacitus wrote that some parts of Germany were still primeval forests and bogs. There were fewer of these a millennium later, as Richard and his remaining companions headed for Villach after a day struggling between boulders and slipping on the ice in the pass, perhaps to spend the night. They must have shared a sense of relief having crossed the Alps, but it was still a murky journey through forests on roads that had been feared in Roman times, providing the very stuff of medieval nightmares. They galloped along the north side of the Ossiacher See, past the Benedictine abbey at Gerlitzen and into the valleys of Carinthia. As they passed the various town walls, they heard the watchmen at the gates ask them to identify themselves and their destinations at Feldkirchen, at St Veit past the palace of the Duke of Carinthia, and finally at Friesach.

Friesach was the objective, with its two competing markets, each one under a different bishop, its castle and, most important, its silver mine. This is the intelligence Richard extracted from the monks at Moggio or otherwise on the road, because Friesach was one of two towns in central Europe that had been contributing to the boom in silver coinage since the 1170s. The historian Peter Spufford describes the other silver-mining town of Freiberg in Germany as like the Californian gold rush towns in the 1850s – camps of hopeful prospectors from every nation in the world, and the hangers-on who are attracted anywhere to prey on those who are suddenly rich: the prostitutes, the gaming houses, the spivs and the petty crooks. There is no reason to believe that Friesach was any different. Even today, still squeezed inside its medieval walls, it has churches from denominations all over Europe, a legacy of the melting pot it once was. It was an anonymous place where a few Templars and pilgrims could easily disappear into the background.

Friesach belonged to the bishop of Salzburg rather than the surrounding region. It was a wealthy town with a mint large enough to use the local silver and more imported from Hungary to create the Friesacher *pfennig*, coins that turned up all over Europe. The walls and moat were built a few years after his visit, but Richard and his companions rode into the town square with the twin towers of the ancient fortress towering above them. Once again, nothing went according to plan.

Richard's group had moved quickly north, but the news of his shipwreck and disguise had moved faster. One of the 'ministers' or indentured barons of the duke of Austria, Friedrich III of Pettau, had dashed from Salzburg and was in Friesach waiting for them. As soon as they realized they were being sought, Richard's companions put into effect a plan they had clearly been practising. Baldwin of Béthune was to stay in Friesach and draw attention to himself by spending lavishly, while Richard took William de l'Étang – or in some accounts not even him – and the boy who spoke German, and set off as fast as he could in the evening towards Vienna. Freidrich, meanwhile, seized Baldwin and the rest of the party. Once again Richard had slipped through the fingers of his pursuers.

Now there were only three of them, and nearly 200 miles between them and the Danube, beyond which lay Bohemia – but to get there they would have to race ahead and skirt Vienna before the news of his escape in Friesach reached the ears of the duke of Austria. Richard's fever was also now much worse.

What followed was a desperate ride of three days and nights, without stopping for food or rest, which would have exhausted anybody, let alone somebody suffering from a potentially deadly bout of dysentery. They galloped past the Forchtenstein castle near Neumarkt, then swung north-west along the road to cross the River Mur just after Teufenbach. They crossed to the south bank again near the Magdalenenkirche at Judenberg, then rode along the north bank past Knittelfeld, through Bruck an der Mur, all the time aware that the roads and inns were being watched. And as they headed north, Richard and his two companions must have considered the fate of one of their Irish predecessors on the road to Vienna. The pilgrim St Colman had been arrested outside the city on his way to the Holy Land and accused of spying, and was put to death on 13 October 1012. It was a worrying precedent.

Their exhausting ride took them past the first wintry vineyards along the old Roman road across the plain that is now the site of Wiener Neustadt until, over the hill, the city of Vienna was suddenly ahead of them, with the great archipelago of islands and channels nearly a mile across that then made up the River Danube beyond. Richard would not have been impressed with the city with its smoking chimneys and wooden one-storey hovels, without a proper city wall and with its thousand or so inhabitants setting up their huts outside the city as well as inside. The palace of the Babenberg dukes loomed in the distance, almost the only stone building in the whole city – the urban retreat of Leopold of Austria – and possibly Richard allowed himself a moment's regret for the way he had behaved over the Austrian banner on the walls of Acre.

The city had to be avoided and, since Richard was now at the very limits of endurance, sweating with fever, he simply had to rest. The Roman road points directly towards that spot on the river, east of Vienna, where there was almost certainly a ferry in the twelfth century, and a key crossing place in medieval times. So they carried on towards the ferry, and then turned off to the left and headed to the tiny village of Erdberg, barely a village at all. There was no mention now of William de l'Étang, and it is possible he was sent on ahead to negotiate with the ferryman or to ask for an escort sent ahead by Henry the Lion. Richard found an inn on the road that approached Vienna from the east, sent the boy to buy some food and collapsed into bed.

Erdberg was later to be a whole village of inns, and may have been the name – in the twelfth century spelt 'Ertpurch' or 'Erdpurc' – for a fortified ring or rampart beside the Danube owned by the wives of the dukes. Even then it seems to have been an area where traders from Russia, Byzantium and Hungary would keep their wagons and horses. Leopold enforced strict rules about trading in Vienna – only Austrians had the right to sell there – which meant that a vigorous trade between visiting merchants and locals had grown up between Erdberg and the city, with whole sprawling encampments of Germans and Hungarians, together with their market stalls, gathered around the new cathedral of St Stephen outside the eastern gates.

Over the years, a tradition has grown up in Vienna that Richard made an unlucky error in his choice of inn. Next door happened to be the Jägerhaus (hunting lodge) or Rüdenhaus, where Leopold kept his hounds. Since this coincidence was not instrumental in Richard's arrest, perhaps he might be excused; but it has allowed generations of Viennese historians to argue about where the inn was. The Rüdenhaus was finally demolished in 1880, but it does mean that we may know something about where Richard finally collapsed. A plaque commemorating the event remains to this day: it is at what is now 41 Erdbergstrasse, but the evidence is now that the Rüdenhaus was actually further towards the river, surrounded then by fields, woods, kitchen gardens and hovels. Even so, if you visit there today, you can see how the main road snaked from this vicinity downhill via the ancient Rochus Market – perhaps where the boy found the food he had been sent to buy – overlooking the edge of the city.

The presence of the boy in the market attracted attention, speaking German with a strange accent and evidently having access to considerable sums of money. He needed to change money because the silver coins he carried were minted in Syria and would have caused a stir in any small suburban market, let alone this one. But, according to Ralph of Coggeshall, he was also noticeably puffed up by his sudden importance – holding himself 'too courtly and too proudly' – standing between life and death for a secret king. He was asked who he was, and he replied that he was the servant of a very rich merchant who was coming to the city in three days – Richard had clearly reverted to the identity of Hugo. This seemed to satisfy his questioners, and the boy dashed back to the tiny inn and urged Richard to leave immediately, but he was just too ill.

For three days, the boy made daily visits to the market, each time attracting more attention, and on the last of these he made the fatal error that led to Richard's arrest. This time, so the chroniclers say, he took with him Richard's ornate gloves with a royal insignia – it was freezing, and it seems likely that Richard lent them to him – and stuck them in his belt as he wandered around the stalls. It was too much for Leopold's men, watching in the market, as others like them were watching all over southern Europe for the king of England. The boy was seized and taken into the city. It was 21 December, the feast day of St Thomas the Apostle.

The chroniclers gloss over exactly how the boy was persuaded to tell the soldiers where Richard was staying, but the methods used were clearly brutal: Ralph of Coggeshall suggests they included torture and threats to cut out his tongue. Whatever, they were sufficient. He then disappears from the pages of history, another crucial player too ordinary for chronicles – except for this chance conjunction – whose name and fate we will never know.*

What happened next, like most of this story, is disputed by the chroniclers. Was Richard arrested as he slept, as some say? Was there a fight, as others insist? Was he arrested, as the French chroniclers say, while he was cooking at the spit? Ralph of Cogge-shall's main source, the chaplain Anselm, was presumably now in the clutches either of Friedrich of Pettau and on his way in chains to Vienna or of Meinhard of Gorz and on his way back to Gorizia, so he would not have been there himself. But still it makes sense to trust Ralph's narrative, and he describes Leopold sending a force of armed men quickly to Erdberg and surrounding the inn. Soon, Richard could hear the clamour of voices outside, and the combination of bravado and panic that infects armed men as they arrive to arrest someone of known ferocity. As a final attempt to rescue the situation, Richard dashed into the kitchen and put on a skivvy's smock and set to work at the spit. There seems to have been no attempt to actually seize him: perhaps it was his fearsome reputation; perhaps it was in the forefront of the minds of Leopold's soldiers that they risked infringing the sacred Truce of God.

According to the French chroniclers, the first search of the inn by Leopold's soldiers found nobody answering Richard's description. Then they questioned the landlord. 'There is no one here like him whom you seek,' he told them, 'unless he is the Templar in the kitchen, now turning the fowls which are roasting for dinner.' Where the English chroniclers emphasized the betrayal of Richard under torture by the boy, the French were more concerned to show the indignity to which Richard had been sunk – captured as a kitchen lad turning the spit, and recognized only because he had forgotten to take off his ring.

Even before one of the soldiers recognized him from Acre, it

---

* One story says that the boy was called Ioldan de la Pumerai, and that he was later taken to England, put on trial and convicted at Winchester.

was clear to Richard that there was no possibility of escape now. Somehow he seems to have persuaded his pursuers that he would surrender, but only to the Duke himself. It would have taken an hour or two for a messenger to reach the Babenberg palace, on the other side of Vienna, and for Leopold to arrive in person. Perhaps it was in this period that Richard cooked the famous meal. But when it was clear that Leopold was nearly there, Richard left the inn – on foot presumably and surrounded by soldiers – and walked down what is now Erdbergstrasse in the direction of the city to meet him. For the first time since their dispute in Acre, Richard and Leopold were brought face to face – and in very different circumstances. Richard, the former hero of Christendom, handed over his sword and submitted to imprisonment. He was less than fifty miles from the border with Moravia and safety.

Like Richard himself, Duke Leopold V was a complex character. He was half Greek and married to a Byzantine princess, part of the same Comnenus family as the Cypriot tyrant Isaac. Like most medieval aristocrats, he was obsessed by power and was the first of his dynasty to unite both Austria and Styria in the same duchy. But there was actually more in common between Leopold and Richard than one might suppose. They were both thirty-five, both obsessed with Jerusalem – Leopold went to Palestine twice – and both combined a shrewd political ability with a love of poetry and singing. Leopold was a patron of one of the first German minnesingers, Reinmar of Hagenau, who had accompanied him on crusade, just as Blondel had accompanied Richard. He was patron also of the greatest German poet of the age, Walther von Vogelweide, who scribbled away about the simple faith of the God of Love – the antidote to the imminent collapse of Christendom – in the wooden streets of Vienna and described Leopold's court as 'a joyous palace of music'. He was also known as Leopold the Virtuous, which could betray a hint of priggishness, but this may just refer to the virtuous impact that the events of 21 December 1192 were going to have on his own city of Vienna as a result of the enormous ransom that was to come.

There was no reason, beyond Richard's outrageous snobbery and greed at Acre, why they should not have enjoyed each other's company. There is even a hint from Ralph of Coggeshall that they did: he explained that the Duke was 'very pleased and treated the king with honour'. This was no ordinary prisoner for Leopold, and he must have been alive to both the possibilities and the risks to his own position. Normal behaviour with a noble prisoner of this kind would be to accept his oath not to escape and to treat him like a guest. With one eye on his own reputation, Leopold informed Richard that relations of Conrad of Montferrat were plotting against his life and that this therefore was protective custody. But there was still an almost supernatural fear of Richard's powers, and Leopold ordered soldiers with drawn swords to be at his prisoner's side day and night.

Richard must have been taken on horseback down what is now Erdbergstrasse, through the Rochus Market, which had so fatefully provided his meals for the past three days, and through the camp of traders outside the city. He crossed the ditch known as Möhrung (dirt), which marked the entrance to Vienna, and entered the Hoher Market, wondering probably how such backward-looking hovels could support a market of what looked like enormous wealth, with its stalls laden with fabrics from Flanders, glass and spice from Venice, amber from Russia, salt from the Alps, as well as the wine that made the city so rich. And from there he was taken to Leopold's palace, next to the tournament area known as Amhof. As Richard would have seen for himself on that short journey, and his companions also when they arrived under guard from Friesach, Vienna was an extraordinary city, perched between east and west – the meeting point of crusaders from the west and Russian merchants from the east. It was the place where the Holy Roman Empire in the north met the world of Italian rivalry and naval power in the south. It was a cosmopolitan place of the kind he loved.

It is hard to know whether he spent the night with Leopold, but later that same day or early the next, still suffering from the after-effects of fever, he set off with an armed escort past the Irish and Scottish monks at Schottenkloster to the west of the city, and along the north bank of the Danube towards the wealthy city of Krems. It was another two more days of riding before they reached the Wachau valley, and lonely Dürnstein Castle, perched high on the rocks above the river. The Danube raged past at this point in the distant valley, and as Richard rode silently by, he may well have wondered at the extraordinary twists of fate that had taken him from the height of fame and adulation to the depths of degradation in a space of just two and a half years. His imprisonment could mean the end of everything: his throne, his dynasty, his wealth and quite possibly his life. There might be no recovery. It must have been a Christmas of despair, made all the more poignant by the awareness that nobody had the slightest idea where he was.

Far away in Rome some weeks later, or so the tradition goes, Queen Berengaria was in the market and was shocked to see a familiar belt of jewels on sale that she knew had belonged to her husband in Acre.* It was her first hint that something had gone terribly wrong with Richard's journey home.

---

*There are documents in existence that record the money that Berengaria borrowed in Rome, which she agreed to repay at the annual fair at Troyes in Champagne.

7. Blondel's Song

The love that's captured me,
Insists that I now sing.

Blondel de Nesle, 'L'amours
dont sui espris', Chanson XI

'The story has always sounded too good to be true, but on the
spot it's impossible to doubt it.'

Patrick Leigh Fermor on the legend of Blondel at Dürnstein,
A Time of Gifts, 1977

Those English and Norman crusaders who left Palestine in the
autumn of 1192 had now been home for many weeks – the ones
who made it home – spreading the news that Richard planned to
celebrate Christmas back at his own court. There was an expect-
ancy in the great cities of Western Europe. London was particularly
worried since the latest peculiar atmospheric conditions had made
the Northern Lights visible again: those who were rich enough to
have glass windows saw the red reflection and dashed outside
thinking there was a fire. It seemed an eerie omen of disaster. Paris
was also nervous, as Philip's propagandists prepared to counter whatever stories the king of England brought home with his companions.
When the news arrived in early December that Richard's ship had
been sighted heading for Brindisi, special watches were organized in
the Channel ports. In Dover, Folkestone and Deal, people gazed
into the mist, awaiting his arrival.

Eleanor made sure she was in England for Christmas. These
final weeks of her son's absence would be the most dangerous, in

many ways, as the various power-brokers jockeyed for position, ready for his return. But as Advent turned into Christmas and there was still no sign of his ship – or any news that he had even succeeded in reaching his wife and sister in Rome – the nerves of the governors across Richard's empire became seriously strained. There were disturbing reports of storms and shipwrecks in the Mediterranean. If one of the storms turned out to have claimed Richard's life, then there would be a new monarch and hopefully an orderly handover of power, but the uncertainty – the carefully balanced decision about when to shift allegiance to John – made anyone in a position of responsibility feel acutely insecure.

We can only guess what was passing through Richard's mind as, still struggling with the effects of fever, he trudged on horseback with a large contingent of soldiers along the bank of the fast-flowing Danube. Exhaustion and despair must have been close to the surface, but he could imagine only too clearly the feelings of those he trusted most back home. Reports of Richard a few months later describe his extraordinary sense of balance and per-spective, and the humour and energy with which he tackled his predicament, but in those first few days of humiliation – when the full extent of his failure and its possible consequences must have come home to him – imprisonment would have been hard to bear.

Dürnstein was Leopold's choice, and not just because it was relatively inaccessible and extremely imposing.* It was too danger-ous to keep Richard in Vienna – who knew what focus for revolt he might represent – and the wooden Babenberg palace was not appropriate for holding him. It was not Leopold's main home, which was outside the city, and it was anyway only two storeys high, and far too small. Leopold was preparing to celebrate Christ-mas there and had already had to rent local houses for his guests. There was no space for a prisoner, however important. But the lords of the newly built Dürnstein were also his most powerful and

---

*Dürnstein means literally 'dry rock', which conveys something of its inaccess-ible position. There is another castle called Dürnstein just near Friesach, where Richard came so close to arrest.

trusted barons, the Kuenrings – the word means 'minister'. The Kuenring family was from Saxony and was not therefore bound to any of the other local aristocracy. They could provide the perfect place in which to hide an eminent prisoner until his fate could be negotiated.

The journey to the Wachau valley, with its steep hills of brown vines – now probably under snow – was slow and difficult. Richard had been parted from the boy he had travelled with, and William de l'Étang was either under arrest himself or in Bohemia on his way to the court of Henry the Lion in Saxony. What money Richard possessed had been stolen by the soldiers who arrested him, along with the Great Seal of England, which he was carrying with him. They in turn had handed him over to a detachment of soldiers described as 'foreign' who knew nothing about him, except that he was extremely dangerous. The chronicles describe his guards as keeping up the precaution of drawn swords around him day and night.

It is possible that he was ignorant of his eventual destination, as he watched the horses dragging the barrels of wine and the other goods from the east on barges up and down the river as they passed. So he rode, half frozen, into the small town of Dürnstein with relief tempered by the imposing sight of the castle high on the rocks north of the road – stronger and more impressive than anything else he had seen so far in Austria. There was probably a glimmer of guilt already apparent among Richard's captors. One of the conditions of the eventual agreement between Leopold and the emperor was that Richard should be forced, as a condition of his release, to persuade the Pope to absolve them for the sin of capturing a returning crusader. For this reason at least, he was probably welcomed with some civility by Hadmar II von Kuenring, the lord of Dürnstein.

The Kuenrings later became one of the most powerful families in Austria, but Hadmar was only the third generation of the family to attach itself to the dukes, and he was extremely ambitious. He was bolstering his reputation and power base by founding monasteries and towns, and Dürnstein itself – planned by his father,

Albero III – dominated the Danube, giving him strategic views for miles up and down the river. He was exactly the same age as Richard and Leopold, and his wife, Euphemia, rejoiced in the nickname of Hunde. The only surviving picture of him dates from five centuries after his death, but it portrays him with a jutting, determined-looking beard and brutish features.

There was another reason to suppose that Hadmar would have made Richard welcome, apart from the pride that a social climber might have felt at having a king as his prisoner, and that was that they already knew each other. Hadmar had been at the siege of Acre with Leopold, and they had returned to Austria in disgust together after the incident of the banner. The Austrian sources emphasize how well Richard was treated, and it was the tradition in the twelfth century to consider high-born prisoners as honoured guests. Their value for ransom depended, after all, on their staying healthy. English sources, on the other hand, describe Dürnstein as crude and squalid.

Richard was almost certainly conducted from the town by Hadmar up the rocky and probably icy track that led to the castle, through the gate into the bailey and then right into the keep and inner courtyard. It seems likely that he was held in the north-eastern corner of the castle, overlooking the sheer cliff over the forests north of the Danube. The prison cells were in the same block, though he must have been in something more comfortable, but the position would have impressed upon him – and been intended to – that his predicament was hopeless, high above the river in an unknown, snow-covered land.

Richard arrived in Dürnstein on Christmas Eve or Christmas Day and would have been allowed to celebrate Christmas either in the chapel of St Michael by the river at the foot of the mountain – for some reason churches associated with hills and mountains tend to be dedicated to the Archangel Michael – or in the tiny chapel in the castle over the eastern walls, still recognizable in the ruins to this day. He may have attended all three traditional masses of a medieval Christmas Day, the Angel's Mass at midnight – if he arrived in time – followed by the Shepherd's Mass at dawn and the mass of the Divine Word later in the morning. He would undoubtedly have attended the Christmas banquet at Hadmar's court, and enjoyed the Yule boar – his first proper meal since Erdberg or even before – together with the familiar acrid stench of tallow winter candles and of old rushes on the floor.

The main meal in the twelfth century was usually eaten around 10 a.m. It followed a ritual washing of hands in water bowls brought by the servants and, in wealthy or pretentious households such as this one, was announced by a trumpeter. It was eaten from big wooden trenchers, one between two people, eaten with their hands and their own knives, before the remaining bread was given to the dogs, the stinking water from the pots carried away through the hall, and the household had dispersed to hunt or play, before sunset, supper and music. Warmth and music were universal elements of Christmas celebrations across Europe, with a Yule log big enough to burn until Twelfth Night, cut down the previous Candlemas and dragged up from the forests and into the castle hall. This is the background to the legend of Blondel's song: music, minstrels and a Christmas banquet – and the faint possibility, as European peasants liked to believe – that at the height of Midnight Mass, the cattle outside would go down on their knees to worship.

As Richard was taking stock of his prison, and realizing how likely it was that none of his friends had any idea of his whereabouts, Leopold's messengers were riding as fast as they could to the emperor, who was spending Christmas at Hordhausen near Nuremberg. The news must have reached him a few days after the first Christmas festivities, because on 28 December – just a week after Richard's arrest in Erdberg – he was in Bamburg dictating a letter to Philip Augustus in Paris – more evidence that he was acting on Philip's request when he had ordered his vassals to take Richard captive on his return.

To any other eyes it would be an explosive letter. 'Henry by the grace of God, Emperor of the Romans and ever august, to his beloved and special friend Philip, the illustrious king of the Franks,' it began, and then the bombshell. 'We have thought it proper to inform your nobleness by means of these presents that while the enemy of our empire and the disturber of your kingdom, Richard, King of England, was crossing the sea for the purpose of returning to his dominions, it so happened that the winds brought him . . . to Istria.' There then followed a detailed account of the chase, Richard's escape and his capture by the Duke of Austria 'in a humble house in a village in the vicinity of Vienna'. The letter finished: 'We know that this news will bring you great happiness . . . Inasmuch as he is now in our power, and has always done his utmost for your annoyance and disturbance, what we have above stated we have thought proper to notify to your nobleness, knowing that the same is well pleasing to your kindly affection for us, and will afford most abundant joy to your own feelings.'

The letter gave an enormous time advantage to the French. It certainly caused delight when it arrived in Paris after a ten-day journey through frozen Europe. Philip immediately dictated a reply, urging Henry to keep his prisoner secure until they had a chance to consult. Then he wrote another letter to the one person likely to be even more excited than he was: John, who was spending Christmas in Cardiff. And finally, he wrote to Richard himself, via Leopold, denouncing him and declaring war against him.

England at New Year and people were still nervously scouring the Channel for Richard's return. But in the first fortnight of the year the rumours began to spread that the king had been taken into captivity on his return journey. On 11 January John received the letter from Philip with mounting excitement. He set off immediately and as quietly as possible to cross the Channel to meet the French king, where he promised to divorce his wife and marry Philip's sister Alys – still locked in a castle in Normandy, for her mistake of satisfying the lusts of Richard's father. He also did homage to him for Normandy and the other dukedoms and counties of the Angevin empire in France, and may have done homage for England too. This possibility shocked the English chroniclers, partly because of the precedent it set and partly because of the evidence it provided that John would now promise almost anything to take the English throne.

That same day, Pope Celestine was writing a New Year letter to the rulers of Europe from Rome, urging them to put aside their differences and make peace with each other. It seems clear that he had not yet heard the news of the fate of his most famous crusader.

In Paris, William Longchamp heard about Richard's disaster as well. He claimed he had seen a copy of the letter that arrived at the French court, and set off as quickly as he could for Germany. Hubert Walter, the Bishop of Salisbury, who had left Richard's ship in Corfu and was then in Italy, also heard the rumours and raced north to Rome to see the Pope, before travelling on to find the king. But the first confirmation of the rumours in nervous England came in letters to the members of the Great Council from the chief justiciar, Walter of Coutances, who had been celebrating Christmas as Archbishop of Rouen, the capital of Normandy. Enclosed in his missive, packed with biblical quotations trying to do justice to the extremity of the situation, were copies of the emperor's letter to Philip. It was the custom in those days of uncertain roads to send more than one copy of vital letters via different messengers. The Archbishop of Rouen had clearly used what informal networks he possessed either to steal a copy of the letter in Paris or to have it seized on the road.

The news was greeted in England with horror and rage. There was a particular animosity towards the Austrians. 'They are savages who live more like wild beasts than men,' said the Dean of St Paul's, the chronicler Ralph of Diceto. 'Frightful in their speech, squalid in their habits and covered in filth.' One outraged abbot announced that he would search for the king until he found him or discovered certain knowledge of him.

Even before the emperor's letter had arrived in Paris, four parties from Austrian territories had set out to meet Henry at Regensburg on the Danube, once the biggest city in Germany. Meinhard of Gorz went with the prisoners he had taken in Udine; Leopold himself went from Vienna; the prisoners taken in Friesach went too; and finally Richard was escorted in the same direction, leaving on 28 December and arriving on 6 January. Richard therefore came face to face with the emperor for the first time on Twelfth

Night. Either through nerves, guilt or rage, or some combination of the three, Henry angrily refused to look at him. It seems to have been this act of petulance that did most to raise Richard's spirits, convincing him that he was dealing with a novice in the art of diplomacy.

Richard's arrest had actually come as a miraculous opportunity for Henry. His first attempt to invade Sicily had been an expensive disaster, and he was facing a brewing challenge to his power from the princes of the lower Rhineland and the powerful archbishops of Cologne and Mainz. Rumours were flying that Henry, Duke of Brabant, might be better suited as emperor – theoretically the Holy Roman Emperor was an elected position. But now Henry held this vital and lucrative pawn, or he would once he could persuade Leopold to part with the prisoner. Not only was Richard a possible financial solution to his difficulties, but holding the most famous prisoner in Europe gave him an immediate status that could not be ignored.

In fact, Henry had been dealing with an awkward situation similar to that faced by Richard's father after the murder of Thomas Becket a generation before. There had been a grumbling argument through the summer between two rival princes over who should be the new bishop of Liège. The emperor had tried to impose a third candidate of his own when, on 24 November – less than a month before Richard's arrest – one of the other two was murdered in France by trained assassins disguised as German refugees. It looked suspiciously as if the murder had taken place on the emperor's orders. Henry VI was temperamentally unsuited to compromise and Richard's arrest seemed likely to provide him with the resources and the status to avoid having to make one. Still, Richard was not in imperial custody yet. Almost as soon as he had arrived in Regensburg, with its famous stone bridge, a suspicious Leopold sent him back to Dürnstein for safe-keeping.

In England, Eleanor and the Great Council were aware that they were likely to face an imminent invasion led by John and Philip – certainly of Normandy and probably of England too – but they had a more immediate problem. They needed to open negotiations for Richard's release as soon as possible, just to show that he would be home eventually. But it was also unclear who was actually holding him, or where he was being held. If the Archbishop of Rouen had secret networks that he could consult, or secret messengers who could listen at the courts of Europe – and it seems certain that he did – he sent desperate instructions to them now.

Having sent their own special emissary to the emperor – Savaric de Bohun, the new Bishop of Bath, who was a cousin of Henry's – the Great Council met in Oxford on 28 February, and decided first to make sure all the English aristocracy renewed their oaths of fealty to Richard, and second that it would send its own official representatives to find the king. Two abbots, of Boxley and Robertsbridge in Sussex, were duly sent across the Channel with letters from Eleanor and instructions to search Swabia and Bavaria. Three weeks later, on 19 March, they stumbled across Richard on the road to Speyer, near Ochsenfurt, with an imperial escort, on his way from Würzburg back to the emperor's strongholds on the Rhine. With him was William Longchamp, restored to royal favour and to his old pomposity, who had himself happened upon him a few days before.

This is the official story about how Richard was found. Conventional history now dismisses the legend of Blondel singing under the tower of Dürnstein in the night and dashing to England to raise the alarm. Even so, it is a surprisingly resilient story and it does still provide an answer – albeit a misty and romantic one – to the question of how Longchamp and the abbots managed so coincidentally to be in the right place at the right time. It is also a story that has been lovingly embellished in the centuries since.

There are complicated versions of the legend of Blondel singing under Dürnstein tower, involving jailors' daughters, castellans and dramatic escapes. But the classic story that most people know is the one in which Blondel disguises himself as an ordinary minstrel and hears a familiar voice replying high in the castle tower. In Agnes Grozier Herbertson's classic version for children, published in 1911, she described the scene: 'Upon one side of the valley were great rocky hills, and on one of these stood a sombre castle, black and grim, and of an aspect most terrible.' It is even the north tower that she accurately marks out for Blondel's attention, having been told that the song he is singing earlier in the day has been heard wafting down from the mysterious prisoner held there. In the Herbertson version, Blondel sings verses that Richard had written himself and hears the king's voice echoing back the second verse.

'Art thou there, my faithful Blondel,' says a voice afterwards.

'Blondel replied with great joyfulness: "It is I, Sire, for I have sought thee and have now found thee."'

That is the legend in a nutshell, explaining how – having travelled across Germany and Austria in search of Richard – his minstrel finally discovers him by singing underneath his cell in Dürnstein Castle. But actually, the earliest surviving version of the Blondel story has the encounter the other way around, with Blondel overhearing the song wafting down from the tower. This early version of the story was written down around 1260, about seventy years after the events it describes, which is almost certainly beyond living memory. The author of the strange manuscript that includes it, known simply as the Minstrel of Reims, might conceivably have been alive when Richard was captured, might have heard the story at first hand from those who were there, but both are pretty unlikely. Nor should we put too much historical weight on a document that also claims Eleanor of Aquitaine had an affair with Saladin.

The Minstrel of Reims describes how Blondel heard about a mysterious prisoner held in one of the castles after he had searched for Richard for over a year – or four months in one version of the manuscript. The story describes Blondel wandering about the castle grounds, asking local people if they know about any prisoners, and finally hearing rumours of one believed to be a 'gentleman and a great lord':

When Blondel heard these words, he was very glad, and it seemed to him in his heart that he had found the man for whom he had been looking, but he showed no signs of this to his hostess. That night he slept very well, and he awoke at daybreak. When he heard the guard sound reveille, he arose and went to the church, to ask for God's help. Then he went to the castle, and spoke with the chastelain, saying that he was a minstrel, and would very much like to stay with him if he was willing . . .

Blondel plays his music in the castle and carries on doing so throughout the winter, being unable to find out who the prisoner is. The climax of the story takes place at Easter, when Richard sings and Blondel overhears him in the garden:

Near the tower, Blondel looked around him, thinking that he might, by chance, see the prisoner. As he was doing this, the king looked through an archer's slot, and saw Blondel. He thought about how to make him recognise him, and he remembered a song that they had made up together, which only the two of them knew. He began to sing the opening words loudly and clearly, for he sang very well, and when Blondel heard him, he knew certainly that this was his lord. In his heart he felt greater joy than he had ever felt, and he left the garden, and went to his room, where he reclined, picked up his vielle, and began to play, singing of his joy at having found his lord. Blondel stayed until Pentecost, making sure that no one within the castle knew what he was trying to do . . .

So he packed and left and went to England to raise the alarm, and when the king's friends heard the news, 'they were overjoyed, for the king was the most generous man who ever spurred a horse'.

A century later, the story had reversed itself into the shape that it has today. The *Ancient Chronicles of Flanders*, written in the mid-fourteenth century, calls the castle Brissac and gives the minstrel his full name, Jean Blondel, and this time it is Blondel who strolls under the tower and sings the verse of the song that is overheard by the imprisoned king. In another version of the same document, the castle is called Frisac and Blondel is Norman. A century later, the French chronicler Jehann de Raveneau was using this same version, where Blondel is overheard, emphasizing that Blondel was a '*ménestral de France*'.

But what did Blondel sing? This is the question that historians of music have pondered for almost as long as the story has been in circulation. Needless to say, none of the early manuscripts are very precise about it – the Minstrel of Reims simply mentions a song – but since then antiquarians have dashed to fill that silence by simply asserting what their contemporaries wanted to hear. There seems to have been no argument about this, no question of marshalling evidence; instead, they set out the verses as if they were telling their readers something that had never been questioned.

The first hint that there might be some record of the missing song came in a book by the first president of France's mint, Claude Fauchet, in 1581 in his *Recueil de l'Origine de la Langue et Poésie Française*, and it was said to be a song written by Richard himself, originally for Marguerite, Countess of Hennegau. Fauchet did not see fit to quote this, but the gap was filled by a romantic novel that rediscovered the legend in the eighteenth century. Marie-Jeanne L'Héritier de Villandon was one of a group of aristocratic French women who were reinventing the fairy-tale form. She wrote only one volume of her successful 1705 novel about Blondel's mission, *The Dark Tower*, but she included an introduction about the original story in which she claimed she had culled her information from a probably mythical long-lost document from 1308. This missing document was the source she used to claim that the song was in Occitan and called 'Domna vostra beutas':

> Your beauty, lady fair,
> None views without delight;
> But still so cold an air
> No passion can excite;
> Yet this I patient see
> While all are shunn'd like me.

To which Richard replied:

No nymph my heart can wound
If favour she divide,
And smiles on all around
Unwilling to decide;
I'd rather hatred bear
Than love with other's share.

Actually, Blondel wrote in Old French not Occitan, and this song is a mixture culled from various sources, with five verses, some of which are taken from Blondel's Chanson III ('A l'entrée de la saison') and some from Richard's own song, which he wrote later in prison (see Chapter 8).

It was these verses that were quoted by Thomas Percy in his *Reliques of Ancient English Poetry*, the 1765 collection that some claim marked the beginning of the Romantic movement in England, and it was then used by the composer and song collector Charles Burney in his influential *General History of Music* (1776–89). Percy, the son of a grocer, became Bishop of Dromore. He claimed that most of his collection came from a seventeenth-century document – now in the British Museum – that he acquired from a friend in Shropshire, having saved it from destruction when he found it 'being used by the maids to light the fire'. Burney recognized that the source for 'Domna vostra beutas' was the introduction to Mademoiselle L'Héritier de Villandon's novel, but says that the English translation came from there, when actually it didn't.

Oddly enough, *The Dark Tower* actually included a completely different song in the story itself, and this one has also filtered through into tradition, though its eighteenth-century roots are obvious. It was translated into English in 1896 for Frederick Crowest's book *The Story of British Music*, under the title 'Fierce in me the fever burning':

Fierce in me the fever burning
Strength and confidence unmanned
Eyes, though dark their sight is turning,
Yet discerning

Through the gloom Death's pallid hand
Grimly stretched across from out the spectral land;
Then came my Love so bright and true,
And Death and fever quickly withdrew.

That is what Richard is supposed to have sung, to which Blondel replied:

I know with full assurance
The Woman's gentle care
Brings comfort, hope, endurance
In time of deep despair.

There then followed three more verses along the same lines, after which the two of them are supposed to have improvised another one. *The Dark Tower* imagined a major duet through the walls of Dürnstein.

This is all fantasy of course. There is no evidence for the song itself as a historical event, apart from the unreliable Minstrel of Reims, and even the successors of romantics like Prosper Tarbé have had to give way to the overwhelming silence of all the contemporary sources. None of them, not the English, French or German contemporary chronicles, mention Blondel's role in Richard's imprisonment. But it is an unforgettable story, and rich enough in its mythic symbolism to stand for a whole variety of ideals in recent history. That is reason enough to cling to the tale. But there are also good historical justifications for taking a second look at Blondel and his part in finding the king.

A visit to the castle where Richard found himself at Christmas 1192 might make anyone think afresh about the story. It is fascinating, for example, that twentieth-century versions focus on the north tower of Dürnstein, where Richard was probably held. There is even a path along the rocks under the trees far below where it is still possible to imagine a troubadour creeping at dead of night. Of course this is not evidence that Blondel actually sang under the north wall. On the other hand, there is good reason to believe that Leopold chose Dürnstein as Richard's prison simply because it was so remote and inaccessible, so that nobody would know where he was. Yet somehow William Longchamp and the abbots of Boxley and Robertsbridge were able to find out enough to stumble upon him on the road to Speyer in the middle of March. Richard spent only three months in Dürnstein, and part of that time being ferried to Leopold's meetings with the emperor, but someone revealed to the English where he was. Blondel's story was at least a convenient tale that successfully obscured the question of how they knew.

To understand the meaning of the legend in a little more detail, we have to step back and look at the role played by troubadours and *trouvères* in Richard and Blondel's generation. It was of course primarily to write songs that would be taken up by minstrels and jongleurs, and to entertain in court circles, but there were other, more subtle roles which have only become clear over the last century since scholars have rediscovered their work. The truth is that *trouvères* had an important political role to play as the propagandists of the twelfth century. That is why, the moment Richard ran into trouble with his reputation, he settled down and wrote a song about it. When the French disapproved of his decision not to attack Jerusalem, Hugh, Duke of Burgundy, wrote a vitriolic song that was then sung around Outremer and presumably taken home by the minstrels in the crusader camps to France to sing there. When Richard heard it, he spent precious time away from negotiations and military preparations to write his own in reply.

His generation was steeped in this musical culture, where music made things happen by moulding opinion. Leopold wrote songs, and so did the Emperor Henry VI, into whose hands Richard was about to fall. Longchamp was constantly commissioning songs that praised his own uniqueness. In prison later, Richard would be writing songs about his situation. This was a generation where the song contests, so beloved of the troubadours, extended into the world of court politics and diplomacy.★ 'I wouldn't give a fig for your arm, because it looks like a goat's leg,' sang the Catalan troubadour Guillem de Berguedà against a rival. He later composed a cycle of songs against the Bishop of Urgel, accusing him of being a eunuch, a lecher, a rapist and a sodomite. It made sense for lords to welcome troubadours, and to put the most lavish hospitality at their disposal, otherwise it might be them lampooned in the next song.

Songs with a political or satirical purpose were known in Occitan as *sirventes*, and the doyenne of the *sirventes* style was the troubadour Bertran de Born, the minor nobleman from Périgord who had dubbed Richard *Oc et Non* (Yes and No). It was Bertran whom Raymond V of Toulouse turned to in order to commission a war song to rally his friends in 1181, and whose enthusiastic paeans of praise for war earned him a place in Dante's *Inferno* a century later. Bertran had been a close friend of Richard's elder brother, Henry the Young King, and, though he was reconciled with Richard later in life, he was his bitter opponent for much of his career. This is how he introduced his gentle goading:

> When I see in the gardens, waving silk
> Of banners, yellow, indigo and blue,
> And with delight the neighing horses
> And the merry songs of the jongleurs,
> As they play their viols, tent by tent,
> With trumpets, horns and clarions –
> Then I want to write a powerful song,
> Enough for even King Richard to hear.

The reason troubadours and their equivalents in other parts of Europe were welcomed at courts anywhere across the Continent

---

★ 'It is indeed fitting,' went one of Raimbaut d'Aurenga's competitive verses, 'that one who is skilled in singing should sing in a good court . . . for the blind and the deaf must know that I, of the twenty of us who will be in the lodging, shall carry off the honours.'

was not just to ask them to sing, but for their hosts to give them something in exchange: their own news, their achievements, their vitriol against their neighbours and opponents – knowing that the troubadour could turn these into a song that would be taken up by the minstrels in his or her circle, and sung widely down through society and at other courts, to the discomfort of their enemies. Troubadours were collectors, editors and pedlars of gossip, opinion and news. They could inform or provoke, they could make or break reputations – and they did. Troubadours were inveigled into drumming up support for the Third Crusade, and many of them accompanied the Third and Fourth Crusades themselves – in fact some of Blondel's fellow *trouvères* never came home.

Blondel was therefore one of an elite group of musicians and songwriters who used popular culture to broadcast their news and their own informal links – right across Europe – to pass on information. So it is not a peculiar juxtaposition, having a mere minstrel search for a king. That was the role that Blondel and his colleagues would have played, listening and gossiping, and Richard was, after all, one of their own – not the only troubadour prince in Europe, but the most celebrated and the most generous patron of others like him.

But there is another clue about the meaning of the story of Blondel's song. It is the Archbishop of Rouen's informal networks that so efficiently produced a copy of a private letter between the emperor and the king of France, copied to every member of the Great Council of England. The archbishop, the Cornishman Walter of Coutances, was at the time acting as chief justiciar of England – Richard's first minister of the realm – and intelligence was his responsibility. He needed to know Richard's whereabouts, and needed to know urgently, so it seems reasonable to expect that he used what networks he possessed to find out.

Espionage is the unspoken element of the story of Richard's arrest that historians have left out until now, partly because they dismiss the story as a tale for children and partly because there is so little evidence about medieval spying. Yet you can read the clues throughout this story. They are there in the tale that Richard disguised himself as a bedouin in order to spy on Saladin's troops. They are there in the immense care that Richard took to sail from Acre without being seen, and in his realization that every port on the north coast of the Mediterranean had watchers who would recognize him and pass the news to those who wanted to do him harm. We can read into his behaviour, and that of his companions, in their disguise and precautions, just how widespread these networks of watchers were. Richard was particularly adept at military espionage, using scouts to intercept Saracen caravans on their way to Egypt, just as his father's justiciar Ranulf Glanville successfully used them to outwit the king of Scotland and his forces in 1174. We might not quite be able to call them spies at this stage in history, we might not know how they were organized, who they reported to or how they were paid, but the story strongly implies their presence nonetheless.

Then there was the mysterious business of the capture of one of the copies of the emperor's letter to Philip, presumably seized by a paid agent sent by the archbishop to watch for imperial messengers on the road. It is impossible eight centuries later to know what kind of secret organization he managed, how informal and how freelance it was, but we can assume they had some arrangements at their disposal. Richard's reign saw the beginnings of the official royal messenger service, known as Nuncios Regis. Within a generation, they were a paid service attached to the court and wearing a uniform of blue and russet.★ They may well have employed more freelance servants, listening in foreign ports and in the courts of foreign princes, or watching on the potholed roads.

By the reign of Edward I, two generations later, the English court was recording payments to large numbers of people on secret missions, and we can only assume they were doing so without formally recording it in Richard's day. Later the same year that

---

★We even know the names of Richard's official messengers attached to the court in England. They were called Hamelin, Lucas, Walwan and Roger le Tort.

Richard spent in prison, in 1193, Philip's invasion plans for England
were captured on the road by messengers in the same way. Two
decades later, in 1213, there are records of John rewarding two
sailors from Seaford who captured messengers with letters sent to
England by Philip Augustus, and then setting about the very
modern business of forging replies from those they were addressed
to and sending them back to mislead the French. 'Diplomacy and
theft were almost synonymous,' wrote Richard Deacon in his
History of the British Secret Service.★ Walter of Coutances was clearly
not above a little diplomacy on the muddy road from the Rhine
to Paris. This kind of activity took place below the radar of history,
and we can only guess what happened to the unfortunate imperial
messenger.

Blondel's story seems to be an alternative version of how the
news of Richard's whereabouts was discovered. It is a tale that
may originally have been designed to obscure espionage or perhaps
it is all that remains of a genuine story of espionage. Either way,
Blondel's song has spying at its heart and that is how we should
now understand it. The first of these alternatives is that the story
was a myth deliberately constructed to hide the real story of
intelligence and betrayal that allowed the English government to
discover what had happened to the king, and his movements
afterwards, so that Longchamp and the two abbots could run across
him so coincidentally on the road. In this version, it was perhaps
a story told half jokingly, half seriously, to avoid the truth.

If the Blondel story was fabricated, it was at least a tale that
borrowed from traditions that were already in circulation and
attached to other names. You can find elements of it in the myth
of Orpheus, another musician who used the power of music to
find the one he loved in the underworld, but it was also there in
a contemporary story about Richard's illegitimate brother William
Longspee and a knight called Talbot. When her father died on
crusade in 1196, the wealthy eight-year-old heiress of the Earl of

---

★ He also says that espionage was usually used against the English at this time,
rather than by them. I find this very hard to believe.

Salisbury was hidden away with relatives in Normandy. Talbot, who may have been Longspee himself, is said to have searched for her for two years disguised as a troubadour. His beautiful singing opened the doors and, when he returned to England, he brought Ela with him and presented her to King Richard. She married Longspee, who became the new Earl of Salisbury.

Then there was the story of the Duke of Lothringe, Ferry III, kidnapped and imprisoned in a castle a long way from home. When he heard a roofer singing a song about his disappearance, he identified himself with the aid of his ring, and the message reached his wife, who raised the alarm. Then there was the medieval baron Von Geroldseck, taken prisoner while hunting and forced to travel to a strange castle, where he eventually heard the sound of a familiar horn blown by a servant. The servant turned out to be one of his old faithful retainers, and they escaped together. Both are stories recorded in the fifteenth century that were supposed have happened in the twelfth century.

They may have been versions of a much older folk tale that became attached to the story of Richard's imprisonment to fill an obvious gap. There is a Japanese fairy story about an emperor of Japan called Takakura and his favourite concubine, Kogo, who was a gifted singer and musician. The jealous empress had her father kidnap Kogo and hide her away, and the emperor became ill with worry. A knight called Nakakuni, who loved both emperor and concubine, searched the whole country, playing her favourite melody on his flute. Finally, outside one house, he could hear a stringed instrument echoing the same tune from inside and knew she was there. If the same story was told about Richard's brother Longspee – and maybe about others – then minstrels and troubadours, or those disguised as them, had the power in contemporary stories to find hidden people, just as they had the power to tell the truth in song. It would have been a useful device to hide the messier business of finding out where Richard was in prison. The Japanese story suggests that the original folk version of the Blondel story had Blondel singing first, and using the power of music. In fact, the existence of a different version the other way around implies that there was after all some kind of historical event that eventually metamorphosed into a more traditional story.

This is the second possibility: that it was not just a story that obscured espionage but one that is based on some kind of real event involving a troubadour or minstrel. If so, it would have been possible because of the unique social position enjoyed by troubadours and minstrels to go anywhere and ask anything. They would be welcomed into the dourest and most distant castles, like Dürnstein, with relief – bringing the promise of song and entertainment after months of kicking the dogs by the hearth on wintry evenings – where almost any other visitor might be treated with great suspicion. They would be there by the fire as the local lord and his family and servants discussed their hopes, plans and local events. All they needed to do was to listen: troubadours were stateless wanderers who often provided valuable intelligence to princes. There was even a tradition that Richard was allowed to receive them during his imprisonment.

Blondel may not have sung under the castle walls, but the story might still be all that remains of the real role that he actually played, making his own way home across Europe from Palestine – maybe even via Dürnstein – listening and watching and sending messages back to Rouen, London or Winchester. Blondel was from Picardy, after all, in the critical border region between the Ile de France and Normandy. He may have paid homage to the French king during his time in Paris. Maybe his role in undermining the machinations of the king of France needed to be disguised. But then Philip was well known for his disapproval of and meanness to minstrels and jongleurs, so perhaps Blondel intervened on Richard's behalf as a blow struck for the European community of troubadours and musicians. Either way, the source of the intelligence might actually have been a minstrel, who might even have been Blondel. And even if the moment of mutual recognition was not at the foot of a tower, it might have been across a great hall some time in the New Year of 1193.

★

There is one more thought that provides a little confirmation that Blondel's story is based on a real but forgotten event. Christmas was not the same feast in the Middle Ages that it is today. It lasted twelve days and presents – if they were exchanged at all – were given in the New Year. But medieval Christmas was still a time of festivity and feasting, and it was especially linked with mystery plays and minstrels. The best houses always had minstrels at Christmas, and chanting carols, but it was also the time of year when people wore disguises, when men dressed as women and vice versa, and when the Lord of Misrule was unleashed. Medieval Christmas was an upside-down world, where masters served servants, sexes exchanged dress, everyone dressed up in disguises, where boys were appointed as bishops for the season and you could even imagine a topsy-turvy story like a king imprisoned in a tower.

The real story behind Blondel's song may be long beyond unravelling, but the events that really took place – if any did – happened at Christmas. The continued existence of these elements of medieval Christmas – the musician in disguise, able to reveal the hiding place of a missing king – is some evidence that this story originally had a genuine date, and may have more seeds of authenticity than is sometimes assumed.

8. Prison

'God willing, you shall learn the might of our victorious eagles and
shall experience the anger of Germany: the youth of the Danube who
know not how to flee, the towering Bavarian, the cunning Swabian,
the fiery Burgundian, the nimble mountaineer of the Alps.'

Frederick Barbarossa's letter to Saladin on the eve of the
Third Crusade, 1190

'Today a king, tomorrow a captive; today in power, tomorrow in
prison; today a free man; tomorrow a slave. Be wise, therefore, ye
judges of the world, come and see the words of the Lord – see a king
made wretched, a proud man humbled, a rich man beggared.'

Chronicle of Melrose

The Emperor Henry VI succeeded his father, Frederick, when the
latter collapsed and died while leading the German contingent to
the Third Crusade so suddenly in Asia Minor. Henry was pallid,
intellectual, coldly inhuman and immensely ambitious. He was
known to be a brilliant chess player and he had no beard: both seemed
to his contemporaries to be evidence of icy rationality. He was also
in a political tangle, accused of assassinating one of his own bishops
and struggling to retain the respect of the German princes despite
the disastrous collapse of his invasion of Sicily. He needed Richard
partly because of the ransom he might provide and partly because
of the authority his capture would give him over his own vassal
princes. But there was another, more historic reason why he might
have been delighted to have the king of England at his mercy. This
was the chance to deal with an ongoing sore in the relations between

England and the empire that went back two generations and could be summed up in five words: the hand of St James.

People in the twelfth century were fascinated by relics. There was the shrine of the Magi in Cologne, the loincloth of Christ and the swaddling clothes of the infant Jesus in Aachen, and two heads of John the Baptist in Constantinople alone. The possession of relics, partly because of their aura of sanctity, partly because of their money-raising powers, was the cause of numerous squabbles, resentments and outrageous thefts. One of Longchamp's opponents, Bishop Hugh of Lincoln, was once shown the sacred arm of Mary Magdalene at the Abbey of Fécamp and horrified the monks by unwrapping it and trying to cut off a piece. When the knife was too blunt, he bit off two mouth-sized chunks, which he handed to his biographer for safe-keeping, explaining that after eating the body of Christ at the mass, the finger of Mary Magdalene was hardly worth comment. It was the spirit of the times.

The hand of St James the Apostle had been among the most precious possessions of the Holy Roman Empire – the rest of St James's arm, from which it had become detached, was in Torcello near Venice – and one of the most valued in the collection of crown jewels belonging to the Emperor Henry V, who had been married to Richard's grandmother Matilda. When the emperor died childless in 1125, Matilda's father, King Henry I of England, ordered her to abandon her German lands and come home (she had been his heir since 1120 and the disastrous sinking of the White Ship and the drowning of her only legitimate brother William, along with much of the royal household). Whether it was in compensation for these lands, or because she felt it was her right as widow, Matilda took possession of the imperial crown jewels and the most important relics, including the Holy Lance, which was supposed to have pierced the side of Christ.*

---

*It was standing next to the lance in Vienna 800 years later that the young Adolf Hitler is supposed to have had his vision of his own destiny. The lance was removed by American troops in 1945 and only handed back to Austria by President Eisenhower.

Somehow the Archbishop of Mainz managed to persuade her to hand back most of these, including the lance – promising to support her candidate in the imperial election – and she left them with him. But she still made her return journey to England with two imperial crowns, one of them made of solid gold and weighing so much that it had to be supported on silver rods when it was worn. Also in her baggage was the hand of St James, which was given with much ceremony to Reading Abbey, where it joined other holy items, such as the hair of the Virgin Mary, the foreskin of Christ and a bit of the rock that Moses struck, and soon became the centre of a series of miracle stories. More than a quarter of a century later, Frederick Barbarossa wrote to Matilda's son Henry II, asking for the hand to be returned. Henry's reply was a highly evasive letter that promised ambassadors were on their way to give the emperor his answer. As it turned out, they were also laden with gifts to try to disguise their negative reply.

Richard had used the solid gold crown at his own coronation, where two earls were employed to hold the weight. Now, as a prisoner, he was finally at the mercy of the Holy Roman Emperor, and almost certainly had been carrying home relics from Palestine himself. Henry was also impatient about his delayed ambitions, reviving claims that the Holy Roman Empire was overlord of the whole world and planning a second invasion of Sicily as a bridgehead for expansion around the Mediterranean. The relics and crown jewels were a critical part of his claims. He would not have lost the opportunity to demand their safe return.

There is no record that the missing relics were discussed – it may have been an embarrassing subject for public consumption for both the English and the Germans. Nor has the information survived about what relics Richard was carrying with him back from Palestine. The escort of Templar knights he had been given at every stage of his journey home implies that he may have been carrying something of importance – perhaps one of the pieces of the True Cross that he had been given just before his second abortive march on Jerusalem.★ He was definitely carrying the Great Seal of England, which had been found around the neck of the drowned seal bearer in Cyprus in 1191 and returned to him, and which he kept with him throughout his captivity. These issues were the unreported, hidden aspects of the negotiations that were to take place between Richard and Henry. In public, the emperor could not draw attention to the fact that Richard had been anointed using the regalia of the Holy Roman Empire because it might give him claims in the eyes of the German princes. Nor could he be seen to capitalize too much on the capture, because Richard was a returning crusader and ought to have had the protection of the Truce of God. The emperor had to portray his detention of the former hero of Christendom as a clear duty, given the terrible accusations against him. It was therefore necessary to put Richard on trial.

Before he could do this, he had to reach agreement with Leopold, and Leopold was clearly nervous that, once he surrendered his main asset by handing Richard over to the Germans, he was liable to lose out. He had nervously steered Richard back to Dürnstein and spent the next six weeks negotiating at a distance – negotiations that were critical to the future of Germany, England, France, Sicily and even the Byzantine empire. Leopold finally met Henry on 14 February, at Würzburg. Würzburg was the crossroads of central Europe: this was the place where the main east–west trade route met the main north–south pilgrimage route from Denmark to Rome.

Leopold and Henry agreed between them that Richard should be asked to pay 100,000 silver marks, of which the Duke of Austria would take half. This was a huge sum, somewhere around a fifth of the combined wealth of all the people and institutions of

---

★ If you wander among the treasures of the Hofburg in Vienna today, you will find any number of pieces of True Cross left behind by the Hapsburg Empire – the heir of the Holy Roman Empire – but none of them match the description of the distinctive cross that Richard found at Beit Nuba.

England. The word ransom was studiously avoided and the payment was disguised as a dowry for Richard's niece Eleanor of Brittany, who would be betrothed to one of Leopold's sons. They also agreed that the Cypriot tyrant Isaac Comnenus should be released from his silver chains, together with his daughter, who was now in England or Normandy. But that was not all. Richard would be given the following demand: that he must provide Henry with fifty fully armed galleys, plus 100 knights and fifty crossbowmen, and that he should come himself – together with another 100 knights and fifty crossbowmen – to help Henry invade Sicily, and should stay there until either the conquest was successful or Henry let him go. To make sure that the 'dowry' was paid in full, Richard would be forced to hand over 200 hostages, fifty of whom would be passed on to Leopold. In the meantime, 200 German hostages would be sent from Henry to Vienna to make sure he kept his side of the bargain. It was decided that Richard's trial would take place on Palm Sunday at Henry's Imperial Council in Speyer.

The imperial entourage consisted of anything up to a thousand people, and it moved weekly and sometimes daily around the empire. Different emperors had tended to favour different palaces, such as the one at Aachen, near the octagonal church where they were traditionally crowned, or at Hagenau, with its classical library, or at Worms, with its spectacular Romanesque cathedral. Speyer also had a massive and recently finished Romanesque cathedral; it was here that Henry's mother, sister and forebears were buried, and an empty space in the vault marked the spot where his father's body would have rested had it not disintegrated in the searing Turkish heat.

It was in Speyer on 20 March that Richard came face to face with the emperor for the second time. With the imminent arrival of princes from all over his empire, Henry once again became nervy and impulsive. Exactly what passed between them has not been recorded, but it seems clear that, among other things, Richard refused the terms of the ransom and that Henry threatened his life.

Richard did not succumb to the pressure, but he must have known that his life was not in danger. There was no way that Henry would sacrifice his most valuable pawn. It was at least possible that the conversation was about relics. If it was, Richard refused these demands too, though the coronation regalia was returned later to Germany, which implies they were discussed at some stage. The disputed hand stayed where it was, however. In fact a mummified hand was found in an old iron chest by workmen digging at Reading Abbey in 1786 and is now in St Peter's Church in Marlow.

The following day, everything was ready for the trial. The great hall was decked out with the finest tapestries, as the princes and their entourages took their places according to precedence.* Conrad of Montferrat's brother Boniface, convinced of Richard's guilt, was among the princes and barons crowding into the room, but there were those on Richard's side too. There was his dark and thick-set brother-in-law, the ageing rebel Henry the Lion of Saxony, as well as other members of his more immediate entourage: Savaric, Bishop of Bath, the abbots of Boxley and Robertsbridge, the Norman chaplain William of St Mary l'Église, the tall, handsome figure of Hubert Walter and, next to him, the short, misshapen William Longchamp. Also there was Richard's nephew Otto of Brunswick, sent expressly by Eleanor to the congress to be with her favourite son.

It was critically important for both Henry and Richard that they should make a good impression. Henry had to demonstrate his largesse, his fairness and his power. He may have been emperor, but this was not a hereditary position. Although the same family tended to fill the role, the barons and bishops in the hall were also electors who voted emperors on to their thrones. Thanks to the affair of the assassination of the Bishop of Liège, Henry was aware

*This was in itself a delicate business. A century later, the Archbishop of Cologne challenged his fellow Archbishop of Mainz to a duel over who had the right to sit next to the emperor.

that he was fighting for his own title.★ The trial was among other things an opportunity to demonstrate in front of his vassals his ability to have the former hero of Christendom in his power and to humiliate him. But it was an even more critical occasion for Richard. It was his first chance to reply to his critics and answer the accusations that had been filtering across Europe. He must have relished the moment also because he knew that a show trial like this, before the flower of German chivalry, suited his particular talents precisely – his love of show, rhetoric and performance. For all his contradictions, his pride and his occasional cruelty, Richard's qualities were never so apparent as during the early weeks of his imprisonment. The chroniclers consistently mention his calmness, optimism and humour in the face of ruin, and the trial at Speyer was in some ways his finest moment.

An expectant silence fell on the illustrious company as the charges were put directly to Richard. He had betrayed the Holy Land by making peace with Saladin. He had plotted to kill Conrad on the eve of his coronation as king of Jerusalem. He had treacherously demolished the defences of Ascalon. He had also broken agreements with the emperor, which probably referred to the alliance with Tancred of Sicily. But Richard, handling his own defence, rose to the occasion bravely, brilliantly and convincingly. 'I know nothing that ought to have brought on me this ill-humour,' he said, rising to reply with reasons for Philip's anger, 'except for my having been more successful than he.' He told the assembly the full story of the crusade, from the attack on Messina to the final agreement with Saladin and the reasons for his return. The murder of Conrad of Montferrat 'is foreign to my character,' he said. 'I have not hitherto evinced such a dread of my enemies as men should believe me capable of attacking their lives otherwise than sword in hand.'

★Elections were surprisingly common in medieval Europe, but not absolutely sacrosanct. 'I order you to hold free elections,' Henry II wrote to the monks of Winchester in 1173, 'but nevertheless, I forbid you to elect anyone except Richard my clerk.'

It was a bravura performance, explaining in detail his restraint in refusing to take Jerusalem without the means to consolidate that success. He also defended the gifts he had exchanged with Saladin. 'The king of France received some as well as myself. These are civilities which brave men during war perform towards one another without ill consequences,' he said. 'It is said I have not taken Jerusalem. I should have taken it, if time had been given me; this is the fault of my enemies, not mine, and I believe no just man could blame me for having deferred an enterprise (which can always be undertaken) in order to afford my people a succour which they could no longer wait for. There, Sire, these are my crimes.'

'When Richard replied,' wrote Philip's court poet, William the Breton, 'he spoke so eloquently and regally, in so lionhearted a manner, that it was as though he had forgotten where he was and the undignified circumstances in which he had been captured, and imagined himself to be seated on the throne of his ancestors at Lincoln or at Caen.'

Richard wrought a minor miracle at Speyer. At the start of his trial, he was the villain – the renegade hero who had abandoned Jerusalem to Saladin and murdered his political opponents. But while he was on his feet, articulating his defence and his hopes and plans for Palestine, it became clear that the mood of the German princes listening had shifted decisively in his favour. This was not what Henry had intended, and he was achingly aware he could not ignore their sympathy. He also seems to have been moved himself.

Richard was making the most of his chivalric training in Poitiers all those years ago, and he ended his speech by walking towards the emperor's throne and kneeling before him. It was an agonizing moment for Henry, quite different from the scene he had imagined, aware that the barons in the room were now overwhelmingly sympathetic to Richard and his plight. But he really had no choice. With tears streaming down his face, Henry rose from the throne, went over to Richard's kneeling figure, lifted him up and gave him the kiss of peace. It was in effect the dismissal of the accusations. Many of the audience wept.

The following day, Leopold formally handed over his prisoner to the emperor, and the terms of the proposed ransom that was not a ransom were revealed. This time, it was couched not as a dowry but as a payment for bringing about a reconciliation between the emperor and Richard's brother-in-law Henry the Lion of Saxony. The demand was set at 100,000 marks, plus a loan of fifty galleys and 200 knights for a year. Once again, the terms carried a clear implication that the king of England was somehow a vassal of the emperor, but Richard had no option but to accept. He believed that he would be released as soon as the first hostages arrived from England, and the ransom terms were sent straight home via William of St Mary l'Église. He sent another flurry of letters about the arrangements via Hubert Walter and the two abbots, and another letter to the Prior of Canterbury, asking him to borrow the entire ransom from the cathedral's treasury.

Richard was being optimistic, and not just about the over-stretched resources of Canterbury Cathedral. Once the German princes had returned home, satisfied that their sympathy with Richard was now shared by the emperor, Henry began to reconsider. He remembered that he had been requested urgently by Philip Augustus not to do anything with the prisoner until they had consulted. It was reasonable to assume that the French would be willing to pay a considerable sum to keep Richard in prison, and it made sense to find out how much. He was also worried that his prisoner had too many sympathizers at the court in Speyer. So instead of allowing him to prepare for his return to England, Henry sent Richard under close guard to Trifels Castle, high in the mountains to the west of the city, and put him in solitary confinement.

Trifels was a fearsome place, towering above the small town of Annweiler and surrounded by forests in the heart of the ancestral lands of Henry's Hohenstaufen family. It was a region of bogs and marshes, where bandits and wild men lived on roots and berries. Trifels was designed to hold prisoners who were considered traitors against the empire. Imprisoning Richard there was not just un-pleasant and uncomfortable, it also implied that he was a betrayer and that the accusations stood after all. So did the constant presence of soldiers with drawn swords, which were a deliberate insult to Richard's integrity. As the most secure fortress in the empire, Trifels was also the place where the imperial crown jewels were kept – or what remained of them after Matilda's return to England. The irony would have escaped neither prisoner nor jailer that the man who had inherited some of the most precious heirlooms the empire possessed was now locked up in the very place where they ought to have been.

Richard spent about five bitter days and nights imprisoned in Trifels, under guard the entire time. The conditions of his incarceration were not recorded: whether he was able to gaze down on the Rhine and feel the fresh mountain air on his face, or whether he was condemned to sit in his cell – perhaps even within shouting distance of the most notorious political prisoners of the Holy Roman Empire. But he was rescued at this point by the intervention of William Longchamp, still at Speyer after the others had returned to England.

Longchamp had never lost the approval of the king, but it would clearly take more than that to recover his former status back in England, especially since the story of his near seduction by the Dover fisherman had spread around the kingdom. On 1 April he asked to see Henry and managed to persuade him that it would be better for both sides if Richard was not incarcerated in Trifels. The two of them then hammered out an agreement whereby Richard would be allowed to return to the court, from where he would be released as soon as the hostages had arrived and the first 70,000 marks had been paid. Relieved, Richard was released to Hagenau, and was able to discuss further with Longchamp – his great fund-raiser before the crusade – how the ransom might be found.

Longchamp was then sent back to England with a stack of letters urging the great families of England to find the money as fast as they could. One particularly effective letter, which reveals some of Richard's desperation, publicly urged the fund-raisers to let him know exactly how much each of the English barons contributed, 'so that we may know how far we are bound to return thanks to each'. There were further letters to Normandy, Aquitaine and the other parts of the Angevin empire, but both Richard and Longchamp must have been aware that England was the key. It was by far the richest corner of Richard's lands, and it also possessed a sophisticated tax system, fine-tuned by the Norman kings, and particularly by Richard's father, that was far more detailed and effective than almost anywhere else in Europe.

By the time Longchamp had left, news of the terms of the ransom had reached Paris, to the horror of Philip, and he had sent a furious letter remonstrating to Henry. Why had the emperor taken such trouble to inform Paris so early about Richard's arrest if Philip had no interest in the matter? Yet suddenly the ransom had been agreed without any reference to him at all. Philip also offered to help Henry by asking the Archbishop of Reims to mediate between him and the German dukes who were most enraged by the death of the bishop-elect of Liège. The emperor did not accept or reject this offer, which effectively pinpointed Henry's most urgent diplomatic needs, but agreed to meet Philip at Valcouleurs on St John's Day, 24 June.

Enormously relieved that Richard had been found and that there was at least a plan in place to bring about his release, Eleanor and the justiciars in England were now mainly concerned about what John would do. It was known at the English court that he had paid homage to Philip for Normandy and had promised to divorce his wife and marry the poor abandoned French princess Alys. Philip was now also overlord for the rulers of Artois, and therefore had access to Boulogne, which meant that for the first time he could threaten England by sea. The combination of Philip and John was very dangerous for Richard's deputies, especially as John was now back in England, having arranged for a force of Flemish mercenaries to join him, and was asserting his claim to the throne.

Before the two abbots had sent back their messages, or before the news from Blondel – or whatever espionage the Blondel story was obscuring – John was able to claim that Richard was dead, and to insist that he had had special information along these lines from Paris. This was contradicted by Eleanor and the Great Council in England, and – to their relief – most of the leading figures of the realm had sided with them. William the Marshal and Geoffrey of York, now securely in his archbishopric, both firmly denied that Richard was dead, so John's first major move fell flat. His request for help from the king of Scotland, William the Lion – who had been generously treated by Richard in 1189 – was firmly rejected.

Eleanor knew how important it was not to drive her youngest son into open revolt. But without consulting him, and while he was relaxing between Good Friday and Easter Day 1193 – a week after Richard's show trial – she and the justiciars set in motion a secret plan to close the Channel ports and muster a home guard along the south coast of England, ordering them to use whatever tools they had to hand for weapons. It was not the first, or the last, time that that coast was defended by agricultural tools because of a shortage of weapons.* Prayers were said daily in places of worship for the safe return of the king.

When the abbots reached Richard on the road on 19 March, he had questioned them closely about events in England, and they were able to tell him a little of John's behaviour. Richard's response was devastating and reported back home: 'My brother John is not the man to win lands by force if there is anyone at all to oppose him.' For all his resentments and shifting loyalties, John was probably the wittiest and most intelligent of the brothers, but for the rest of his life he never quite played the remark down.

Even so, by the following month, fighting had broken out simultaneously in three parts of Richard's empire. An uprising in Poitou by the Court of Périgord and some Gascon nobles was successfully beaten back by Berengaria's brother Sancho. And in England the advance guard of John's mercenaries were arrested as

* The most recent occasion involved the Home Guard in the autumn of 1940, when most of the rifles in the British Army had been left behind on the beaches of Dunkirk.

they landed; those who managed to land later were driven back into John's castles at Windsor and Wallingford by forces loyal to the justiciars. John was saved by the return from Germany of Hubert Walter, who brought with him Richard's proposal that there should be a truce for six months. The garrisons were on the brink of surrender, but the truce went ahead, although John was forced to hand over both castles to his mother – as well as Peak Castle in Derbyshire – until the truce was over.

But in Normandy Philip took personal charge of his own small invasion force with great success. The castellans in charge of the strategic castles that Henry II had so exhaustively strengthened along the Norman border were in an awkward position. Richard might never return, and his obvious successor had all but handed over Normandy to Philip. If Richard was never released, John would shortly be their overlord and too enthusiastic a defence in the name of his predecessor might prove extremely unwise. On the other hand, if Richard was freed, then their future would depend on their successful defence against the French. It was a difficult decision, and it meant that the vital frontier castle of Gisors was probably most exposed, since Gisors was nominally part of Alys's dowry and might be returned to Philip at any moment. The castellan of Gisors chose the French camp and he surrendered to Philip on 12 April. Back in England, this was considered an act of supreme treachery. Three other castellans, some of whom had been on crusade with Richard, also gave up as soon as they heard the news.

The surrender of Gisors opened the road to the Norman capital at Rouen, and Philip advanced with twenty-three siege engines to link up with an allied Flemish army under Count Baldwin VII of Flanders. In the confusion of their arrival, Robert, Earl of Leicester – one of Richard's comrades from the defence of Jaffa – managed to slip into the city and take charge of its defence, and to great effect. When Philip had collected enough of his forces to send a message to Rouen demanding its surrender, the earl replied that the city gates were open and Philip could walk in whenever he wanted. Fearing an obvious trap, Philip refrained. He had been prevented from mounting a full-scale invasion because of the reluctance of his barons to attack the lands of a returning crusader, and he also knew that his forces were not sufficient to take Rouen if it was defended with any kind of passion. He therefore abandoned the attempt, burning his siege engines and emptying his wine casks into the Seine, and retreated to Paris – threatening to return with enough troops and a rod of iron.

Despite Philip's failure at Rouen, other parts of his army had advanced all the way to Dieppe. He had gathered a fleet together at Wissant, but held back from an invasion of England until he could persuade more of his own barons to take part. If Henry could be prevailed upon to hold Richard a little longer – and if Philip could scrape together a bigger fleet – then there was still time.

The French advance had been checked and England was temporarily peaceful, but the situation was extremely unstable. John took the opportunity to meet his mother in London, passing on all the disastrous rumours he had heard in Paris about the fate of his brother. And it was probably at this point that Eleanor wrote her bitter appeal to the Pope. The letters were actually written not by her but by her husband's former clerk Peter of Blois, and copies were only found among his papers in the seventeenth century. Some historians dismiss them simply as exercises in rhetoric, drafted for Peter's own amusement, and that may be so. But there is some evidence that Eleanor actually composed them, perhaps with his help, because the Pope seems to have replied to the second letter. If they were really written by Eleanor, they are an extraordinary revelation of her personality – at the same time powerful and furious as it is pleading and a little querulous, as she castigated Pope Celestine for his inaction and begged him to intervene on behalf of her favourite son. 'My very bowels are torn away from me,' she wrote, angry that she had been dragged back to public life so exhaustingly.

I have lost the staff of my old age, the light of my eyes. The kings and princes of the earth have conspired against my son, the anointed of the lord. One keeps him in chains while the other ravages his lands; one holds him by the heels while the other flays him. And while this goes on, the sword of St Peter reposes in its scabbard . . . Why do I, a wretched creature, delay? Why do I not go that I may see him whom my soul loves, bound in beggary and irons? At such a time as this, how could a mother forget the son of her womb . . . ? Yet I fluctuate in doubt for if I go away, I desert my son's kingdom which is afflicted on all sides with fierce hostility . . . Once the Church trod upon the necks of the proud with its own strength, and the laws of emperors obeyed the sacred canons. Now things have changed: no one dare murmur about the detestable crimes of the powerful, which are tolerated, and canonical rigour falls on the sins of the poor alone.

To this devastating indictment, goading the heir of St Peter for being so pusillanimous against the emperor, there seems to have been no reply. Actually the Pope had responded to Richard's arrest by excommunicating Leopold and threatening Philip with an interdict over the whole of France if he should attack Richard's lands. He even threatened the English, rather unfairly, if they failed to raise whatever ransom was required. But his weakness in the face of imperial pressure was all too obvious. Celestine was now eighty-seven and imperial troops were in his own papal territories; his injunctions to them were ignored. There had been no condemnation for the jailer himself.

The second letter opens as she styles herself, unforgettably, 'Eleanor, by the wrath of God, Queen of England, Duchess of Normandy and Count of Anjou', and begs Celestine to be 'a father to a pitiable mother'. But the third appears to be a reply to an admonishment from the Pope for her tone, and is couched in terms of an apology: 'I beseech you, O Father, let your benignity bear with what is an effect of grief rather than of deliberation. I have sinned and used the words of Job. I have said that which I would that I had not said, but henceforth I put my finger on my lips and say no more.'

For the intellectuals of northern Europe in particular, Germany seemed determined to take control of both the temporal and the

1. Three generations of English kings: (clockwise from top left) Henry II, Richard I, Henry III and John (from a thirteenth-century manuscript).

2. A French troubadour or possibly a jongleur (from a thirteenth-century manuscript). Historians of music do not know for certain what instruments the troubadours used, or indeed if they used any at all. Jongleurs were paid to spread the troubadours' songs as widely as they could.

3. Lancelot and Guinevere kiss for the first time, watched by Galahad (from a manuscript of Arthurian legends, c. 1315). The twelfth century was a romantic age of sexual and emotional awakening.

4. Minstrels below the table, with some romantic hand-holding on the table above (from a fourteenth-century French Book of Hours).

5. A crusader knight (from the twelfth-century Westminster Psalter).

6. (Left) The coronation
of Richard I
(a miniature from *Flores
Historiarum* by
Matthew Paris,
1250–52).

7. The king and his entourage set off on crusade
(from a 1250 history of Jerusalem).

8. (*Above*) Richard's neglected queen, Berengaria of Navarre, in effigy on her tomb at L'Epau Abbey.

9. (*Left*) Philip Augustus, Richard's former passionate friend, carved on Rouen Cathedral.

10. Philip shocks the English by leaving Palestine before the end of the crusade (from *Grandes Chroniques de France*, c. 1335–40).

11. *Richard I the Lionheart at the Battle of Arsuf,*
14 September 1191: this was the only pitched battle Richard ever fought
in his life (nineteenth-century oil painting by Feron Eloi Firmin).

12. The engraver Gustave Doré's view of Richard's dramatic assault from the sea at Jaffa (from J.-F. Michaud's *Bibliothèque des Croisades*, 1877).

13. Richard's arrest in a kitchen outside Vienna, as the German chroniclers recorded it.

14. Arrested in disguise by two soldiers, Richard kneels before the clean-shaven emperor (from *Liber ad honorem augusti* by Petrus de Ebolo, 1195–6, a contemporary German chronicle now in Switzerland).

15. The scene of Blondel's song: Dürnstein and its castle as it was in 1650.

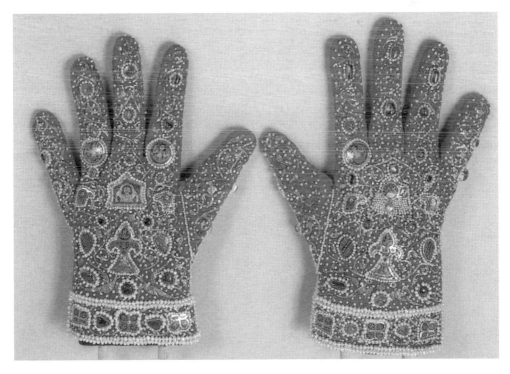

16. Ornate gloves played a key role in Richard's arrest. These gloves were looted by Emperor Henry VI from the Sicilian treasury and incorporated into the imperial coronation robes.

17. *The Pedlar* by Charles Alston Collins, 1850. This Victorian painting shows Berengaria's horror as she discovers Richard's belt on sale in a market in Rome.

18. Behind the Holy Family is Vienna as it was in the fifteenth century; the walls were built with the money from Richard's ransom (detail from the Schottenmeister altar, after 1469).

19. Two scenes from Richard's life: languishing in prison and then attacking Philip in Gisors (from a thirteenth-century document).

20. Richard's emotional speech at Speyer in March 1193
(from a nineteenth-century print by Werthmann).

21. Richard's legendary encounter with
the lion (from a sixteenth-century
woodcut).

22. One of Blondel's songs (from a
thirteenth-century song collection
in Paris).

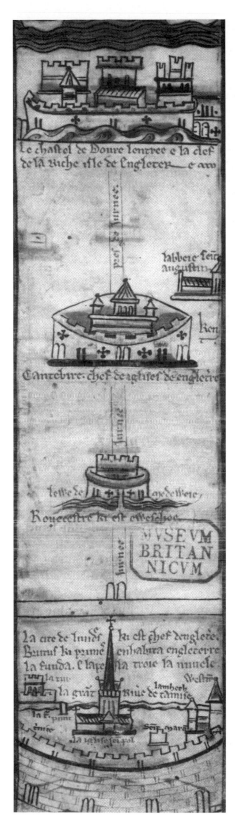

Le chastel de Doure lentree e la clef
de la riche isle de Engletere. e.xxx

por huittel

labbeie sei[n]t
augustin

Cantrebire chef de eglise de engletere

ken

lewe de ...... de Mede[.]wee

Rouecestre ki est eveschee

MVSEVM
BRITAN
NICVM

La cite de lundes ki est chef denglete[r].
Brutus ki prime enhabita engleterre
la funda. E la[....] la troie la nu[m]cle

la riue Westm

la grā riue de tamise lamb[e]th

la t[....] pont

la ...... la eglise sei[n]t pol sei[n]t mar...

24. (Above) Coins changing hands.

23. A thirteenth-century map of Watling
Street, Richard and Eleanor's route home,
showing Dover, Canterbury, Rochester
and London.

25. Old London Bridge, late eighteenth century, as the bridge would have appeared for much of the medieval period. It was half built when Richard reached the city in 1194.

26. Salisbury Cathedral, the English version of the new Gothic style.

27. Richard's half-brother William Longspee, the first to be buried in Salisbury Cathedral.

28. Richard's effigy on his tomb, now empty, at Fontevrault. The effigy is not necessarily a likeness, but it may be a guide to his appearance. The clothes provide some idea of contemporary fashion.

29. Blondel's song as a classic children's story, this time from Agnes Grozier Herbertson's 1911 book *Heroic Legends*, showing the troubadour as he creeps under the tower at Dürnstein. The story of Richard's imprisonment is still a familiar element of other legends, like that of Robin Hood, thanks largely to Sir Walter Scott's novel *Ivanhoe*.

30. *Robin Hood and His Merry Men Entertaining Richard the Lionheart in Sherwood Forest* by Daniel Maclise. The meeting shown in this Victorian oil painting is entirely mythical, but Nottingham and Sherwood Forest were in fact Richard's first objective on his return to England.

spiritual affairs of the whole of Europe. John of Salisbury, who was exiled along with Becket a generation before and had dominated the intellectual life of Western Europe after the death of Abelard, had urged England and France to work together to resist Frederick Barbarossa's plans for European domination, and his growing influence over the papacy. 'Who made the Germans judges over the people of Christ?' he asked, contrasting the world of freedom and justice in Western Europe with the tyranny of Germany. For the barons of Eleanor's generation, the emperor's imprisonment of the king of England was a further twist in the tale of growing German hubris.

Eleanor's rage was shared across all Richard's dominions, but she had added reason to be angry. Richard was her favourite, and the entire crisis in government – which threatened everything she had worked towards – was on her shoulders at the age of nearly seventy; she may have doubted her ability to stand the strain. But most of all, she had a personal horror of imprisonment. She had been incarcerated in Old Sarum by her husband for sixteen miserable years, at the end of which she had effortlessly taken over the reins of power in the empire. Her first act in 1189 had been to release all the prisoners in England, because, she said, she knew what it was like. Eleanor hated prisons, and something of this horror is reflected in the letters.

Free at least to move around the court at Hagenau and Worms, Richard began to receive queues of visitors: barons, bishops and clerks from England – seeking advice, providing information, asking permissions – and dignitaries from foreign countries too. They were followed by a stream of letters passing from Worms to the English court, some of them arriving intact, some of them replaced by downright forgeries. 'However many times we send messages to you in England with orders for you, you are only to believe those which concern our own honour and advantage,' Richard wrote to Walter of Coutances. 'Those which do not affect our honour or profit are not to be believed.'

It was an imperfect way of running his kingdom. Even when

the letters were genuine, they were liable to disappear on the road, seized by the agents of foreign powers, just as the emperor's original letter to Paris had been. The journey to see him down the Rhine was also fraught with difficulty. The Bishop of Chester was ambushed by thieves even before he got to Germany, resting near Canterbury on his way to Dover. The feeling against Longchamp was still strong enough to suspect his brother-in-law Matthew of Clare, the castellan of Dover Castle, of complicity.

But despite all the enormous difficulties, and the frustration and concerns that he must have had, Richard was astonishingly optimistic in prison. In some ways it is one of the most potent testimonies to his character. He may have had flaws as a husband, he may have left his own kingdom almost bankrupt after his short reign, but under overwhelming pressure he kept his nerve enough to inspire those around him – from the two abbots onwards. 'No tribulation could cloud the countenance of this most serene prince,' wrote Ralph of Coggeshall, the chronicler with the sources closest to Richard at the time. 'His words remained cheerful and jocund, his actions fierce or most courageous as time, place, reason or person demanded.'

The number of visitors astonished and unnerved his captors, and there was evidently a considerable amount of work to be done – advisers and ambassadors to consult with, letters to write, orders to issue and proclamations to seal. But there was time on his hands too. The chronicles report that he spent some of this on the castle walls, and devoted considerable effort to getting his jailers drunk, testing his strength against theirs by wrestling with them and playing practical jokes on them. Ransom was a legitimate chivalrous demand – though perhaps not for crusaders on the way home – and Richard took his vows seriously. He would have been given wide freedom around the court on condition that he did not try to escape. He even sent to England for his hawks, which were dispatched to Germany so that he could go hunting. The English government accounts, known as the Pipe Rolls, have an entry for 'scarlet cloth and green cloth and hauberks and capes of doeskin and of lamb's wool and three silver cups brought to Germany, £44 11s 2d'.

There were other entertainments too. Like Richard, the emperor was a songwriter. Henry had learned to write songs in Italy in his early twenties. His palace on the hill at Hagenau – where Richard had lodged after his release from Trifels – had the full array of minnesingers and minstrels, as well as an impressive library of classical authors, and brand new wall-paintings illustrating Barbarossa's part in the Third Crusade. Despite John of Salisbury's warnings, Henry presided over a sophisticated and cultured court and Richard must have loved the colour, the music, the great red gold pinnacles on the towers of the Hohenstaufen castles. He must have enjoyed the ladies reading French aloud to each other in the garden, the food and drink provided each day by the stewards and cupbearers in the great hall, with the most luxurious dishes that medieval kitchens could provide – roast peacock, salted herring from the Baltic, braised heron or even, occasionally, roast dolphin.*

In a court that valued music and romance, it is hardly surprising that the legends that wove themselves around Richard in prison should have been about these – including the famous story about how he earned his 'Lionheart' nickname. The tales tell how Richard was arrested by King Modred of Almain (Swabia) when he and his friends refused to share their roast goose in a wayside inn with a wandering minstrel. They gave false names and were imprisoned for espionage. In prison, Richard was loved by the king's daughter Margery, who smuggled herself night after night into his cell and helped him survive two crucial trials of strength.

The first of these was when he played a game of 'pluck-buffet'

---

* The most ingenious twelfth-century dish was probably a pie with living birds: when the pastry was broken open the birds would fly out – first the small ones and then the larger hunting birds not far behind, which would chase them up to the ceiling of the hall.

– exchanging blows – with Modred's gigantic son Ardour. Having survived Ardour's tremendous blow, he asked permission to rebuild his strength by eating and to return the blow the following day, and he spent the evening in his cell coating his hand with wax. When he struck Ardour on the cheek with his wax-covered fist, Ardour was killed instantly. Modred was furious, not so much about the death of his son but about the seduction of his daughter, and Richard was forced to face another trial. His only request to Margery was for forty of her silk handkerchiefs. So when a hungry lion was released into his cell, Richard protected his arm by wrapping it with the handkerchiefs, and then thrust his hand into the lion's throat and pulled out its beating heart. The lion fell dead, and Richard thanked God, strode out into the great hall in front of all the barons of the court, and there he sprinkled salt on the heart and ate it before their horrified gaze.

The story of the lion seems to have originated in a German manuscript called *The Romance of Richard the Coeur de Lion*, written sometime before 1250, but there may have been an earlier version that has been lost. Richard seems actually to have been identified with lions for most of his adult life, described as the 'lion-hearted prince' by the historian Giraldus Cambrensis. What is most interesting about the story is how much the popular imagination – and probably Richard's own – linked him with King Arthur. Modred or Mordred was originally King Arthur's enemy and nemesis in the legends, and the story of the exchanged blows with Ardour sounds very like Sir Gawain and the Green Knight – right down to the magical garments of protection – which was to become such a critical story in the development of English literature nearly two centuries later. Not just King Arthur either: the mythical Irish hero Cuchulain was also said to have torn a lion's heart out from its throat.

Richard may have been transforming himself into a hero of folklore, but the facts of his imprisonment were all too real. There must have been moments of despair for him, and probably the news that some of his fellow crusaders – those he had fought alongside at Acre – had surrendered their Norman castles to Philip without a fight was among the worst. It may have been then that Richard put pen to paper and wrote one of the only songs of his to have survived: 'Ja nus hons pris' (No one who is in prison). It was written both in Old French and Occitan and was addressed to his half-sister Marie of Champagne, the mother of Henry of Champagne – now king of Jerusalem – and the patron among others of Chrétien de Troyes. It starts '*Ja nus hons pris ne dira sa raison Adroitement, se dolantement non*' (see Appendix):

> No one who is in prison sees his fate
> With honesty; for all he feels is sad –
> But he can still compose a hopeful song.
> I am so rich in friends, but poor in help:
> They should be ashamed if, for my ransom,
> I lie here one more year.

The song was written in a popular form, perhaps because that was how he wrote, but he may also have intended it – like the good troubadour that he was – to be taken up and sung across Europe by other minstrels to help raise the ransom. It is unclear whether he wrote it to comfort himself, to amuse his cultured relatives or to reach a wide audience. Perhaps it was a little of all three.

It is also recognizably his song: you can detect the peculiar mixture that made up Richard's personality – a hint of pride, but a flash of ironic humour as well. Once again, it is almost impossible to pin down Richard's contradictions. The awareness of his own importance is here, but at the same time he is not ashamed to wrestle with the servants responsible for his imprisonment. It was a contradiction summed up by his old adversary the troubadour Bertran de Born after he was released in a poem called 'Now Comes the Pleasant Season': 'I like the custom which the lion has, that is not cruel to a conquered thing, but is proud against pride.'

The biggest mystery about the song is the final lines, which are obscure and hard to translate – as well as being more like a private accompanying note to the song – and therefore tend to be left out of the translations:

> Sister, Countess, your sovereign right
> May God preserve, and guard the one I claim
> For whom I suffer here.

These are clearly addressed to his half-sister Marie of Champagne, and they are followed by two even more obscure final lines:

> I do not speak of the lady of Chartres,
> The mother of Louis.

Who did he mean? The 'one I claim' could conceivably have referred to his wife, though it is not clear why Marie of Champagne might have a role in guarding her – unless Marie was visiting Poitiers at the time, where Berengaria was. It may have been his sister Joanna, though again it is not clear why his imprisonment was on her account. There is one other possibility, which is more likely, that this means Henry of Champagne, Marie's eldest son and Richard's nephew, whom he had left behind as king of Jerusalem. If so, it would be clear why there might be some link in Richard's mind between their two fates. As for the mother of Louis, this refers to their sister Alix, whose son Louis was the new Count of Chartres and Blois, and was for dynastic reasons tied in allegiance to the French. But why mention her at all, except in a wry way to make clear which 'Sister, Countess' he was referring to? Somehow you feel that these mysterious lines might provide a key to some of the unanswered questions about how Richard could have been condemned to prison so far from home.

If Richard had melancholic moments, he generally kept them hidden with activity. He wrote to the Old Man of the Mountains, asking for a deposition clearing him of blame for the murder of Conrad of Montferrat, though the reply to this letter, which still exists – and granting his wish – has been dismissed as a forgery. He even sent his own armour back to England, so that it could go on a fund-raising tour around the country. On 30 March he had written the first of a string of letters to his mother, asking her to take personal control of the fund-raising and to appoint Hubert Walter to the vacant position of Archbishop of Canterbury. 'Nothing apart from my own freedom matters more than this does,' he said, hinting later in the letter that there might be some advantages in his predicament that he would not have wanted to miss. His strategic mind was exploring diplomatic opportunities.

But then news reached him of the planned meeting between Philip Augustus and the emperor, and he realized that all his plans could be undermined if the conference was allowed to go ahead. Once Henry was in France, the likelihood was that there would be an agreement – perhaps backed by large payments from Philip – that would keep him in prison or, worse, transfer him to a prison in France. It was vitally important that the meeting should not happen. Summoning his key advisers, Richard and the English government began a dramatic series of diplomatic manoeuvres to regain the initiative.

Richard had reason to believe, correctly, that the emperor's eventual ambition was to curb the growing power of France and reclaim French territory for the empire. He guessed, correctly again, that there was an opportunity to persuade Henry of how useful a long-term relationship with England would be in comparison to one with France. Throughout the early summer of 1193, he also worked to build links with some of the emperor's most difficult princes of the Lower Rhineland, in particular working closely with his now ageing brother-in-law in Saxony to build new relationships with his fellow rebels, while at the same time negotiating trading links with England. Just as Philip had understood that Henry needed more than anything to heal the political rift inside the empire, this was where Richard's efforts were devoted. But it was Richard who achieved it, managing to transform himself into a crucial asset for Henry as he battled to regain the trust of his vassal princes. Powerful north German princes and prelates were now confirmed English allies – Conrad and Adolf, respectively archbishops of Mainz and Cologne; Henry, Duke of Limburg and his son Simon, the bishop-elect of Liège; Henry, Duke of Brabant; and Dietrich, Count of Holland. The vital meeting with the German barons and bishops was organized for the emperor around Midsummer's Day, and so instead of meeting Philip Augustus at Valcouleurs, Henry was meeting his former rebels at negotiations that were managed and facilitated by Richard and the English diplomats.

Richard then requested that the court that had heard his case in March be reconvened at Worms, also meeting in a palace next to a massive and recently finished Romanesque cathedral, beside one of the biggest synagogues in continental Europe.* For the second time, the leading princes of the empire were able to discuss Richard's imprisonment. Once more Longchamp and Walter, the short and the tall, stood by Richard during their five-day deliberations. Also with him for the occasion were Baldwin of Béthune and Hubert Walter's co-justiciar, William Brewer.† It was here that the final moves in the English diplomatic game were concluded. Henry swore to the assembled prices and bishops that he was innocent of the murder of the short-lived bishop-elect of Liège, and promised a new election for bishop. The general settlement also included a renegotiation of the terms of Richard's ransom. He would now be freed once the emperor had received 100,000 silver marks plus hostages for another 50,000 which had to be paid within seven months of his release. These 50,000 would be waived if Richard was able to achieve something too secret to be recorded, but it may have been a full reconciliation between the emperor and his most implacable opponent, Henry the Lion of Saxony. As well as all the diplomatic effort, it had cost Richard the promise of another 50,000 silver marks to make sure the meeting at Valcouleurs did not take place. Again, he was in no position to bargain.

Once the news of the agreement reached Paris, it seemed to Philip – as it must have seemed to Richard – that release was only

---

* This had been finished in 1174 and survived until the Nazi Kristallnacht in 1938.
† William Brewer was the man who founded the beautiful Mottisfont Abbey in Hampshire, still a haven of green peace and quiet.

a matter of days away. He then sent his famous message to John: 'Look to yourself, the Devil is loosed.'

Walter Scott's novel *Ivanhoe* imagines John receiving this message at a tournament in Ashby de la Zouch and going white with fear. In reality, a terrified John made his way quickly to the coast and fled across the Channel to Paris. Once he had left, his estates in England were confiscated by the justiciars and his remaining supporters abandoned to their fates. To seal his dependence on the French, John also handed over the key fortresses in Touraine that his father and brother had so painstakingly developed. It was then that Philip began to conceive the contempt for John that was to characterize their difficult relationship for the rest of their lives. And then, finally, Pope Celestine acted on Richard's behalf. He excommunicated both Philip and John for attacking a returning crusader.

Longchamp and William Brewer travelled separately to Paris to negotiate a proper truce with Philip. It made sense to Philip to consolidate his gains while he could plan something more dramatic, and the treaty signed at Mantes on 9 July allowed him to keep all the lands he had gained, and Richard agreed to pay Philip 20,000 silver marks in four instalments after his release. Once the castles had been handed over formally to him, Philip also promised that he 'receive the king of England into his favour and make request to the emperor for his liberation'. Probably nobody at the negotiations expected Philip to fulfil this part of the bargain, but it might prove important later.

One of the agreements was that a series of castles in Normandy would be handed over to John. This was clearly in Richard's interest because it provided a lure to extract John from the influence of Philip's court in Paris. Once the treaty had been signed, messages from Germany urged John to take possession of his new castles. But it was a measure of the distrust with which he was regarded that the castellans refused to hand them over to him, and he returned in a rage to Paris.

★

Philip was preparing a far more dramatic move, and had been making preparations ever since his withdrawal from Rouen. He knew that a full-scale invasion of England would require allies and probably also a bigger fleet than he had available. Since his wife, Isabella, had died giving birth to stillborn twins just as they were preparing to leave for the crusade in 1190, three years before, he had been weighing up the most advantageous marriage.* Having briefly considered and dismissed Richard's widowed sister Joanna, he had finally come to the conclusion that a diplomatic marriage with Denmark would have great advantages. Not only was King Cnut VI's eighteen-year-old sister, Ingeborg, said to be extraordinarily attractive, but his naval strength dominated the southern Baltic. Cnut also had the added advantage of a distant claim on the English throne, because his ancestor had been the famous King Cnut, who ruled England until his death in 1035 – the same claim that had led the Norwegian Harald Hardrada to invade England back in 1066. The marriage was arranged swiftly and Ingeborg arrived in France with her household, chaperoned by the Bishop of Roskilde, on 15 August. Philip finally met his new bride in procession in Arras with an enormous range of gifts. Together they were taken to Amiens, where they were married in the cathedral, and Ingeborg was crowned queen of France by Philip's uncle the Archbishop of Reims. There then followed one of the most extraordinary, unexplained events of medieval history.

The first sign of trouble came in the middle of the ceremony, when Philip was seen to go deathly pale and begin to tremble. He recovered shortly afterwards and the rest of the festivities continued without difficulty. But after the king and his new queen retired for their wedding night behind closed doors, something happened so dreadful – at least in Philip's mind – that he was prepared to do anything to rid himself of her. He was prepared to abandon his

---

*Philip had married his first wife, Isabella of Hainault, in 1180, when she was only ten. The wedding was not consummated for some years and was disrupted when one knight pushed the crowd at Saint-Denis, upsetting lamp oil all over the wedding guests. Philip tried to divorce her four years later, but she wandered barefoot in public around Senlis until he agreed to take her back.

whole alliance with Denmark, and with it his invasion plans, just to dissolve the marriage and unstitch himself from his saintly new bride. At dawn the next morning, he sent Ingeborg back to the Bishop of Roskilde and the other Danish envoys, but they refused to take her and hurried out of France. Three months later, he had the marriage dissolved by some compliant bishops, one of whom was Conrad of Montferrat's old friend Philip, Bishop of Beauvais.

What happened on Philip's wedding night is one of those infuriating historical mysteries from which we are completely excluded. Nobody witnessed it except for Philip and Ingeborg and they disagreed about the basic facts. All we know is that Philip always claimed that the marriage was not consummated and Ingeborg said it had been. His own official explanation was that he realized they were fourth cousins and too closely related, but even the Pope said this was not too close. It was hard, in those days, for the interwoven European aristocracy to marry anyone more distantly related than that.★ It remains a complete mystery, but there are some clues.

Three years later, still with Ingeborg haunting his life in France – refusing either to go home or to become a nun – Philip married Agnes de Méran, the daughter of Berthold, Count of Méran, which was in the Rhineland. He had no wedding night problems and may actually have already been having an affair with her at the time of his wedding to Ingeborg. Sources close to him used to say that Agnes had bewitched Philip in Amiens and made him regard his new wife with horror. Sorcery in those days was often used as a shorthand for sexual difficulties, and it seems possible that Philip found he was impotent on his wedding night.

Philip was a fastidious man, obsessively nervous about disease and so puritanical in his own court that he fined anyone swearing twenty sous, or – if they did it again – had them thrown fully clothed into the Seine. It may be that Ingeborg's unique

★ Theoretically, anyone related in the fourth degree – with the same great-great-grandparents – could not get married, and 'affinity' included godparents. The Church was even pressing for seven degrees. But in practice this was normally ignored, simply because of the difficulty of finding anyone of sufficient rank, and because of the potential that diplomatic marriages had to bring peace.

combination of saintliness and sexuality unnerved him – she was 'beautiful in face, more beautiful in soul', according to the chron- iclers. We know that Philip originally found her attractive, but something happened between them that led him to believe he had been cursed in some way, and it was such a disturbing experience that he regarded her with absolute revulsion ever after. It was a tragic story for Ingeborg, who was also strong-minded enough not just to refuse to return humiliated to Denmark but to spend the next twenty years imprisoned in one castle or convent after another, demanding that she be given her rights as queen and desperately selling her last clothes and jewels so she could afford to live.

The whole business with Ingeborg defies political explanation, but it seems to have occurred to Philip in the days after his disastrous wedding night that he might anyway have made a more advantageous marriage, to Henry VI's cousin Constance of Hohen- staufen, and thereby built the alliance with the emperor. As soon as he had dispatched Ingeborg's household so cruelly, he sent emissaries to Germany to propose marriage to Constance instead, assuming that his marriage to Ingeborg could be dissolved on the grounds of non-consummation. To his rage, they returned to inform him that Constance had already secretly married Henry of Brunswick, the son and heir of Henry the Lion of Saxony. Richard seemed to have quietly achieved the diplomatic breakthrough in Germany, and sealed the new understanding between Saxony and the imperial court with a secret marriage with the emperor's cousin, heiress to the Count Palatine.

Pope Celestine may have barely stirred himself in response to Eleanor's impassioned letters pleading for his support for her son's release, but he did act to rescue Richard's wife and sister, who were still trapped in Rome. He organized an escort of cardinals and sent them to Berengaria and Joanna, who were taken safely as far as Genoa. There they took a ship to Marseilles and were met, also through the intervention of the Pope, by King Alfonso II of Aragon, who ruled the coast of Provence. He led them safely into the charge of the very man who, Richard had been told, was waiting to arrest him in the south of France, Raymond of St Gilles, the son and heir of Raymond V of Toulouse. Raymond had also been returning from Rome and had with him a powerful force of soldiers, and he escorted Berengaria and Joanna – both then twenty-seven – as far as Poitiers.

Their journey had unforeseen consequences because of the unexpected romance that grew up on the journey between Raymond and Joanna. By the time she reached Poitiers, in true chivalric style, they were in love. A surprised Richard consented to the marriage and it took place in 1196, bringing – after the death of Raymond's father the following year – peace between Richard and his most difficult neighbour in the south. The matter of Raymond's previous wife, already abandoned in a convent, was quietly brushed aside.

In Poitiers, Berengaria settled down to organizing her own fund-raising efforts on behalf of her husband. It must have been an enormous relief to her to be home. She had been crowned queen of England in Cyprus and had spent almost no time at her new husband's side, except briefly in Acre, when he was almost delirious with fever in the final months of their stay in Palestine. Richard may then have been in the middle of his infatuation with the Cypriot princess, or he may, under the influence of al-Adil, have been experimenting with more exotic forms of love. He may just have been distant and aloof. Either way, it was already clear to Berengaria that she would have to battle for a place in her husband's heart.

The old queen of England, her mother-in law, Eleanor, was now dominating the empire. It is true that the political crisis had drawn her unwillingly into that position, but Berengaria must still have wondered quite what her new life was destined to entail. She would not have known, though she might have guessed, that not one of Richard's copious letters to his mother from captivity mentioned her at all.

9. A King's Ransom

'As the earth grows dark when the sun goes down, so the face of the kingdom was changed by the absence of the king. All the barons were disturbed, castles strengthened, towns fortified and ditches dug.'

Richard of Devizes, *Chronicon de Rebus Gestis Ricardi Primi*

'And do you know what will befall the king if he is not cured of his wounds, and does not hold his land? Ladies will lose their husbands, hapless maidens will be orphans, many knights will die; and the lands will be laid waste. All these ills will result because of you.'

Chrétien de Troyes, *Percival*

Blondel and Richard's more literate crusaders would have been familiar with the new story of romance and spirituality that had emerged from the court of Champagne in the years before Richard's coronation. Chrétien de Troyes was among the first of the *trouvères* of northern France, and his extraordinary tales of the quest for the Holy Grail – built around the court of King Arthur – were rapidly spreading across Western Europe. Chrétien had probably borrowed the stories from a Welsh writer called Bleheris, in a book given him by his patron, Philip, Count of Flanders, who had died outside Acre just before it fell. But he gave them life – the Knights of the Round Table and the intricate mystery of their parallel search.

At the heart of the Grail romance was the haunting and mysterious figure of the Fisher King, the wounded monarch whose affliction – whether it is an actual wound or just Philip Augustus-style impotence – meant that his land had become sterile and wasted.

The forests had died, the crops were parched and the rivers had run dry. To heal the land, Percival, Lancelot and Galahad have first to heal the king, and that requires them to seek out the Grail. Their purity and character are tested along the way, and – just as in the old tradition of the Courts of Love – the constant testing of their dedication adds to the quest.

The nature of the Grail is different in different accounts. Sometimes it appears to be the cup that held the blood of Christ or the chalice used at the Last Supper. Sometimes it is the Celtic cauldron of rebirth and sometimes even a precious stone from the crown of Lucifer when he was flung out of heaven. The legends are probably based on much more ancient tales – probably Celtic (Percival is usually described as Welsh) – but the Grail quest has all the hallmarks of the twelfth century: dedication and purity for a great quest, the mystery and excitement of hidden or forgotten knowledge, and a luminous sense of romance that could just as well be sexual as it is spiritual. That is the atmosphere that Blondel and Richard grew up with, and – as you would expect from the age of chivalry – the answer to the quest is often something very simple, such as a polite question.

'In the night, God had restored the streams to their proper channels in the country,' wrote Wauchier de Denain in his *Conte del Grail*, 'and all the woods, it seems, had turned green as soon as he had asked why the lance bled.' Chrétien's *Percival* was abandoned in mid-sentence, and the French poet Wauchier was attempting to finish the story during the events described in this book.

Richard's subjects in England had, at this time, been enjoying unprecedented wealth – the first windmills were appearing across the countryside and the burgeoning wool trade was drawing in silver money from all over Europe. But they also knew all about the waste land. Those who were old enough could remember the civil war between Stephen and Matilda in the 1140s had seen the country descend into banditry, terror and disorder and left villages, as one chronicler put it, 'standing lonely and almost empty'. Now the prospect of the waste land returning to England seemed all too imminent. Their king was wounded, in the sense that he was imprisoned by a powerful emperor in a distant land. And, as a result of that wound and Richard's absence, England was perched on the edge of a similar descent into disastrous civil war. Even if that was avoided, its wealth seemed certain to be sucked away to pay for his unprecedented ransom.

The threat of civil war had temporarily receded, now that John's ambitions seemed to have been checked, but it had been replaced by the threat of invasion. Eleanor, the consummate politician, was in charge for the time being. But she was elderly and there was also a subtle but unmistakable jockeying for position, even among the justiciars, who must have realized that – should Richard's return be delayed too long – they would have to make the leap of allegiance at some point to his brother, or risk losing everything because they had stood aloof from the winning side. The Bishop of Durham, Hugh de Puiset – the co-justiciar who had been stripped of his power so humiliatingly by Longchamp in 1190 – had been ordered to raise the siege of John's remaining castle at Tickhill just as he was about to take it. It was whispered that even Walter of Coutances and William the Marshal had been careful not to prosecute their military operations against John too forcefully.

England's noble families all now knew the talk about the king's brother – his greed and unreliability, and how he had lost his head and fled to France, handing over much of Normandy to Philip. They knew how John's mercenaries had behaved, turning the territory between his castle at Windsor and Kingston into a small waste land of their own. But Richard had no legitimate children and John was the *de facto* heir, and the prospect of living under his rule was looming and disturbing.

Then there was the question of money. Those close to the English government knew about Richard's diplomatic success in Germany, how he had detached Baldwin, Count of Flanders, from the French side, and the new network of alliances with the princes and prelates of northern Germany – promising valuable trade concessions across the Baltic in the future. But they also knew that these agreements were based on large sums of money, over and above the ruinous ransom, that had been promised by Richard in the future. As well as that expenditure, the justiciars had embarked on urgent fortifications to protect the most vulnerable parts of the coast from the expected invasion by Philip and the French. Large sums had been spent strengthening the castles at Dover and along the coast from Pevensey to Chichester, Winchester, Porchester, Southampton and Corfe, as well as Bristol and Gloucester, to guard against an incursion from John's sympathizers in Wales.

Richard had asked to meet Walter of Coutances face to face, and the chief justiciar made the uncomfortable journey across the Channel and down the Rhine to see him. While he was on his way, Richard replaced him with his trusted Hubert Walter, now also Archbishop of Canterbury. Walter of Coutances had taken over the reins of the country with great skill at a moment of unique danger for England, and – by doing so – had twice missed the opportunity he craved of becoming Archbishop of Canterbury himself. Hubert Walter was criticized for his pride and ostentation, and for his lack of holiness, but as an administrator he was absolutely inspired. He set about overhauling England's comparatively sophisticated systems of government. They were going to face their sternest test yet.

The country he took over was united behind Richard in a way it had been for no previous monarch since the Norman invasion. The great divisions of language remained in place – the French and Latin of the ruling classes and the emerging English of those they ruled – but this seems to have been the generation when England finally became English, rather than an uneasy coexistence of Saxons and Normans. They must have been aware of how rarely Richard had even crossed the Channel. They could hardly have overlooked the impact on their pockets of the Saladin Tithe to pay for his crusade. But they remained enormously proud of their king, still as far as they were concerned the hero of Christendom. That may be one reason why this enormous ransom was eventually paid.

Also, England was not a waste land yet. It was a country that had benefited from the stability of Richard's father and his efforts to codify and systematize the legal system. Its increasing wealth was admired, though its peculiarities remained a source of dis-approval on the Continent. The English vice, then as now, was alcohol. Writing in Paris a little later, Jacques de Vitry – later Cardinal-Bishop of Acre – outlined the drawbacks of all Europe's nations. The French were proud and effeminate, he said; the Germans were angry and obscene; the Lombards greedy and cowardly – and the English were drunkards and had tails.★

But if they drank more than their neighbours, they could at least afford it. The trade in wool was already making England wealthy, feeding the burgeoning cloth industry in Flanders. The trade in wheat was packing the ports of East Anglia, the mines of the West Country were extracting tin and lead, and the silver coins in payment were flooding into England from all over the known world. A new generation of water mills, many of them investments by the Templars, was appearing all over the countryside, symbols of twelfth-century enterprise. Staffordshire was already producing ceramic plates and cups. The merchant guilds of London were emerging and London was growing into its new status as an immensely rich, self-governing financial centre, and had embarked, under Peter Colechurch, on one of the most extraordinary engin-eering achievements of the century: the nineteen stone arches spanning 906 feet of the new London Bridge.

But for all that wealth, the ransom was an immense amount of money. It was far from clear, even with Hubert Walter's adminis-trative skills, whether this country of forests, abbeys and small farms would be able to afford to pay for their king and bring him home.

So, by the summer of 1193, it was clear that the bill for Richard's ransom was going to cost his empire 150,000 silver marks, most of which would come from England. This was not just because of England's wealth, but because England's tax system was far superior to the one in Normandy, Aquitaine or Brittany, and was the only

---

★ It was a long-standing joke among the continentals that the English had tails. Quite what this meant – and it was unlikely to have been meant literally – has been lost in the mists of time.

administrative system capable of raising anything approaching that sum.

How much was 150,000 marks? The exact currency stipulated in the agreement was silver marks of Cologne, the best and most reliable in Europe. This meant that the ransom was going to amount to just over thirty-five tons of silver. In English currency, even the initial downpayment of 100,000 marks was going to be worth £66,666 thirteen shillings and four pence (though the only official currency at that stage was the penny). This was an era when sheep cost a penny and pigs cost sixpence, where footsoldiers serving abroad for the king were paid twopence a day, and where the normal annual rent for cottages was sixpence a year. At that rate of pay, it would have taken the average footsoldier just over 32,000 years to pay the ransom on his own. The value of the whole ransom, £100,000, might provide you with the purchasing power of perhaps £2 billion today. But it is impossible to work out an exact equivalent, given that government in the twelfth century was so much smaller. The 150,000 marks was about three times anything the English government had raised in any previous year – and, of course, it had to be raised over and above the annual administrative costs of the kingdom. It was as if the current British government were suddenly expected to pay a one-off fee of over a trillion pounds, or three times their annual expenditure. It might not be impossible, but it would be extremely painful.

Richard's letter to his mother of 19 April, addressed to 'his dearest mother, Eleanor, Queen of England, and his justiciars and all his faithful men in England', explained that 'our dearest Chancellor, William, Bishop of Ely' – the indefatigable Long-champ – had arranged for his release from the dungeon at Trifels. It also set out the king's instructions for raising the initial 100,000 silver marks. England's administrative machinery swung into action, with a special request from Richard to the justiciars, which they must have read with a sinking feeling, to set an example by their own generosity.

The justiciars themselves were excluded from the business of collecting the ransom. The Great Council, meeting in the first week of June in St Albans, assigned this task to Hubert Walter and Richard, Bishop of London, plus William, Earl of Arundel, and Hamelin, Earl Warenne. Apart from the new Archbishop of Canterbury, the other three trustees were elderly and highly respected figures. They were also three of the only members of England's ruling elite who had managed to avoid being implicated in the deposing of Longchamp as chief justiciar in 1191 – though Warenne's daughter was John's mistress at the time, which complicated matters. In recognition of the crucial role that London's financial centre would play, Henry FitzAilwin – the formidable first mayor of London – was appointed as the fifth trustee. Through FitzAilwin, the sixteen interlocked families that dominated the business of London – including the Farringdons, Bukerels, Basings, Blunts and Viels – were, in this way, drawn into the business of raising the money. When it was raised, the ransom was to be locked away in London under the seals of Eleanor and Walter of Coutances.

When Eleanor and the other trustees sat down to work out how to raise the money, the task seemed immense. It was widely believed that England had already been stripped bare by the Saladin Tithe and the heavy taxation to finance the crusade. Even the initial downpayment of 100,000 marks was a sum beyond anything that had been calculated before. They decided not to entrust the task to the exchequer, perhaps because of a conflict of interest between the demands of the ransom and the needs of the government, and set up a parallel organization called *Scaccarium Redemptionis* or the Exchequer of Ransom.

The formidable English tax system owed its existence to Richard's father and his tireless devotion to the details of government, but the development of the new kinds of tax that were required – and which marked the future of taxation the world over – owed as much to the imprisonment of his son and the involvement of Hubert Walter's administrative wizardry.

What had once been fines for holding illegal tournaments or 'wastage of hunting' – cutting down forests illegally – became under Richard's rule simply fees paid to the government. At the same time, the old feudal fees were still central, though cash was becoming increasingly important in the economy too. Customs like *heriot* – the right of the lord to take your best horse or cattle from your family in death duty – were turning into cash payments or being abandoned completely. Or *merchet*, paid to the lord on the marriage of your daughter. The old customs – that sowers were entitled to a basketful of the seed they sowed, or the cowherd to the first seven days of milk from a cow after it had given birth – were going the same way. It was a new economy of coins and money rather than hereditary obligation, and it was a source of some regret to those who saw the old world beginning to disappear in a welter of silver pennies and rising prices. A generation before, payment for a knight's fee – the land held by a knight in return for military duties – had been a simple matter of giving the time or, maybe, occasionally just paying the money. Now knights were being granted fractions of a knight's fee, and in practice these could only be paid for in cash. That was the background on which the trustees had to work out how to raise an unprecedented sum. They decided there were broadly five possible sources, and they decided to use all of them.

The first of these was known as *scutage*. This was the levy on anyone holding land as a knight, and was traditionally in lieu of military service in time of war. Knights owed forty days a year in military support or training, and for the ransom – which was a defence of the king, after all – this was set at twenty shillings per knight's fee.

The second was an early form of income tax, which took a percentage of revenues and movable property. This tax represented the future, and had been developed by Henry's brilliant exchequer officials Nigel of Ely and his son Richard FitzNigel. The Saladin Tithe had set up mechanisms for assessing it, based on local juries who would work out what their neighbours owed. The ransom tax was set at a quarter of the annual income and a quarter of the movables of every freeman, above the rank of villein. In the case of the much poorer parish clergy, without any obvious means of earning money, it was set at a tenth.

The third source was from the churches and abbeys, which were asked to hand over all their gold and silver. Or, in the case of monastic orders that were theoretically forbidden gold and silver – like the Cistercians – the proceeds of their wool output for the year, their most substantial realizable asset. This was intended as a loan: the Exchequer of Ransom promised that all gold and silver plate would eventually be paid for, and in fact this promise was kept in 1195. Eleanor had the right to claim 10 per cent of everything that was paid towards the ransom, which she sensibly refused to exercise. But she did occasionally intervene to rescue particularly precious pieces of Church treasure – like the golden cup belonging to the monks of Bury St Edmunds, which she arranged to be returned to the abbey. Treasure from England's churches would not be taken again until the reign of Henry VIII.

The fourth source of money was a direct appeal to the loyalty of Richard's office holders at every level of society. Lists of these donors were sent regularly to the king in captivity. Even William the Lion, the king of Scots, sent 2,000 marks. It was made known that the most generous of them all had been Richard's close friend Baldwin of Béthune, his companion on the exhausting journey through central Europe, who had been arrested in Friesach but was now home again. Even the poor were asked to donate what they could. 'No subject, rich or poor, was overlooked,' wrote the chronicler William of Newburgh.

Finally, there were the financiers. Mayor FitzAilwin imposed a special tax on London for the ransom, but the bulk of this demand fell on the Jewish community, many of them among the wealthiest people – though also the most oppressed – in England.

We are in sensitive territory here. Jews had been under the 'special protection' of kings since the days of Charlemagne, but were banned from nearly all professions except moneylending, which was also forbidden to Christians under canon law. It is a myth that Jews were the only bankers in England. The Templars and Lombards were beginning to rival the Jewish bankers as financiers to the nobility, though it is hard to tell because most loans to the king were not included in the official balance sheets, and were excluded from the Pipe Rolls that recorded most of the other financial transactions of government. But there is no doubt that, despite their precarious position in society, some of the Jewish community were extremely wealthy, representing – or so it was believed – up to a third of the movable wealth of the nation.

But this was the relatively tolerant twelfth century, and the Jewish community, while not exactly integrated into society, had been involved in finance at every level, as well as their own academic and literary life. But it was a precarious tolerance, as they discovered in the terrible events after Richard's coronation, when one of the most brilliant rabbis in Europe – Jacob of Orléans – was killed after being caught up in the post-coronation massacre in London. But there was no doubt that one of the main reasons for the royal protection of the Jewish community was that princes required the services of generous bankers. When they deemed it appropriate, they also felt they had the right to exact considerably more than they would from their Christian subjects. Only a few years before, in 1185, the money owed to the richest man in England, the financier Aaron of Lincoln, was simply seized by the crown when he died. The first proceeds of this and his liquid wealth were sent over to Normandy to help in the military stand-off with Philip Augustus in February 1187, and the whole amount was lost when the vessel carrying it sank in a storm somewhere between Shoreham and Dieppe.* The danger was that, at times of economic difficulty – when popular discontent focused on the activities of bankers, as it has from time to time throughout history – it was convenient to direct that rage at the Jewish community, already the subject of such discrimination, and their opulent houses so obvious in the heart of the financial districts of most of the biggest cities.

There were special laws forbidding the charging of interest over 43 per cent, though most people were paying between 10 and

---

* The government set up a special *Scaccarium Aaronis* to gather in all his debts, and this turned out to be such a complex business that it took them twenty years to bring in the whole £15,000.

20 per cent a year. This was still a sizeable sum and there had also been an explosion of borrowing in the years leading up to the ransom, as many people borrowed small sums – sometimes for pilgrimages, sometimes to go on crusade – often from their local abbey, though often actually managed on their behalf by experienced Jewish financiers. The anti-Semitism stirred up at the time of Richard's coronation was partly the result of religious mania before a crusade, but partly – especially in the case of the outrage in York – fuelled quite deliberately by minor aristocratic families who were heavily in debt. The culmination of the 1190 murders in York was the ritual burning of the debt bonds in the nave of York Minster, lit with a flame from the candles on the high altar.

It seems likely that a special tax of 3,000–5,000 marks was earmarked as the Jewish contribution to the ransom – for the time being. Richard's companion from the shipwreck, Philip of Poitou, escorted the wealthiest Jewish financiers of Winchester to London, presumably to help them lend further large sums. There may also have been a special tax on gold, which would have hit the goldsmiths and early bankers particularly hard. It was a dangerous moment for them. They had to be seen to be playing their part in raising the ransom. But if they were forced to pay too much, and found themselves having to call in loans as a result, the riots of 1189–90 might be unleashed again on a wider scale, and the whole focus of frustration at the enormous tax burden would be directed at them.

The major administrative burden of the ransom fell on the bishops in the case of raising the money from the clergy, and on the sheriffs for everyone else, along with their usual duties of revenue collection, writs, juries, prisons and arranging for visits by the justices. But the engines of English administration were soon grinding away. The local juries were meeting, and the bailiffs were at work. Soon the accounts of the ransom payments – long since lost – must have been recorded on pipe rolls, sewn together at the head like the great roll of the exchequer. The ransom office organized itself in parallel to the exchequer, using a great cloth in the form of a chess board – a form of abacus – across which sheriffs from every county were expected to justify their accounts.

These accounts were also recorded using tally sticks, nine inches of wood – usually hazel – with the big numbers recorded in different sized and shaped notches on one side, and the small numbers in the same way on the other. Once the sum was agreed, the tally stick was split in two, then half was given to the sheriff as a receipt and half kept as evidence of payment, with the name written across the break so that it would match if ever it had to.

One reason why England was better able to afford the ransom than contemporaries might have expected was that – for the first time in history – it was beginning to suffer the first signs of serious inflation. The replacement of all those feudal customs and obligations with silver pennies, and the unprecedented flood of coinage from all over the world to pay for English exports, had meant that there was beginning to be too much money in circulation chasing too few goods – the classic recipe for rising prices. It was the only region of Europe that was affected in this way. Since the 1160s, in the lifetime of the king, some agricultural prices had risen by about 130 per cent. Oxen, which had cost three shillings in the 1170s, were now priced at double that. Wheat was over two and a half times as expensive. Knights were now paid twice what they had received a generation before.

The English were encountering this phenomenon for the first time and had little idea what was causing the prices to rise. But for landlords who were receiving fixed rents from their tenants – as many of them were – this was about to be a serious problem. Increasingly and inexorably, their incomes were beginning to dwindle compared to the prices they had to pay. Nearly everyone else in this overwhelmingly rural society was producing food of some kind, and their incomes were rising, and then being gobbled up by rising rents. This burgeoning inflation would be the great driver of the process that was also ending feudal payments in peppercorns or crops, and demanding higher and higher rents in cash, and it would continue for over a century. With rising prices, rising rents and loans called in to pay for the ransom, it was also a

dangerous period for those small artisans and farmers on whom the
burden of the ransom would eventually fall.

Much of the silver was paid in the form of treasure that was melted
down into ingots, but a sizeable proportion came in silver coins.
These could have been from anywhere in the world, but were
mainly the new silver pennies instituted by Henry II's mint master
Isaac the Jew, who was immortalized rather unflatteringly as a
character in Sir Walter Scott's novel *Ivanhoe*.★ These standard coins
were made of 92.5 per cent pure silver, known later as 'the ancient
right standard of England', which survived until the 1920s. Each
coin, even in Richard's reign, carried a simple picture of a bearded
monarch and the legend HENRICVS. They were reliable and widely
copied around Europe.

   As this money poured in all over the country, under the watchful
eye of Eleanor and her officials, it was making its way by cart under
armed escort to London. From there it was taken to St Paul's
Cathedral, where it was put into massive chests and locked in the
crypt – the venue for London's triannual folkmoot in bad weather
– near the tomb of Ethelred the Unready, under heavy guard, and
sealed with the seals of Walter of Coutances and Eleanor herself.
It was yet more recognition of the financial status of London.

   St Paul's was not quite the unusual choice it might seem,
because, as one of the largest buildings in the world, it was the
social, political and administrative centre of London. The St Paul's
Cross outside the cathedral, with its banks of seats around it, had
been the venue for the Folkmoot that had decided the fate of
Longchamp in 1191. The bell towers at the west end of the
cathedral were used as prisons. The vaults alongside those which
held the chests of silver were rented out, one to a local carpenter,
another to a wine merchant. Behind the high altar, the jewels on
St Erkenwald's tomb were supposed to cure eye problems and

★ The chronicler Ralph of Diceto, then Dean of St Paul's, praised Isaac rather
as the English praised Mussolini for getting the trains to run on time, on the
grounds that he had managed for once to make the coins round.

were used for that purpose. The foot of the first prebendary of Islington, sculpted on the base of one of the main pillars, was the standard measure of twelve inches used by the city. The nave above the silver – still unfinished – echoed to the sound of hundreds of conversations and the clack of hurrying feet as the city did its business. The font was becoming used as a counter for settling debts. There were drunkards sleeping on benches by the door of the choir. One pillar near the great west door was used by people looking for work. The south aisle of the nave was used by moneylenders, the north aisle for selling horses, and the central nave was known as the venue for gossip.★ Old St Paul's was already the third cathedral on the site, and was considerably larger than the later building by Sir Christopher Wren, and it was what it had traditionally always been: the beating heart of London.†

But while the silver was mounting up, there remained the question of the hostages whom Richard had agreed to provide – initially 200 of them – both to the emperor and to Leopold in Vienna. Eleanor had been asked to take particular responsibility for their recruitment and dispatch to Germany. If the records of how the money was raised are now sparse, that is nothing to the silence that has descended over the difficult business of persuading the leading families of the land to send their sons as hostages for the remainder of the ransom. After all, hostages could not just be chosen at random from the population. They had to be worth something themselves, should it come to the point that the king's ransom was not forthcoming. The bitter disputes, the refusals and the appeals that must have taken up so much of Eleanor's time have nearly all but disappeared from the pages of history.

We know that Eleanor set out her decision about how to proceed at the Great Council meeting in Ely. Here it was decided

---

★In later centuries this became known as Duke Humphrey's Walk. Layabouts, hopeless gossips and people who had nowhere better to go at dinnertime were said to be 'dining with Duke Humphrey'.

†Wren is supposed to have arranged for his grave ('If you seek my monument, look around') to be on the spot where the high altar had been in the twelfth century.

in more detail which great families should send their sons, and how the resulting appeals would be heard. In the event, the final agreement at Worms stipulated that Richard would have to find only sixty hostages for the emperor and seven for Leopold, which was more achievable. The decision was taken, probably by Eleanor, that it would make political sense for the list to be headed by the two most eminent people in the government, the chief justicier and the Chancellor – then still Walter of Coutances and William Longchamp. This was probably also a ruse to persuade Longchamp to stay abroad longer, knowing that his reappearance would almost certainly cause trouble. If it was, it was less than effective, because Richard had already sent him back to England with messages and instructions that he should accompany the chosen hostages to Germany.

Others on the list included Berengaria's younger brother, Fernando of Navarre, and Henry of Saxony's eldest son, Otto, who had been managing affairs in Aquitaine in Richard's absence. Otto was a favourite nephew of Richard's: Richard had made him Earl of York, made strenuous efforts to have him named heir to the throne of Scotland and would later intrigue to have him succeed Henry VI as Holy Roman Emperor. Other hostages included Otto's younger brother, William of Winchester, Richard's friend Baldwin of Béthune and Bishop Savaric of Bath. There was also the four-year-old son of a nobleman called Roger de Tosny, a cousin of the Count of Hainault, who removed the boy from Eleanor's care later as she passed through with the hostages on their way to Germany. Another hostage – this time destined for the contingent bound for Austria – was a knight called Hugh de Morville, probably the very same person who had, as a young man, kept the spectators and monks back from Canterbury Cathedral while his three friends murdered Thomas Becket. His inclusion on the list was perhaps a sign of final acceptance by English society twenty-five years later.

The negotiation to choose hostages was particularly arduous, but it became obvious quite early on what the main problem was. Longchamp's reputation as a pederast made it quite impossible for some families to accept the idea of putting their young sons into his care. Over and over again, the same message was conveyed to Eleanor. If it was a question of daughters, they would be quite happy for Longchamp to accompany them to Germany, but since it was sons they preferred to err on the side of safety.

Longchamp headed straight back to England after the end of the Worms court meeting. It would be his first visit since the embarrassing incident with the fisherman when he was trying to escape disguised as a woman. He probably dreaded his arrival as much as his successors in the English government did, but he had been given a task to perform – and letters from the king might have been expected to smooth his reception. In the event, it was even colder than he could have anticipated.

He landed in Ipswich and spent the night in the village of Hitcham, sending a message to Abbot Samson at Bury St Edmunds that he would like to hear mass at St Edmund's shrine the next day. Longchamp must have felt that this was a suitably unthreatening and low-key way of announcing his arrival, but it was not to be. Samson believed he was still under excommunication and ordered that no services should take place at the abbey in Longchamp's presence. When Longchamp reached there the next day, the priest stood motionless and silent at the altar until the miserable Chancellor had been ushered outside again.

He then set out towards London, but was refused entry to the city at the gates. A flurry of messages passed backwards and forwards between him and the justiciars, who finally agreed – along with Eleanor – to meet him in St Albans and to receive the letters from Richard. When they finally all reached the agreed spot, Richard's new government refused to give him the traditional kiss of greeting. Worse, they refused even to let him deliver his messages until he had assured the entire party that he came 'not as a justiciar, not as a legate, not as Chancellor, but as a simple bishop and messenger from the lord king'.

Richard's messages included a list of bishops and nobility he wanted to join him in Germany, and they confirmed that Longchamp had been appointed to take the hostages back there. It was clear that something would have to be said, and Eleanor took it upon herself to say it. There were absolutely no circumstances, she said, in which she would entrust him with her own grandson – in this case, Henry of Saxony's youngest son, William of Winchester. Once Eleanor had said so, the other justiciars followed suit. There was really no way they could persuade the hostages to go if they had to go with him. For Longchamp, this was a complete humiliation. The meeting broke up without agreement, and Eleanor wrote to Richard advising him to recall his Chancellor. Some weeks later, Longchamp was making his way back down the Rhine alone. Whether as punishment or consolation, he was even relieved from his role as a hostage himself and his place was taken by a man called Baldwin Wake.

Richard may have been popular in England, but it was impossible to impose the equivalent of a 25 per cent income tax – higher even than the UK basic rate is today – on a country that had never encountered such an idea before without dissent. The contemporary chronicler William of Newburgh described how the fund-raising progressed:

The royal officers accelerated the business throughout England, without sparing anyone; nor was there any distinction made between clergy and laymen, secular or regular, citizen or husbandman; but all indifferently were compelled to pay the stipulated sum for the king's ransom, either in proportion to their substance or the amount of their revenues. Privileges, prerogatives, immunities of churches and monasteries, were neither pleaded nor admitted. Every dignity, every liberty was silent; nor had any one licence to say: 'Such, and so great am I; have me excused' . . .

The records of exactly where the money came from have disappeared, but it seems clear that the local juries charged with the task of assessing the tax that every freeman should pay had an exhausting and difficult task. The bailiffs who were then expected to collect this unprecedented tax, many of them appointed by Henry II in the massive root and branch reform of the institution twenty years before, must have had an even more difficult time. If individuals simply refused to pay, the bailiffs would have had some means of applying local pressure and military support that could have enforced the settlement. But if more than a handful refused, and if those refusals included anybody with any local standing and power, the bailiffs would have had no redress. For territories under the control of barons who were sceptical about the whole operation – even actively intriguing for their own reasons for John to succeed – the business of collection must have been completely impossible. We can only imagine the favouritism, the settling of old scores and the lassitude with which some of the juries must have gone about their work.

By the high summer, two things were becoming clear. One was that the money was failing to pour in nearly as fast as was expected, and the other was that there was a political price to pay. This was obvious to anyone, especially in the cities, and came in the form of frustration – not so much at the obvious inequalities (that belongs to later in history) but rage at the corruption at the top, as the great landowners colluded with juries to decide what people should pay and then wriggled out of payments themselves. Or extracted their own payments from their tenants. It was anger that seems to have overlooked the role of their absent king, but focused on his ministers and barons. This is the pattern you find in the Robin Hood legend, set at this time, which retains a reverent attitude to the law and extends a poignant hope towards the king, who would return like Odysseus to Ithaca or Christ to the temple – cleansing and righting wrongs. 'I love not man in all the world/ so well as I do my King,' says Robin in an early version of the ballad.

This attitude was deepened by the news that John had forged a copy of the royal seal, imposed a swingeing tax on his own tenants in the name of the Exchequer of Ransom, but had kept the money himself.

This mounting rage was not directed at the social system. It was aimed at the behaviour of lords and landowners, not at their existence. It was a fury that was stoked by the attitude of the

Church, as they handed over their precious plate and chalices for melting down. Some of their wealth was not just luxury for the government to take as it pleased; it was holy relics without price. Abbot Samson dared the exchequer to take any of the jewels off the shrine at Bury St Edmunds, where Longchamp had recently been dismissed. 'The fury of St Edmund can reach those who are absent and far away,' he warned. 'Much more will it strike those who are present and desire to strip his shirt from him.'

Peter of Blois wrote to his old friend the Archbishop of Mainz complaining about the effects of the ransom. The Germans, he said, 'Those children of perdition, were levying a treasure that would not be drawn from the royal exchequer, but from the patrimony of Christ, the pitiful substance of the poor, the tears of widows, the pittance of monks and nuns, the dowries of maidens, the substance of scholars, the spoils of the Church.'

There was particular trouble in York, where Richard's half-brother Archbishop Geoffrey was demanding that his canons contribute a quarter of their incomes, although the original demand had been for only a tenth. They refused and accused him of trying to undermine the freedom of the Church. The argument became confused with disputes over the appointment of the new Dean of York, three candidates for which seem to have been appointed at the same time.★ When he heard about the squabble, Richard asked Geoffrey to visit him in Germany to discuss the issue face to face, but as soon as he had set out on the road, the canons launched a protest about the ransom money, stripping the altars, silencing the bells and locking York Minster. Geoffrey turned straight round and ordered them to open it again.

Similar tensions were emerging all over the country. There were also demagogues emerging in the cities. One of these was William FitzOsbert, a social reformer and campaigner against 'royal extortion', characterized by his magnetic style and his long flowing

---

★ One was John of Béthune, brother of Richard's great friend and companion Baldwin. Another was Richard's clerk, Philip of Poitou, who had also been shipwrecked with him.

beard, who began making long speeches under St Paul's Cross, castigating the city leaders for their oppression of the poor. It was the tax on income imposed on London for the ransom by the new mayor that particularly enraged him. His regular harangues from outside the cathedral gathered momentum in the following months until, two years later, London erupted with an uprising of small traders and artisans under his leadership. When this collapsed a few hours later, he took refuge in the church of St Mary-le-Bow, from where Hubert Walter had him dragged out, tried and hanged. The evidence is contradictory, but it is possible that he was hanged in chains from a tree at Tyburn, now Marble Arch, which would have made him the first of tens of thousands to be put to death at that spot over the next six centuries. Wherever it was, splinters from his scaffold were treasured as holy charms.*

One of the problems was that the biggest moneylenders, just as the Jewish community feared, were being forced to pay considerably more than was comfortable, and to loan more to the Exchequer of Ransom. That meant they were often forced to call in their loans, and simple self-preservation meant that these were the ones to people furthest down the social hierarchy. When small landowners were losing their land or their homes because they could not afford to pay back loans that were not even due, you had a recipe for widespread social rage and misery. And although there were many Christian moneylenders, the whole business of the ransom seems to have accelerated the spread of anti-Semitism in England.

Sometimes the only option for indebted landowners who had lost their estates was to escape into the forests, traditionally set aside for the king for hunting. In times of political or economic difficulty, the forests increasingly became the gathering place for the dispossessed, for bands of armed poachers and other outlaws, for younger sons who could not be supported at home, for ordinary thieves, heretics and millenarian fanatics. Forests were dangerous places,

---

* St Paul's Cross, the scene of London's folkmoots, lasted rather longer. It was pulled down and replaced by an elm tree by Parliament in 1643.

dark and mysterious havens of magic and gloom where you might risk enchantment by the little people, or face the jaws of a monstrous worm or even – if you were very lucky – catch a glimpse of King Arthur and his knights riding through the trees by torchlight.*

The great outlaws of the age all spent time in the forests. Eustace the Monk, for example, went from being a traditional outlaw in the forest to an admiral helping the French invade England. And Fulk Fitzwarin from the Welsh marches – whose full-scale rebellion was to set the scene for the signing of the Magna Carta a generation later – was enraged by favours shown to his local rivals and also ended up in the forest.† Fulk had actually been brought up in the royal court and was a friend of Richard's, and he invented his own style of banditry, attacking only property that belonged to John.

Centuries later, historians placed one of the most famous outlaws of all time in this period of English history: a limbo time without a monarch and with increasing resentment of the power of the wealthy. By the time Sir Walter Scott was writing *Ivanhoe* before 1819, he was able to conjure up a tale in which Robin Hood and his outlaws sided with a mysterious knight in disguise who turned out to be Richard himself, hurrying to undo the wrongs imposed on the country – and on the Jewish community in particular – by John, his allies and the evil Templars.

The true identity of Robin Hood has never been discovered. We know that his first mention in literature was in 1377 in William Langland's classic *Piers Plowman*, in which a drunken priest criticized himself for knowing the rhymes of Robin Hood better than he knew his prayers. The legend itself is much older than that. The *trouvère* Adam de la Halle wrote a song in the 1260s called 'Jeu de Robin et Marion'. By then the legend must have been so widespread that many people – and not all of them criminals – were nicknamed 'Robinhood'.

---

*Sir John Conyers is supposed to have killed a dragon in the forests near Darlington during Richard's reign. So the legend goes.

†As with Robin Hood, Fulk's name was borrowed by rival outlaw groups. When one robber did so in his own lifetime, Fulk hunted him down and forced him personally to behead the rest of his gang.

Unfortunately for those of us who would prefer our legends to be based on solid fact, there is little evidence to date Robin Hood's activities to the period of Richard's imprisonment. That, however, was the consensus in the seventeenth century, thanks partly to the work of the Scottish historian John Major, who explained that Robin Hood would 'allow no woman to suffer injustice'. 'The robberies of this man I condemn,' he wrote. 'But of all robbers, he was the humanest and the chief.' By then, Robin was said to have been born in 1160 in Loxley – in Yorkshire or Nottingham-shire or possibly even Warwickshire – and called Robert Fitzooth. He was also supposed to have used the title, perhaps ironically, of the Earl of Huntingdon. He died, so the story goes, at Kirklees Monastery on 18 November 1248 at the age of eighty-seven. In 1690 his gravestone was still in what had been the monastery grounds, with an almost indecipherable inscription – in spelling unknown to antiquarians – that said:

> Hear undernead dis laitl stean,
> Laiz Robert earl of Huntingtun.
> Near archir ver az hie sa geud
> And pipl kauld im Robin Heud.

Little John was supposed to have been exiled to Ireland, though there was also a grave claimed to be his in Hathersage in Derbyshire.*

Doubts about this story emerged when it became clear that Robin's complex genealogy had actually been invented by the anti-quarian William Stukeley in 1746 and that, underneath the Kirklees gravestone, the earth had not actually been disturbed. Most of the stone disappeared in the nineteenth century, despite Victorian rail-ings, because the navvies working on the Yorkshire & Lancashire Railway believed that fragments from it could cure toothache.

---

* The grave was opened in 1764 and a thirty-inch thigh bone extracted, which was put in the window of the home of the parish clerk. It was stolen from there by the antiquarian Sir George Strickland.

Since then, a series of possible candidates for Robin Hood have been culled from the legal records. The most promising was a fugitive in the Yorkshire assize roles for 1225–6 called Robert Hod or Hobbehod, who may also have been the outlaw Robert of Wetherby, who was eventually hanged. The man who hunted him down, Eustace of Lowdham, had been deputy sheriff of Nottingham and later became the sheriff. There was also a Robert FitzOdo from Loxley, who was stripped of his knighthood in the 1190s. The sheriff of Nottingham from 1209 to 1224, Philip Mark, was known for his own robberies, false imprisonments and seizure of land.

Oddly enough, the real Earl of Huntingdon in the period of Richard's imprisonment was the brother of William the Lion, the king of Scots. David, Earl of Huntingdon, took part in Richard's coronation and shortly afterwards married the sister of Ranulf, Earl of Chester. This is a peculiar coincidence because the fourteenth-century poem *Piers Plowman* talks about 'the Rymes of Robyn Hood and Randolf Erl of Chestre'. There are no mentions of the earl in official records at all while Richard was away, which may mean he was also on crusade. And in fact, David was actually outlawed in 1212, accused – quite correctly – of taking part in a plot to kill John, and he sided with the barons against the king in 1215.

But all this is some way from the Robin Hood of legend, the gentleman thief, kind to women, stealing from the rich and giving to the poor. Modern commentators believe the original was either an entirely mythical figure of fertility – a cross between Robin Goodfellow and the Green Man, pricking the pride of pompous aristocrats by playing practical jokes – or an outlaw perhaps at the beginning of the thirteenth century, or possibly both. But the consensus is for an early date to allow the legends to grow up enough for Robin Hood, Maid Marian, Little John and the rest to take the absolutely central role they did later in English culture.

But even if Robin Hood was not a historical figure at all, it was an intelligent guess to lodge him in legend in the uncertain period of doubt and heavy taxation during Richard's imprisonment. He is a cultural figure who belongs to a period of outrage – when the old feudal obligations were disappearing, and the lure of silver coins was drawing the ambitious away to the cities, where money seemed to be flooding into the pockets of the new urban traders, and punitive taxation was impoverishing the small farmers, while it was accumulated by the rich and powerful. The tenacity of a Robin Hood legend set in the 1190s, subtly siding with the absent king against the corrupt forces trying to take his place – lodged in the royal forests and outside the corrupted law – says more about the way that period was regarded in the seventeenth century than it does about Robin Hood himself, but there is an element of truth in it. People were prepared to pay the ransom, but as long as everyone paid – and not everybody was paying. Robin Hood is a story about the drift of money from farmers to merchants, and a hero – living in the territory of the wounded king, in the murky upside-down world of the forests – who was prepared to do something about it.

One of those who fell victim to Robin Hood, or the outlaws who provided the pattern for him, was Hugh of Nonant, the Bishop of Coventry, who had appointed himself John's senior propagandist, and led the campaign to persuade the barons that Richard was dead. Since John had fled to the French court, Hugh's position had become increasingly delicate – and even more so since his brother Robert Brito had refused to be a hostage on the grounds that he was a pledged supporter of John's. All too soon, the message that Hugh must have dreaded arrived: a summons from Richard to visit him in Germany. Very sensibly, he loaded himself up with all the money he could, but he was robbed of everything on the road near Canterbury. Longchamp's brother-in-law, still castellan of Dover Castle, was again suspected of complicity and was excommunicated.

Two worries dominated the minds of the English government by the beginning of September 1193. One was that there was still no firm date for Richard's release, even though they had long since accepted the principle of the ransom and agreed its sum as many as three months before. The other was that still not nearly enough money was coming in.

You have to sympathize with the officials of the Exchequer of Ransom. England had the most sophisticated system of taxation in Western Europe, but it was still rudimentary compared to modern systems, and the most important tax – the 25 per cent – had barely been tested before. There was no census of the kingdom, no economic data about incomes and production were available, and the voluminous Domesday Book survey of landholding was over a century old. It really was impossible to predict how much money should be forthcoming, even before the horse-trading at local level between the juries, the bailiffs and the barons.

Perhaps it should not have been a surprise to them, then, that the main disappointment was the paltry sum that had been forthcoming from the 25 per cent tax on income and movables, which seems to have raised a meagre £7,000. If it had been administered faultlessly, the authorities had believed it would raise £25,000. It was probably organized along the lines of the old system set up by Henry II, yet even this should have yielded £12,000. It was soon apparent that more taxes were going to be needed. A second tax round was imposed on anyone with property valued over ten shillings (known as the 'Ten Shillings and Upwards Tax'). Some months later – at the Great Council meeting in Nottingham in April the following year – a third round of taxes was set out, including a tax of two shillings per landowner per hide. This was a very old-fashioned tax, based on the Danegeld introduced by the Anglo-Saxons and known as *carucage*. Its efficiency can be judged by the fact that the Exchequer of Ransom was forced to use the Domesday Book, despite its age, as the basis for working out who owned what.

There was also the idea of a fine on some of those who had supported John in 1191, including a special fine on the people of York of 200 marks, for their role in the anti-Semitic slaughter of the same year. Eleanor sent emissaries to Anjou and Aquitaine with special requests to some of the abbeys in Angevin lands on the Continent. This was obviously heeded, especially in Normandy –

which felt especially threatened by the French – and where the people of Caen finally gave even more money than the people of London.

The local coinages were continuing to circulate among peasants and small businesses, and were probably increased to compensate for the loss of all that silver. But when the moneylenders were forced to call in loans to pay the extra demands of the Exchequer of Ransom, that hardship – on top of the extra tax the small landowners were having to pay – came as an enormous burden on the class that borrowed most: the minor aristocrats, the landowners, the emerging middle classes, the small traders. It was they who bore the brunt of the ransom, and they directed their rage not against the king or his advisers, but against the people who had lent them money.

The obvious pressure on the Jewish community also seems to have been high on Hubert Walter's agenda. He set up a belated inquiry into the events in 1190 and 1191, intended to bring the leaders of the murderous riots to justice, and the whole adminis-tration's stance on Jewish affairs was put into better order partly as a way of regulating bank lending, and partly as a way of protect-ing the nation's Jews better than before when the ransom was having the side-effect of putting them in danger. William of St Mary Église was given the job of supervising Jewish affairs and joint Christian–Jewish committees were set up in seven cities where Jewish financiers were working. Records of debts were to be pro-tected and financiers were asked to take an oath on the Pentateuch to conduct their banking openly.

But there was another payback expected from them as well. In March 1194 Walter organized a major conference of Jewish finan-ciers in Northampton, with representatives of the Jewish com-munities from all over the country, to work out how much more they could afford to pay and lend to the ransom. It must have been especially poignant to all those who attended that there were no representatives left from the cities that had suffered the worst anti-Jewish violence in 1190 – York, Stamford, Dunstable, King's Lynn and Bury St Edmunds.

But that is to leap ahead by six months, because it was actually September 1193 when these matters first came to a head. The feast of Michaelmas in September was the end of the farming and therefore of the financial year, when all around the country, reeves were called upon by the bailiffs to account for the yield of the manors they were responsible for. It was the moment the Exchequer of Ransom began to take stock and realized just how far the yield was falling short. It also marked the arrival in London of a number of German emissaries from the emperor, sent to find out how the ransom-raising was progressing. They inspected the great chests under St Paul's, looked at the Pipe Rolls of the Exchequer of Ransom, checked through the tally sticks and seem to have had a riotous visit to London for a month. Some time in late October or early November – the date was not recorded – the preparations seemed to the emissaries to be complete enough to allow them to take delivery of the first tranche of the ransom. Eleanor and the other trustees must have been present to make sure that their valuable charge was safely dispatched.

This was the time when London began to assume its pre-eminence among the English cities, while the government was increasingly based a little to the west at Westminister. So it was from Westminster Palace, with the great medieval hall built by William Rufus and the cathedral built by Edward the Confessor, that Eleanor and her entourage set out for the ceremony of handing over the largest tranche of silver to the Germans. Eleanor was in her early seventies and must have been carried in her litter along the 'Royal Street', what is now Whitehall, with the leper hospital of St James across the fields to her left, a figure of legendary veneration and fascination to everyone standing transfixed as she passed by.

At the hermitage of St Catherine in the small village of Charing, she turned right into Akeman Street, with a glance perhaps down the road to the west towards what is now Piccadilly. Akeman Street, also known as the Strand, was not yet the magnificent road built by the Templars with palaces along either side. It was still a Saxon track with open spaces and bushes along it, with a view down to the sandy edge of the river and its wharves to the right, and construction taking place to build the first of the great houses that would soon line the road. Past the fields and occasional cattle drover, she came to the dairy farm that marked the beginning of the parish of Danish merchants and seafarers, and St Clement Danes Church, with its tomb of Cnut's son Harold Harefoot. Then past the new Temple Church in the distance to her right – scene of her recent encounter with her husband's illegitimate son Geoffrey of York – and on down the gentle slope to the bridge over the River Fleet, with its small ships and lighters packed together, with their square sails furled, jostling in the current below Baynard's Castle next to the Thames. Then through Ludgate and up the hill towards St Paul's, with its great square tower soaring above it.

It was an excitable city, filled with soldiers, banners and crowds of the usual mixture of traders, artisans, prostitutes, beggars, quacks and street performers, with pigs and horses in the street, and the workshops crowded at eye level as she passed by, and the overhanging upper storeys, painted in bright red, blue or black above them. And Eleanor herself was the main object of excitement – Eleanor and the money.

The great chests filled with silver in the crypt were emptied and their contents put into boxes and barrels, and then carried up through the cathedral and out of the door in the south transept, where the wagons and packhorses were waiting. From there it was a short but slow journey, surrounded by soldiers and fascinated Londoners, down to the dock at Queenhithe, then London's most important wharf, and much frequented now that it was also home to London's first public lavatory. As the wagon wheels crunched along the stone streets, the sound of dancing songs known as carols from St Paul's choristers on the top of the cathedral tower wafted over the hunched houses to speed the ransom on its way.

It is hard to work out exactly how much was sent to Germany at Michaelmas with the emissaries and, presumably, a powerful armed force of English soldiers. It was probably rather more than half of the initial downpayment of 100,000 silver marks, mostly in ingots – the melted-down treasures of churches across the land – and in barrel upon barrel of silver coins, tied to wagons and horses.

It may have been the whole 100,000 marks. But we can be certain that, in this small fleet of ships, the consignment of at least fifteen tons of silver began its long journey down the Thames estuary, across the North Sea and down the Rhine – in precisely the opposite direction to the usual flow of silver coins cascading north across Europe to buy English wool and wheat.

Eleanor and her officials from the Exchequer of Ransom stood on the dock at Queenhithe, watching the fleet manoeuvre past the half-completed London Bridge and sail up the river on the tide. As they held their breath for its safe passage across the sea, they must also have been praying that this would finally succeed in wresting a clear date for Richard's release from the emperor.

The emperor was delighted with the arrival of the first tranche of silver. He was even more pleased to hear from his emissaries of the detailed preparations being made in England to raise the rest, and of the wealth of London – Europe's boom city – where it was being held. But now it came to the point of actually agreeing a date for the release of his priceless captive, Henry was in a dilemma. Should he stick to his word, or would holding on to Richard longer prove equally valuable to the French?

For the rest of November the emperor agonized over the decision, weighing up the diplomatic possibilities. But there was now a powerful contingent of English diplomats at his court and they were pressing on his own officials the benefits of a long-term alliance with England, reminding him of his ultimate ambition to subject France and the rest of continental Europe to the old boundaries of the empire, as it was in the days of Charlemagne. Finally the imperial court made its decision, and the following letter arrived in London in early December:

Henry by the grace of God, Emperor of the Romans, and ever august, to his dearly beloved friends, the archbishops, earls, barons, knights, and all the faithful subjects of Richard, illustrious King of England, his favour and every blessing. We have thought proper to intimate to all and every one of you that we have appointed a certain day for the liberation of our dearly beloved friend, your lord Richard, the illustrious King of the English, being the second day of the week next ensuing after the expiration of three weeks from the day of the nativity of our lord, at Speyer, or else at Worms; and we have appointed seven days after that as the day of his coronation as King of Provence, which we have promised to him; and this you are to consider certain and undoubted. For it is our purpose and our will to exalt and highly honour your aforesaid lord, as being our special friend.

Whether Eleanor entirely trusted Henry or not, this was definitely hopeful. The coronation of Richard as king of Provence was only a gesture – Henry had absolutely no power to enforce his jurisdiction around Arles and Marseilles – but it was a useful one. It would strengthen Richard in his southern territories, and it would surround Philip Augustus even further. It was intended as a special mark of imperial affection, and an outward symbol of the new alliance between England and Germany.

So it was that on 20 December – exactly a year since Richard's arrest in Vienna – Eleanor set off from Queenhithe herself with the rest of the original 100,000 marks downpayment. She was accompanied by another powerful force of soldiers, plus bishops and barons and the sixty-seven hostages, and travelled across the North Sea and down the Rhine. It was an arduous winter journey for a woman in her seventies and they arrived exhausted at the imperial court on 17 January the following year. With every mile they progressed, Eleanor's suspicions of the emperor deepened.

The payment of such an unimaginable sum of money, when it was still unclear whether Henry VI would actually release Richard at all, was a painful gamble for Eleanor. She would not then have understood that she was also helping the English economy. Removing a quarter of the nation's money from circulation ought perhaps to have provided just the deflationary shock that England needed to calm the inflation that was beginning to eat its way into everyday life, although there is no evidence that it actually did yet. On the other hand, taken together, the vast ransom plus the other large payments that followed in later years – the enormous sums spent to secure the post of Holy Roman Emperor for Richard's favourite nephew, Otto – eventually did the trick. Early the next century, the rising prices fell back to more manageable levels.

Taxation for Richard's ransom had a profound effect on English government. The accounts may have long since disappeared – and may even have been destroyed by those who felt embarrassed by the public record of their generosity to Richard when his brother was on the throne. But it marked the beginning of a shift from feudal payments to the very start of taxing income. The English would have to wait just over 600 years before the first proper income tax was instituted, and then it was set at only 10 per cent. When it finally arrived, just for eighteen years, to pay for the Napoleonic Wars, those who paid it so grudgingly might have reflected that the tax took its first tentative steps to release a king from prison.

All that survived as a record of the greatest tax ever imposed on England were those wooden tally sticks, the receipts and raw material for the accounts, which marked each transaction for the ransom. They may have survived, along with all the other tally sticks that were used by the English administration for centuries, kept in large, useless piles around the Palace of Westminster long after they had become redundant antiques. By the early nineteenth century they were simply stored in heaps in the room that had originally been the Court of the Star Chamber under King James II, and when it was decided to restore the courtroom for other uses in 1834, the Westminster clerk of works was ordered simply to get rid of the tally sticks however he could.

On 16 October his workmen put them into the stove in the House of Lords, which overheated and set fire to the panelling. As a result, the receipts from Richard's ransom, nearly six and a half centuries later, contributed to the disastrous fire that left the Houses of Parliament a smouldering heap of rubble. The conflagration was immortalized in an extraordinary painting by the young J. M. W. Turner, and all that remained of the old medieval Palace of Westminster, except for Westminster Hall, where Eleanor held her councils, was burned to the ground. It was replaced by the neo-

Gothic structure, along with Big Ben, that represents a nineteenth-century medievalist's view of what the Age of Chivalry should have been like.

10. The Return of the King

Venison and fowls were plenty there,
With fish out of the river.
King Richard swore, on sea or shore,
He ne'er was feasted better.

The Ballad of Robin Hood

Sumer is icomen in
Lhude sing cuccu!
Groweth sed and bloweth med
And spingth the wude nu
Sing cuccu!

contemporary English verse

As soon as Eleanor arrived at the German court with the hostages and the rest of the first 100,000 silver marks, her worst fears were realized. As she had been making her journey down the Rhine, Philip and John were hatching a final plan to keep Richard in prison. Their offer was generous enough to severely tempt the emperor to change his mind about Richard's release and the alliance he had been planning with him to isolate the French. Philip and John's letter reached Henry only a few days before Eleanor arrived. It offered him £1,000 a month for as long as he kept Richard captive, or £80,000 to keep him in prison until the autumn, which meant the end of the next military campaigning season – by which time, they believed, they would have achieved their objectives. Alternatively they offered to match the entire

English ransom to keep Richard permanently incarcerated or – better still – hand him over to them.

Henry was also furious about the secret marriage between Henry of Brunswick, Richard's nephew and Henry the Lion of Saxony's eldest son, and Constance of Hohenstaufen – which made Henry of Brunswick Count Palatine by marriage – and blamed Richard for failing to prevent it. But the emperor was not completely at liberty simply to decide one way or the other whether to abandon the ransom agreement and keep him in prison. It was the assembly of German princes and bishops that had agreed to the ransom, and it was impossible for Henry to change that without bringing them into the discussion. So he postponed the date of Richard's release and summoned the imperial princes to meet him in Mainz at Candlemas on 2 February. He also showed Richard the letter from his brother and former passionate friend. History does not record Richard's reaction.

This was the news that greeted Eleanor as she arrived at the German court at Speyer in mid-January. In fact, many of the princes had already arrived there for the date the emperor had set – 'three weeks after the nativity of our Lord' – for Richard's release and his coronation as king of Provence a week later. Richard's freedom seems to have been more constrained now, and Eleanor – bitterly angry – does not seem to have been allowed to see him.

So, for a third time, Richard prepared to face the German assembly of princes and bishops to plead for his liberty. Henry knew from experience what Richard's powerful eloquence was capable of, but this time also Richard had woven a diplomatic alliance of princes and prelates who were prepared to support him. By his side, facing the court, was the familiar sight of the faithful Longchamp, but also Walter of Coutances and Savaric of Bath. His mother was in the hall as well. Richard used his speech to appeal particularly to the bishops, and called on them to vindicate the sanctity of an oath made and to protect a warrior who was still returning from crusade. At the critical moment he brought out the letter he had received from the Old Man of the Mountains, the shadowy leader of the Assassins, clearing him of any complicity in the murder of Conrad of Montferrat. There was applause at the end of his speech as Richard laid his hat at the feet of the emperor. Adolf de Altena, the archbishop-elect of Cologne, rose in his seat in support. Once again, there was weeping in the court. Richard had 'the eloquence of Nestor, the prudence of Ulysses,' according to one chronicler.

It soon became clear that Richard's new northern alliance was now working together on his behalf. Adolf of Cologne and Conrad of Wittelsbach, the Archbishop of Mainz, both urged the emperor to dismiss the emissaries from Paris and to honour his ransom agreement. 'The empire, lord emperor,' they said, 'has been sufficiently defiled by the unworthy imprisonment of a most noble king. Do thou not fix an inexpiable stain upon its honour.'

They were joined by an unexpected ally. Leopold of Austria was anxious to bring Richard's imprisonment to an end, partly to salve his conscience about the original arrest and partly to get his hands on his considerable share of the ransom money. He and Richard went through a show of reconciliation after the court broke up in deadlock, followed by nearly two days of feverish negotiations between the English and the Germans – 'anxious and difficult,' according to Walter of Coutances – with the two German archbishops acting as go-betweens.

Henry realized that he had been outmanoeuvred, but he was determined to extract whatever further concessions he could from the situation. He therefore made one final demand: that Richard should resign his kingdom and all the possessions of the Angevin empire to Henry, and receive them back as a vassal of the Holy Roman Empire. Perhaps this offer was actually intended to break the negotiations, giving Henry an excuse to accept the money from Philip and John; perhaps it was a genuine attempt to lock Richard into the alliance that he had always intended. Either way, it was completely unacceptable. How could the ancient crown of England, let alone the rest of the hard-won empire, be handed over to the Germans? It was unthinkable.

Except, Eleanor wondered, it was a potential way out of the

impasse. She had all but broken England with the effort of raising such an unimaginable sum, a hefty proportion of which was still theoretically at least in her possession, under the guard of her soldiers, even if it was at the imperial court. If it was necessary to make this meaningless and illegal gesture to the emperor just to release her son from his clutches, then perhaps it was worth the indignity. Her message to Richard, via his advisers, at the end of the day on 3 February was a strong recommendation to accept. And with enormous reluctance, he did so. When the court reconvened, Richard knelt at the emperor's feet and turned England from an independent kingdom into an outpost of the empire and promised payments to the emperor as his vassal of £5,000 a year.

The details of Richard's homage to the emperor were suppressed in England, though his coronation regalia was still sent from England to Germany later in the year in big chests, returned at last to Trifels. Those who had witnessed it were silent about it, and it was only written about by historians after Richard's death, with the additional information that Henry had released Richard from his promise on his deathbed. It was barely mentioned again in English history, but it rankled. Two centuries later, when the Emperor Sigismund was visiting Henry V of England, the Duke of Gloucester took a boat out to meet the visitor's ship on the tide as it arrived in Dover and, with a drawn sword, demanded that the emperor should not set foot in England until he had given up his claim to the overlordship. The whole embarrassing incident has been excised from history by the English ever since, but the German chroniclers remembered it – and so did the emperor.

At 9 a.m. on 4 February the remainder of the first 100,000 silver marks were finally handed over, and the two German archbishops conducted Richard formally into the custody of his mother. Mother and son were reunited for the first time since Sicily and, with enormous relief, his ordeal was over. Eleanor had told the Pope that worrying about the imprisonment of her favourite son had meant she had been 'worn to a skeleton, a mere thing of skin and bones'. She had described him as 'the staff of my old age, the light of my eyes'. Now at last he was free.

But the worry was not quite at an end. Eleanor deeply distrusted the emperor and she had made preparations so that, once Richard was finally released, they could leave almost immediately. Perhaps Henry had withdrawn the promise to crown him king of Provence; perhaps Richard preferred not to stay for the extra week. Either way, when a well-wisher advised Richard to go immediately, the coronation was forgotten in the haste to leave Mainz. Before he left, he wrote to his nephew Henry of Champagne and the other rulers in Outremer, promising that – if he could achieve peace at home – he would return to Acre at the agreed time. The Mainz court and the collective princes of the Holy Roman Empire also dispatched a letter to Philip and John, as agreed during the negotiations, that they expected everything taken from Richard while he was in captivity to be returned to him, and threatening that they would do everything they could to enforce this demand.

Once he heard the news that Richard had been released, Philip realized that this was his last chance and mobilized his armies. That same month, John surrendered the whole of Normandy east of the Seine to him, except for Rouen and some key castles. It was now time for Philip to take possession, and in the weeks ahead the towns of Evreux, Neubourg and Vandreuil also surrendered to him. Soon he was in control of both banks of the Seine all the way to Rouen. Time was clearly running out for the defenders.

Meanwhile, Eleanor and Richard set off with the English soldiers on boats back up the Rhine, and sure enough, as soon as they had left, the emperor changed his mind and sent out armed parties to find Richard, arrest him again and bring him back. He also sent urgent letters to Philip, informing him of this and urging him to send out naval patrols to try and intercept him in the English Channel. But it was too late. By then Richard and his mother were well on their way north to Cologne, where they spent three days as guests of the new archbishop, who – as provost of Cologne – had been one of the members of the court who had spoken up for Richard during his original trial in 1193. Richard and Eleanor were his guests at mass in the cathedral on 12 February, when Archbishop Adolf joined the choristers and sang the mass for 1 August: 'Now I know that God has sent his angel and taken me from the hand of Herod.'

Once they had gone far enough up the river and into the territories of his new network of allies in northern Europe, Richard could afford to pay his respects to some of the princes responsible for setting him free. The whole purpose of the alliance had been only partly about his freedom and only partly about trade; the main purpose was to isolate the French while Richard secured his inheritance. To that end, the promised pensions to the various princes and prelates now had to be delivered. Henry, Duke of Brabant, was given the rent from the manor of Brampton in Huntingdon. The Archbishop of Cologne got the rent from the manor of Soham in Cambridgeshire. By 16 February Richard was in Louvain; by 25 February he was in Brussels. He and his mother were entertained by the Duke of Brabant to a sumptuous banquet in his castle in Antwerp, where Eleanor sat in pride of place on Richard's right.

Antwerp was also the main port in the vicinity, and here he met the English fleet sent to collect him from Rye, including his favourite galley, *Trench-le-Mer*, under the command of Stephen de Turnham, the admiral who had conducted Berengaria and Joanna from Acre to Rome. From there, they sailed immediately down the coast of what is now Belgium to the coastal port of Zwin, these days a silted-up nature reserve but then the vital seaway to the port of Bruges. It is not clear why Richard and Eleanor did not make their way back to England as quickly as they could. Perhaps the weather was too bad. But it is possible that they were only too aware of the threat from Philip's naval patrols – as requested by the emperor – now that the French controlled the ports of Dieppe and Tréport. It would have been too ironic for Richard to fall once more into the hands of a malevolent king. But the potential of naval strategy was now exercising his mind, and he may also have wanted to survey the strategic possibilities of the nearby islands. Whatever the reason, Richard spent the next five days sleeping on board the ship and making brief forays along the coast.★

On 12 March, more than five weeks after his release, he finally weighed anchor and slipped across the North Sea in the night. Their small convoy landed at Sandwich in Kent early the next morning. It was a bright and beautiful spring day.

The arrival of the king and his mother after all this time came as a complete surprise, not just in Sandwich, but everywhere else. There was nobody to greet them as they stepped off the ship, and no arrangements for conducting them to their capital. Instead Richard went on foot to Canterbury to pay his respects at the tomb of Thomas Becket. From Canterbury, he set out on horseback – with Eleanor presumably in a litter – along the Pilgrim's Way to London, the old Roman road of Watling Street, and as they did so, the news began to spread. The first signs of spring in England welcomed the king home, and the ploughmen whispered as they passed that the beautiful sunshine was a good omen for the rest of Richard's reign. The blossom was out in the Forest of Blean, north of Canterbury, and from there Richard and Eleanor made an increasingly noisy procession through Ospringe, Sittingbourne, Newington and Rochester, where Hubert Walter had arrived to greet them, together with an enormous crowd of excited people.

At Rochester, they stayed briefly at the castle and Richard consulted with his new chief justiciar. Then it was back on to Watling Street to Strood – past the new hospital for pilgrims – to Dartford, where they crossed the River Darent at the ford. On top of Shooters Hill, they were able to get their first glimpse of London in the distance. An hour or so later, they were making their way down the Old Kent Road, past the gardens and vineyards and the new inns that were growing up south of the Thames for the burgeoning pilgrim trade. Chaucer's famous Tabard Inn, where Watling Street met the Roman Stane Street, was not yet built, but

---

★ It was the intention of Richard and his successors to fight their decisive naval action against the new French navy in these waters, and the plan worked. The first English naval victories at Damme in 1213 and Sluys in 1340 were fought there.

there were others like it, clustering around the ponds for watering horses and cattle coming from the southern markets and into London. As they reached the south bank of the river, Richard caught his first glimpse of the new London Bridge,★ now stretching part of the way across the river. It was a very different city from the one he had left four years before.

'Faster than the winds flew, [came] the report of the king's long-expected but almost despaired of return,' wrote the chronicler William of Newburgh. By the time Richard and Eleanor's increasingly unwieldy procession had reached the church of St Mary Overie (now Southwark Cathedral) on the south side of the river and was preparing to cross the old wooden bridge next to Peter Cole-church's half-built stone structure, news of their arrival had reached London. People were on the streets and the city had been cleaned and decorated for the occasion, with rushes lining the route.

Winchester was still the capital of England when Richard was young, but now it was clear that London overshadowed it thanks to its sheer scale and wealth. It was an increasingly independent city that governed itself, with Henry FitzAilwin — one of the trustees of Richard's ransom money — as its powerful mayor. It had flexed its political muscles to depose Longchamp as chief justiciar, siding with the rebels, and would do the same in 1216 by inviting the Dauphin Louis over to take the throne, just as it played a role in deposing Charles I during the English Civil War four and a half centuries ahead. The city was already repeating the radical slogan of William FitzOsbert, 'Londoners will have no king but their mayor.' Even in four years, and though it still had a population

---

★London Bridge took thirty-three years to complete. It was built on massive isles erected with enormous difficulty across the river. The first structure on it, in the middle, was a chapel dedicated to Thomas Becket, which eventually housed Peter Colechurch's tomb. It is not absolutely clear how far across the river the bridge would have reached by early 1194, but the evidence is that the northern half was built first. When a northern arch was discovered by archaeologists in 1920, it had the date 1192 carved on it, which implies that the bridge stretched only halfway across the river at that time.

of only 40,000, London had grown immeasurably in wealth as its trading and financial tentacles had stretched out towards the Baltic, Palestine and beyond.

The Germans in Richard's entourage were immediately struck by the city and told the king, had the emperor known, things would have turned out very differently. 'For really, if he could have known of these English riches, he would not easily have believed that England could be exhausted of its wealth,' they told the king. 'Nor would he have thought of sending thee away without an intolerable amount of ransom.'

What Richard's companions would have seen as they wandered around London in the days to come was its enormous energy: the splendour of the great houses outside the city walls in the suburbs of Holborn, the clatter of mills in the meadows in Finsbury and Moorgate, the chaos of the hue and cry as citizens dropped everything to chase thieves down the narrow streets, the menace of the gangs of apprentices or wealthy youths moving around the streets in defiance of the 9 p.m. curfew tolled from the church of St Martin le Grand. They would have smelt the tanneries and breweries and trodden in the piles of stinking horse dung washed eventually down into the river, along with an unpleasant concoction of fish heads, rotting meat and sewage.

There were also the horses parading at Smithfield on Fridays, the football games on the fields outside the city, and, since this was now Lent, the jousting games on fields outside the walls every Sunday. The visitors would have missed the events of Shrove Tuesday, when boys brought their fighting cocks to school. But they must have sat by the River Walbrook, which divided the city between rich and poor, and where the inhabitants of the city skated in the frozen winters, and tested out some of London's civilized innovations – the public cookshop by the river and the public lavatory at Queenhithe dock.

They were probably as divided about what they saw as contemporary commentators were. On the one hand, there were the attractive wooden two-storey houses, the upper floors stretching over the street and their bustling workshops at street level. Then there was the evidence of thought behind the intricate rules – about the mesh of fishermen's nets, or the 'just price' that merchants should charge for food and luxuries – designed to protect people's livelihoods from unfair or unsustainable competition. On the other hand, there were the savage dogs that hung around St Paul's Cathedral at night, the rogue salesmen forced to eat their own rotten food in public and the pigs wandering the streets at will.* Becket's friend and biographer William FitzStephen loved everything about the city except 'the immoderate drinking of foolish persons and the frequent fires'. Meanwhile his West Country colleague the chronicler Richard of Devizes saw only the 'jesters, smooth-skinned lads, moors, flatterers, pretty boys, effeminates, pederasts, singing and dancing girls, quacks, bellydancers, sorceresses, extortioners, night-wanderers, magicians, mimes, beggars, buffoons . . . Therefore, if you do not want to dwell with evil-doers, do not live in London.'

It was a city of different nationalities – French diplomats, Italian bankers, Baltic traders – all crowded together in the eating houses, gambling with dice in the taverns or cheering the theatre shows at Skinner's Well and Clerkenwell, just outside the city walls, and, more than anything else, buying and selling – fish in what is now Old Fish Street, loaves in Bread Street, chickens in Poultry, corn in Cornhill, while ships and barges crowded the wharves from the mouth of the River Fleet at what is now Blackfriars down to Longchamp's Tower of London.

It was now 16 March. Richard had been back in England for three days, moving in the opposite direction to the pilgrims. He and Eleanor now crossed the Thames by the old wooden bridge and entered a city in the mood for celebration, with carpets and mats and tapestries hanging out of all the upper windows they passed, with decorations on every wall, and the sounds of cheering, the blowing of Saracen horns and carol music. Royal entries into cities were marked by carol singing, as well as dancing – with

---

* The pigs from St Anthony's Hospital had bells around their neck and were allowed to wander and dig for food where they liked.

garlands on the heads of girls, old women leading them into the dances, and the more serious-minded clergy tut-tutting on the edges in disapproval. With the music and colour, and himself as the centre of worshipful attention, this must have been one of the supreme moments of Richard's life. The phrase 'Merry England' ('*Anglia plena jocis*') had been coined less than half a century before, and it was this kind of occasion – with its dancing, colour and banners fluttering on the breeze – which underpinned it.

Richard and his mother processed side by side to St Paul's Cathedral, where they held a crowded and colourful service of thanksgiving, with the music echoing under the great vault of the still-uncompleted nave. London made the most of Richard's return and the privilege of marking his first formal stop. They had paid for it and they felt they deserved it. Richard never visited London again, but his fund-raising, his absence and his ransom had all converged to lay the foundations of a proud and powerful city. It must have occurred to Eleanor during the service, as she looked around the red and gold painted decorations all over the cathedral walls, that the stone slabs under her feet were all that divided the enormous congregation from the silver being amassed in the vaults, ready for the next instalment of the ransom payment.

After the service and the procession down to Westminster, they were 'hailed with joy upon the Strand,' according to the Dean of St Paul's, the historian Ralph of Diceto. Two days later, they rode north to St Albans and went on to give thanks at the shrine of St Edmund the Martyr at Bury St Edmunds, the same abbey that Longchamp had been ejected from the previous year. Having paid his tribute to the English saints, it was time for Richard to restore order in his kingdom.

Londoners had turned out in delight and could see with their own eyes that Richard was alive. When the news reached John's castles, which had been confiscated by the Great Council in February but were still holding out, most of them surrendered immediately. John's castellan at St Michael's Mount died of shock when he heard the news.

John had sent secret messages, via his envoy Adam de St Edmund, to his English castles the month before, ordering them to prepare for siege. Adam, however, had been followed and arrested in London on 9 February by the mayor's agents. But even without the message, two of John's castles still held out – Nottingham and Tickill in Yorkshire. The garrison at Tickill sent two knights to find out for certain whether Richard was really in the country, and, when they heard beyond a shadow of doubt that he was, they surrendered. But Nottingham was tougher.

Richard reached Nottingham two days after the service in St Paul's. It is one of those peculiarities of folklore that, although there is no evidence that Robin Hood actually operated during these critical four years of Richard's absence, history confirms the legend that Nottingham Castle was Richard's first excursion on his return. In fact the siege was led by two of the names associated closely with Robin Hood in the very earliest reference to the legend: Ranulf, Earl of Chester, and David, Earl of Huntingdon, the brother of the king of Scots. The king's arrival outside the besieged castle was heralded with trumpets and horns, but the defenders were not taken in by what they believed to be a trick and they fought on. As Richard stood watching the siege, two of those next to him were suddenly hit by arrows and he ordered an immediate assault. He took part in the attack himself, wearing only a light coat of chain mail and with a large shield carried in front of him. In his first military operation since Acre, part of the outer bailey of the castle was taken, along with some other buildings, which were burned down deliberately by the garrison during the following night.

The next day, he changed tactics, erecting a large gallows in full view of the castle and bringing up the siege engines. When there was still no sign of surrender, he changed tack again, offering the garrison safe conduct for two of its defenders, so there could be absolutely no ambiguity about their intentions if they fought on knowing that the king had in fact returned.

'Well, what can you see?' said Richard as they were ushered into his tent. 'Am I here?'

When they reported back to the castle, the garrison finally surrendered.* The lives of nearly all of them were spared, on the condition that they paid hefty ransoms. The exception was Hugh of Nonant's brother Robert Brito, who had refused to be a hostage on the grounds that he owed his allegiance to John. Richard ordered that he should be starved and imprisoned. He died in Dover Castle the following year.

With the remaining rebel castle now safely in his hands, Richard went to Sherwood Forest, which he had never seen before. He and his mother stayed in the royal hunting lodge, now a ruin known as King John's Palace. It was this visit, according to the legends, that brought him face to face with Robin Hood. Then it was time for a marathon four-day meeting of the Great Council of England, in the great hall of Nottingham Castle.

One of the main items on the agenda was the failure of the Exchequer of Ransom to raise the outstanding money, and it was here that the extra taxes were imposed. The council also decided that the amounts the officers of the realm had paid for their positions in 1189 – right down to the level of sheriff – had not actually bought them their positions outright, but simply leased them. Now they would have to be paid for all over again. A few months later, as a result of discussions in Nottingham, England finally legalized tournaments. This was another fund-raising tool: there would be entrance fees and licence fees. Richard's illegitimate brother William Longspee, soon to be Earl of Salisbury, was appointed as their director.†

Other outstanding issues included what to do about anyone

---

*We actually know the names of the two envoys: Foucher de Grendon and Henry Russel.

†The first tournaments in England did not bode well for the future. When eighty wealthy young knights gathered near Bury St Edmunds for a tournament and came to the town looking for lodgings in the evening, they were put up and fed rather reluctantly by Abbot Sansom. But afterwards they so disturbed the town by oafish drinking, dancing and singing, finally breaking down the town gates to escape in the middle of the night, that – on the advice of Hubert Walter – the abbot had every one of them excommunicated.

who had openly taken John's side, notably the case of his chief propagandist, the Bishop of Coventry, Hugh of Nonant. He was restored to grace for the fee of 2,000 silver marks, but he sensibly decided to go into exile in Normandy and live in seclusion, where he died on Good Friday 1198. His sins were considered so grave that local churchmen were unwilling to hear his final confession. 'After a long illness and unbearable suffering,' wrote one chronicler, 'he closed a miserable life by a well-deserved death.'

John was ordered to appear before the Great Council within forty days, and a new Great Seal of England was ordered to replace the one that had endured such adventures in the sea off Cyprus and in the hands of Richard's jailers in Austria. The new seal carried Richard's revised emblem of three golden lions on a red background, which have been in the royal coat of arms ever since.

Richard's advisers spent the final day of the council meeting persuading him that he needed some kind of public demonstration that he was still king. He was initially unwilling, but finally agreed to a crown-wearing ceremony in Winchester while the fleet and army gathered in Portsmouth. So on Easter Day, 17 April, wearing what remained of his coronation regalia, Richard processed from St Swithun's Priory to the cathedral, led by his friend William, king of Scots, carrying a ceremonial sword, and followed by the earls, barons and knights and an enormous crowd. His mother met him in the north transept on a specially built dais that allowed her and her ladies to survey the unprecedented scene.

For nearly a month Richard waited impatiently in his new naval base at Portsmouth. This was built on land owned by Jean de Gisors, who had shifted his allegiance to Philip and had therefore forfeited it to the crown. Richard was preparing a fleet of nearly 100 ships for sail. He appointed William of St Mary Église to take charge of the new dockyard and to make Portsmouth the focal point from which to manage the defence of Normandy. He then finally set sail for Barfleur, the fleet laden with soldiers, provisions and siege engines, on 12 May. He never returned to England.

★

From Barfleur, Richard and his mother processed to Caen, followed by an ever-growing crowd, who were dancing and singing: 'God has come again in strength/It's time for the French king to go.' From there it was on to Bayeux. There were now so many people in the narrow streets that, William the Marshal said later, if you threw an apple in the air, it would have landed on someone's head. Richard hurried ahead of his army, together with his mother, to Lisieux, where he stayed in the house of the local archdeacon, John of Alençon – the messenger sent by his mother to Acre to urge him to come home – and went to bed early. But the news from Philip's siege of Verneuil preyed on his mind and he could not sleep. It was then that a figure appeared outside on foot in the evening light and asked to see Eleanor. It was John, who had slipped out of Paris earlier in the day and was in a state of 'abject penitence'. Very nervously, the archdeacon woke the king.

'Why do you look like that?' asked Richard. 'You have seen my brother. Don't lie – I will not reproach him. Those who have driven him on will soon have their reward.'

So John was finally ushered into his brother's presence and fell sobbing at his feet. Richard raised him up and kissed him, just as his father had done to him after his own rebellion at the age of sixteen. 'Don't be afraid, John, you are a child,' he said. 'You have got into bad company and it is those who have led you astray who will be punished.'

He asked the archdeacon if there was anything to eat and ordered that the large salmon presented to him by the citizens of Lisieux the day before should be cooked in John's honour. 'The king is straightforward and merciful,' the archdeacon told John later, 'and kinder to you than you would be to him.'

As Richard pressed on towards Verneuil the next morning, sending his mercenaries ahead to cut Philip's supply lines, John went back to Evreux, invited the French officials to dinner and had them murdered, before announcing that he now held the town for Richard. Not surprisingly, Philip never forgave him. He immediately abandoned his siege, marched to Evreux, sacked it and destroyed its churches. It was a sign that the conflict was becoming particularly embittered, to the miserable impoverishment of any of the ordinary people who happened to get in the way.

There then followed four solid years of manoeuvre and counter-manoeuvre as Richard pushed Philip's forces back slowly from the land he had taken in Normandy, while Philip in turn distracted him from this by fomenting trouble in Aquitaine and the south. It was a strategic joust between two of the master strategists of the age. It saw Richard investing vast sums in a new, impregnable castle in the River Seine near Rouen known as Château Gaillard. He described the castle as his 'daughter'. It was an ironic boast given that he had cared so little about fathering any real children that, a year after his release, he had still not sent for Berengaria. 'He took such a pleasure in the building,' wrote William of Newburgh, 'that, if I am not mistaken, if an angel had descended from heaven and told him to abandon it, that angel would have been met with a volley of curses and the work would have gone on regardless.'

Richard's diplomatic noose around France also began to tighten; Savaric of Bath was even made Chancellor of Burgundy. It was a period that also saw the development of Richard's military tactics, with the Genoese crossbowmen and his force of 300 Saracen soldiers brought home from Outremer – shocking evidence for Richard's enemies of his admiration for Muslim culture – going into action on his behalf all over the Angevin empire.

'How is your conscience, my son?' Bishop Hugh of Lincoln asked him early in 1195.

'Very easy,' Richard is supposed to have replied.

'How can that be when you live apart from your virtuous queen and are faithless to her?'

It was a rhetorical question, but shortly afterwards Richard had his famous encounter with the hermit who urged him to abstain from the 'sin of Sodom'. Later that day he became ill with one of his periodic nervous collapses. Berengaria was still on her dower lands near Le Mans, spending her time helping the poor – the 1190s was a time of terrible famine in Europe, exacerbated by the constant clashes between Richard and Philip – and now, finally, Richard summoned her to him and they spent Christmas together in Poitiers.

There were moments of truce. During one of them, Philip's sister Alys was finally released from her years of imprisonment for the sin of having been seduced by Richard's father. But later in 1195 the emperor was writing impassioned letters urging Richard to continue the war, and renouncing the remaining 17,000 marks of the ransom to help him to do so. Henry reminded Richard that he was now an imperial vassal and must not make peace with Philip without his consent. With this letter from Henry, the ransom payments finally stopped. The rest was never paid.

But where Richard and Philip were well matched as strategists, Richard was the pre-eminent military mind of his generation, and step by step the Angevins seized the upper hand. In July 1194 at Fréteval he came close to capturing Philip, seizing his wagon train, along with his treasure and archives, and an incriminating document with the names of Angevin subjects who were prepared to swap sides. In 1198 Philip was chased to Gisors by Richard's mercenary captain Mercadier, and fell into the river as a bridge collapsed under him. Forty of his knights were drowned.

Richard's strategy to secure his southern dominions was enormously helped by the unexpected love between his sister Joanna and Raymond of St Gilles – also a well-known womanizer with a reputation for cruelty – who had now succeeded his father as Count Raymond VI of Toulouse. Richard and Berengaria were in Rouen Cathedral in October 1196 for the wedding. There was also an unexpected bonus when Mercadier captured Richard's great enemy Philip, Bishop of Beauvais, Conrad of Montferrat's friend, the versifier who had execrated him in Palestine, and probably the man who hated him most in the world. It was God's way, said Richard, of saying who was right and who was wrong.* When

---

* What he actually said was, 'It is not we who have done this, but God and my right.' The phrase 'God and my right' continues to this day as the motto of the British royal family, 'Dieu et Mon Droit'.

the Pope sent his legate Cardinal Peter of Capua to ask Richard for his release, Richard lost his temper. His diatribe was remembered years later by William the Marshal:

By my head, he is deconsecrated, for this is a false Christian. It was not as a bishop that he was captured but as a knight fighting and fully armed, a laced helmet on his head. Sir hypocrite, what a fool you are! If you had not been an envoy I would send you back with something to show the Pope which he would not forget. Never did the Pope raise a finger to help me when I was in prison and wanted his help to be free. And now he asks me to set free a robber and an incendiary who has never done me anything but harm. Get out of here, sir traitor, liar, trickster, corrupt dealer in churches, and never let me see you again!

Peter of Capua fled to Philip's court in Paris, telling him that he was afraid he would have been castrated if he had stayed a moment longer. Richard went to bed and refused to see anyone. His mother later arranged diplomatically for the bishop to escape from Château Gaillard and be given asylum in Aquitaine. He was to play an active role on the French side, mace in hand, during the Battle of Bouvines in 1214. But the pressure from Rome was mounting for some kind of agreement that might facilitate another crusade, and Peter of Capua finally managed to negotiate a truce, so that Richard and Philip could meet. They finally did so in January 1199, Richard on a ship on the Seine and Philip remaining on horseback on the bank. It was a stiff and suspicious conference and the former passionate friends never met again.

Although the emperor had cancelled the rest of the ransom, the story of the money did not end there. It was Henry's plan to use his vast windfall of silver to carry out a successful invasion of Sicily, which he claimed in the name of his wife, Constance. This was a critical part of his vision of an enlarged Holy Roman Empire that would dominate the Mediterranean just as it dominated central Europe. He could now afford to pay and equip an enormous army to do what he failed so ignominiously to do in 1190–91.

Only a fortnight after Richard's release, Henry had another stroke of luck. The king of Sicily, Richard's unexpected ally Tancred of Lecce, died suddenly. His heir was his four-year-old son, who was crowned by the ageing Pope Celestine as William III in a desperate attempt to prevent the emperor from encircling the papal lands in the middle of the Italian peninsula. This was the moment to act, and three months later Henry was marching across the Alps.

The kingdom of Sicily extended over much of what is now southern Italy and by October Henry was ready to cross to the island, taking Palermo on 20 November. The emperor made a generous agreement, offering the child king the principality of Taranto, and invited William and his mother and sisters to watch his own coronation in Palermo on Christmas Day 1194. The following day, near Ancona, Constance gave birth to their son, Frederick, the man destined to crown himself king of Jerusalem and who would later be known as *Stupor Mundi* – the Wonder of the World. Three days later, Henry's advisers discovered a conspiracy against him in Palermo – or said they had discovered one – and all the leading figures of Sicily, including William and his family, were blindfolded, sent to Germany and imprisoned. William's mother and sisters were eventually released and lived in exile in France. Nobody knows what happened to William, though it is said that he returned much later to Sicily under the name Tancredi Palamara but was arrested in Palermo and executed in 1232.

Henry had the tombs of Tancred and his predecessors opened to remove their jewels and regalia. As many as 150 packhorses were loaded up with treasure and taken to Trifels, where Richard had been briefly imprisoned. They included the Sicilian coronation robes that were used in later centuries by the emperors themselves, and are still on public display in Vienna. As for Excalibur, which Richard had presented to Tancred, Henry seems to have over-looked it in the treasury in Palermo and it has never been seen again.

Vast quantities of silver from the ransom that fuelled the emperor and his army now ended up in Sicily, so much that it allowed

Henry to launch a new silver coinage there. In fact, all over Europe
the English silver began to circulate – either in its original form or
melted down into new coins – making its way along the trade
routes to Venice and the East, and often back to England again.
When the leaders of the Fourth Crusade handed over their money
to pay for the enterprise in Venice a few years later, they did so in
sterling silver from England. Hoards of Richard's ransom still
appear sometimes on the Continent.

As Henry was embarking on his successful invasion, the Austrian
share of the ransom money had also arrived in Vienna. Leopold
immediately put it to work to pay masons to build a proper stone
wall to defend the city and a new military colony on the marshy
plain of Steinfeld to the south, called Wiener Neustadt. The new
town was designed as a major fortification to prevent incursions
from Hungary and was laid out like a parallelogram, with four
main streets converging on a rectangular plaza in the centre, and a
canal that took river water into the city and into a moat between
the inner and outer walls. With its strong new walls, the money
also transformed Vienna from a small outpost of Western Christendom into a splendid trading city. The influx of stone masons had
a more lasting effect. Once they were lodged in Vienna, they
began to be employed to rebuild the city's wooden houses in
stone, changing its character for ever.

One of the last letters Richard wrote after his second coronation
in Winchester, before leaving for Normandy, was to the Pope,
asking him to put pressure on Leopold of Austria to liberate the
hostages and to return his part of the ransom. By June 1194 the
elderly Celestine was openly intriguing against the emperor and
there was no point in pretending otherwise – imperial agents were
imprisoning or slitting the throats of the agents of the Pope. So
finally Celestine did as he was asked. He sent Adelard, Bishop of
Verona, to remonstrate with the Duke of Austria, urging him not
just to pay back the money but to go on crusade for the same
length of time that Richard had spent in prison. It was a tough
year in Austria, with a succession of floods and plagues, but Leopold
resisted the injunction. He had already spent 26,000 marks and

was expecting another 20,000 when Richard's niece Eleanor of Brittany arrived, as agreed, to marry his son. In fact, seven months after Richard's release, he was becoming nervous that Eleanor would never arrive and he sent one of the hostages – Baldwin of Béthune – home to England with a message for Richard, threatening to execute the other hostages unless she was sent.

The threat worked. Baldwin set off back towards Austria in December, bringing with him not just Eleanor of Brittany but also the Cypriot princess, Isaac Comnenus's daughter, who had been released under the same agreement. He was in Germany when a message reached him that changed everything, and he turned straight round and took the two princesses back to England.

What had happened was that, the same day that the emperor's young son had been born, 28 December, Leopold had fallen from his horse while he was out riding near Graz and the horse had crushed his foot. The following day the foot was black and his surgeons advised an immediate amputation. Unfortunately for Leopold, nobody in his entourage could summon the strength of mind necessary to carry out the painful operation. Not even his son, Frederick, was prepared to do it, and the smell from the gangrenous limb was growing worse. Eventually Leopold was forced to hold an axe against his ankle himself, while a servant drove it through his leg with a mallet. The amputation took three heavy blows, and by then it was too late. The gangrene had spread upwards.

When he realized the Duke was dying, Adalbert, Archbishop of Salzburg, hurried to his bedside and heard his full confession, which included a promise to return the hostages and the 4,000 marks left of the ransom money that had not yet been spent. Leopold died on 31 December and was buried in the habit of a Cistercian monk. At the graveside in Heiligenkreuz, Adalbert forced Frederick to repeat his father's deathbed oath. One of Leopold's minnesingers, Reinmar of Hagenau, wrote a moving song about his death. 'Summer has come,' he wrote, but 'what use to me this time of bliss, since he of all joys Lord Liutpolt in earth lies, who never for one day I saw sorrowful.'

At least one of Leopold's hostages had a lasting effect on his hosts. The first Arthurian story in German about Lancelot, a poem in rhymed couples called *Lanzelet* by the Swiss priest Ulrich von Zatzithoven – which has Lancelot kidnapped as a baby and raised as a sea fairy – was translated from an Anglo-Norman manuscript brought to Austria by Hugh de Morville. Hugh was the hostage who was probably the same man who had helped to murder Thomas Becket in his youth, and was expiating his sin – not just by acting as a hostage for the king but by spreading the Grail legend across Germany.*

Tancred and Leopold were not the only ones to die. It is a strange irony about the story of Richard's imprisonment, but within five years many of the leading figures in the tale were dead.

The first to go was Saladin. He had intended to make a pilgrimage to Mecca as soon as Richard left Palestine, but – although he was completely exhausted – first he had to visit Damascus, where he found four years of work that had built up there without him while he was with the army. His health began to fail through the winter of 1192, and on 19 February 1193 – while Richard was still in Dürnstein – he came home with a fever from a bitterly cold day out meeting returning pilgrims. On 1 March he became unconscious. Two days later, while most of his closest associates had left his bedside to seize power, and as the words from the Koran were read over him – 'There is no God but God and in him do I trust' – he opened his eyes briefly, smiled and died. Saladin was devout, trustworthy and merciful, but his legacy did not survive him. The empire he had built began to crumble under the combined rule of his seventeen sons and the unity of the

---

* There is rather an odd twist to the Grail story, at least as far as this book is concerned. The anonymous author of *The High Book of the Grail*, early in the thirteenth century, wrote that it had been written for 'the lord of Neele' – Jehan II de Nesle, one of the candidates for being Blondel – who was among the small group of Grail enthusiasts who joined the Fourth Crusade but bypassed Constantinople, and went on almost alone to Syria in 1204.

Islamic world was fractured. Acre did not fall to the Muslims until
1291.*

In Germany, Richard's brother-in-law Henry the Lion had been
reconciled to the emperor as part of Richard's diplomatic intrigue.
They were due to meet the month of Richard's release, but the
Duke of Saxony fell off his horse shortly before and was taken to
the monastery of Walkenried. Believing this to be a trick, the
emperor postponed their meeting. But the day before Easter 1195,
Henry the Lion had a stroke. He died in August in Brunswick
Castle and was succeeded by his son Henry, now also Count
Palatine.

In northern Syria Isaac Comnenus, the former ruler of Cyprus,
died suddenly and mysteriously, apparently poisoned. He had been
released at last from the Hospitaller castle of Marqab as part of the
ransom agreement and had made his way directly to Constantinople, where he began to collect allies for an attempt on the
Byzantine throne. His death took place in the summer of 1195, as
he tried to involve the Sultan of Konya in his plot.

Eighteen months later saw the end of William Longchamp, still
chancellor of England, sent on yet another mission by the king –
this time to put his case to the Pope in a dispute with Walter of
Coutances over the ownership of the land where Château Gaillard
was being built. But Longchamp was sick by the time he reached
Poitiers and died there in January 1197. He was buried in a nearby
Cistercian abbey, but his heart was taken to Ely – where he had
been bishop – and was buried in front of the altar. He was mourned,
according to the chronicles, by nobody except his loving chaplain
Milo.

But there was more death to come. The next surprise took place
in Acre, where Richard's nephew Henry of Champagne, left
behind as king of Jerusalem until he could return to Outremer,

---

*When the French general Henri Gourand arrived in Damascus in 1920, in
command of the allied army of occupation, he went straight to Saladin's tomb
and announced, 'Saladin, we have returned! My presence here consecrates the
victory of the cross over the crescent.' History remains on the side of Saladin
for his humane inspiration to future generations.

was facing an attack on Jaffa by Saladin's brother al-Adil – part of a series of skirmishes with some recently arrived German crusaders. On 10 September 1197 he gathered what troops he could in his palace courtyard in the city and reviewed them from a window in the upper gallery. While this was happening, some envoys from Pisa offering reinforcements were ushered into the room. Henry turned to greet them but, for a brief second, he forgot where he was and stepped backwards. As he hurtled out of the window, his dwarf servant Scarlet grabbed his clothes in a desperate attempt to rescue him, but Henry was a large man and he was too heavy, and Scarlet was carried out of the window and on to the pavement below. Both were killed instantly.

His heartbroken widow, Isabella, with three small daughters – one of them by Conrad of Montferrat – was still heiress to the throne of Jerusalem, but the barons could not decide whom she should marry. On the advice of Richard's friend the Archbishop of Mainz, they finally offered the throne and Isabella to the recently widowed King Amalric of Cyprus, the older brother of Guy of Lusignan. So the beautiful Isabella found herself married off for the fourth time, but even her fourth husband did not last long. He died in 1205 in Acre after eating too much fish. She reigned in her own right briefly and died shortly afterwards at the age of only thirty-three, and was succeeded by Conrad's daughter Maria, then only thirteen.

At the height of his powers, wealthy beyond his dreams thanks to Richard's ransom, and still in Sicily planning his crusade, the Emperor Henry VI was also feeling unwell. In the spring of 1197 he had uncovered another plot to assassinate him – almost certainly with the tacit support not just of the Pope but also of his wife, Constance. The next six months were spent in the brutal hunting and execution of the rebels: one of them was skinned alive and another one crowned using iron nails through the temple. Then, on 28 September 1197, Henry died unexpectedly of fever – probably malaria – in Messina. On his deathbed, he offered to compensate Richard for the money that had been paid. He was only thirty-one. Pope Celestine seized his opportunity for revenge and forbade the burial of his body until the ransom money had been returned.

Henry's son, Frederick, was only three, and was too young to be elected to the position of Holy Roman Emperor. The Archbishop of Cologne and his northern allies invited Richard to Germany to take part in the election, but he decided not to go. Perhaps it was just too soon after his release to face a visit to the land of his imprisonment. Instead he sent two of his comrades from the journey across the Alps, Philip of Poitou and Baldwin of Béthune, to represent him. Before the election there were even rumours that Richard would be offered the imperial throne himself. In the event, two rival elections were held, the first early in 1198. One of them elected Henry VI's younger brother, Philip of Swabia, with the support of the king of France; he was assassinated a few years later. Three months later, in June 1198, and packed by Richard's northern allies, the German court elected Richard's favourite nephew, Otto of Brunswick, who was already both Earl of York and Count of Poitou. Payments in silver to facilitate his successful bid began flowing once more out of England and down the Rhine. He was crowned Otto IV in Aachen later that month. 'O splendid deed of a splendid man,' wrote one French chronicler about Richard at the time, 'who acquired the empire of the whole world for his nephew.' But although Otto did rule outright for some years, the ensuing struggle between the rival claimants to the imperial throne lasted fifteen years and devastated large parts of Germany, causing widespread inflation and famine.

Six months before, on 8 January 1198, Pope Celestine finally died in Rome at the age of ninety-four. His enemies whispered that this had been caused by complications from syphilis. The cardinals elected the vegetarian and teetotaller John de Salerno to succeed him, but he refused the position. After another round of voting, Celestine's successor was named as the 38-year-old Lotario de Segni. He took the title Innocent III and became one of the most powerful and ambitious Popes of the Middle Ages. His first act was to allow the burial of Henry VI's body, which had then been decomposing for eight months. His second was to crown the child Frederick II as king of Sicily at the age of four. He then took up the cause of abandoned wives and widows like Philip's Ingeborg of Denmark, Raymond VI's Beatrix, now shut up in a convent, and Richard's Berengaria.

The curse of Blondel's song, which saw the deaths of so many players in the saga within five years of Richard's release, had certainly afflicted Richard's friends and allies – Longchamp, Henry the Lion, Henry of Champagne and Tancred of Sicily. But most of all, it had destroyed his enemies. One by one, those who were responsible for his imprisonment, or who had failed to act to shorten it, had died.* He also had reason to be satisfied with his progress in France, forcing Philip back in Normandy, securing Aquitaine and his southern possessions. But it was an intense, exhausting and increasingly bitter process. Richard's strategy, isolating Philip with his intricate diplomatic alliances across northern Europe, was paying off. But Philip's strategy – encouraging dissent inside Aquitaine and the south – was effective too. So it was that, in March 1199, with the peace negotiated by Peter of Capua agreed, Richard marched south to deal with the growing difficulties there, including the disaffected Aimar, Viscount of Limoges.

Tradition has it that Richard's visit to the viscount's castle at Chalus-Chabrol was a greedy bid to seize some treasure that had been discovered there, but modern scholarship has undermined the story as a deliberate piece of misinformation. The dispute with Limoges was an old-fashioned one between vassal and overlord, part of the complex series of competing strategies that was drawing in castles and territories right across what we now know as France.

After supper on 26 March, when the daylight was beginning to fade, Richard left his tent to join Mercadier outside the walls of the castle, to give orders to the sappers who were tunnelling underneath and to practise with the crossbow. He was not wearing

---

*This did not affect absolutely everybody. Philip Augustus lived until 1223, dying at the age of fifty-seven. Meinhard of Gorz lived until the grand old age of seventy-three, reigning until 1231.

any armour, except for an iron helmet, though as usual a large shield was carried in front of him. When he reached the castle – actually just a tiny stone tower containing just two knights and a handful of soldiers – he was told that nobody inside had summoned up the nerve to show themselves on the walls all day, except for one man with a crossbow, who was protecting himself with nothing except a frying pan. And suddenly there he was again. As the courageous crossbowman shot off another bolt, Richard could not help applauding, and was therefore just a fraction of a second late before ducking behind the shield. The bolt penetrated his left shoulder.

Not wanting to cause any alarm, Richard went back to his tent as calmly as he could as though nothing had happened. He tried to pull out the bolt himself, but it just broke off in his hand. A surgeon arrived and removed it by the flickering light of torches, fighting his way through the excess fat on Richard's torso, and bandaged up the wound. On closer examination, the bolt turned out to have been shot originally from his own side, collected up and returned from whence it came.

Richard knew all about gangrene. He had seen it creep into the wounds too many times to have any illusions when the signs began to appear clearly on his own shoulder, and he knew he was going to die. He wrote to his mother – now withdrawn from the world at the abbey in Fontevrault – and urged her to come as quickly as she could. In the meantime he stayed in his tent, allowing only four people inside, to make sure the news did not leak out. When the castle fell a few days later, he asked to see the crossbowman with the frying pan – known variously as Peter Basil or Bertrand de Gurdon – and he was ushered into the tent.

'What wrong have I done you that you should kill me?' he asked.

'With your own hand you killed my father and two brothers and you intended to kill me,' said Bertrand. 'Take your revenge in any way you like. Now that I have seen you on your deathbed I shall gladly endure any torment that you may devise.'

Richard forgave him and set him free. He then confessed his sins and was given the last rites. He died at 7 p.m. on 6 April, at the age of forty-one. It was just five years and three weeks since he had landed at Sandwich. After his death, Mercadier recaptured Bertrand the crossbowman and had him flayed to death.

Richard left his jewels to his favourite nephew, Otto, now Holy Roman Emperor, and asked for his brain and entrails to be buried at Charroux, on the border between Poitou and Limousin, his heart at Rouen and the rest of his body – together with the crown and regalia he had worn in Winchester Cathedral – at Fontevrault at his father's feet. The saintly Hugh of Lincoln, Richard's self-appointed father confessor, was near enough to Fontevrault to preside over the funeral mass on Palm Sunday, and hurried north as soon as it was over to break the news to Berengaria.

Eleanor had arrived in time, but John was too late. He had received an urgent message from his mother, sent in Richard's final hours, telling him to take control of the treasure fortress of Chinon. He arrived after the funeral was over and hammered on the door of the abbey, demanding to be allowed to see his brother's tomb. He was told that the abbess was away and nobody could be admitted without her permission. Instead he stood on the porch with Bishop Hugh, took the amulet from his neck and told him that, as long as he owned it, the Plantagenets would never lose their empire. Hugh urged him to trust in God not in stones. Three days later, John was subjected to a long sermon from the bishop about the difference between good and bad kings, and shocked the congregation by interrupting to tell him to hurry up because it was dinner time.

William the Marshal took the news to Hubert Walter, then in Normandy. Late at night, four days after Richard's death, he knocked on his lodging door in Vaudreuil and immediately began discussing the problem of the succession. Hubert Walter wanted Richard's nephew Arthur of Brittany to succeed, but the Marshal wanted John. 'So be it then,' said Walter. 'But mark my words, Marshal, you will never regret anything in your life as much as this.'* Walter pursed his lips with disapproval as he crowned John as Duke of Normandy in Rouen shortly afterwards. The ducal lance slipped through John's fingers as it was handed to him, because he was laughing so much with his friends in the pews opposite, and clattered on to the flagstones.

Richard's last days had coincided with a crisis in the short marriage of his sister Joanna and Raymond VI of Toulouse, which – despite its romantic start – had become bitterly unhappy. She had already given birth to one son, the future Raymond VII – another nephew of Richard's destined to play a heroic role in the next century – and was pregnant again. But her husband had abandoned her to deal with his barons and she had fled for protection to her brother. Joanna managed to find Eleanor, still in Aquitaine after Richard's funeral, and was told the terrible news of her brother's death. This seems to have been the final straw for her. She went to Fontevrault, demanded to be made a nun – despite being married and pregnant – and she and the baby both died during the birth a few months later in Beaucaire in September 1199. The child lived long enough to be christened Richard.

Her husband married again later – the Cypriot princess, finally released on Richard's death, whom he had met in Marseilles on her way home and for whom Richard had conceived such a passion in Palestine. But even that marriage did not last. Raymond abandoned her in favour of the sister of the king of Aragon and she returned home to Cyprus, tried and failed to overthrow the Lusignans, and went into exile in Armenia. Historians never recorded her name, but something of her compelling character and brilliance still lingers somehow behind the basic outlines of her life. On the flimsy grounds that he was her third cousin, Leopold VI, Leopold of Austria's successor, made another failed claim to Cyprus during the Fifth Crusade in 1217.

Richard's older half-sister Marie of Champagne, the patron of

---

*Hubert Walter died exhausted in 1205, one of the most successful administrators in English history. He was buried in Canterbury Cathedral and the head of Saladin was carved on his tomb.

troubadours and *trouvères*, had died the previous year of a broken heart when she had heard the news of her son Henry's death on the flagstones of his palace in Acre. Her second son, Thibaut, married Berengaria's sister Blanca in Chartres in 1199, and gave birth to one of the most important troubadours of medieval Europe: Thibaut of Champagne. He grew up to be one of the fathers of French literature and was, incidentally, an ancestor of the current Spanish royal family.

Eleanor came out of retirement for one final journey, across the Pyrenees at the age of seventy-eight to collect her granddaughter Blanche of Castile — Richard's niece — who was to seal the truce with Philip Augustus by marrying the Dauphin Louis.* Blanche would prove to be the formidable mother of St Louis IX. Her escort was Mercadier, who was killed in a brawl on the way home.

On 6 March 1204 Richard's precious Château Gaillard fell after Philip's soldiers had managed to climb in through the lavatory in a new extension built by John. Three weeks later, Eleanor died in Fontevrault, where she was buried next to her second husband and her favourite son. Normandy fell to the French shortly afterwards.

Berengaria lived out her long widowhood in Le Mans — constantly urging John to pay her the pension money he had promised — and became known for her work with the poor.† Until the end of her life she styled herself as 'most humble former Queen of the English'. When she died in 1230, her effigy was of a woman with long flowing hair, dressed as a virgin bride, with her feet resting on a lion, and a small dog underneath it — a symbol of faithfulness. Her remains were rediscovered in 1960 hidden under the floor of the former chapterhouse of the abbey at L'Epau that she founded.

Richard's remains, along with those of his parents and his sister Joanna, were dug up during the French Revolution in 1789 and

---

* In fact the agreement was to marry Blanche's sister Urraca, but when Eleanor arrived in Castile she said the French would never accept a queen with a name like that and chose Blanche instead.

† 'When these clouds that have overcast our serenity shall disperse, and our kingdom shall be full of joyful tranquillity,' wrote John to her in 1214, 'then the pecuniary debt owed to our dear sister shall be paid joyfully and thankfully.'

scattered in the fields – a fate that befell the bones in most of the royal tombs in France. The abbey where they were buried was converted into a prison and remained one until 1963, when the tombs were restored. His heart, which was said to be unusually large when it was removed from his body, was exhumed in 1842 and can now be seen in the Rouen Museum.

Richard's death sent shock waves across Europe, particularly among the troubadour culture that he had so encouraged – but even they recognized his faults. 'Ah! Lord God! You who are merciful, true God, true man and true life, have mercy,' went the lament written by the troubadour Gaucelm Faidit. 'Pardon him, for he has great need of your compassion. Do not consider his sins, but remember how he was going to serve you.'

There is no doubting Richard's vanity, his occasional cruelty and his undoubted brutality. But there are aspects of him that remain heroic – his tolerance, his generosity, his imagination and his sheer determination. It is easy to see how contemporaries were staggered and horrified by the news of his death in his prime of life. This is how the chronicler Roger of Howden paid tribute to him:

His valour could no throng of mighty labours quell, whose way and onward progress no obstacles did retard, no roaring, no rage of the sea, no abyss of the deep, no mountains, no roughness of the path by rocks made rugged, no windings of the road, no devious unknown track, no fury of the winds, no clouds with showers drunk, no thunders, no dreadful visitations, no murky air . . . at the same moment that the will is born, the result is born as well.

The city walls of Vienna, built with the proceeds of Richard's ransom, had a long and eventful history. They were strengthened and extended constantly, holding off the Ottoman Turks until 1683, even used by the revolutionaries of 1848 to defend the city against the forces sent to suppress them. Because of this, the 1848 revolution hastened their demise and the new Austrian emperor, Franz Joseph I, finally had them demolished in 1857.

There then followed a battle between the city of Vienna and the imperial Austrian government, both of which claimed the strip of land where the wall and the defensive space in front of it had been for so many centuries. The imperial government won this dispute and sold the land, building the Ringstrasse – the great inner ring road that dominates the heart of Vienna to this day – along the outside of where the wall used to stand. The proceeds from the sale were used to build some of the great nineteenth-century buildings that are the pride of Vienna still. They include some of the most stately architecture in Europe: the opera house and the great museums and galleries, and the new wing of the Hofburg Palace, including a museum to house the imperial crown jewels and the state robes looted from Sicily by Henry VI. Seven decades later, the city of Vienna and the government were still fighting over the money, and claiming compensation for it. They continued to do so until the Anschluss and the Nazi takeover.

Perhaps it would have pleased Richard that so much of the money paid to release him from prison was used for institutions that still house some of the greatest paintings in the world – Brueghel, Dürer and Rubens – and still echo to the music of Gustav Mahler and to the waltzes of the Strauss family.

11. The Very Last Day of Chivalry

'At his death, the entire world fell into chaos.'

the German chronicler Otto of St Blaise on the death of the
Emperor Henry VI

'Who can doubt that such goodness, friendship and charity came from
God? Men whose parents, sons and daughters, brothers and sisters, had
died in agony at our hands, whose lands we took, whom we drove
naked from their homes, revived us with their own food when we
were dying of hunger, and showered us with kindness even while we
were in their power.'

Oliverus Scholasticus on Sultan al-Malik-al-Kamil, al-Adil's son,
who supplied the defeated Christian army with food during the
Fifth Crusade

It is March 1226, more than a quarter of a century later. Although
it is daylight outside in the English county of Wiltshire, it is cold
and dark inside the unfinished shell of Salisbury Cathedral, the full
flowering of the English version of Gothic. The wind and rain are
lashing the brand-new walls of golden stone, driving through the
unglazed arched windows that normally fill the building with light,
and guttering the candles in the chandeliers that hang down the
nave. There are flashes of lightning.

The cathedral is packed with some of the most powerful princes
and bishops in the land, up near the high altar in fine red cloaks,
which they pull more warmly around them in the cold and damp.
Their ladies are behind them in the transepts, with wimples on
their heads, and long gowns in bright blues and greens scraping

the floor. There are some bare-headed girls, and behind them in the nave are the men-at-arms, holding banners that flutter in the wind, and swords that flash in the nervous candlelight.

Behind them too are the shopkeepers and townspeople of the most famous new town in England – which has been taking shape within sight of the new cathedral – the guildsmen and masons who have been lovingly shaping the carvings, the freemen and merchants who are making Salisbury their own. In the lightning flashes, you can see the unfinished paintings along the walls, the saints, monsters and Bible stories picked out in ochre, red and gold, with texts that describe them in English painted on the back of the stalls.

It is the funeral of Richard's last surviving brother, William Longspee, Earl of Salisbury, sometime official in charge of England's tournaments and one of the five dignitaries who laid the foundation stones of this revolutionary new building a mere six years before. He has died in mysterious circumstances at the age of fifty-seven after a successful military campaign in Gascony, the only part of Richard's continental inheritance that remains. He leaves behind four sons, four daughters and a youthful countess, the young heiress who had been discovered in hiding by a knight disguised as a minstrel – a contemporary echo of Blondel's song.

The eighteen-year-old king, John's son Henry III, is unwell and in Marlborough. The chief justiciar, Hubert de Burgh, is mysteriously absent as well. But there in the nave are William de Mandeville, the Bishop of Winchester, the Earl Marshal – the son and heir of William the Marshal, former Regent of England – and the Bishop of Salisbury, Richard le Poore. It was le Poore's dream of the Virgin Mary that led to the risky decision to build the new cathedral here in marshy Mary's Field, and six years later – plus 40,000 tons of stone on makeshift scaffolding, 15,000 tons of oak and 400 tons of lead for the roof – it has become a reality.

But also in the congregation are the last of the old generation, those men who fought alongside Longspee on the Third Crusade, veterans who may not have been able to read or write, but who have seen the Saracens on the march, witnessed the magic of a Sufi wanderer on the dusty roads of Europe, braved the storm-tossed Mediterranean by the stars, seen the towers of Rome and Salerno, and the tomb of the Magi in Cologne. These are men who have witnessed with their own eyes the giants of the recent past – Saladin, William the Marshal, Thomas Becket, Eleanor of Aquitaine and, above all, Richard the Lionheart, for one brief decade the king of England and the pride of Christendom.

The crowds part a little for them as they go by, because everyone knows who they are, these last few survivors of a golden age. They are listened to with respect because of what they have done and seen, and because of the stories they can tell of the great days before the interdict – the terrible spiritual punishment levelled on the country under King John, now lying unmourned in his tomb in the nave of Worcester Cathedral, before the military disasters that broke the umbilical cord with Normandy and shattered the Angevin empire. And they are discussing these things as they watch the masses said for Longspee before he is lowered into his crusader tomb. Because this is the end of an era, at least as they see it: the very last day of chivalry.

They are also discussing Longspee himself – his luck in his marriage, his luck at the Battle of Damme, where he destroyed the French invasion fleet in 1213, his judgement about where to place his loyalty in the last few turbulent decades, how he stuck with his half-brother King John at Runnymede for the sealing of the Magna Carta, and way beyond the point where normal loyalty might have left him in the cold. And even when John's rage and cruelty became too overwhelming, when he took the side of the Dauphin Louis – rampaging across the English countryside in 1216 – Longspee had managed to escape the consequences just by announcing he would go on crusade.

Then there was his luck on the recent journey home from Gascony, struck by a tremendous storm – like this one, lashing the cathedral walls – which tossed them for days in the English Channel. The stars were invisible, and the crew gave up all hope of steering the ship. In desperation, the earl ordered all their goods and weapons thrown overboard to make the ship lighter. It was pitch dark, and just as hope was finally disappearing over the side with them, a strange thing happened. The whole crew could suddenly see a bright light at the top of the mainmast, which transformed itself into a beautiful woman standing there calmly in the storm. Longspee took this as a sign from the Virgin that they would survive. Sure enough, they were driven ashore on an island called Ré, and took another boat to Cornwall. But just like his older brother Richard, he was soon to discover how dangerous it was to be too long abroad. Like Odysseus' wife, Penelope, his own wife, Ela, had been surrounded by the most forceful and persuasive suitors. Ela held them at bay, but the king's justiciar, the ambitious Hubert de Burgh, was particularly forceful in pressing the suit of his nephew.

Enraged by this, Longspee eventually decided to complain to the teenage king. Henry soothed the two barons and forced them to eat dinner together, but it was Longspee's last meal. He became ill on the journey home and, by the time he had reached Salisbury, he knew that he was dying. He summoned the bishop, who gave him the final sacraments, and he died on 7 March. Those who have turned out for his funeral – Hubert de Burgh conspicuous by his absence – are debating whether or not he was poisoned.*

They are also remembering the story of Longspee's marriage, and perhaps now even comparing it to the famous story of Blondel's song and his search for the missing king. It is impossible to know whether they were aware of the Blondel story by then, or whether they knew the truth behind Richard's discovery – the Christmas espionage by a troubadour – but the chances are that there were those among them who knew both tales. Probably also the death of Richard's last brother was persuasion enough to share them again. They must have pointed out that it was almost exactly twenty-seven years since Richard's unexpected and disastrous

---

*There is some evidence that he was. In 1791 a group of antiquarians opened his tomb and found Longspee dressed in furs and robes that had bleached white with age. Curled up inside his empty skull was a dead rat. The rat was finally given a post-mortem in the twentieth century and was found to have died of arsenic poisoning, possibly an unexpected second victim of Hubert de Burgh.

death. Had he lived, he would have been sixty-eight – perhaps drawing to the end of a successful reign consolidating the empire, though since his father died at fifty-six and his brother John at forty-eight, perhaps even Richard would have succumbed to old age by now.

Various questions must also have occurred to them. How would Europe have been different if Richard had lived? Would the Fourth Crusade have been diverted so successfully to attack Constanti-nople if Richard had been involved? Would he have allowed the unholy cooperation between the Pope and some of Philip's hungriest young aristocrats to launch the Albigensian Crusade against the unique culture of southern France? Would he have used his undoubted strategic genius to see, before anyone else, where these trends were leading?

They would not have been able to provide answers, any more than we can. But they were aware that they were living in a world that had changed out of all recognition since their youth, since those heady days of hope when England had reached into the very bottom of its purse to bring their king home. Something had happened to the world of tolerance, troubadours and tournaments – those underpinnings of the world of chivalry and courtly love – in which they had grown up. Since Richard's release and untimely death, Europe had plunged into an era of brutality – one that subsequent generations would associate most closely with the word 'medieval' – of intolerance, torture and suppression. Some of those present would have approved of the 'pious' spirit of the age, but others of those older relics of the past would look back to the debates, the love songs, the European culture of *fin' amor*, and regret its passing. There may even have been those present who traced its demise to the arrest of the hero of Christendom in 1192.

What had gone wrong? It is true that some of the disasters that struck Europe were the direct result of Richard's arrest. The wars in France had deepened in their bitterness, especially after his death. In 1202 John took twenty-two of his captives from his successful defence Mirebeau castle in Anjou back to Corfe Castle in Dorset and deliberately starved them to death. He also probably murdered his own rival – his admittedly infuriating nephew Arthur of Brittany – by throwing him into the Seine at Rouen during a drunken rage. Others were the result of the emperor's death, as the rival claimants to the throne – Otto, Philip and the child Frederick and their supporters – battled it out in Germany, causing inflation and a succession of despoiled harvests, followed by catastrophic famines. The bodies of those who had starved to death lay in piles in the fields and villages. But some of the disasters were entirely natural or supernatural. The year after Duke Leopold's death, there were disastrous floods in Vienna. And by the River Mosel, a gigantic ghost of a long-forgotten king appeared and warned that the empire faced disasters and misery ahead. The worst hit region of Germany was Thuringia, where the court of the margrave Henry I had been the centre of courtly literature. The attack on courtly culture and music was not yet direct, but that would come too.

But something else was in the air besides war. A new kind of intolerance was beginning to corrode the gentle spirit of the age that had moulded Richard and Blondel. It had been a period when the closest adviser to Alexander III, Pope for twenty-two years, had been a rabbi, and when the doctor of Henry I, King of Castile, had been Jewish. The papal household had been managed by Jews throughout the twelfth century. Since the days of Peter Abelard, Europe's intellectuals had enjoyed their set-piece public debates with Jews, Muslims and heretics alike. But it was not to last.

As so often in history, a renewed spirit of persecution came as people began to project their own loss of innocence on to their children, to imagine that these were uniquely threatened by dark, often sexual, possibly demonic forces within their own society. The first signs of the new brutality emerged during Richard's lifetime as an obsession across Europe with the dangers to children from their own underworld. The first hint of what was to come had been the discovery in a shallow grave in 1144 of the child William of Norwich, almost certainly the victim of a cataleptic fit and buried prematurely by his relatives. When there were reports

of a local Jewish man seen with a sack in the neighbourhood of
the discovery, the story began to circulate that William was the
victim of kidnap and ritual murder by Jews. The story was so
clearly outrageous that local magistrates made strenuous efforts to
protect the Jewish community, but it was too late. Little William
eventually got his own plaque in the cathedral, followed by veneration as a Christian martyr, and he was soon the heart of a new
persecuting cult.

Similar stories began to filter through the consciousness of
Western Europe. In an age when impoverished peasants were still
known to send their unwanted children into the forests to die, it
became convenient to blame the local Jews. There were more
rumours of ritual murders of children in Gloucester in 1168, where
a child called Harold had been murdered and thrown into the
Severn, followed by Blois in 1171, Bury St Edmunds in 1181 and
Bristol in 1183. At the same time, it was increasingly believed
that Jews were sexually voracious – the heart of an international
conspiracy to sacrifice children – and that even leprosy was a sexual
disease that engorged the sexual organs of sufferers and sent them
out wildly in pursuit of the innocent.

But there were other factors at work as well. Increasingly, as the
Church and state began to centralize, their officers saw themselves
as the bastions against the forces of subversion – heretics, Jews and
lepers were interchangeable. They were all in their interconnected
ways symptoms of the Devil working to subvert the Christian
order or, as one cleric put it, 'Islam within'. This was a phrase that
was coming increasingly to be applied to homosexuals, a particular
obsession of the preacher Peter the Chanter from Notre-Dame in
Paris. It was he who revived the myth that homosexuals had died
on the first Christmas night, because the pure revelation of God
on earth had destroyed those who commit crimes against nature.★

★ Twelfth-century jokes imply that homosexual activity was widespread but
tolerated. When St Bernard of Clairvaux threw himself on the body of a dead
boy but failed to revive him, the satirist Walter Map – who particularly disliked
the Cistercians – joked that this was extremely unlucky: monks often threw
themselves on boys, he said, but when they got up again, the boys got up too.

It was no coincidence that people began seeing demons more regularly. Western Europe shivered at the sinfulness of their neighbours.

Lepers became official targets early, as stories spread about their mythical sexual appetite. But by the early fourteenth century, royal agents were torturing and burning lepers to extract confessions of a plot to poison wells all over France – an attempt, as it turned out, to seize the revenues of the leper houses for the royal treasury. In 1179 the Third Lateran Council – a conference of the whole Catholic Church in Rome – removed all the legal rights of lepers, making them legally dead. But even then the Pope had called for tolerance towards Jews 'on the grounds of humanity alone'.

Even that was not to last. In 1199, the year Richard died, Pope Innocent III was demanding that 'no Christian ought to presume . . . wickedly to injure their persons, or with violence to take away their property, or to change the good customs which they have had until now in whatever region they inhabit'. But a new intolerance was institutionalized by his Fourth Lateran Council in 1215. Despite the bitter divisions between bishops supporting different claimants to the imperial throne, they still managed to agree a whole raft of measures that sowed the seeds of intolerance across Christendom. Jews had to wear a horned cap and a distinctive yellow circle on their clothing. Lepers had to carry bells. Prostitutes had to dress with a red cord. Philip Augustus had already outlawed debate on religious matters between Christians and Jews, which had been the very stuff of twelfth-century culture, and this was extended across Europe in 1233.

Europe did not succumb immediately to anti-Semitism. In England, the regency for John's child heir Henry III, led by William the Marshal, refused to follow the instructions from Rome about the Jews.* All over Europe, large sections of the population refused to join in the persecution and in England and France even lobbied

---

*It seems to have been the destiny of the English to chafe against instructions from Rome then, just as they do against those from Brussels now. In fact, the two cities play parallel roles in English history.

the court on their behalf. The famously independent-minded Emperor Frederick II, Henry VI's son, later set up a commission to inquire into the ritual slaughter of children by Jews and found there was absolutely no evidence for it.

But the repression only intensified. In England the Warden Justices of the Jews, set up by Richard and Hubert Walter in 1194, soon disposed of their one Jewish member. John's administration raided the Jewish treasure-houses while insisting that Jews were under royal protection. 'If I give my peace even to a dog, it must be kept inviolate,' he said, rather unconvincingly, in 1203. Hubert Walter saw himself as responsible for protecting them, but when he died in 1205 the floodgates opened and the houses of the richest Jews were confiscated and given to royal favourites. Finally, three generations later, in 1291, Edward I expelled the entire Jewish population of England as the simplest way to avoid his debts.

This rising anti-Semitism was driven partly by their enforced role of moneylenders in the days when the word 'usury' was used to define any lending of money for interest. Rage at bankers and anti-Semitism have always been closely and unnecessarily linked, and the impact of Richard's ransom – when many Jewish bankers were forced to call in their debts, to the misery of those affected – certainly fanned the flames in England and Normandy. Even Leopold of Austria's Jewish mint-master Schlom, charged with the task of turning Richard's ransom into a silver currency, was murdered by fifteen crusaders who happened to be passing through the city. The link between the Jewish community and banking had made many Jewish families extremely wealthy, but it was a dangerous kind of wealth because the whole idea of money and banking remained deeply controversial, and charging interest was still condemned by the Church. It was considered unnatural for money to breed money, when the crops or goods it was based on did not behave in the same way. The close connection between Jews and moneylending was making them increasingly vulnerable, even though many Jewish families did other things and they were far from being the only moneylenders in the market.

★

We should not exaggerate the tolerance of the twelfth century. The European pogroms against the Jews began, after all, with the First Crusade in 1095, and even the open-minded debates could be a nerve-racking experience for the Jewish theologians on the other side. But there were other dangerous shifts as well. The disaster that was overtaking Europe's Jewish communities was mirrored by the suppression of heresy, and of the Cathars in particular. Catharism is said to have begun in the tenth century with a peasant priest called Bogomil who preached that the world was overwhelmingly evil, and the solution was penitence, simplicity and prayer. His followers were expelled from Byzantium in 1110 and wandered Dalmatia and Serbia before reaching Italy and France, their new ideas brought West by returning crusaders. But its origins are mysterious and it may simply have emerged in various different forms spontaneously in Western Europe.

It was a Christian-based religion of peace, non-violence and equality between men and women that also embraced reincarnation. Like the southern Occitan culture that moulded Richard's upbringing and gave birth to courtly love, Cathars particularly venerated St Mary Magdalene as one who turned away from the world and they set great store by purity. Those who reached the highest priestly levels were known as 'perfects' – women as well as men – and they abstained completely, not just from violence but also from sex. Even so, the rising forces of intolerance taught that – like Jews and the lepers – heretics possessed prodigious and unnatural sexual appetites.

Catharism grew rapidly in some of the most socially advanced regions of Europe – the bustling financial centres of Champagne, the trading cities of northern Italy, but also across the Languedoc region of France, with their independent-minded towns, their sexual equality and their tolerant culture of music and *fin' amor*. In turn, Eleanor's and Richard's generations had ignored the Cathars, and had been taught to do so by enlightened churchmen like Peter Lombard, a future Bishop of Paris. We need heresy, he said, 'both because of their teaching, but because they stimulate us as Catholics in our search for the truth and for a proper understanding of everything in the world'. Even so, heretics could expect the same punishments as traitors, and the lands and property of anyone who failed to hunt them down would also be forfeit. It was to be a tempting prospect for landless younger sons of the aristocracy.

The Cathars had established themselves so firmly in the south of France that, in 1165, they were able to hold open public debates with the bishops of Toulouse and Albi. And when a papal mission arrived in Toulouse ten years later, the locals felt safe enough to jeer. By then they were organizing their own network of bishops across the region to deal with their burgeoning congregations. Many of the leading aristocratic women in the south led Cathar religious houses. The court of Raymond VI of Toulouse, briefly Richard's brother-in-law, was a tolerant mix of Cathars, Jews and orthodox Catholics. One contemporary in the city noted that nobody could be arrested 'for reason of adultery, fornication or coitus in any store or house he or she rents, owned or maintained as a residence'. Jews there were allowed to own property and hold public office. In nearby Béziers, the chief magistrate was Jewish. In Narbonne and Nîmes, many of the vineyard owners and most important merchants were Jewish as well. One of Raymond's previous wives, also a relative of Eleanor's, was said to have secretly conducted a Cathar service in the same chapel where the Pope was celebrating mass. At one unforgettable Sunday mass in Albi cathedral, the bishop and chapter found themselves alone and without any congregation at all. For some powerful churchmen, the situation was intolerable.

This was also a period when the centralized Church was turning its back on women again and found the influence of the powerful women behind Cathar society particularly threatening, so the early years of the thirteenth century saw a concerted attempt to win back ground from the Cathars. The new initiative began with a series of public debates led by St Dominic, the founder of the Dominican order of friars. The debates drew audiences of thousands but had little impact, and Raymond of Toulouse consistently refused the instructions from Rome to oppress his own people. It was the beginning of a period of unprecedented brutality.

St Dominic's debates, and the subsequent murder of a papal legate, set the scene for one of the most destructive events of the Middle Ages. A group of ambitious and land-hungry young aristocrats from northern France marched south to suppress the Cathars in a long and brutal struggle known as the Albigensian Crusade. It marked the end of the era of tolerance ushered in a century before by Peter Abelard and the troubadours, culminating in the destruction of Béziers in 1209 by Simon de Montfort, from a noble family just outside Paris – heir through his mother of the earldom of Leicester – and the head of the Cistercian monastic order, Arnold Amaury. As the 'crusaders' stormed into the city, ironically on the feast of St Mary Magdalene – the patron saint of southern culture and tolerance – Amaury was asked how they could tell the heretics from the faithful Catholics. 'Kill them all,' he is supposed to have said. 'God will know his own.' As many as 20,000 men women and children, Catholic and Cathar alike, were slaughtered together, almost 2,000 of them sheltering in churches.

Even in tolerant Toulouse, the White Brotherhood, formed by the local bishop, dressed in dark robes with a large white cross, and marched with torches through the streets at night, attacking the homes of Jews and Cathars. It was the White Brotherhood that sang the Te Deum around the foot of the largest human bonfire of the age, when Amaury and Simon de Montfort burned 400 Cathars from Lavaur on May Day 1211. The leader of the defenders in the city, Aimery of Montréal, had hosted the debates a few years before and was in the town to protect his sister, who was one of the leading Cathar women and one of the most loved and hospitable in Languedoc. Simon had him hanged and had her thrown down a well and stoned to death.

Raymond's dithering leadership and hopeless military skills meant that Occitan culture provided little organized resistance. But his son Raymond VII – Joanna's son and Richard's nephew – was a different animal, returning from the Lateran Council in the winter of 1216 and rallying the Provençal nobles to defend Toulouse against Simon de Montfort. It was then that Simon was finally killed by a stone from a siege engine fired by a band of fighting women. But for all his inheritance of leadership and military flair, Raymond then came up against Richard's niece Blanche of Castile – another granddaughter of Eleanor of Aquitaine – now the widow of Philip's Dauphin and the devoted regent of France in the name of her son, Louis IX, the future crusader St Louis. She watched in Paris as Raymond VII was scourged as part of the agreement to end the Albigensian Crusade. She presided over the agreement whereby Raymond's only daughter was forced to marry one of her brothers-in-law. When Raymond died in 1249, his place as count was therefore taken by one of the uncles of the king of France, and when his daughter died childless forty-two years later, Toulouse and most of Languedoc were ruled directly by the French kingdom.

But in another sense, the crusade was still not over. Village by village, town by town, a new inquisition – organized primarily by Dominicans – rooted out all that remained of Cathar culture over the next century, tearing apart the social fabric, using torture to extract each succeeding series of confessions and denunciations, flushing the last terrified Cathars out of hiding and burning them on the pyres. Repression was now the spirit of the age. In 1233 even the orthodox leaders of the southern Jewish community denounced the followers of the great Jewish philosopher Maimonides to the inquisition as part of their own crusade against heresy.

Mathematicians like Maimonides were increasingly attracting suspicion because their ideas had come from the Arab masters. Arabic numerals were 'infidel knowledge'. Zero was even banned by the Church in 1229, though its vital importance to traders who needed to use it to balance their books while their cargoes were still at sea ensured its survival. It became a kind of underground symbol of the freedom to trade.★

★ The Church was also worried about how easy it was to use zero in fraud. The simple business of adding zero to a figure multiplied it by ten. But the suspicion of 'infidel knowledge' also counted and continued. Even in 1648 the tomb of the great mathematician Pope Sylvester II – the man who had introduced Arabic numerals to Western Europe – was being opened by orders of the Vatican to cleanse it of devils.

Again, it is hard to push this idea of a new intolerance too far. The culmination of the First Crusade at the end of the eleventh century had been the viciously bloody capture of Jerusalem by the Christians and mass slaughter inside what had been a city shared peacefully by three religions. It may have been the uncivilized influence of the crusades – the Church had traditionally tried to reduce violence, even in the twelfth century making great efforts to organize local truces for four days every week – but churchmen now appeared to have been inoculated against the revulsion towards war. The Muslim world, with the humane example of Saladin, clung to a tradition that remained in some ways more tolerant, sometimes amazing those of their Christian opponents on the receiving end of their generosity and superior learning, but there were fewer and fewer exemplars of peaceful thinking. One of the very few was Francis of Assisi, a wealthy eighteen-year-old apprentice merchant and would-be troubadour in the year of Richard's death. His determined poverty and message of peace were accepted by Innocent III, when so many similar movements were condemned, partly because the meeting between the two of them – culminating in the Pope sending Francis off to have a bath – gave the Pontiff obsessive dreams.

Why this extraordinary collapse of the ideals of the Twelfth-century Renaissance? Was it the sheer success of the Cathars? Was it the greed of the nobility, and especially their younger sons – in 1204, after all, most of the Fourth Crusade was diverted to attack the Christian city of Constantinople? Was it – as some historians say – that persecution was a useful means by which the new administrators for the increasingly centralized machineries of state could advance themselves? Was it simply the triumph of the scholars around Lotario de Segni, the future Innocent III, with their vision of a corrupted Christendom rescued by a powerful Church? Or was it perhaps that the corrosive spirit of the crusades would inevitably turn inwards? It was probably all those factors, but still that is not quite enough of an explanation for why the century that gave us some of our great civilizing institutions –

including universities, love songs, trial by jury and the feminizing cult of the Virgin Mary – should have petered out in such a bloodbath.

One reason was undoubtedly a backlash against some of the effects of the new coins circulating down through society and the slow break-up of Europe's feudal ties – the luxuries from all over the known world, the fine clothes worn by urban dwellers of all classes, the widespread irritation at the greed of the monasteries as well as the moneylenders.* It was almost as if money could buy and value anything. The queen of Georgia even tried to bypass the whole business of crusading by offering Saladin 200,000 dinars for the Holy Cross. It was regarded as most unseemly. A century later, Dante would link usury with sodomy in the same circle of hell, both of them associated with unregulated greed. The fastest-growing cities, London, Paris and Vienna, were soon to be condemned by preachers for their association with greed and homosexuality. The emergence of silver coins and moneylending on such a wide scale – spread across Europe by Richard's enormous ransom – was one of the main agents of social change, and there were those among the aristocracy, whose peasants had fled beyond their reach to the freedom of the cities, who bitterly resisted it.

Even more important was the way this newly plentiful supply of silver – some of it from Richard's ransom – fed into a new determination by princes to centralize and regulate their own coinage. Philip Augustus was among the first to close his local mints to promote his own silver coinage from Paris. Richard's silver was soon turning into coins in Austria via the new mint in Vienna. Although the non-silver local tokens and *méreaux* continued to fuel local exchange, minted sometimes by cathedrals or charitable enterprises, the new centralization of power across Europe meant that administrators were intolerant of any kind of money but their own. Over the following century, there was a

---

* The monks of St Swithun's in Winchester grovelled in the mud before the elderly Henry II to complain that their bishop had forbidden three of their customary thirteen dishes a day.

slow withdrawal of local currencies, until some centuries later economists began to share the suspicion of the princes and talk of 'bad money' driving out 'good'. Yet the trouble with silver coins was that they did not tend to circulate to peasants. It was the beginning of the end of the great twelfth-century prosperity.

All this fed into the sense at the beginning of the new century that the Christian world was in decay. The humiliating loss of Jerusalem, the failure of the Third Crusade to win it back and the arrest and accusations against its leader – all seemed to imply that God had turned against Christendom. If God had not seen fit to reward the crusaders with success on his behalf, then maybe there was something deeper wrong with their way of life. Some German contemporaries blamed the failure to recapture Jerusalem on the original sin of Richard's arrest, though it was a sin rather after the fact. It was a further symptom of 'Islam within', and brought with it a growing sense of their own internal imperfections and those of their society. There is no doubt that the shock of Richard's failure to take Jerusalem, and the fragmentation of Christian Europe that resulted from his imprisonment – as well as the pressure that his ransom caused the Jews of England and Normandy – were at least part of the process that was sweeping away the old twelfth-century European culture of tolerance and learning.

As fear and despair spread around Europe in the early years of the thirteenth century, in the face of war, inflation and starvation when the next generation increasingly seemed to be symbols of innocence and hope – then the determination to protect them from what were perceived as predatory Jews, heretics and lepers became all the more pressing. It was a small step from there to the spiritual hysteria behind the Children's Crusade in 1212.*

If Richard had lived, probably the Angevin empire would have survived intact, perhaps linked by a sturdy alliance of princes and

---

*The Children's Crusade was the tragic and bizarre departure of thousands of children from all over northern France and western Germany, aged six upwards, who believed that they could succeed in the liberation of Jerusalem when their parents had failed. Many were turned back on the roads to the south, but many also managed to reach Marseilles and were never seen again.

prelates across northern Europe. Richard's alliance was smashed at
the Battle of Bouvines in 1214, where his old enemy the Bishop
of Beauvais was back in action with his mace. If Richard had been
there, the chances are that the battle would never have taken place,
but if it had, it might have gone the other way.

Would he have seen the Albigensian Crusade for what it was?
Probably not, but he might have perceived the strategic threat it
posed, and it is unlikely to have succeeded without at least his tacit
support. But would the new age of intolerance have been a little
muted as a result? Richard was guilty of his own brand of brutality
– the murder of the Saracen prisoners outside Acre in 1191 – and
it is hard to imagine that he would have stayed so aloof from his
own age. On the other hand, it is difficult to see Richard embracing
the relative puritanism of his French counterpart. There is evidence
that he was planning to settle down closer to Berengaria – the two
of them bought a house together on the Continent – but Richard
would probably have clung to the world of songs, music and
courtly culture that the new age was beginning to frown on, and
if he had done so then others would have too. He was planning
to go back to Palestine. If he had done so, and captured Jerusalem,
perhaps the corrosive sense of collective unworthiness that afflicted
Western Europe might have been dispersed.

Meanwhile, a new generation of musicians was emerging, determined to take the music of people like Bernart de Ventadorn and
Blondel and make it respectable. Within decades, preachers were
beginning to put aside their disapproval of minstrels and use songs
in their sermons. Music was beginning to lose its dangerous,
romantic edge. A manuscript of *trouvère* music in the British
Library, dating from the middle of the thirteenth century, includes
the songs of Blondel and his contemporaries, but some of the
words have been scrubbed out and replaced with religious ones.
Even the troubadours were beginning to find themselves edged
out. Walther von der Vogelweide, the pioneering minnesinger,
did not find favour with Leopold VI of Austria. Under Richard's
nemesis Leopold V, Walther had described Vienna as a 'joyous
court of the muse'; now he was forced to leave.

Blondel's contemporaries also became increasingly respectable. The Chastelain de Coucy, Guy de Ponceaux, joined the Fourth Crusade and died in 1203 on his way – as he believed – to Palestine. Gace Brulé was given a pension by the famously puritanical Philip Augustus, and lived out his old age in exile in Brittany, collaborating with Richard's great-nephew the young Thibaut of Champagne, the leading troubadour of the next generation. Conon de Béthune also joined the Fourth Crusade, negotiating on behalf of the crusaders and deputizing for the new Byzantine emperor, Baldwin of Hainault, in his absence. He died in 1219 or 1220 as the lord of a small region of Turkey. Jehan II, Lord of Nesle, almost certainly not in fact Blondel – though he may have written songs – even joined the Albigensian Crusade.

Andreas Capellanus and Richard's aunt Marie de France – the great romantic writers of the age – both confessed their mistakes at the end of their lives: courtly love had been ungodly and they no longer believed in its tenets. The literature of the Holy Grail disappeared in a generation. There are some suggestions that it had been forbidden. And at the same time, the new intolerance was closing the door to the inspirations behind it – the great resource of learning in the Arab world, and the great Arab and Jewish translations of the classics. The Albigensian Crusade also dispersed some of the troubadours of Languedoc, partly because their aristocratic patrons were Cathar heretics or because they were heretics themselves. 'It is no wonder to me, Rome, if people fall into error,' wrote the Toulouse troubadour Guilhem Figueira, 'for you have plunged the whole world into trouble and war.' The Provençal troubadours who survived adapted to the new spirit, but though their culture continued in new forms in northern France, Germany, Spain and Italy, they were always hankering after their forefathers, who, they believed, still had something new to say. The thirteenth-century Bertran Carbonel from Marseilles was so much part of the new commercial world that he could compare his love for his lady to investment in the hope of profit.

As for Blondel, the facts about the end of his life are even more sparse than those about its beginning. In the song collections written out half a century later in the great libraries of the world, the initial verse of Blondel's Chanson VIII ('De la pluz douce amour') appears in other songs, which is evidence that it had become very famous and familiar. There is a William Blondel recorded as having been given land in England by Richard after his return, but there is nothing else to connect the two names. Blondel de Nesle's great friend Gace Brulé died in Brittany and it may be that he did too, though the references to him in the oldest documents as a 'gentleman of Arras' might imply a retirement there instead. He is generally believed to have lived until 1220, but it is really only tradition that says so. Apart from his songs, and the occasional reference to him in the songs of the next generation, and of course the strange legend that has kept his name alive, Blondel fades out of history.

William the Marshal lay dying throughout April and early May 1219. He was one of the great self-made figures of the age, and regent of England in the name of John's child, Henry III. When he knew he was facing death, he had himself rowed up the Thames to his favourite manor of Caversham next to the river, and lay there for some weeks giving away his goods, slowly divesting himself of his powers, and arranging for his funeral in Westminster Abbey and his burial in the Temple Church in London, where his effigy can still be seen. As he lay in his room just before death, wearing the white cloak of the Templars, he found his mind wandering back to the tournament fields in France in his youth. It was there that he and Henry the Young King had won their reputations and where he would sing carols as he waited to be called into the lists.

'Shall I tell you something extraordinary?' he said to his friend John of Earley, next to his bed. 'I have a great desire to sing.'

'Sire, sing,' said John, 'and throw your heart and mind into it. If it comforts you then it will be well done.'

'Quiet, John, such singing would not be good for me. The people here would think me mad.'

Very reluctantly, beside the bed, where the silk pall from Wales that would cover his coffin lay beside him, his daughter Joan was persuaded to sing instead and, with tears in her eyes, she sang about love. It was a fitting end for one of the most colourful characters of the age of light and *fin' amor*. It was also a final glimpse of his world of culture and openness, where music had the power to find missing kings, and where it could speed regents into the next world.

Epilogue: The Legend of Blondel, Reprise

'O Richard! Oh, my king! The universe abandons you.'

Michel-Jean Sedaine, *Richard Coeur de Lion,* 1784

It is 21 October 1784 and there is a thrilling atmosphere as the waving feathers and rustling skirts, the velvet coats and powdered wigs make their way through the great six pillars at the front of the Comédie-Italienne, one of the most fashionable theatres in Paris. There is nothing quite like the first night of a comic opera by Grétry and Sedaine, and this brand-new theatre – just near the modern Opéra – has the exclusive right to perform comic operas in the heart of the city. Inside the Comédie-Italienne, the chandeliers of candles are reflecting on the mirrors and gilt that cover the green walls of the auditorium. The thirty-two musicians are tuning up and crowding in is a mixture of the gentry and street brawlers of the boulevard des Italiens and rue du Favart, many of them paid by the authors to cheer or by their rivals to hiss.

Samuel Johnson, the great lexicographer, has seven weeks to live. But Mozart is working on the first glimmerings of what will eventually become *The Marriage of Figaro*, the only rival of that whole decade to the operatic extravaganza the audience will witness tonight at the Comédie-Italienne. Schiller is hard at work on some of the most romantic works of German poetry; Goya is experimenting with his first successful paintings. A new romantic age is in the air and will shortly turn the world upside down.

But this opera straddled past and future. Grétry and Sedaine were masters of the comic form, and their masterpiece, *Richard Coeur de Lion* – their most successful collaboration – was both medieval and romantic at the same time. As the curtain rose on the opening night, the fascinated audience could see the stage dominated by Gothic castle walls. They thrilled to the full-scale assault of these in Act 3, but what they brought away with them more than anything else — even more, perhaps, than the romantic story of Richard's imprisonment and rescue by Blondel – were the costumes. The production had dressed the actors not so much in authentic medieval garb, but in what medieval troubadours ought to have worn if they had been practising their art in the eighteenth century. Their plumes and lace were soon afterwards popularized by Queen Marie Antoinette, Grétry's greatest fan, as *'le style troubadour'*.

Sedaine's libretto took the old story to some wild and eccentric places: the opera included a romance between Richard and a foreign princess and another between Blondel and the prison governor's daughter, neither of which has any basis, even in legend. But none of that mattered to the audiences that flocked to see the performances night after night, as they rediscovered the power of the story of Blondel's song for the first time in centuries. What they saw was the same story of love, friendship, loyalty and determination that has haunted people ever since, but they also had a particular interpretation that would guarantee trouble for the opera in Paris in the years ahead.

The audiences cheered the new smokeless lamps used to imitate the rising moon, and the critics adored what they saw. 'The romance song sung by Blondel and King Richard,' said one, 'reminds us of those so sweet and touching melodies that one still finds in our southern provinces like monuments which testify that they were the cradle of our minstrels and troubadours.' They longed for it to be true, retelling it for children, dramatizing it and versifying it constantly over the next decade on both sides of the Channel and in Germany too. But the medium-term outlook for Grétry and Sedaine's masterpiece was not so good. Its gentle royalist sentiment — loyalty to kings — was about to become extremely unfashionable. Nearly three months after the storming of the Bastille, in October 1789, the French royal family joined a celebration which included songs from *Richard Coeur de Lion* — including a performance of Blondel's song from the opera 'O, mon

Roi! L'univers t'abandonne.' When the news of this cosy royal occasion filtered out, and its royal song, rumours began to circulate in Paris that it had constituted a demonstration against the new revolutionary regime – even that the new *tricolore* had been trampled in the orgy of royalist sentiment that Blondel's song had unleashed.

It proved to be a turning point in the relationship between the royal family and the new rulers of France. The new regime banned the opera in 1791 – in fact, it was banned again by the brief revolutionary regimes of 1830 and 1848 – and just three months before the last performance of *Richard*'s first run, King Louis XVI and his family were captured as they tried to escape from the country. Soon those who saw the first night, and who wept over Blondel's efforts on behalf of his king, would reflect that their own king was in prison himself, and had no minstrel to rescue him. Blondel's song had contributed to the series of events that led to the execution of the royal family.

But although the opera itself was banned, the legend did not disappear so easily. Until Grétry and Sedaine, the tale had been the province only of serious historians. Antiquarians like Jean de Notre Dame, the brother of Nostradamus, and those who followed him, treated Blondel's song as historical fact. The French librarian Claude Fauchet, first president of France's mint, published his collection of ancient songs and chronicles in 1581 and explained that the story of Blondel by the Minstrel of Reims was a real, forgotten event. 'When all those who played a role in the [lives of] kings Philip Augustus and Richard Coeur de Lion were gone, nothing was heard any more of Blondel,' he wrote, adding sadly, 'He had been forgotten.'

The first sign that the story was coming back into fashion was the publication in 1705 of Marie-Jeanne L'Héritier de Villandon's anonymous novel, *The Dark Tower*, the source for both versions of the song that Blondel and Richard are supposed to have sung. She understood how to reinject the mythic power into the dry bones of the tale. It was she who moved the events to Linz and added in the romantic twist with blossoming love between Blondel and the jailer's daughter. It was also this book that was used as the source for the Blondel story in the *Bibliotheque Universelle des Romans* in 1776, probably written by the Marquis de Paulmy. His version in turn fell into the hands of the composer André Ernest Modeste Grétry, who exclaimed that 'never was a subject more proper for musical treatment'.

The French Revolution just five years after the first performance of *Richard Coeur de Lion*, and the execution of Grétry's royal admirer, should have nipped the old legend's revival in the bud. When one contemporary writer argued that the Blondel story never really happened, he was proclaimed a revolutionary hero. Yet the story survived in popular culture, because there was another message in Sedaine's plot, along with rescuing royalty, and it chimed in with the first glimmerings of the romantic movement. Richard was portrayed as a noble, poetic figure – an artist king liberated by the power of music. Even in Sedaine's libretto, it is clear that Blondel's achievement was not just about faithfulness and loyalty – though it certainly was that:

> *Un troubadour*
> *Est tout amour,*
> *Fidélité, constance,*
> *Et sans espoir de recompense.*

'And without hope of reward,' sang Blondel, but the opera was not just about the servile business of sacrificing yourself for the good of a king. It was also about the sheer power of music. Sedaine's Richard was a creative force that must be freed. So when the revival of royalty in turn made a revival of the opera possible, it was still remembered with some passion, and *Richard Coeur de Lion* was staged again with enthusiasm in 1806, when Napoleon Bonaparte crowned himself emperor. His empress, Josephine, even adopted *le style troubadour* herself, and it infused French women's clothing with a medieval swagger for a generation, creating a widespread taste for gold bracelets, puffy sleeves, lace veils and outrageous collars.

For the Victorian antiquarians who searched for the real Blondel for the next two generations, the story retained this ambiguity – on the one hand about old-fashioned faithfulness, on the other hand about the power of art and creativity. For the Picardy song-collector Prosper Tarbé in the 1860s, it was a story of friendship as much as anything else between France and England. Tarbé was writing in a period of thawing relations between the old enemies – France was about to suffer the indignities of the Franco-Prussian War – and the love between a French minstrel and an English king was important to him. Perhaps this was why he devoted so much of his time to proving that it was a true story, clinging to the hope that L'Héritier de Villandon's mythical 1308 document – which she claimed to have used to write *The Dark Tower* but which has never come to light – was real. Tarbé imagined Richard and Blondel 'under the sky of Palestine, united together by heart and by mind'.

The twentieth century shifted the emphasis of the story back on to love, as musicians and musicologists began to rediscover the literature and music of the troubadours and *trouvères*. The term 'courtly love' was only coined by Gaston Paris as recently as 1883, and the rediscovery of the Courts of Love fed through into a series of collections of Blondel's songs with long commentaries in French and German – for some reason, the *trouvères* have not appealed so far to English antiquarians. This time there was no expression of regret, as there had been from Fauchet's generation, that the song that Blondel must have sung was missing from the manuscripts.

Manly love, faithfulness, friendship and determination were also what the story meant for the contemporary English children's writers of the early twentieth century. This was the Middle Ages as if they had been written by Lord Baden-Powell. In fact, his classic 1908 *Scouting for Boys* uses Blondel's story as his prime example of self-sacrifice – not just on Blondel's part, but on Richard's too, for leaving 'his kingdom, his family, and everything to go and fight against the enemies of the Christian religion'. The passage appears right next to his 'Knight's Code', which enjoins new scouts to 'be always ready with your armour on, except when you are taking your rest at night'. But inevitably what had seemed to the Edwardians an innocent, though passionate, friendship between minstrel and king became evidence for Richard's homosexuality – an idea first put forward in our own day by the historian J. H. Harvey in 1948 as 'breaking the conspiracy of silence'. The story's loss of innocence, so to speak, is the main reason why Blondel and his song have been dropped from children's literature in recent generations.

But the other romantic meaning behind the story remains, and it is more closely related to themes that Blondel himself might have understood – faithfulness to love itself, and a determination to sing despite the consequences. In Grétry and Sedaine's opera the romantic theme is apparent in the references to Orpheus, who took his lyre into Hades to rescue his wife from the Underworld. 'Impelled by love, Orpheus opened up Hades,' Sedaine has Blondel sing. 'Perhaps the gates of these towers will open to the tones of friendship ' Richard here was not so much a king who has been unjustly imprisoned as an artist whose genius demands his release.★ It was the romantic theme repeated in Byron's *Lament for Tasso* a generation later – that genius must be set free – and which became developed in the Blondel story over the following century. Soon searching for your king became a metaphor for seeking out your own creativity or conscience. For the American poet James Russell Lowell, writing in *Atlantic Monthly* at the height of the American Civil War, the Blondel story was about finding your own nobility in the midst of war, compromise and self-seeking politicians. It was not Blondel's role in rescuing the king that was praised, it was his commitment to values beyond himself and beyond the business of ordinary politics, wrote Lowell:

★ In Blondel's day, 'genius' was simply the Latin for 'daemon', our personal guardian through life, sometimes understood as a psychic animal companion. By the Romantic movement, 'genius' had become our inner creative gift. In a sense, in this story, Blondel was playing the role of Richard's daemon.

Yes, I think I do see: after all's said and sung,
Take this one rule of life and you never will rue it,
'Tis but do your own duty and hold your own tongue,
and Blondel were royal himself, if he knew it!

Later versions of Blondel's song, like this one, more self-consciously refer to the situation they are in. In the middle of the nineteenth century, the Viennese poet Johann Gabriel Seidl, author of what was originally the Austrian national anthem and is now the German one, wrote his own romantic version with the chorus 'Seek in faith and you will find'. This was a neat summary of the Romantic movement's understanding of the meaning of the Blondel legend, and it was later set to music by Robert Schumann:

Peering through the metal railings,
In the pale moonlight's shine,
Stands a minstrel with his zither
Next to Castle Dürrenstein.
He gently tunes it, picks his words,
And then begins to sing, though blind,
His instincts tell him gently:
Seek in faith, and you will find!

King Richard, hero of the East,
Are you lost below the wave?
Must your sword rust in the sea,
Or you decay in a distant grave?
Seeking you down every road,
Your minstrel wanders unresigned,
For instincts tell him gently:
Seek in faith, and you will find!

We can never know for certain what the story of Blondel's song meant to Blondel himself, if indeed he ever knew anything about it. It is a tale so rich in meaning that every generation has understood it slightly differently. They warm to its evocation of faithful friendship, its echo of the Parable of the Lost Coin, but at its heart there still remains the kernel of something else: the idea that creativity and music have their own power – to reveal genius, and disclose secrets and hiding places, and to make the truth clear. It is that ambiguity in its meaning, those conflicting messages about the meaning of greatness and the purpose of life, that perhaps have given it such resonance so many generations later.

Strangely enough, this message – that our duty is to our own inner spark of creativity – would also have been understood by the author of 'Ma joie me semont', who wrote eight centuries ago that his heart urged him to sing 'and I dare not ignore/the wishes of my heart'.

Appendix: Richard's Prison Song – Written in Captivity, Summer 1193

Ja nus hons pris ne di— ra sa rai - son a- droi -te-
mais par con-fort puet il fai - re chan- çon. Mout ai d'a-

ment ; s'en - si com do-lans non ; Honte en a-vront, se por
mis, mais po -vre sont li don.

ma re - an - çon sui ces deus y - vers pris !

No one who is in prison sees his fate
With honesty; for all he feels is sad –
But he can still compose a hopeful song.
I am so rich in friends, but poor in help:
They should be ashamed if, for my ransom,
I lie here one more year.

They know this all too well, my home, my lords,
The English, Norman, Poitevin, Gascon:
I never had a friend who was so poor
That I would leave them in their prison cell.
I do not sing these words to criticize –
Yet I am still in prison here.

The ancient saying I now know too well:
In prison, death: no family nor friends.
Because they leave me here for lack of wealth,
I grieve my fate, but grieve for them still more –

When I am dead, they will have their remorse
If I am too long here.

It's no wonder that my heart is sad
When my own overlord torments my lands.
If he remembered what we both agreed
And held back, knowing what we swore,
You would not see me held in chains so long,
Nor stay in prison here.

They know this well, Tourains and Angevins –
Those youthful gentlemen so strong and rich –
That I am far away, in hostile lands.
They loved me so, but have not loved enough –
There'll be no tournaments held on their fields
While I'm in prison here.

Comrades I loved, and those I still do love,
My lords of Perche and also of Caieux:
Tell them, song, that they have not proved friends.
My heart was never false or vain to them.
But they'll be criminals if they still fight me
While I am lying here

Sister, Countess, your sovereign right
May God preserve, and guard the one I claim
For whom I suffer here.

I do not speak of the lady of Chartres,
The mother of Louis.

Notes and Sources

Prologue: The Legend of Blondel

p. xxvii There are many different versions of even the 'classic' Blondel legend. The story entitled 'Richard and Blondel' in Agnes Grozier Herbertson, *Heroic Legends* (London, 1911), gives perhaps the best Edwardian account. The past half-century has become more wary, though the story was still to be found in its most popular form in the Ladybird children's series in L. Du Garde Peach, *Richard the Lion Heart* (Loughborough, 1965), which points out that 'unfortunately the story is not true'. It rather depends what you mean by 'true'.

p. xxix The manuscripts with Blondel's songs are in the Bürgerbibliotek in Bern (No. 389), the British Library in London (Egerton 274), the Biblioteca Estense in Modena (No. 45 R 4, 4), the Bodleian Library in Oxford (Douce 308), the Bibliothèque de l'Arsenal in Paris (no. 5198), the Bibliothèque Nationale in Paris (Nos. 844-847, 1591, 12 615, 20 050 and 24 406 and nouv. acq. 1050), the Biblioteca Comunale in Siena (H X 36), the Vatican Library (No. 1490) and in Leiden (BPL 2785, fragments). There is a reproduction of 'The Manuscript of the King' (Bibliothèque Nationale No. 844) in Johann Beck, *Les Chansonniers des Troubadours et Trouvères, publiés en facsimile*, Vol. II, Le Manuscrit du Roi (London, Oxford and Philadelphia, 1938).

1: The Courts of Love

By far the most comprehensive modern study of Richard's life and generation is John Gillingham, *Richard I* (Yale, 1999), which is unequivocally on Richard's side in the long academic dispute about whether Richard deserved to overshadow his brother John in traditional history. I have relied heavily on his books, others of which are listed in the Select

Bibliography. For a more traditional view, but from the same standpoint, see Kate Norgate, *Richard the Lionheart* (London, 1924). For the opposite point of view, strongly expressed, see Terry Jones and Alan Ereira, *Medieval Lives* (London, 2004), pp. 228–31.

p. 1 'To leap up on errands . . .': see C. S. Lewis, *The Allegory of Love: A Study in Medieval Tradition* (Oxford, 1936), p. 7.

p. 1 'Were the whole world . . .': see the translation from the *Carmina Burana* in Friedrich Heer, *The Medieval World: Europe 1100–1300*, trans. Janet Sondheimer (London, 1962), p. 154. The *Carmina Burana* includes some of the earliest recorded melodies by the minnesingers: see also translation in Helen Waddell, *The Wandering Scholars* (6th edn, Harmondsworth, 1954), p. 236.

p. 2 The classic account of the feudal system and how it worked is in Paul Vinogradoff, *Cambridge Medieval History*, vol. 3 (Cambridge, 1924), but a more up-to-date version is in S. Reynolds, *Fiefs and Vassals* (Oxford, 1994). The system tended to be more flexible on the Continent at this time – especially in Aquitaine, where the old Roman laws of property still prevailed. The dukes of Normandy managed to claim that Normandy was not a fief and they were not vassals, and it was an argument over his homage to the king of France for Normandy that eventually led John to lose it altogether in 1204. It was Philip Augustus, king of France from 1180, who managed to establish a more unambiguous position for himself as overlord of the lands in what is now France. In this he was building on the propaganda of his grandfather Louis the Fat, who set out the principle that the king was nobody's vassal, because he was a vassal of the long-dead St Denis. On the spread of manorialized agriculture, see R. Bartlett, *The Making of Europe* (London, 1993).

p. 2 'it was openly said . . .': *The Anglo-Saxon Chronicle*, trans. and ed. G. N. Garmonsway (Letchworth, 1953), p. 265.

p. 3 Eleanor of Aquitaine has been very well served by recent biographers: see Amy Kelly, *Eleanor of Aquitaine and the Four Kings* (Harvard and London, 1950); Marion Meade, *Eleanor of Aquitaine: A Biography* (London, 1977); Alison Weir, *Eleanor of Aquitaine, by the Wrath of God, Queen of England* (London, 1999); and, most recently, Douglas Boyd, *Eleanor: April Queen of Aquitaine* (Stroud, 2004).

p. 5 'I give my pride . . .': this was recorded by Giraldus Cambrensis, and there is a discussion of it in Gillingham, *Richard I*, p. 257.

p. 5 'He was bad to all . . .': this comes from the anonymous author of the *Gesta Henrici Secundi*. Alison Weir collects a useful selection of historians' contradictory opinions about Richard: see her *Eleanor of Aquitaine*, pp. 199–201.

p. 5 slightly overweight: the evidence for this comes from the trouble Richard's doctor had extracting the crossbow bolt that eventually killed him from his shoulder in 1199 – see Gillingham, *Richard I*, p. 266n.

p. 5 'While thus almost continually trembling . . .': see Giraldus Cambrensis, *The Topography of Ireland*, ed. J. O'Meara (Harmondsworth, 1982), pp. 195–6.

p. 6 'By the grace of God . . .': Giraldus Cambrensis, *The Autobiography of Giraldus Cambrensis*, trans. and ed. H. E. Butler (London, 1937).

p. 6 William the Marshal: see David Crouch, *William Marshal: Court, Career and Chivalry in the Angevin Empire 1147–1219* (London and New York, 1990).

p. 7 'When two nobles quarrel . . .': see Morris Bishop, *The Penguin Book of the Middle Ages* (Harmondsworth, 1971), p. 88.

p. 9 The Twelfth-century Renaissance: see, for example, Christopher Brooke, *The Twelfth Century Renaissance* (London, 1969); and R. N. Swanson, *The Twelfth Century Renaissance* (Manchester, 1999). The first major work on this subject was C. H. Haskins, *The Renaissance of the Twelfth Century* (Cambridge, Mass., 1927).

p. 9 'Greece had the first renown . . .': see Colin Morris, *The Discovery of the Individual 1050–1200* (London, 1972), p. 50.

p. 9 Peter Abelard: see M. T. Clanchy, *Abelard: A Medieval Life* (Oxford, 1997).

p. 11 Bernard of Clairvaux: see B. James, *St Bernard of Clairvaux* (London, 1957).

p. 13 Peter the Venerable: see Swanson, *The Twelfth Century Renaissance*, pp. 53–4. The scholars in Toledo in Spain, one of the most international and open-minded cities in Europe, were Robert of Chester (English) and Herman of Carinthia (Austrian). 'By his coming': see Waddell, *The Wandering Scholars*, p. 131.

p. 14 'that we may fulfil . . .': see Colin Morris, *The Discovery of the Individual 1050–1200* (London, 1972), p. 144.

p. 15 'God knows that I never wanted . . .': ibid., pp. 116-17.

p. 15 Catharism and women: this was not universal. Some Cathars said that women were entirely the creation of the demiurge and were polluting to any of their so-called *parfaits* (perfects) if they so much as touched them.

p. 16 Black madonnas: see Ean Begg, *The Cult of the Black Virgin* (London and Boston, 1985).

p. 17 Santiago de Compostela guidebook: see Gillingham, *Richard I*, pp. 34–5, taken from J. Viellard, *Le Guide du Pèlerin de Saint-Jacques de Compostelle* (Macon, 1938).

p. 18 Marie de France: the exact identity of the author of the *Lais* has never been discovered, but the consensus is that she was the abbess sister of Henry II and therefore Richard's aunt. See Marie de France, *Lais*, ed. Jean Rychner (Paris, 1973). For Chrétien de Troyes, whose patron was Eleanor's daughter Marie de Champagne, see notes for p. 209.

p. 18 *fin' amor*: see Lewis, *The Allegory of Love*. For a brief introduction, see Pamela Porter, *Courtly Love in Medieval Manuscripts* (London, 2003).

p. 19 Andreas Capellanus: quotation taken from translation by John Jay Parry (New York 1941), p. 29.

p. 19 Courts of Love: there is a continuing dispute about whether Eleanor actually ever saw her daughter Marie of Champagne again after the end of her marriage to Marie's father, Louis VII, let alone presided over the Courts of Love with her – though there is evidence that Marie and Richard were close. For the view that the Courts and Andreas Capellanus's description of their rulings were satirical inventions that never actually took place, see, for example A. Weir, *Eleanor of Aquitaine*, pp. 181–2. For a more equivocal view, see Melrich V. Rosenberg, *Eleanor of Aquitaine: Queen of the Troubadours and of the Courts of Love* (London, 1937). For the view that life imitates art, see John W. Baldwin, *Aristocratic Life in Medieval France: The Romances of Jean Renart and Gerbert de Montreuil, 1190–1230* (Baltimore and London, 2000), p. 265.

p. 22 The evidence is that Occitan culture . . .: see Ruth Harvey, 'Courtly Culture in Medieval Occitania', in Simon Gaunt and Sarah Kay (eds.), *The Troubadours: An Introduction* (Cambridge, 1999), p. 23.

p. 22 Jean Renart: see Christopher Page, *Voices and Instruments of the Middle Ages: Instrumental Practice and Songs in France 1100–13000* (London, 1987), p. 35.

p. 22 Women troubadours: see Tilde Sankovitch, 'The Trobairitz', in Gaunt and Kay (eds.), *The Troubadours*. This particular verse was quoted by Deborah H. Nelson in F. R. P. Akehurst and Judith M. Davis, *A Handbook of the Troubadours* (Berkeley, 1995).

p. 23 Beaucaire festival: see Harvey, 'Courtly Culture in Medieval Occitania', in Gaunt and Kay (eds), *The Troubadours*, p. 12.

p. 23 Mainz festival: see Joachim Bumke, *Courtly Culture, Literature and Society in the High Middle Ages*, trans. Thomas Dunlap (Berkeley, 1991), pp. 203–6.

p. 24 Treviso festival: from Rolandino of Padua, *Muratori*, Book 1, Chapter 13, taken from G. G. Coulton, *Life in the Middle Ages*, Vol. III (Cambridge, 1929), pp. 47–9.

p. 25 since the eighteenth century . . .: see, for example, Paul de Rapin-Thoyras, *History of England* (London, 1732).

p. 25 he used to share a bed . . .: see Chapter 3, p. 55. The story of sharing a bed with Philip Augustus is in Roger of Howden's *Gesta Henrici II et Ricardi I*, ed. William Stubbs (Rolls Series, 1867), Vol. II. The first modern assertion that Richard was bisexual was in J. H. Harvey, *The Plantagenets* (London, 1948, 1967), pp. 65–6. There is a full discussion of the case against Richard's homosexuality in Gillingham, *Richard I*, pp. 263–6.

p. 25 when he was married . . .: this is the story of the hermit's warning and is in Roger of Howden's *Chronica Magistri Rogeri de Hoveden*, ed. William Stubbs (Rolls Series, 1868–71), Vol. III, pp. 288–90.

p. 26 'I am romance . . .': see Baldwin, *Aristocratic Life in Medieval France*, p. 153.

p. 26 Peter the Chanter and the 'sin of Sodom': see John W. Baldwin, *The Language of Sex: Five Voices from Northern France around 1200* (Chicago, 1994), pp. 44–5. It is also true that unnatural sex for Peter the Chanter included masturbation and anything that wasn't in the missionary position.

p. 27 Bertran de Born: see *The Poems of the Troubadour Bertran de Born*, trans. C. W. Wilson (London, 1897).

p. 27 swearing: 'But let your communication be, Yea, yea; Nay, nay: for whatsoever is more than these cometh of evil' (Matthew 5: 37; see also James 5: 12). Equally II Corinthians 2 uses the phrase to refer to someone who is undecided about committing to Christ.

2: *The Age of Light*

Almost nothing has been published about Blondel de Nesle in English, and only a handful of his songs have ever been rendered into English – though there are English versions of many of the most famous troubadour songs. The most up-to-date guide to Blondel scholarship is undoubtedly Yvan G. LePage, *L'Oeuvre Lyrique de Blondel de Nesle* (Paris, 1994), which includes all the songs and has a comprehensive introduction, though I come to a different conclusion about Blondel himself. There is generally very much more in print about the southern troubadours than their northern counterparts, but the best guides to troubadour scholarship are Simon Gaunt and Sarah Kay (eds), *The Troubadours: An Introduction* (Cambridge, 1999); and Christopher Page, *The Owl and the Nightingale: Musical Life and Ideas in Medieval France 1100–1300* (London, 1989). The latter is out of print, but anyone who wants a longer collection of troubadour songs in English might consult Angel Flores (ed.), *An Anthology of Medieval Lyrics* (New York, 1962).

p. 29 'From just before . . .': Hilaire Belloc, *The Old Road* (London, 1904).

p. 29 'My lady is like . . .': see Lepage, *L'Oeuvre Lyrique de Blondel de Nesle*. Translations are revisions by the author unless stated otherwise.

p. 30 Note on the stone used for the Gothic cathedrals: Jean Gimpel, *The Cathedral Builders* (Salisbury, 1983).

p. 31 Note on Buddhism: Friedrich Heer, *The Medieval World: Europe 1100–1300*, trans. Janet Sondheimer (London, 1962), p. 128.

p. 31 Silver coins: for the story of the discovery of silver at Christiansdorf and the implications of that, see Peter Spufford, *Money and Its Use in Medieval Europe* (Cambridge, 1988), pp. 109f.

p. 31 By far the most comprehensive guide to the growth of trade in medieval Europe is Peter Spufford's *Power and Profit: The Merchant in Medieval Europe* (London, 2002).

p. 32 *Renovatio monetae*: see Bernard Lietaer and Stephen M. Belgin, *Of Human Wealth: Beyond Greed and Scarcity* (Boulder, 2004). See also Luca Fantacci, 'Complementary Currencies: A Prospect on Money from a Retrospect on Pre-modern Practices', presented for publication to the *Financial History Review*; and Luca Fantacci, 'Moneta universale e locale', in *Storia della moneta immaginaria* (Venice, 2004).

p. 33 London skeletons: see Robert Lacey and Danny Danzinger, *The Year 1000: What Life was Like at the Turn of the First Millennium* (London, 1999), p. 9. The average London woman in the twelfth century was seven centimetres taller than her Victorian counterpart.

p. 33 Blondel's songs: see note for p. xxix.

p. 34 Blondel's accent: see L. Wiese, *Die Lieder des Blondel* (Dresden, 1904), and Le Page, *L'Oeuvre lyrique de Blondel de Nesle*, pp. 45–7.

p. 34 'clumsy, uncouth and doomed to disappear . . .': see Frederick Tingey, *History, People and Places in the North of France, Picardy and Artois* (Bourne End, 1978).

p. 35 Champagne fairs: see Spufford, *Power and Profit*, pp. 63–4, etc.

p. 35 Bishop of Trier: see Morris Bishop, *The Penguin Book of the Middle Ages* (Harmondsworth, 1971), p. 261.

p. 36 Prosper Tarbé: see his *Les Oeuvres de Blondel de Neele* (Reims, 1862).

p. 37 Nesle as the birthplace: see Wiese, *Die Lieder des Blondel*.

p. 37 Jehan II: see Holger Petersen Dyggve, *Trouvères et protecteurs de trouvères dans les cours seigneuriales de France* (Helsinki, 1942).

p. 38 Nesle town hall: conversation with Pierre Le Roy.

p. 38 Birth date: conversation with Pierre Le Roy. Despite considerable research, I have not been able to track down an original source for the 1155 date, though it is even quoted on CDs of medieval music.

p. 39 Kings employed boys . . . : see Page, *The Owl and the Nightingale*, p. 94.

p. 39 'speak and rhyme well . . .': quoted in Terry Jones and Alan Ereira, *Medieval Lives* (London, 2004), p. 49.

p. 39 The music of the troubadours: see Margaret Switten, 'Music and Versification', in Simon Gaunt and Sarah Kay (eds), *The Troubadours: An Introduction* (Cambridge, 1999), pp. 141f.

p. 40 William IX etc.: see Stephen G. Nichols, 'The Early Troubadours', ibid.

p. 40 'wailing, thin, miserable . . .': Peire d'Alvernha's song reviews thirteen troubadours, none of them politely – it is this song that is the basis for the idea that Bernart de Ventadorn was the son of a kitchen maid. See ibid., pp. 21–2.

p. 40 'Little Hugh . . .': see Ruth Harvey, 'Courtly Culture in Medieval Occitania', ibid., p. 17.

p. 41 loosen their clothing . . .: see Page, *The Owl and the Nightingale*, p. 1. There are nine volumes of parchment in the council library at Douai, composed around 1320 by a Dominican friar as a commentary on the Psalms, which include this description of preparing to perform medieval music: 'For see, a minstrel wishing to play the fiddle takes off his outer clothing, adjusts his inner garments, takes the belt off his tunic, puts down his hood, smoothes down his hair and puts a woollen cap on top of it.'

p. 41 Raimon Vidal's visit to Dalfi d'Alvernhe: see Ruth Harvey, 'Courtly Culture in Medieval Occitania', in Gaunt and Kay (eds), *The Troubadours*, pp. 12–13; also Page, *The Owl and the Nightingale*, pp. 46–51.

p. 41 John of Salisbury: see ibid., p. 4.

p. 42 Diet of Mainz: see note for p. 23.

p. 43 Remembering her face . . .: the second verse from Blondel's Chanson XI, 'L'amours dont sui espris'. See Le Page, *L'Oeuvre de Blondel de Nesle*, pp. 197f.

p. 43 Someone should sing . . .: the first verse of Chanson IV, 'Bien doit chanter'. See ibid., pp. 93f.

p. 43 In the season . . .: the first verse of Blondel's Chanson IX, 'En tous tans ue vente bis'. See ibid., pp. 171f.

p. 45 song 'Ver pacis apperit': see Theodore Karp, entry on Blondel de Nesle in *New Grove Dictionary of Music and Musicians* (London, 1980).

p. 46 Giraut de Borneil was considered the leading troubadour in his lifetime: see Ruth Harvey, 'Courtly Culture in Medieval Occitania', in Gaunt and Kay (eds), *The Troubadours*, p. 16.

p. 46 If Blondel was in Paris . . .: the English tradition constantly returns to the idea that Blondel was a teacher of poetry. Thomas Warton, *History of English Poetry* (London, 1775–81).

p. 46 Arras: see Deborah H. Nelson in F. R. P. Akehurst and Judith M. Davis, *A Handbook of the Troubadours* (Berkeley, 1995).

p. 46 'Gentleman of Arras . . .': see Tarbé, *Les Oeuvres de Blondel de Neele*.

p. 47 'Ma joie me semont': Blondel's Chanson XIV. See LePage, *L'Oeuvre de Blondel de Nesle*, pp. 241–4.

3: Paris and Jerusalem

My main sources for Paris in the 1180s have been the wonderful details in Mildred Prica Bjerken's *Medieval Paris: The Town of Books* (Metuchen, 1973). But Alexander Neckham, Richard's exact contemporary, was also in Paris then, and his reminiscences are also very useful. See Urban Tigner Holmes, Jr, *Daily Living in the Twelfth Century: Based on the Observations of Alexander Neckham in London and Paris* (Madison, 1953). The classic account of the Third Crusade is Sir Stephen Runciman's *A History of the Crusades*, Vol. 3 (Cambridge, 1954), but more recent works give a broader context. See for example, Andrew Wheatfield's *Infidel: The Conflict between Christendom and Islam 683–2002* (London, 2003).

p. 49 'The golden age comes round . . .': see John Gillingham, *Richard I* (Yale, 1999), pp. 107–9. The anthem has been recorded in *Music for a Lion-hearted King: Music to Mark the 800th Anniversary of the Coronation of Richard I of England*, Gothic Voices, director: Christopher Page (Hyperion), 1989.

p. 49 Chastelain de Coucy: from Christopher Page, *The Owl and the Nightingale: Musical Life and Ideas in Medieval France 1100–1300* (London, 1989), p. 27.

p. 49 the kingdom of France: the kings claimed theoretically to be descended from Charlemagne but preferred not to stress the matter, partly because some of their vassals were even more closely related and partly because the Germans claimed to be his successors as emperor. See R. Morrissey, *Charlemagne and France: A Thousand Years of Mythology* (London, 1997), pp. 66–7.

p. 50 'paradise on earth . . .': see Friedrich Heer, *The Medieval World: Europe 1100–1300*, trans. Janet Sondheimer (London, 1974), p. 255.

p. 50 rue saint-Christofle: see Holmes, *Daily Living in the Twelfth Century*, p. 66.

p. 50 stone pavements . . .: the walls and foundations of Philip's new castle on the site of the Louvre have been recently excavated and can be seen, very impressively, underneath the great art gallery.

p. 51 St Louis and the chamber pot: see Morris Bishop, *The Penguin Book of the Middle Ages* (Harmondsworth, 1971), pp. 230–1.

p. 51 'make a crow laugh . . .': see John W. Baldwin, *Aristocractic Life in Medieval France: The Romances of Jean Renart and Gerbert de Montreuil, 1190–1230* (Baltimore and London, 2000), pp. 192–3.

p. 51 beyond the pockets of scholars: there is, however, one intriguing reference in the accounts list of the Paris scholar Gerard of Abbeville, written in the flyleaf of a twelfth-century book, which includes a payment for 'a servant girl and binding'. See R. H. and M. A. Rouse, 'Expenses of a Mid-thirteenth Century Paris Scholar', in L. Smith and B. Ward (eds), *Intellectual Life in the Middle Ages: Essays Presented to Margaret Gibson* (Hambledon Press, 1992), p. 219.

p. 51 pastries: see Holmes, *Daily Living in the Twelfth Century*, p. 80.

p. 52 The student's day: see Bjerken, *Medieval Paris*, pp. 90f.

p. 53 Music teaching in Paris: see Nan Cooke Carpenter, *Music in the Medieval and Renaissance Universities* (Oklahoma, 1958), p. 48.

p. 53 'Well, you won't mind . . .' see Helen Waddell, *The Wandering Scholars* (London, 1927), p. 135.

p. 54 Note about students' graduation: see Bishop, *The Penguin Book of the Middle Ages*, p. 286.

p. 54 Philip Augustus: see J. W. Baldwin, *The Government of Philip Augustus* (Berkeley, 1986), pp. 356–9.

p. 54 Philip's attitude to swearing: see Baldwin, *Aristocratic Life in Medieval France*, p. 201.

p. 55 'Philip so honoured him . . .': see Roger of Howden, *Gesta Henrici II et Ricardi I*, ed. William Stubbs (Rolls Series, 1867), Vol. II, p. 7.

p. 55 *vehementem* . . .: see Ann Trindade, *Berengaria: In Search of Richard the Lionheart's Queen* (Dublin and Portland, 1999), p. 71. This is a useful discussion to balance against the one in Gillingham, *Richard I*, pp. 263–4. Dr Mark Philpott has pointed out to me that Roger of Howden is also quoting I Samuel 18: 1–2 ('. . . that the soul of Jonathan was knit with the soul of David, and Jonathan loved him as his own soul.'), and is making parallels with the story of the passionate friendship between

David and Jonathan. Whether this was because Jonathan was also trying to irritate his father, like Richard, or because of the passion between men isn't so clear; it may have been both. We do not, after all, describe David as 'homosexual' because of his passionate friendship with Jonathan.

p. 56 Battle of the Horns of Hattin: for a popular account, see James Reston Jr, *Warriors of God: Richard the Lionheart and Saladin in the Third Crusade* (London, 2001).

p. 56 Saladin: see Hamilton Gibb, *The Life of Saladin* (Oxford, 1973).

p. 56 Templars: the market is crowded with books about the Templars, ranging from the timidly academic to the wildly apocalyptic. For an introduction that treads a middle way, see Karen Ralls, *The Templars and the Grail: Knights of the Quest* (Wheaton, 2003).

p. 56 The Second Crusade: see Alison Weir, *Eleanor of Aquitaine, by the Wrath of God, Queen of England* (London, 1999), pp. 65–9; and other biographies of Eleanor of Aquitaine for discussion about exactly what happened while she was there and if there is any truth in the rumours about her affair with Raymond of Antioch.

p. 56 Baldwin IV: see Stephen Runciman, *A History of the Crusades*, Vol. 2 (Cambridge, 1952), pp. 436f.

p. 58 *poulains* and life in Outremer: see Joshua Prawer, *The World of the Crusaders* (London, 1972).

p. 60 'I am only the lieutenant . . .': see Reston, *Warriors of God*, p. 124.

p. 63 'I can offer you . . .': H. E. Mayer, *The Crusades* (Oxford, 1988), p. 34.

p. 63 When the disastrous news . . .: the story of Richard's taking of the cross is in Ralph of Diceto, *The Historical Works of Master Ralph of Diceto, Deacon of London*, ed. William Stubbs (Rolls Series, 1876), Vol. II, p. 50; see Gillingham, *Richard I*, p. 87.

p. 64 The Bonmoulins conference: William the Marshal believed that Richard and Philip had stitched up an agreement beforehand, as did Ralph of Diceto. It is not clear what Henry was really up to here. See Kate Norgate, *Richard the Lionheart* (London, 1924), pp. 81–3, for the view that he was actually intending to supplant Richard with John.

p. 64 'Now at last I must believe . . .': from Ralph of Diceto, *The Historical Works of Master Ralph of Diceto, Deacon of London*, Vol. II, p. 58; see Gillingham, *Richard I*, pp. 95–6.

p. 65 'By God's legs, do not kill me . . .': an anecdote of William Marshal's. See *Histoire de Guillaume le Maréchal*, ed. P. Meyer (Paris, 1897–1907), Vol. 3, ll. 8831–50.

p. 65 blood flowed suddenly: the story is in *Gesta Henrici Secundi*.

p. 66 'Thank you, sire . . .': see David Crouch, *William Marshal: Court, Career and Chivalry in the Angevin Empire 1147–1219* (London, 1990).

p. 66 The coronation: there is a detailed description in Roger of Howden's *Gesta Henrici II et Ricardi I*. See Gillingham, *Richard I*, pp. 107–8.

p. 66 The crown jewels and the Empress Matilda: see p. 181.

p. 67 The pogroms against Jews: see Cecil Roth, *A History of the Jews in England* (3rd edn, Oxford, 1964), pp. 19–25.

p. 68 William Longchamp: there was no sense in the twelfth century that someone was 'homosexual' – or, in the case of Longchamp, congenitally predisposed towards boys. He was accused simply of the practice, but then it was becoming common to accuse political opponents of deviant sexual practice, so who knows.

p. 68 'would fight for anything . . .': *Chronicles and Memorials of the Reign of Richard I*, ed. William Stubbs (Rolls Series, 1864).

p. 68 office holders: for details of the payments made by Richard's leading officers, see Gillingham, *Richard I*, pp. 115–18.

p. 69 'I would sell London itself . . .': quoted by Richard of Devizes and William of Newburgh, *Historia Rerum Anglicarum*, ed. R. Howlett (Rolls Series, 1884), Vol. IV, Ch. 5.

p. 69 Mayor of London: see p. 111. This self-government status was confirmed with the help of John.

p. 70 hand of St James: see note for p. 181. The reference to the gold is from C. Coates, *The History and Antiquities of Reading* (London, 1802).

p. 70 Frederick Barbarossa: see the description of his death in Runciman, *History of the Crusades*, Vol. 3, p. 17.

p. 71 fearsome regulations . . .: the regulations appear in Roger of Howden's *Gesta Henrici II et Ricardi I*.

p. 72 the grave of King Arthur: in 1962, the archaeologist Ralegh Radford excavated on the spot where the monks were supposed to have found the tomb. He found that the earth there had been dug to a great depth, that the hole had been filled up again and that the soil included chips of stone from a building dated to about 1190. He also found the rough stone lining of an early grave at the bottom of the hole.

p. 73 the cry of a hawk: see Gillingham, *Richard I*, pp. 130–31.

p. 74 The disagreements in Sicily (and also Excalibur): see Roger of Howden, *Gesta Henrici II et Ricardi I*, Vol. II, pp. 126–38.

p. 74 'in the time it takes . . .': see Gillingham, *Richard I*, p. 135. The quotation is from Ambroise, *L'Estoire de la Guerre Sainte*, trans. M. J. Hubert and J. La Monte (New York, 1941).

p. 75 Berengaria: the classic, but very dated and highly unreliable, account is in Agnes Strickland's *The Lives of the Queens of England from the Norman Conquest*, Vol. I (London, 1840; republished Bath, 1972). See also Trindade, *Berengaria*.

4: Acre

The main sources I used for the Third Crusade were, again, Sir Stephen Runciman's *A History of the Crusades* and John Gillingham's *Richard I* (Yale, 1999). For the period in Cyprus, my main source was G. Jeffery, *Cyprus under an English King in the 12th Century* (Cyprus, 1926), and others listed below. For the atmosphere of twelfth-century Acre I've relied on D. Jacoby's detailed descriptions in 'Crusader Acre in the Thirteenth Century: Urban Layout and Topography', in *Studi Medievali*, Series 3, Vol. 20, 1979, as well as the diverse writings of Joshua Prawer.

p. 77 the Great Seal: Roger of Howden, but see also Lionel Landon, *Itinerary of Richard I* (London, 1935), which has an appendix on the Great Seal, pp. 173f.

p. 77 Isaac Comnenus: the story of Isaac and his daughter, who is not named in any of the chronicles, is told in H. Fichtenau, 'Akkon, Zypern und das Lösegeld für Richard Lowenherz', *Archiv fur Österreichisches Geschichte*, CXXV (Vienna, 1966).

p. 78 Richard's wedding: see Roger of Howden's *Gesta Henrici II et Ricardi I*, ed. William Stubbs (Rolls Series, 1867), Vol. II, pp. 166–7.

p. 78 invasion of Cyprus: the best source is Ralph of Diceto, *The Historical Works of Master Ralph of Diceto, Deacon of London*, ed. William Stubbs (Rolls Series, 1876).

p. 79 'the flower of the world . . .': Ambroise, quoted in Gillingham, *Richard I*, p. 155.

p. 79 'God's own sling . . .': the minstrel Ambroise said that Richard had brought tons of sons to fling at Acre with him from Cyprus. Ibid., p. 160.

p. 80 'when Richard came . . .': quoted in James Reston Jr, *Warriors of God: Richard the Lionheart and Saladin in the Third Crusade* (London, 2001), p. 171.

p. 82 Acre was also a divided city: see Joshua Prawer's 'Crusader Cities', in Harry Miskimin, David Herhily and A. L. Udovitch (eds), *The Medieval City* (Yale and London), 1977, pp. 179ff.

p. 82 sugar cane, bananas, etc.: see Joshua Prawer, *The Latin Kingdom of Jerusalem: European Colonials in the Middle Ages* (London, 1972).

p. 83 And the banks were re-establishing . . .: for the development of medieval moneychanging, see Peter Spufford, *Power and Profit: The Merchant in Medieval Europe* (London, 2002), pp. 38–41.

p. 83 even the priests rented . . .: Jacques de Vitry, quoted in Andrew Wheatcroft, *Infidel: The Conflict between Christendom and Islam 683–2002* (London, 2003), p. 195.

p. 83 appalling translation problems . . .: see Kate Norgate, *Richard the Lionheart* (London, 1924). The full quotation, by Saladin's secretary, was: 'The number of barbaric tongues among these people from the West is outrageous, and outdoes everything that can be imagined Sometimes, when we take a prisoner, we can only communicate with him through a series of interpreters – one translates the Frank's words to another, who translates them again to a third.' The Arabs described anyone in the Christian army as a Frank.

p. 84 Leopold's banner: the main source for this incident is Richard of Devizes, *Chronicon*, ed. and trans. T. Appleby (London, 1963). There is a full discussion of it in Gillingham, *Richard I*, pp. 224–5. For the conversation between them, see also A. W. A. Leeper, *A History of Medieval Austria* (London, 1941), pp. 277–8.

p. 84 'The time limit expired . . .': see Gillingham, *Richard I*, pp. 167–70. Christian contemporaries did not criticize Richard for this wholesale slaughter, but the Arabs were horrified. Briefly, for a month afterwards, Saladin killed any on the Christian side taken captive.

p. 85 'the Muslim world never quite forgot . . .: though this was true, they also respected Richard for his 'judgement, experience, audacity and astuteness'. See C. Hillenbrand, *The Crusades: Islamic Perspectives* (Edinburgh, 1999), p. 336.

p. 85 'Never have we had to face . . .': see John Gillingham, *The Life and Times of Richard I* (London, 1973), p. 121.

p. 86 'elderly laundresses . . .': Ambroise, *L'Estoire de la Guerre Sainte*, ed. Gaston Paris, trans. M. J. Hubert and J. La Monte (New York, 1941).

p. 86 Battle of Arsuf: see Gillingham, *Richard I*, pp. 175–8. For a fuller study of Richard's military tactics, see David Miller, *Richard the Lionheart: The Mighty Crusader* (London, 2003).

p. 87 'a wide path . . .': see Gillingham, *The Life and Times of Richard I*, p. 133.

p. 87 'With God's grace . . .' see Gillingham, *Richard I*, p. 181, quoting Roger of Howden's *Chronica Magistri Rogeri de Hoveden*, ed. William Stubbs (Rolls Series, 1868–71), Vol. III, p. 130.

p. 88 orgiastic drinking sessions . . .: Ambroise's biased account says, 'Those who were present assured us that they danced through the late hours of night, their heads bedecked with flowers, entwined in garland and in crown; beside wine casks they sat down and drank until matins had rung, then homeward made their way among the harlots.' Quoted in Gillingham, *The Life and Times of Richard I*, p. 143.

p. 89 Conrad's assassination: there is a full discussion about the Assassins and who ordered Conrad's death in Gillingham, *Richard I*, pp. 197–201. The French believed that Richard had been behind the death, though a letter from the leader of the Assassins, now believed to have been forged, exonerated him.

p. 89 Saladin and the Assassins: see Gillingham, *The Life and Times of Richard I*, pp. 146–51.

p. 90 'You see the licentiousness . . .': ibid., p. 153.

p. 90 'It is the custom of kings . . .': see Gillingham, *Richard I*, p. 20.

p. 91 'The time has come to stop . . .': ibid., p. 183.

p. 92 'You are the father . . .': the chaplain was William of Poitou. See Gillingham, *The Life and Times of Richard I*, p. 156.

p. 92 The hermit of Beit Nuba: see Norgate, *Richard the Lionheart*, p. 243.

p. 93 Army council decision: the decision not to attack Jerusalem shocked the whole of Europe, with the French blaming Richard, while the English chroniclers – see Roger of Howden – blamed the Duke of Burgundy. See Gillingham, *Richard I*, p. 206.

p. 93 'Do not be deceived . . .': ibid., p. 210.

p. 94 'it was the only thing . . .': quoted in Reston, *Warriors of God*, p. 285.

p. 94 'Are any of them still living . . .': from Ambroise, *L'Estoire de la Guerre Sainte*, Vol. II, ll. 114–26, quoted in Norgate, *Richard the Lionheart*, pp. 249–50.

p. 95 'In every deed . . .': see Reston, *Warriors of God*, p. 296.

p. 95 'This sultan is mighty . . .': Richard's joke was recorded by the Arab chronicler Baha ad-Din and was made to Saladin's chamberlain, Abu Bakr. See Gillingham, *Richard I*, pp. 213–14.

p. 95 'What of the king . . .': Richard de Templo, *Itinerarium Peregrinorum et Gesta Regis Ricardi* in *Chronicles and Memorials of the Reign of Richard I*, ed. W. Stubbs (Rolls Series, 1864), trans. Helen Nicholson as *Chronicle of the Third Crusade* (Ashgate, 1997), p. 366. See Gillingham, *Richard I*, p. 215.

p. 95 'My only object . . .': see Reston, *Warriors of God*, p. 297.

p. 96 Henry promised to arrest him . . .: see Roger of Howden, *Chronica Magistri Rogeri Hoveden*, ed. William Stubbs (Rolls Series, 1868–71), Vol. III, p. 167.

5: Setting Sail

The main source I have used for events in England during Richard's absence is J. T. Appleby, *England without Richard* (London, 1965). The description of Richard's route was constructed from descriptions of twelfth-century seamanship: for example, Robert Gardiner (ed.), *The Age of the Gallery: Mediterranean Oared Vessels since Pre-classical Times* (London, 1975).

p. 97 Gace Brulé song: see Samuel N. Rosenberg, and Samuel Danon, *The Lyrics and Melodies of Gace Brulé* (New York and London, 1985).

p. 97 The story of Regnault: this is from a late-thirteenth-century document called *The Roman du Castelain du Couci*. See Sylvia Huot, 'Troubadour Lyric and old French Narrative', in Simon Gaunt and Sarah Kay (eds), *The Troubadours: An Introduction* (Cambridge, 1999), pp. 274–5.

p. 98 'We who were there . . .': Ambroise, quoted in John Gillingham, *Richard I* (Yale, 1991), p. 4.

p. 99 one in twelve . . .: for a fuller discussion about the army and its casualties, see David Miller, *Richard the Lionheart: The Mighty Crusader* (London, 2003).

p. 100 'At every stage of his journey . . .': see Richard of Devizes, *Chronicon*, ed. and trans. J. T. Appleby (London, 1963).

p. 103 'I have long been aware that your king . . .': this is in Ambroise, *L'Estoire de la Guerre Sainte*, ed. Gaston Paris, trans. M. J. Hubert and J. La Monte (New York, 1941). Gillingham, *Richard I*, pp. 16–17, believes it is an imaginary conversation, but there is some evidence that this was genuinely the opinion of his Arab opponents. It also seems that Ambroise himself was on the same trip, so may well have been there – or at least nearby.

p. 103 Isaac Comnenus' daughter: see note for page 77. See also Ann Trindade, *Berengaria: In Search of Richard the Lionheart's Queen* (Dublin and Portland, 1999), p. 92.

p. 104 one spy slipped aboard . . .: see Bernard le Trésorier, *Le Continuation de Guillaume de Tyr*, ed. M. R. Morgan (Paris, 1982). See also P. W. Edbury, *The Conquest of Jerusalem and the Third Crusade* (Aldershot, 1996).

p. 105 'O, Holy Land . . .': see Richard de Templo, *Itinerarium Peregrinorum et Gesta Regis Ricardi* in *Chronicles and Memorials of the Reign of Richard I*, ed. W. Stubbs, trans. Helen Nicholson as *Chronicle of the Third Crusade* (Ashgate, 1997).

p. 105 John in the English Channel: see G. G. Coulton, *Medieval Panorama: The English Scene from Conquest to Reformation* (New York, 1955) p. 325.

p. 106 'twinkling with a kind of blood-stained light . . .': see William of Newburgh, *Historia Rerum Anglicarum*, ed. R. Howlett (Rolls Series, 1884).

p. 107 'Planting vines, Marshal?': see David Crouch, *William Marshal: Court, Career and Chivalry in the Angevin Empire 1147–1219* (London, 1990), p. 72.

p. 107 'The laity found him . . .': see William of Newburgh, *Historia Rerum Anglicarum*, Book IV, Chapter 5.

p. 109 The arrest of Geoffrey of York: see Ralph of Diceto and Giraldus Cambrensis. See also Appleby, *England without Richard*, pp. 72–3.

p. 110 Hugh of Nonant and the monks: ibid., p. 27.

p. 110 'Let's go to London and buy . . .': ibid., p. 81.

p. 112 'He was as pale . . .': see Richard of Devizes, *Chronicon*, quoted in Amy Kelly, *Eleanor of Aquitaine and the Four Kings* (Harvard and London, 1950), p. 293.

p. 112 Longchamp and the green dress: these stories were taken from a letter by Hugh of Nonant which was reproduced in Roger of Howden's *Gesta Henrici II et Ricardi I*, ed. William Stubbs (Rolls Series, 1867). See the discussion in Gillingham, *Richard I*, p. 228.

p. 114 'All applauded him . . .': see *Annals of Roger de Hoveden*, trans. Henry T. Riley (London, 1853).

p. 114 'It is meet for the servants . . .': see Richard of Devizes, *Chronicon*, p. 420, quoted in Kelly, *Eleanor of Aquitaine and the Four Kings*, p. 296.

p. 115 William Fitzhugh and the Messina agreement: see Gillingham, *Richard I*, pp. 229–30.

p. 116 Eleanor's council meetings: see Roger of Howden, *Gesta Henrici II et Ricardi I*.

p. 116 'The Chancellor fears the threats . . .': see Richard of Devizes, *Chronicon*, p. 434.

p. 117 'wherever she passed . . .': ibid., quoted in Alison Weir, *Eleanor of Aquitaine, by the Wrath of God, Queen of England* (London, 1999), p. 282.

p. 118 Roman military writers . . .: see Gardiner (ed.), *The Age of the Galley*. According to Gillingham, *Richard I*, p. 231, the Pisan authorities forbade sailing after 30 November in the twelfth century.

p. 118 *Franchenef*: see H. E. Mayer, 'A Ghost Ship Called the *Franche Nef*: King Richard I's German Itinerary', *English Historical Review*, February 2000.

p. 118 The capacity of Richard's ships: see Richard W. Unger, *The Ship in the Medieval Economy 600–1600* (London and Montreal, 1980), pp. 123–4.

p. 118 Anchors: see David Jacoby (ed.), *Trade, Commodities and Shipping in the Medieval Mediterranean* (Aldershot, 1997), section XII.

p. 119 'showing the ropes': see Gillian Hutchinson, *Medieval Ships and Shipping* (London, 1994), p. 112.

p. 119 Poseidon and Artemis: see Gardiner (ed.), *The Age of the Galley*, p. 213.

p. 120 regular sailings from Venice: see Jonathan Sumption, *Pilgrimage: An Image of Medieval Religion* (London, 1975), pp. 185f.

p. 120 its historic base at Portsmouth: see John Gillingham, 'Galley Warfare and Portsmouth: The Beginnings of a Royal Navy', in *Thirteenth Century England VI, Proceedings of the Durham Conference 1995*, ed. Michael Prestwich, R. H. Britnell and Robin Frame (Woodbridge, 1997).

p. 121 Saewulf and Richard's route: see Gardiner (ed.), *The Age of the Galley*, pp. 211–15. I am assuming that Richard took the normal fast route used in the twelfth century. It is possible, but very unlikely, that he made a dash via the open sea.

p. 121 'The voyage from Rhodes . . .': Gonzalez de Clavijo in 1403, quoted ibid.

p. 122 the area of limbo: see Weir, *Eleanor of Aquitaine, by the Wrath of God, Queen of England*, pp. 72–3.

p. 122 Corfu: see H. Jervis, *A History of the Island of Corfu and the Republic of the Ionian Islands* (Amsterdam 1852; reprinted 1970).

p. 123 heading for Brindisi: see Roger of Howden, *Chronica Magistri Rogeri Hoveden*, ed. William Stubbs (Rolls Series, 1868–71), Vol. III. p. 194.

p. 125 But where: there is a longer discussion in Gillingham, *Richard I*, p. 231, about Richard's deliberations about where to land.

p. 125 the Straits of Gibraltar: in *Richard the Lionheart* (London, 1924), p. 265, Kate Norgate wonders why he did not go that way, but as John Gillingham says (*Richard I*, p. 231), the knowledge about the currents there and how they affected medieval seafaring has only been available recently.

6: *Disguise*

This is the most obscure chapter when it comes to historical documents. Our knowledge of the events of Richard's journey across central Europe come from two main sources originally. One is the chronicler Ralph of Coggeshall, who seems to have received his information from Richard's chaplain, Anselm, who was actually with him for much of the journey. This description is confirmed by details in other accounts, so seems reliable. The other main source is the letter sent by the Emperor Henry VI to Philip Augustus in Paris, the text of which is in Roger of Howden's *Chronica Magistri Rogeri Hoveden*, ed. William Stubbs (Rolls Series, 1868–71). What I have tried to do is to fill in the gaps by including some of the local legends and German-language documents that do not contradict those sources, and by retracing the journey – or our best guess about which direction Richard went – on the ground. Once again, the most detailed discussion is in John Gillingham, *Richard I* (Yale, 1999).

p. 127 Jean de Joinville: from Norbert Ohler, *The Medieval Traveller*, trans. Caroline Hillier (Suffolk, 1989), p. 45.

p. 128 pirates: see Nigel Cawthorne, *Pirates: Blood and Thunder on the High Seas* (London, 2003).

p. 129 sea battles: see Gillian Hutchinson, *Medieval Ships and Shipping* (London, 1994), p. 146f.

p. 130 alternative accounts: the main account of Richard's battle with the pirates is in Ralph of Coggeshall, *Chronicon Anglicanum*, ed. J. Stevenson (Rolls Series, 1875), and since he is relying on an eyewitness, we probably should believe him. But Roger of Howden describes a simple financial negotiation in *Chronica Magistri Rogeri Hoveden*, Vol. III, p. 185.

p. 131 the number of companions: the main list of these is again in Ralph of Coggeshall's *Chronicon Anglicanum*. Other names become apparent as the story unfolds, though Berlay of Montreuil is mentioned in Lionel Landon, *Itinerary of Richard I* (London, 1935), p. 70.

p. 131 Hubert Walter: see p. 102.

p. 131 medieval galleys: see Robert Gardiner (ed.), *The Age of the Galley: Mediterranean Oared Vessels since Pre-classical Times* (London, 1975). Roger of Howden explained that 'galleys cannot, nor dare not, go by that route [the open sea route from Marseilles to Acre] since, if a storm should arise, they may be swamped with ease, and therefore they ought always to proceed close to land'.

p. 132 'high-necked' and 'Rumanian': from Ralph of Coggeshall, *Chronicon Anglicanum*, p. 53.

p. 132 Lokrum: Richard's landfall on Lokrum is a local tradition in Dubrovnik. The Benedictine monastery was bought in the nineteenth century by the Archduke Maximilian, later assassinated as Emperor of Mexico, and converted into a palace. Kate Norgate calls it Lacroma in her *Richard the Lionheart* (London, 1924), p. 267.

p. 133 Richard considered himself to be a Templar: 'Therefore, I pray you,' he wrote to the Master of the Temple, 'lend me some of your knights and men-at-arms, who will go with me, and when we are far from here, they will conduct me as a brother Templar to my own country': Bernard le Trésorier, p. 249, quoted in Amy Kelly, *Eleanor of Aquitaine and the Four Kings* (Harvard and London, 1950), p. 283.

p. 135 He was making for Saxony: a history written twenty-five years later by an author attached to Baldwin of Béthune's family says this was the intention. See John Gillingham, *Richard I* (Yale, 1999), p. 231.

p. 135 Henry the Lion: see A. L. Poole, *Henry the Lion* (Oxford, 1912).

p. 135 Note on Bertran de Born: the song is quoted in Ruth Harvey, 'Courtly Culture in Medieval Occitania', in Simon Gaunt and Sarah Kay (eds), *The Troubadours: An Introduction* (Cambridge, 1999), p. 8.

p. 136 Pula or Zadar: both Ralph of Coggeshall and Roger of Howden say he landed in Hungary at Zara, though it is not clear – if he did so – why he ended up going so far west. Gillingham, *Richard I*, p. 231, suggests that this is in fact where he planned but failed to land.

p. 137 Aquileia and Tagliamento: for the evidence that he landed between Aquileia and Venice, ibid. William of Newburgh, *Historia Rerum Anglicarum*, ed. R. Howlett (Rolls Series, 1884), confirms that it was on the coast of Istria, which points again towards Trieste. For the Tagliamento, see Gino Vatri, 'Le avventure di Riccardo Cuor de Leone nel Basso Friuli', *La Bassa*, Vol. 46, June 2003.

p. 138 Hugo: the disguise is mentioned in Ralph of Coggeshall, *Chronicon Anglicanum*, p. 54.

p. 138 Gorizia: Ralph of Coggeshall, by far the most reliable witness, says they were heading for Gazara and that this was where they met the count (see below).

p. 138 'It is not Great Britain who will fail . . .': see Norgate, *Richard the Lionheart*, p. 267n.

p. 139 medieval travel: the classic account of the rediscovery of travel is in Hilaire Belloc's *The Old Road* (London, 1904). I have also relied on Ohler, *The Medieval Traveller*. Peter Spufford's *Power and Profit: The Merchant in Medieval Europe* (London, 2002) is a monumental description of trade and transport, though it concentrates on later medieval centuries (see his discussion of medieval roads, pp. 181–7).

p. 140 the importance of bridges: ibid., pp. 176–80.

p. 141 Alpine passes: ibid., pp. 187–91.

p. 141 Emperor Henry IV's crossing: Mary Taylor Simeti, *Travels with a Medieval Queen* (London, 2002), pp. 30–31.

p. 142 the counts of Gorz: the story of Richard's encounter in Gorizia is told by Ralph of Coggeshall but confirmed in German chronicles. See Hermann Wiesflecker, *Die Regesten der Grafen von Görz und Tirol, Pfalzgrafen von Kärnten*, Band 1, 957–1271 (Innsbruck, 1949), pp. 81–2. See also, for the Italian point of view (Gorizia is now in Italy), Sergio Tavano (ed.), *I Goriziani nel Medioevo* (Gorizia, 2001).

p. 144 the direction would have to be Bohemia: see Gillingham, *Richard I*, p. 232.

p. 145 Roger of Argentan: see Ralph of Coggeshall, *Chronicon Anglicanum*, pp. 54–5.

p. 146 The Bavarian chronicler Magnus of Reichersberg: see Gillingham, *Richard I*, p. 232.

p. 147 Val Canale: Aldo Merlo (ed.), *Guida del Friuli*, Vol. VII, *Val Canale* (Udine, 1991).

p. 148 In one inn in Arezzo: see Spufford, *The Power and Profit*, p. 204.

p. 150 the road to Friesach: I am assuming here that Richard and his companions stuck to the most ancient main route through Carinthia.

p. 150 Friesach: this is the town described in the letter from Emperor Henry VI to Philip Augustus. See Roger of Howden, *Chronica Magistri*

Rogeri Hoveden, Vol. III, pp. 185–6. There is a more detailed description of this incident in Norgate, *Richard the Lionheart*. For silver-mining in Friesach at the time, see Peter Spufford, *Money and Its Use in Medieval Europe* (Cambridge, 1988).

p. 150 Friedrich III of Pettau: he is mentioned in the emperor's letter.

p. 151 The road to Vienna: again I have assumed that Richard stuck to the main road.

p. 151 St Colman: see Ohler, *The Medieval Traveller*, p. 71.

p. 151 the great archipelago: the Danube was not then the culverted series of neat rivers it is today at Vienna; the original navigable stream is now the Donaukanal.

p. 152 the tiny village of Erdberg: the site of Richard's arrest was identified as Erdberg by a Bavarian chronicler with ties to Hadmar II (see below). See Gillingham, *Richard I*, p. 232. Ralph of Coggeshall calls it Ganina. For details of the archaeology of Erdberg, see Michaela Müller, *Römische und neuzeitliche Funde aus Wien*, Vol. 3 (Vienna, 2000), pp. 80–82; and Helmut Kretschmer, '800 Jahre Erdberg: Kleinausstellung des Wiener Stadt- und Landesarchiv', *Wiener Geschichtsblätter*, Beiheft 1, 1992, pp. 1–13.

p. 152 where Leopold kept his hounds: the exact location of the capture is not really known, although there is a plaque in the corridor of the house Erdbergstrasse 41 about 'the hunting lodge ("Rüdenhaus") in which Richard I, King of England was captured' – now shared with a sushi bar. When I visited there in 2003, one of the older residents explained to me that they had been taken to see it on a school trip many years before, but told me that the original site was nearer the river. The Dietrichgasse 16 address is given in A. W. A. Leeper, *A History of Medieval Austria* (London, 1941), p. 280n. It is true that the Babenbergs had a hunting lodge in Erdberg, which they also used as a residence from at least the thirteenth century, though the location of the Rüdenhaus at the time was probably not near Erdbergstrasse 41, but in today's block of buildings between Göllner-, Haidinger-, Hagenmüller- and Rüdengasse. This Rüdenhaus was actually one of the oldest and most important buildings in the area. The building, in the shape of a long, four-sided figure, housed the court hunters, the hound masters and hound servants of the sovereign, and was demolished in the 1870s. But most sources suggest that Richard was not captured in such an exclusive house but in a simple inn or hut nearby.

p. 153 the boy in the market: the story is in Ralph of Coggeshall's *Chronicon Anglicanum* and Roger of Howden's *Chronica Magistri Rogeri Hoveden*.

p. 154 Ioldan de la Pumerai: see Thomas Grey, *Scalacronica: A Chronicle of England and Scotland from 1066 to 1362*, trans. Herbert Maxwell (Glasgow, 1907), p. 254. Grey was imprisoned in 1355 in Edinburgh Castle and wrote this history while he was incarcerated.

p. 154 What happened next: Roger of Howden, *Chronica Magistri Rogeri Hoveden*, Vol. III, p. 187, says he was sleeping. French chroniclers emphasize the story about him cooking at the spit, because of his descent to the level of kitchen skivvy. I have followed the account given by Kate Norgate in *Richard the Lionheart*.

p. 154 French chroniclers: see Bradford B. Broughton, *The Legends of Richard I Coeur de Lion: A Study of Sources and Variations to the Year 1600* (The Hague, 1966), pp. 114–15. Otto of St Blaise emphasizes the terrible indignity of the arrest. Other chroniclers, such as Bernard le Trésorier and Alberic of Three Fountains, also mention the kitchen disguise.

p. 155 Richard handed over his sword: Ralph of Coggeshall, *Chronicon Anglicanum*, pp. 54–5.

p. 155 Leopold V. see Leeper, *A History of Medieval Austria*, p. 275.

p. 156 soldiers with drawn swords. a bitter account of the circumstances of Richard's captivity can be found in Ralph of Diceto, *The Historical Works of Master Ralph of Diceto, Deacon of London*, ed. William Stubbs (Rolls Series, 1876), Vol. II, p. 106.

p. 156 medieval Vienna: see the various works of Reinhard Pohanka in particular – for example, *Hinter den Mauern der Stadt – Eine Reise ins mittelalterliche Wien* (Vienna, 1987).

p. 157 Berengaria and the jewels: see Agnes Strickland, *The Lives of the Queens of England from the Norman Conquest*, Vol. I (London, 1840; republished Bath, 1972).

p. 157 Berengaria's loan in Rome: see Ann Trindade, *Berengaria: In Search of Richard the Lionheart's Queen* (Dublin and Portland, 1999), pp. 110–11.

7: Blondel's Song

The proposition that the legend of Blondel is a distant memory of medieval intelligence is mine, but the best source of information about this area is probably J. O. Prestwich, 'Military Intelligence under the Norman and Angevin Kings', in George Garrett and John Hudson (eds), *Law and Government in Medieval England and Normandy* (Cambridge, 1994). An invaluable source for the details of dates and places is Lionel Landon, *Itinerary of Richard I* (London, 1935).

p. 158 the Northern Lights: see William of Newburgh, *Historia Rerum Anglicarum*, ed. R. Howlett (Rolls Series, 1884), Book IV, p. 616.

p. 159 his extraordinary sense of balance . . .: see note for p. 187.

p. 160 The Kuenrings: the family was the subject of a major exhibition, mainly dealing with later generations, in Vienna in 1980. The catalogue includes some information about Hadmar II: Herwig Wolfram, Karl Brunner and Gottfried Stangler, *Die Kuenringer: Das Werden des Landes Niederösterreich* (Vienna, 1981).

p. 160 Dürnstein: see Fritz Dworschak and Willi Schwengler (eds), *Dürnstein* (Dürnstein, 1966).

p. 161 The only surviving picture: see Wolfram, Brunner and Stangler, *Die Kuenringer*, Abs 65.

p. 161 They already knew each other: see Dworschak and Schwengler (eds), *Dürnstein*.

p. 161 the north-eastern corner of the castle: there is a useful plan of the castle in Josef Kallbrunner and Oskar Oberwalder, *Dürnstein an der Donau* (Krems, 1910).

p. 161 Christmas: see G. Newcomb, *A History of the Christmas Festival, the New Years and Their Peculiar Customs* (Westminster, 1843).

p. 162 The main meal in the twelfth century: see Morris Bishop, *The Penguin Book of the Middle Ages* (Harmondsworth, 1971), pp. 154–60.

p. 162 it would be an explosive letter: the letter is in Roger of Howden, *Chronica Magistri Rogeri Hoveden*, ed. William Stubbs (Rolls Series, 1868–71).

p. 163 Letters: the details of when and where these letters were sent are in Landon, *Itinerary of Richard I*, pp. 71–2.

p. 164 Longchamp: see Douglas Boyd, *Eleanor: April Queen of Aquitaine* (Stroud, 2004), p. 287.

p. 164 Walter of Coutances: see John Gillingham, *Richard I* (Yale, 1999), p. 236.

p. 164 'They are savages . . .': Ralph of Diceto, *The Historical Works of Master Ralph of Diceto, Deacon of London*, ed. William Stubbs (Rolls Series, 1876), Vol. II, p. 106.

p. 164 Even before the emperor's letter: see Landon, *Itinerary of Richard I*, p. 72.

p. 165 a miraculous opportunity: see Gillingham, *Richard I*, p. 234.

p. 166 Having sent their own special emissary: the main source for the political response in England and the dispatch of the abbots is Roger of Howden, *Chronica Magistri Rogeri Hoveden*, Vol. III, p. 198.

p. 167 the Minstrel of Reims: I have taken the translation from Robert Levine, *A Thirteenth Century Minstrel's Chronicle* (New York, 1990).

p. 168 *Ancient Chronicles of Flanders*: *Istore et croniques de Flandres*, ed. Mervyn de Lettenhove (Brussels, 1879), p. 74, quoted in Bradford B. Broughton, *The Legends of Richard I Coeur de Lion: A Study of Sources and Variations to the Year 1600* (The Hague, 1966), pp. 125–6.

p. 169 Claude Fauchet: see Prosper Tarbé, *Les Oeuvres de Blondel de Neele* (Reims, 1862).

p. 169 the song: see L. Wiese, *Die Lieder des Blondel* (Dresden, 1904).

p. 169 'Your beauty, lady fair . . .': the source of this was the introduction to Marie-Jeanne L'Héritier de Villandon, *La Tour Ténébreuse et les Jours Lumineux* (Paris, 1705). See Thomas Percy (ed.), *Reliques of Ancient Poetry* (London, 1765).

p. 172 song contests and note about Raimbaut d'Aurenga: see Ruth Harvey, 'Courtly Culture in Medieval Occitania', in Simon Gaunt and Sarah Kay (eds), *The Troubadours: An Introduction* (Cambridge, 1999), p. 20.

p. 173 Guillem de Berguedà: see Catherine Léglu, 'Moral and Satirical Poetry', in Gaunt and Kay (eds.), *The Troubadours*, p. 58.

p. 173 Raymond of Toulouse's war song: see Harvey, 'Courtly Culture in Medieval Occitania', in Gaunt and Kay (eds), *The Troubadours*, p. 21.

p. 173 'When I see in the gardens . . .': Léglu, 'Moral, and Satirical Poetry', in Gaunt and Kay (eds), *The Troubadours*, p. 86.

p. 174 Troubadours were inveigled: see Harvey, 'Courtly Culture in Medieval Occitania', in Gaunt and Kay (eds), *The Troubadours*, p. 9. For their role in the reputation of lords, see Christopher Page, *The Owl and the Nightingale: Musical Life and Ideas in Medieval France 1100–1300* (London, 1989), pp. 43–4.

p. 175 disguised himself as a bedouin: see Gillingham, *Richard I*, pp. 17–18. This was an Arab story, and may say more about their belief in Richard's powers than his actual behaviour. See also J. O. Prestwich in George Garrett and John Hudson (eds), *Law and Government in Medieval England and Normandy* (Cambridge, 1994).

p. 175 Nuncios Regis: Mary C. Hill, *The King's Messengers 1199–1377: A Contribution to the History of the Royal Household* (London, 1961), pp. 11–12.

p. 175 Edward I and John: ibid. pp. 17–18.

p. 176 'Diplomacy and theft . . .': see Richard Deacon, *A History of the British Secret Service* (London, 1969), p. 15.

p. 176 William Longspee and Talbot: see John Thomas Canner, *A History of Chitterne* (private publication, 2002).

p. 177 the Duke of Lothringe (Lorraine) and other stories: Wiese, *Die Lieder des Blondel*. Wiese suggests that the Japanese version was the earliest, and I'm sure he is right.

8: Prison

I have relied on three sources in particular for this chapter. For the negotiations it is John Gillingham's invaluable *Richard I* (Yale, 1999). For the French point of view, and especially the saga of Philip's marriage, it is Jim Bradbury's *Philip Augustus, King of France 1180–1223* (London, 1998). For the legends of Richard's imprisonment, the best source is Bradford B. Broughton, *The Legends of Richard I Coeur de Lion: A Study of Sources and Variations to the year 1600* (The Hague, 1966).

p. 180 Barbarossa's letter: see James Reston Jr, *Warriors of God: Richard the Lionheart and Saladin in the Third Crusade* (London, 2001), p. 115.

p. 180 Chronicle of Melrose: see Broughton, *The Legends of Richard I Coeur de Lion*, p. 113.

p. 180 Emperor Henry VI: see Peter Csendes, *Geschichte Wiens* (Vienna, 1981).

p. 181 Mary Magdalene's finger: see Jonathan Sumption, *Pilgrimage: An Image of Medieval Religion* (London, 1975), p. 35.

p. 181 The hand of St James and Matilda's jewels: see K. J. Leyser, 'Frederick Barbarossa, Henry II and the Hand of St James', *English Historical Review*, Vol. CCCLVI, July, 1975.

p. 183 Leopold and Henry agreed: see Gillingham, *Richard I*, pp. 234–5; and Lionel Landon, *Itinerary of Richard I* (London, 1935), pp. 72–3. The implication of the crossbowmen and knights was that Henry was treating Richard like a vassal.

p. 185 Duel between the archbishops: see Joachim Bumke, *Courtly Culture, Literature and Society in the High Middle Ages*, trans. Thomas Dunlap (Berkeley, 1991), pp. 183–5.

p. 186 the trial of Speyer: see Ralph of Coggeshall, *Chronicon Anglicanum*, ed. J. Stevenson (Rolls Series, 1875), pp. 59–60; and Ralph of Diceto, *The Historical Works of Master Ralph of Diceto, Deacon of London*, ed. William Stubbs (Rolls Series, 1876), Vol. II, p. 114.

p. 186 He had plotted to kill Conrad: see Gillingham, *Richard I*, p. 237. The key Austrian chronicle, the *Marbach Annals*, does not mention the assassination, so it may be that this was not put to him after all.

p. 186 'I know nothing . . .': this is from a letter Richard wrote to Henry, but it seems likely that it is also what he said in court. See James O'Halliwell-Phillipps, *Letters of the Kings of England* (London, 1848), Vol. I, pp. 7–9.

p. 186 'is foreign to my character . . .': see J. H. Harvey, *The Plantagenets* (London, 1948), p. 71.

p. 187 'The king of France . . .': ibid., p. 68.

p. 187 William the Breton: see Gillingham, *Richard I*, pp. 237–8.

p. 188 Trifels: see Ralph of Diceto, *The Historical Works of Master Ralph of Diceto, Deacon of London*, Vol. II, pp. 106–7.

p. 189 the intervention of Longchamp: see Gillingham, *Richard I*, p. 239.

p. 190 'so that we may know how far . . .': Richard's letters are in Roger of Howden, *Chronica Magistri Rogeri Hoveden*, ed. William Stubbs (Rolls Series, 1868–71), Vol. III, pp. 208–11.

p. 190 Eleanor and the justiciars: see J. T. Appleby, *England without Richard* (London, 1965), pp. 101f.

p. 191 'My brother John is not the man . . .': see Gillingham, *Richard I*, p. 236.

p. 192 Gisors: ibid., pp. 240–41.

p. 193 Eleanor's letters to the Pope: the longest version of these is in the very dated Agnes Strickland, *The Lives of the Queens of England from the Norman Conquest*, Vol. I (London, 1840; republished Bath, 1972). I have followed the discussion – arguing that Eleanor was involved in their composition – in Alison Weir, *Eleanor of Aquitaine, by the Wrath of God, Queen of England* (London, 1999), pp. 290–99.

p. 195 'Who made the Germans . . .': see Friedrich Heer, *The Medieval World: Europe 1100–1300*, trans Janet Sondheimer (London, 1962), p. 116.

p. 195 'However many times . . .': see Elizabeth Hallam (ed.), *The Plantagenet Chronicles* (New York and London, 2000), p. 228.

p. 196 Bishop of Chester: ibid.

p. 196 'No tribulation . . .': Ralph of Coggeshall, *Chronicon Anglicanum*, p. 58. See also Gillingham, *Richard I*, p. 254.

p. 196 getting his jailers drunk: ibid., p. 257.

p. 196 'scarlet cloth . . .': see J. T. Appleby, *England without Richard* (London, 1965), p. 118.

p. 197 palace at Hagenau: see Bumke, *Courtly Culture, Literature and Society in the High Middle Ages*, p. 118.

p. 197 pie with living birds: for more on food see ibid., pp. 178f.

p. 197 'Lionheart' nickname and legends: see Broughton, *The Legends of Richard I Coeur de Lion*, pp. 115f.

p. 199 'No one who is in prison . . .': see translations in Gillingham, *Richard I*, pp. 42–3; Caroline Bingham, *The Crowned Lions: The Early Plantagenet Kings* (Newton Abbot, 1978), p. 125; Angel Flores (ed.), *An Anthology of Medieval Lyrics* (New York, 1962), p. 114; and Henry Adams, *Mont-Saint-Michel and Chartres* (Boston, 1904), pp. 219–21, which includes the original Old French. There is a recording in *The Cross of Red: Music of Love and War from the Time of the Crusades*, New Orleans Musica da Camera, directed by Milton G. Scheuermann Jr and Thaïs St Julien, Centaur (CRC 2373), 1998. Richard's other surviving song, addressed to the Dauphin of Auvergne, is translated in Appendix I of Harvey, *The Plantagenets*.

p. 200 'Sister, Countess . . .': there is a quite different interpretation of this in Ann Trindade, *Berengaria: In Search of Richard the Lionheart's Queen* (Dublin and Portland, 1999), p. 109, which says the lines mean 'whom I love so much'.

p. 201 'Nothing apart from . . .': see *Chronicles and Memorials of the Reign of Richard I*, ed. W. Stubbs (Rolls Series, 1865), Vol. 2, pp. 362–3.

p. 202 reconvened at Worms: see Gillingham, *Richard I*, pp. 243–4.

p. 203 'Look to yourself . . .': the famous lines are in Roger of Howden, *Chronica Magistri Rogeri Hoveden*, Vol. III, pp. 216–17.

p. 203 treaty signed at Mantes: details of the agreement are in Landon, *Itinerary of Richard I*, pp. 77–8.

p. 204 Philip's marriage: see Bradbury, *Philip Augustus, King of France 1180–1223*. The discussion about whether Philip's repudiation of Ingeborg might have been because of his impotence comes from here.

p. 206 'beautiful in face . . .': ibid.

p. 207 Joanna and Raymond: see Amy Kelly, *Eleanor of Aquitaine and the Four Kings* (Harvard and London, 1950), p. 330. For why this was such a mistake for Joanna, see Trindade, *Berengaria*, pp. 144–5.

9: A King's Ransom

The main sources I used here are J. T. Appleby, *England without Richard* (London, 1965) and Frank Barlow, *The Feudal Kingdom of England 1042–1216* (London, 1961). The best source of information about England's Jewish community and their role in medieval finance, at least as far as the ransom is concerned, is probably Cecil Roth, *A History of the Jews of England* (3rd edn, Oxford, 1964). As for the question of outlaws, I rely largely on Maurice Keen, *Outlaws of Medieval Legend* (rev. edn, London, 2000).

p. 208 Chrétien de Troyes: see Jean Frappier, *Chrétien de Troyes: The Man and His Work*, trans. Raymond J. Cormier (Athens, Ohio, 1982).

p. 208 the Holy Grail and its meaning: see Jessie L. Weston, *From Ritual to Romance* (Cambridge, 1920). For a modern retelling, see Lindsay Clarke, *Parzival and the Stone from Heaven* (London, 2001). The idea of the waste land was brought into the twentieth century by T. S. Eliot's famous poem.

p. 209 Wauchier de Denain: see Jessie L. Weston, *The Legend of Sir Perceval: Studies upon the Origin, Position and Influence on the Arthurian Cycle*, Vol. 1 (London, 1906).

p. 210 siege of John's remaining castle: see Doris M. Stenton (ed.), *The Great Roll of the Pipe for the Fifth Year of the Reign of King Richard the First, Michaelmas 1193* (London, 1927).

p. 211 urgent fortifications: ibid.

p. 212 150,000 silver marks: see Lionel Landon, *Itinerary of Richard I* (London, 1935), p. 78.

p. 213 three times anything the English government had raised: see N. Barratt, 'The English Revenue of Richard I', *English Historical Review*, Vol. 116, 2001, pp. 635-56.

p. 214 families that dominated the business of London: see Timothy B. Baker, *Medieval London* (London, 1970).

p. 214 Exchequer of Ransom: see A. L. Poole, *From Domesday Book to Magna Carta 1087–1216* (Oxford, 1951), pp. 365–6.

p. 215 ransom tax and the exchequer: see David Sinclair, *The Pound: A Biography* (London, 2001), pp. 100–04.

p. 216 Baldwin of Béthune: see *Histoire de Guillaume le Maréchal*, ed. P. Meyer (Paris, 1897–1907), Vol. III, l. 133.

p. 216 William of Newburgh: see Alison Weir, *Eleanor of Aquitaine, by the Wrath of God, Queen of England* (London, 1999), p. 300.

p. 216 since the days of Charlemagne: though not in England – there is no evidence for Jews in England before 1066.

p. 217 Aaron of Lincoln: see Roth, *A History of the Jews of England*, pp. 15–16. On the time it took to collect his debts, see Poole, 1951, *From Domesday Book to Magna Carta 1087–1216*, p. 422.

p. 217 interest rates: see G. G. Coulton, *Medieval Panorama: The English Scene from Conquest to Reformation* (New York, 1955), pp. 331f.

p. 218 escorted the wealthiest Jewish financiers: see Stenton, *The Great Roll of the Pipe for the Fifth Year of the Reign of King Richard the First, Michaelmas 1193*.

p. 219 tally sticks: see Sinclair, *The Pound*, pp. 103–4.

p. 219 inflation: see P. D. A. Harvey, 'The English Inflation of 1180–1220', in *Past & Present*, No. 61, November 1973. There is some disagreement about exactly when inflation began to take hold. See Barratt, 'The

English Revenue of Richard I', pp. 653ff., for the view that inflation was only really taking off in the 1190s.

p. 220 Isaac the Jew and silver coins: see Sinclair, *The Pound*, pp. 108–9.

p. 220 St Paul's Cathedral: see William Benham, *Old St Paul's Cathedral* (London, 1902). The details about activities in St Paul's come from a century or more later, but there is no reason to suggest they did not apply at this time as well, as they did in cathedrals all over Europe. In fact, in 1385 the cathedral authorities were forced to ban playing ball games inside the cathedral because the windows kept getting broken. One of the first things the chapter did when Notre-Dame was completed in Paris was to ban the sale of wine in the nave. See also Ben Weinreb and Christopher Hibbert, *The London Encyclopaedia* (London, 1983), pp. 778–9.

p. 222 hostages: there is a list in Landon, *Itinerary of Richard I*, pp. 82–3.

p. 222 Roger de Tosny: see Landon, *Itinerary of Richard I*, p. 83.

p. 223 the return of Longchamp: see Appleby, *England without Richard*, pp. 114–15.

p. 224 Baldwin Wake: see Kate Norgate, *England under the Angevin Kings* (London, 1887), p. 326n.

p. 224 'The royal officers accelerated . . .': William of Newburgh, *Historia Rerum Anglicarum*, ed. R. Howlett (Rolls Series, 1884), Book IV, p. 615.

p. 225 'I love not man in all the world . . .': see Maurice Keen, *Outlaws of Medieval Legend* (rev. edn, London, 2000), p. 156.

p. 226 'The fury of St Edmund . . .': see Appleby, *England without Richard*, p. 119.

p. 226 'Those children of perdition . . .': quoted in Amy Kelly, *Eleanor of Aquitaine and the Four Kings* (Harvard and London, 1950), p. 310.

p. 226 William FitzOsbert: see Peter Ackroyd, *London: The Biography* (London, 2000), pp. 51f.

p. 227 forests: strictly speaking, 'forest' was a legal and administrative term for the king's own hunting land. The actual forest stretched over a third of England during the reign of Henry II.

p. 228 Eustace the Monk and Fulk Fitzwarin: see Keen, *Outlaws of Medieval Legend*.

p. 228 Robin Hood: see, for example, J. C. Holt, *Robin Hood* (rev. edn,

London, 1989). The earliest rhymes seem to refer to Edward II, but by his reign it was clear that the name 'Robin Hood' was already widely used.

p. 229 'allow no woman . . .': see John Major, *A History of Greater Britain*, trans. and ed. Archibald Constable (Edinburgh, 1892), pp. 156–7.

p. 229 'Hear undernead dis laitl stean . . .': see Keen, *Outlaws of Medieval Legend*, p. 179.

p. 229 Little John: ibid., p. 182.

p. 230 the real Earl of Huntingdon: K. J. Stringer, *Earl David of Huntingdon 1152–1219: A Study in Anglo-Scottish History* (Edinburgh, 1985).

p. 231 the drift of money: see Sinclair, *The Pound*, p. 112.

p. 231 Robert Brito: see John Gillingham, *Richard I* (Yale, 1999), p. 269n.

p. 232 which seems to have raised a meagre £7,000: James H. Ramsay, *A History of the Revenues of the King of England 1066–1399*, Vol. I (Oxford, 1925).

p. 232 forced to use the Domesday Book: Frank Barlow, *The Feudal Kingdom of England 1042–1216* (London, 1961), p. 389.

p. 233 Hubert Walter and the Jews: see Roth, *A History of the Jews of England*.

p. 234 Akeman Street and Eleanor's journey: see under various headings in Weinreb and Hibbert, *The London Encyclopaedia*.

p. 235 in barrel upon barrel of silver coins: see Peter Spufford, *Money and Its Use in Medieval Europe* (Cambridge, 1988), p. 390.

p. 236 for the rest of November: see Gillingham, *Richard I*, pp. 247–8.

p. 236 'Henry by the grace of God . . .': see Roger of Howden, *Chronica Magistri Rogeri Hoveden*, ed. William Stubbs (Rolls Series, 1868–71), Vol. II, p. 227.

p. 237 King of Provence: see discussion in Gillingham, *Richard I*, p. 247.

p. 237 deflationary shock: depending on whom you believe, inflation seems to have been running at a steady 3 per cent a year in England throughout Richard's imprisonment. See Barratt, 'The English Revenue of Richard I', pp. 653f.

p. 237 the vast ransom: for a discussion of the other major payments in silver from England to Germany, see Spufford, *Money and Its Use in Medieval Europe*, pp. 160–62 and 390–91.

p. 238 tally sticks and the fire at Westminster: see account in A. N. Wilson, *The Victorians* (London, 2002), pp. 9–10.

10: *The Return of the King*

Once again, the main source for the return of Richard to England and Normandy is John Gillingham's *Richard I* (Yale, 1999). For the use of the ransom in Austria, see the works on the history of Vienna by Reinhard Pohanka and also A. L. Poole, 'Richard I's Alliances with the German Princes in 1194', in R. W. Hunt, W. A. Pantin and R. W. Southern (eds.), *Studies in Medieval History* (Oxford, 1948).

p. 240 'Venison and fowls . . .': see Helen Child Sargent and George Lyman Kittredge (eds.), *English and Scottish Popular Ballads* (Boston, 1904), quoted in Amy Kelly, *Eleanor of Aquitaine and the Four Kings* (Harvard and London, 1950), p. 322.

p. 240 'Sumer is icomen in . . .': one of the earliest recorded songs in English and dated variously from 1240 onwards. It is the spring carol that is still sung every year from the top of the chapel tower of Magdelen College, Oxford, at dawn on 1 May.

p. 240 Philip and John's letter: Roger of Howden, *Chronica Magistri Rogeri Hoveden*, ed. William Stubbs (Rolls Series, 1868–71), Vol. III, p. 229.

p. 241 The Old Man of the Mountains: Longchamp sent a copy of the letter home to Ralph of Diceto, but, as we have seen, it is generally agreed to have been a forgery.

p. 242 'the eloquence of Nestor . . .': see *Itinerarium Peregrinorum et Gesta Regis Ricardi* in *Chronicles and Memorials of the Reign of Richard I*, ed. William Stubbs and trans. Helen Nicholson as *Chronicle of the Third Crusade* (Ashgate, 1997), p. 143.

p. 242 'The empire, lord emperor . . .': see William of Newburgh, *Historia Rerum Anglicarum*, ed. R. Howlett (Rolls Series, 1884), Book IV, p. 617.

p. 242 Leopold of Austria's role in Richard's release: see A. W. A. Leeper, *A History of Medieval Austria* (London, 1941), p. 281.

p. 242 'anxious and difficult . . .': that was how Walter described them in a letter to Ralph of Diceto. See Ralph of Diceto, *The Historical Works of Master Ralph of Diceto, Deacon of London*, ed. William Stubbs (Rolls Series, 1876), Vol. II, p. 112.

p. 243 details of Richard's homage: see Gillingham, *Richard I*, p. 248n.

p. 243 coronation regalia: see Lionel Landon, *Itinerary of Richard I* (London, 1935), p. 83.

p. 243 the Duke of Gloucester and Emperor Sigismund: see James Bryce, *The Holy Roman Empire* (London, 1874).

p. 243 'worn to a skeleton . . .': see her letters to Celestine, p. 193f.

p. 244 'the staff of my old age . . .': quoted in Alison Weir, *Eleanor of Aquitaine, by the Wrath of God, Queen of England* (London, 1999), p. 322.

p. 244 the emperor changed his mind: William of Newburgh, *Historia Rerum Anglicarum*, Book I, p. 404, quoted in Kelly, *Eleanor of Aquitaine and the Four Kings*, p. 318.

p. 245 mass in Cologne: see Ralph of Diceto, *The Historical Works of Master Ralph of Diceto, Deacon of London*, ed. William Stubbs (Rolls Series, 1876), Vol. II, p. 114. See also Gillingham, *Richard I*, p. 249n.

p. 245 the promised pensions: see Poole, 'Richard I's Alliances with the German Princes in 1194'.

p. 245 naval strategy: see Gillingham, *Richard I*, p. 250.

p. 246 on foot to Canterbury: see Helen C. Bentwich, *History of Sandwich in Kent* (Deal, 1971).

p. 247 'Faster than the winds flew . . .': William of Newburgh, *Historia Rerum Anglicarum*, Book IV, p. 619.

p. 247 London Bridge: see Patricia Pierce, *Old London Bridge* (London, 2001).

p. 248 'For really, if he could have known . . .': William of Newburgh, *Historia Rerum Anglicarum*, Book IV, p. 619.

p. 248 The main source for London at this time is Becket's biographer William FitzStephen: see his *A Description of London*, trans. H. E. Butler, Historical Association Pamphlets, 1954. See also Peter Ackroyd, *London: The Biography* (London, 2002) and Timothy B. Baker, *Medieval London* (London, 1970).

p. 249 'jesters, smooth-skinned lads . . .': Richard of Devizes, *Chronicon*, ed. and trans. J. T. Appleby (London, 1963).

p. 249 carol singing: see Christopher Page, *The Owl and the Nightingale:*

Musical Life and Ideas in Medieval France 1100–1300 (London, 1989), pp. 89f.

p. 250 'Merry England': the phrase was first used by Henry of Huntingdon around 1150. See G. G. Coulton, *Medieval Panorama: The English Scene from Conquest to Reformation* (New York, 1955), p. 65.

p. 250 John's castellan at St Michael's Mount: see Gillingham, *Richard I*, p. 252.

p. 251 Adam de St Edmund: see Landon, *Itinerary of Richard I*, p. 83.

p. 251 David, Earl of Huntingdon: see K. J. Stringer, *Earl David of Huntingdon 1152–1219: A Study in Anglo-Scottish History* (Edinburgh, 1985) , p. 40.

p. 251 'Well, what can you see?': see Gillingham, *Richard I*, p. 269.

p. 252 Robert Brito: ibid., p. 269n.

p. 252 the tournament yobs: see J. T. Appleby, *England without Richard* (London, 1965), p. 169.

p. 253 Hugh of Nonant's death: ibid., p. 214. The malevolence shown towards him by the chroniclers, most of them churchmen or monks, was not so much because of his political intrigues but because of the incident when he put down his own monks in Coventry with the use of armed soldiers, and his often-repeated and derogatory views about monks in general.

p. 253 three lions: see Landon, *Itinerary of Richard I*, pp. 173f. There is a tradition that he took one lion from his mother and one from his father, with the third lion added on his own account, but there is no evidence for this. See J. P. Brooke-Little, *Boutell's Heraldry* (rev. edn, London, 1973), p. 207.

p. 253 crown-wearing ceremony: see Roger of Howden, *Chronica Magistri Rogeri Hoveden*, Vol. III, pp. 247–9.

p. 253 new dockyard: see Gillingham, *Richard I*, pp. 273–4. See also John Gillingham, 'Galley Warfare and Portsmouth: The Beginnings of a Royal Navy', in *Thirteenth Century England VI: Proceedings of the Durham Conference 1995*, ed. Michael Prestwich, R. H. Britnell and Robin Frame (Woodbridge, 1997).

p. 254 'God has come again . . .': see *Histoire de Guillaume le Maréchal*, ed. P. Meyer (Paris, 1897–1907), Vol. 3, ll. 10352ff.

p. 254 if you threw an apple in the air: see Kelly, *Eleanor of Aquitaine and the Four Kings*, p. 324.

p. 254 'Why do you look like that?': see Gillingham, *Richard I*, p. 285 – the story was remembered later by William the Marshal.

p. 255 'He took such a pleasure . . .': see William of Newburgh, *Historia Rerum Anglicarum*, Book V, p. 34.

p. 255 'How is your conscience . . .': see Agnes Strickland, *The Lives of the Queens of England from the Norman Conquest*, Vol. I (London, 1840, republished Bath, 1972), p. 318.

p. 257 'By my head . . .': see Gillingham, *Richard I*, p. 319.

p. 259 paying for the Fourth Crusade: see Peter Spufford, *Money and Its Use in Medieval Europe* (Cambridge, 1988), p. 161.

p. 259 Wiener Neustadt: see Leeper, *A History of Medieval Austria*, p. 279.

p. 260 'Summer has come . . .': see O. Güntter, *Walther von Vogelweide mit einer Auswahl aus Minnesang und Spruchdichtung* (Berlin, 1927).

p. 261 Saladin's death: see Stephen Runciman, *A History of the Crusades* Vol. 3 (Cambridge, 1954), pp. 76–80.

p. 262 Henry the Lion's death: see A. L. Poole, *Henry the Lion* (Oxford, 1912), p. 101.

p. 262 Isaac Comnenus's death: see H. Fichtenau, 'Akkon, Zypern und das Lösegeld für Richard Lowenherz', *Archiv fur Österreichisches Geschichte*, Vol. CXXV (Vienna, 1966).

p. 262 Henry of Champagne's death: see Runciman, *A History of the Crusades*, pp. 93–4.

p. 263 Henry VI's death: see Gillingham, *Richard I*, p. 311.

p. 264 'O splendid deed . . .': this was from the *Annales de Jumièges*, quoted in Gillingham, *Richard I*, p. 312n.

p. 266 'What wrong have I done you . . .': Roger of Howden, *Chronica Magistri Rogeri Hoveden*, Vol. IV, pp. 82–4.

p. 267 Mercadier recaptured Bertrand the crossbowman: another story says that he was sent instead to Richard's sister Joanna, who had him torn apart by horses. But this is unlikely, because Joanna was otherwise engaged at the time (see p. 268).

p. 267 John and Bishop Hugh: see Marion Meade, *Eleanor of Aquitaine: A Biography* (London, 1977), pp. 406–7.

p. 267 'So be it then . . .': quoted in Caroline Bingham, *The Crowned Lions: The Early Plantagenet Kings* (Newton Abbot, 1978), pp. 147–8.

p. 268 Joanna's death: Ann Trindade, *Berengaria: In Search of Richard the Lionheart's Queen* (Dublin and Portland, 1999), p. 144.

p. 268 The Cypriot princess: see Fichtenau, 'Akkon, Zypern und das Lösegeld für Richard Lowenherz'.

p. 269 Eleanor and Blanche of Castile: see Douglas Boyd, *Eleanor: April Queen of Aquitaine* (Stroud, 2004), pp. 325–7.

p. 269 Berengaria's final days: see Trindade, *Berengaria*, pp. 183–9.

p. 269 John's letter to Berengaria: see Strickland, *The Lives of the Queens of England from the Norman Conquest*, p. 324.

p. 270 'Ah! Lord God! . . .': Faidit's most famous song is quoted in English in Gillingham, *Richard I*, p. 333, and, in a different version, in Bingham, *The Crowned Lions*, p. 128.

p. 270 'His valour could no throng . . .': Roger of Howden, quoted in Bradford B. Broughton, *The Legends of Richard I Coeur de Lion: A Study of Sources and Variations to the Year 1600* (The Hague, 1966).

p. 270 Vienna walls and the Ringstrasse: see Leeper, *A History of Medieval Austria*, pp. 282–3. See also *The Times*, 28 November 1928.

11: *The Very Last Day of Chivalry*

The spirit of the new age is made all too apparent by reading any of the various books on the suppression of the Cathars; for example, Stephen O'Shea, *The Perfect Heresy: The Revolutionary Life and Death of the Medieval Cathars* (London, 2000). I have particularly relied on R. I. Moore, *The Formation of a Persecuting Society: Power and Deviance in Western Europe 950–1250* (Oxford, 1987).

p. 272 Otto of St Blaise: see Joachim Bumke, *Courtly Culture, Literature and Society in the High Middle Ages*, trans. Thomas Dunlap (Berkeley, 1991), p. 3.

p. 275 a dead rat: this can still be seen in the Salisbury and South Wiltshire Museum.

p. 277 William of Norwich: see Cecil Roth, *A History of the Jews in England* (3rd edn, Oxford, 1964), p. 9.

p. 278 'Islam within': see Jeffrey Richards, *Sex, Dissidence and Damnation: Minority Groups in the Middle Ages* (London, 1990).

p. 278 Peter the Chanter: see John W. Baldwin, *The Language of Sex: Five Voices from Northern France around 1200* (Chicago, 1994), pp. 44–5.

p. 279 demons: Christopher Page, *The Owl and the Nightingale: Musical Life and Ideas in Medieval France 1100–1300* (London, 1989), p. 184.

p. 279 leprosy as a sexual disease: R. I. Moore, *The Formation of a Persecuting Society: Power and Deviance in Western Europe 950–1250* (Oxford, 1987), p. 63.

p. 279 William the Marshal and the Jews: ibid., p. 44.

p. 280 Frederick II's commission: ibid., p. 38.

p. 280 anti-Semitism and moneylending: ibid., p. 34.

p. 280 Leopold's mint-master: see Peter Csendes, 'Die Babenberger und Wien', *Wiener Geschichtsblätter*, Vol. 31, 1976.

p. 281 'both because of their teaching . . .': see Friedrich Heer, *The Medieval World: Europe 1100–1300*, trans. Janet Sondheimer (London, 1974), p. 145.

p. 282 'For reason of adultery . . .': see Stephen O'Shea, *The Perfect Heresy: The Revolutionary Life and Death of the Medieval Cathars* (London, 2000), p. 52.

p. 282 Sunday mass in Albi: see Morris Bishop, *The Penguin Book of the Middle Ages* (Harmondsworth, 1971), p. 202.

p. 283 'Kill them all . . .': it is not absolutely clear that he actually said this, but it was widely believed. See O'Shea, *The Perfect Heresy*, pp. 84–5.

p. 283 White Brotherhood: ibid., p. 123.

p. 284 Raymond VII was scourged: ibid., p. 189.

p. 285 the Church had traditionally tried to reduce violence . . .: for the development of the concept of Holy War, see Andrew Wheatcroft, *Infidel: The Conflict between Christendom and Islam 683–2002* (London, 2003), pp. 187f. Even St Augustine of Hippo could see occasions where violence was justified.

p. 285 some of our great civilising institutions: it is true that these all had roots further back in history, but it was the twelfth century when they were formalized. Nor, it does have to be said, was the cult of the Virgin necessarily helpful to women, but it was a crack in the overwhelming maleness of religious culture.

p. 286 Dante would link usury with sodomy: see Colin Spencer, *Homo-*

sexuality: A History (London, 1995), p. 114. Ironically, Dante's own family seems to have made their money from usury.

p. 286 money and cities: see Moore, *The Formation of a Persecuting Society*, pp. 104–5.

p. 286 *méreaux* and local currencies: once again, I am grateful to Bernard Lietaer for making some of his thinking, and the latest academic research on the subject of money, available to me. It can be found in Bernard Lietaer and Stephen M. Belgin, *Of Human Wealth: Beyond Greed and Scarcity* (Boulder, 2004). See also Luca Fantacci, 'Complementary Currencies: A Prospect on Money from a Retrospect on Pre-modern Practices', presented for publication to the *Financial History Review*; and Luca Fantacci, 'Moneta Universale e Locale', in *Storia della moneta immaginaria* (Venice, 2004).

p. 288 make it respectable: see R. N. Swanson, *The Twelfth Century Renaissance* (Manchester, 1999), p. 186. The fourteenth century saw the first attempted revival of troubadour music in the annual Jeux Floraux festivals.

p. 289 'It is no wonder to me . . .': quoted by Michael Routledge, 'The Later Troubadours', in Simon Gaunt and Sarah Kay (eds), *The Troubadours: An Introduction* (Cambridge, 1999), p. 107.

p. 289 Bertran Carbonel: ibid., p. 100. The full verse says: 'Like a man who takes a great risk with his money, out of a desire to make a fortune, and manages to put up with the misfortune he has to suffer because of the profit he hopes for, I have done likewise, lady, since I have given you my heart and body . . .'

p. 290 Blondel's Chanson VIII: see L. Wiese, *Die Lieder des Blondel* (Dresden, 1904).

p. 290 William the Marshal's death: see David Crouch, *William Marshal: Court, Career and Chivalry in the Angevin Empire 1147–1219* (London, 1990), pp. 129–32 and 193–4.

p. 291 she sang about love: see Page, *The Owl and the Nightingale*, pp. 105–7.

Postscript: The legend of Blondel, reprise

p. 292 'O Richard!': from Michel-Jean Sedaine, *Richard Coeur de Lion*, 1784 *Théâtre de Sedaine* (Paris, 1878).

p. 292 Grétry and Sedaine: see David Charlton, *Grétry and the Growth of Opera-Comique* (Cambridge, 1986).

p. 293 '*le style troubadour*': see, for example, Alice MacKrell, *An Illustrated History of Fashion* (New York, 1997).

p. 294 Jean de Notre Dame and Claude Fauchet: the development of the story's treatment by French historians is outlined in Prosper Tarbé, *Les Oeuvres de Blondel de Neele* (Reims, 1862).

p. 296 Lord Baden-Powell: see Robert Baden-Powell, *Scouting for Boys: A Handbook for Instruction in Good Citizenship* (new edn, Oxford, 2004).

p. 297 James Russell Lowell: see 'Two Scenes from the Life of Blondel', *Atlantic Monthly*, November 1863, pp. 576–8.

Select Bibliography

Primary sources

Ambroise, *L'Estoire de la Guerre Sainte*, ed. Gaston Paris, trans. M. J. Hubert and J. La Monte (New York, 1941)

Andreas Capellanus, *On Love*, trans. and ed. P. G. Walsh (London, 1982)

Beck, Johann, *Les Chansonniers des Troubadours et Trouvères, publiés en facsimile*, Vol. II 'Le Manuscrit du Roi' (London, Oxford and Philadelphia, 1938)

Bernard le Trésorier, *Le Continuation de Guillaume de Tyr*, ed. M. R. Morgan (Paris, 1982)

Bertran de Born, *The Poems of the Troubadour Bertran de Born*, trans. C. W. Wilson (London, 1897).

Chrétien de Troyes, *Arthurian Romances*, trans. W. W. Kibber (Harmondsworth, 1991)

Chronica de Mailros, ed. J. Stevenson (Edinburgh, 1835)

Die Regesten der Grafen von Görz und Tirol, Pfalzgrafen von Kärnten, Band I, 957–1271, ed. Hermann Wiesflecker (Innsbruck, 1949), pp. 81–2

FitzStephen, William, *A Description of London*, trans. H. E. Butler (Historical Association Pamphlets, 1954).

Gesta Henrici Secundi in *English Historical Documents 1042–1189*, trans. and ed. D. C. Douglas and G. W. Greenaway (London, 1953).

Giraldus Cambrensis, *The Autobiography of Giraldus Cambrensis*, trans. and ed. H. E. Butler (London, 1937)

Histoire de Guillaume le Maréchal, ed. P. Meyer (Paris, 1897–1907)

Istore et Croniques de Flandres, ed. Mervyn de Lettenhove (Brussels, 1879)

Itinerarium Peregrinorum et Gesta Regis Ricardi in *Chronicles and Memorials of the Reign of Richard I*, ed. William Stubbs and trans. Helen Nicholson as *Chronicle of the Third Crusade* (Ashgate, 1997).

Marie de France, *Lais*, ed. Jean Rychner (Paris, 1973)

Ralph of Coggeshall, *Chronicon Anglicanum*, ed. J. Stevenson (Rolls Series, 1875)

Ralph of Diceto, *The Historical Works of Master Ralph of Diceto, Deacon of London*, ed. William Stubbs (Rolls Series, 1876)

Récits d'un ménestrel de Reims, ed. N. de Wailly and trans. E. N. Stone as *Three Old French Chronicles of the Crusades* (Seattle, 1939). Also trans. Robert Levine, *A Thirteenth Century Minstrel's Chronicle* (New York, 1990)

Richard of Devizes, *Chronicon*, ed. and trans. J. T. Appleby (London, 1963)

Roger of Howden, *Chronica Magistri Rogeri de Hoveden*, ed. William Stubbs (Rolls Series, 1868–71)

Roger of Howden, *Gesta Henrici II et Ricardi I*, ed. William Stubbs (Rolls Series, 1867)

William of Malmesbury, *Historia Novella*, ed. K. R. Potter (London, 1955)

William of Newburgh, *Historia Rerum Anglicarum*, ed. R. Howlett (Rolls Series, 1884)

Secondary sources

Ackroyd, Peter, *London: The Biography* (London, 2002)

Akehurst, F. R. P., and Davis, Judith M., *A Handbook of the Troubadours* (Berkeley, 1995)

Allmand, C. T. (ed.), *War, Literature and Politics in the Late Middle Ages* (Liverpool, 1976)

Appleby, J. T., *England without Richard* (London, 1965)

Arnold, Benjamin, *Medieval Germany 500–1300: A Political Interpretation* (Basingstoke, 1997)

Baker, Timothy B., *Medieval London* (London, 1970)

Baldwin, J. W., *The Government of Philip Augustus* (Berkeley, 1986)

Baldwin, John W., *The Language of Sex: Five Voices from Northern France around 1200* (Chicago, 1994)

– *Aristocratic Life in Medieval France: The Romances of Jean Renart and Gerbert de Montreuil, 1190–1230* (Baltimore and London, 2000)

Barber, Richard, *The Devil's Brood: A History of Henry II and His Sons* (London, 1978)

Barlow, Frank, *The Feudal Kingdom of England 1042–1216* (London, 1961)

Barratt, N., 'The English Revenue of Richard I', *English Historical Review*, Vol. 116, 2001, pp. 635–56.

Begg, Ean, *The Cult of the Black Virgin* (London and Boston, 1985)

Bingham, Caroline, *The Crowned Lions: The Early Plantagenet Kings* (Newton Abbot, 1978)

Bishop, Morris, *The Penguin Book of the Middle Ages* (Harmondsworth, 1971)

Bjerken, Mildred Prica, *Medieval Paris: The Town of Books* (Metuchen, 1973)

Boyd, Douglas, *Eleanor: April Queen of Aquitaine* (Stroud, 2004)

Bradbury, Jim, *Philip Augustus, King of France 1180–1223* (London, 1998)

Bridge, Antony, *Richard the Lionheart* (London, 1989)

Brooke, Christopher, *The Twelfth Century Renaissance* (London, 1969)

Broughton, Bradford B., *The Legends of Richard I Coeur de Lion: A Study of Sources and Variations to the Year 1600* (The Hague, 1966)

Bullough, Vern L., and Brundage, James A. (eds), *Handbook of Medieval Sexuality* (New York, 1996)

Bumke, Joachim, *Courtly Culture, Literature and Society in the High Middle Ages*, trans. Thomas Dunlap (Berkeley, 1991)

Burney, Charles, *A General History of Music* (London, 1789)

Byrne, Eugene H., *Genoese Shipping in the 12th and 13th centuries* (Cambridge, Mass., 1930)

Carpenter, Nan Cooke, *Music in the Medieval and Renaissance Universities* (Oklahoma, 1958)

Charlton, David, *Grétry and the Growth of Opera-Comique* (Cambridge, 1986)

Clanchy, M. T., *Abelard: A Medieval Life* (Oxford, 1997)

Coulton, G. G., *Medieval Panorama: The English Scene from Conquest to Reformation* (New York, 1955)

Crosland, Jessie, *William Marshal: The Last Great Feudal Baron* (London, 1962)

Crouch, David, *William Marshal: Court, Career and Chivalry in the Angevin Empire 1147–1219* (London, 1990)

Crowest, Frederick, *The Story of British Music* (London, 1896)

Csendes, Peter, 'Die Babenberger und Wien', *Wiener Geschichtsblätter*, Vol. 31, 1976

– *Geschichte Wiens* (Vienna, 1981)

Deacon, Richard, *A History of the British Secret Service* (London, 1969)

Dworschak, Fritz, and Schwengler, Willi (eds), *Dürnstein* (Dürnstein, 1966)

Dyggve, Holger Petersen, *Trouvères et protecteurs de trouvères dans les cours seigneuriales de France* (Helsinki, 1942)

Edbury, Peter W., *The Kingdom of Cyprus and the Crusades 1191–1374* (Cambridge, 1991)

Edmondstoune, Duncan, *The Story of Minstrelsy* (London, 1907)

Feavearyear, Albert, *The Pound Sterling: A History of English Money* (2nd edn, Oxford, 1963)

Ferrante, Joan M., and Economou, Georges D., *In Pursuit of Perfection: Courtly Love in Medieval Literature* (Port Washington, 1975)

Fichtenau, H., 'Akkon, Zypern und das Lösegeld für Richard Lowenherz', *Archiv fur Österreichisches Geschichte*, Vol. CXXV (Vienna, 1966)

Flores, Angel (ed.), *An Anthology of Medieval Lyrics* (New York, 1962)

Frappier, Jean, *Chrétien de Troyes: The Man and His Work*, trans. Raymond J. Cormier (Athens, Ohio, 1982)

Gardiner, Robert (ed.), *The Age of the Galley: Mediterranean Oared Vessels since Pre-classical Times* (London, 1975)

Garrett, George, and Hudson, John (eds), *Law and Government in Medieval England and Normandy* (Cambridge, 1994)

Gaunt, Simon, and Kay, Sarah (eds), *The Troubadours: An Introduction* (Cambridge, 1999)

Gibb, Hamilton, *The Life of Saladin* (Oxford, 1973)

Gillingham, J. B., *The Kingdom of Germany in the High Middle Ages 900–1200* (London, 1971)

Gillingham, John, *The Life and Times of Richard I* (London, 1973)

– *Richard the Lionheart* (2nd edn, London, 1978)

– *Richard Coeur de Lion: Kingship, Chivalry and War in the Twelfth Century* (London, 1994)

– 'Galley Warfare and Portsmouth: The Beginnings of a Royal Navy', in *Thirteenth Century England VI, Proceedings of the Durham Conference 1995*, ed. Michael Prestwich, R. H. Britnell and Robin Frame (Woodbridge, 1997)

– *Richard I* (Yale, 1999)

– *The English in the Twelfth Century: Imperialism, National Identity and Political Values* (Woodbridge, 2000)

– *The Angevin Empire* (2nd edn, London, 2001)

Gimpel, Jean, *The Cathedral Builders* (Salisbury, 1983)

Hallam, Elizabeth (ed.), *The Plantagenet Chronicles* (New York and London, 2000)

Harvey, J. H., *The Plantagenets* (London, 1948)

Harvey, P. D. A., 'The English Inflation of 1180–1220', *Past & Present*, No. 61, November 1973

Haverkamp, Alfred, *Medieval Germany 1056–1273*, trans. Helga Braun and Richard Mortimer (Oxford, 1988)

Heer, Friedrich, *The Medieval World: Europe 1100–1300*, trans. Janet Sondheimer (London, 1962; paperback edition 1974)

Herbertson, Agnes Grozier, *Heroic Legends* (London, 1911)

Holmes, Urban Tigner, Jr, *Daily Living in the Twelfth Century: Based on the Observations of Alexander Neckham in London and Paris* (Madison, 1953)

Holt, J. C., *Robin Hood* (rev. edn, London, 1989)

Hutchinson, Gillian, *Medieval Ships and Shipping* (London, 1994)

Jacoby, D., 'Crusader Acre in the Thirteenth Century: Urban Layout and Topography', *Studi Medievali*, series 3, Vol. 20, 1979

Jacoby, David (ed.), *Trade, Commodities and Shipping in the Medieval Mediterranean* (Aldershot, 1997)

James, B., *St Bernard of Clairvaux* (London, 1957)

Jeep, John M. (ed.), *Medieval Germany: An Encyclopaedia* (New York, 2001)

Jeffery, G., *Cyprus under an English King in the 12th Century* (Cyprus, 1926)

Jones, Terry, and Ereira, Alan, *Medieval Lives* (London, 2004)

Kallbrunner, Josef, and Oberwalder, Oskar, *Dürnstein an der Donau* (Krems, 1910)

Keen, Maurice, *Outlaws of Medieval Legend* (rev. edn, London, 2000)

Kelly, Amy, *Eleanor of Aquitaine and the Four Kings* (Harvard and London, 1950)

Knight, Stephen, *Robin Hood: A Complete Study of the English Outlaw* (Oxford, 1994)

Landon, Lionel, *Itinerary of Richard I* (London, 1935)

Leeper, A. W. A., *A History of Medieval Austria* (London, 1941)

LePage, Yvan G., *L'Oeuvre Lyrique de Blondel de Nesle* (Paris, 1994)

Lewis, C. S., *The Allegory of Love: A Study in Medieval Tradition* (Oxford, 1936)

– *The Discarded Image: An Introduction to Medieval and Renaissance Literature* (Cambridge, 1967)

Leyser, K. J., 'Frederick Barbarossa, Henry II and the Hand of St James', *English Historical Review*, Vol. CCCLVI, July 1975

– *Medieval Germany and Its Neighbours 900–1250* (London, 1982)

L'Héritier de Villandon, Marie-Jeanne, *La Tour Ténébreuse et Les Jours Lumineux* (Paris, 1705)

Lofts, Norah, *The Lute Player* (London, 1951)

Loxton, Howard, *Pilgrimage to Canterbury* (Newton Abbot, 1978)

Maalouf, A., *The Crusades through Arab Eyes* (London, 1984)

Marshall, Christopher, *Warfare in the Latin East 1192–1291* (Cambridge, 1992)

Marshall, Fred, 'Blondel de Nesle and His Friends: The Early Tradition of Grand Chant reviewed', *New Zealand Journal of French Studies*, Vol. 5, No. 2, November 1984

Mayer, H. E., *The Crusades*, trans. John Gillingham (Oxford, 1988)

– 'A Ghost Ship Called the *Franche Nef*: King Richard I's German Itinerary', *English Historical Review*, February 2000

McGrail, Sean, *The Ship: Rafts, Boats and Ships from Prehistoric Times to the Medieval Era* (London, 1981)

Meade, Marion, *Eleanor of Aquitaine: A Biography* (London, 1977)

Miller, David, *Richard the Lionheart: The Mighty Crusader* (London, 2003)

Miskimin, Harry, Herhily, David, and Udovitch, A. L. (eds), *The Medieval City* (Yale and London, 1977)

Mitchell, Marian, *Berengaria: Enigmatic Queen of England* (Burwash Weald, 1988)

Moore, R. I., *The Formation of a Persecuting Society: Power and Deviance in Western Europe 950–1250* (Oxford, 1987)

Morris, Colin, *The Discovery of the Individual 1050–1200* (London, 1972)

Nelson, Janet L., *Richard Coeur de Lion in History and Myth* (London, 1992)

Newman, William, *Les Seigneurs de Nesle en Picardie: Leurs chartes et leur histoire* (Paris, 1971)

Norgate, Kate, *England under the Angevin Kings* (London, 1887)

– *Richard the Lionheart* (London, 1924)

Ohler, Norbert, *The Medieval Traveller*, trans. Caroline Hillier (Suffolk, 1989)

Oman, Charles, *The Coinage of England* (London, 1910)

O'Shea, Stephen, *The Perfect Heresy: The Revolutionary Life and Death of the Medieval Cathars* (London, 2000)

Page, Christopher, *Voices and Instruments of the Middle Ages: Instrumental Practice and Songs in France 1100–1300* (London, 1987)

– *The Owl and the Nightingale: Musical Life and Ideas in Medieval France 1100–1300* (London, 1989)

Percy, Thomas (ed.), *Reliques of Ancient Poetry* (London, 1765)

Pierce, Patricia, *Old London Bridge* (London, 2001)

Pohanka, Reinhard, *Wien im Mittelalter* (Vienna, 1998)

Poole, A. L., *Henry the Lion* (Oxford, 1912)

– 'Richard I's Alliances with the German Princes in 1194', in R. W. Hunt, W. A. Pantin and R. W. Southern (eds), *Studies in Medieval History* (Oxford, 1948)

– *From Domesday Book to Magna Carta 1087–1216* (Oxford, 1951)

Powicke, Maurice, *The Loss of Normandy 1189–1204: Studies in the History of the Angevin Empire* (Manchester, 1913)

Prawer, Joshua, *The Latin Kingdom of Jerusalem: European Colonials in the Middle Ages* (London, 1972)

– *The World of the Crusaders* (London, 1972)

– *Crusader Institutions* (Oxford, 1980)

Ralls, Karen, *The Templars and the Grail: Knights of the Quest* (Wheaton, 2003)

Ramsay, James H., *The Angevin Empire* (London, 1903)

– *A History of the Revenues of the King of England 1066–1399*, Vol. I (Oxford, 1925)

Reston, James, Jr., *Warriors of God: Richard the Lionheart and Saladin in the Third Crusade* (London, 2001)

Richards, Jeffrey, *Sex, Dissidence and Damnation: Minority Groups in the Middle Ages* (London, 1990)

Richardson, H. J., *The English Jewry under Angevin Kings* (London, 1960)

Richardson, H. G., and Sayles, G. O., *The Governance of Mediaeval England from the Conquest to the Magna Carta* (Edinburgh, 1963)

Rosenberg, Melrich V., *Eleanor of Aquitaine: Queen of the Troubadours and of the Courts of Love* (London, 1937)

Rosenberg, Samuel N., and Tischler, Hans (eds), *Chanter D'estuet: Songs of the Trouvères* (London, 1981)

Roth, Cecil, *A History of the Jews in England* (3rd edn, Oxford, 1964)

Runciman, Stephen, *A History of the Crusades*, Vol. 3 (Cambridge, 1954)

Scott, Walter, *Ivanhoe* (London, 1819)

– *The Talisman* (London, 1825)

Sinclair, David, *The Pound: A Biography* (London, 2001)

Spufford, Peter, *Money and Its Use in Medieval Europe* (Cambridge, 1988)

– *Power and Profit: The Merchant in Medieval Europe* (London, 2002)

Stenton, D. M., 'Norman London: An Essay', *Historical Association Leaflets*, No. 93 (London, 1934)

Stenton, Doris M. (ed.), *The Great Roll of the Pipe for the Fifth Year of the Reign of King Richard the First, Michaelmas 1193* (London, 1927)

Strickland, Agnes, *The Lives of the Queens of England from the Norman Conquest*, Vol. I (London, 1840; republished Bath, 1972)

Sumption, Jonathan, *Pilgrimage: An Image of Medieval Religion* (London, 1975)

Swanson, R. N., *The Twelfth Century Renaissance* (Manchester, 1999)

Tarbé, Prosper, *Les Oeuvres de Blondel de Neele* (Reims, 1862)

Tavano, Sergio (ed.), *I Goriziani nel Medioevo* (Gorizia, 2001)

Thomson, Janice E., *Mercenaries, Pirates and Sovereigns: State-building and Extraterritorial Violence in Early Modern Europe* (Princeton, 1994)

Tischler, Hans (ed.), *Trouveres' Lyrics with Melodies: Complete and Comparative Edition* (Stuttgart, 1997)

Trindade, Ann, *Berengaria: In Search of Richard the Lionheart's Queen* (Dublin and Portland, 1999)

Turner, R. V., and Heuser, R. R., *The Reign of Richard Lionheart* (Harlow, 2000)

Unger, Richard W., *The Ship in the Medieval Economy 600–1600* (London and Montreal, 1980)

Viellard, J., *Le Guide du Pèlerin de Saint-Jacques de Compostelle* (Macon, 1938)

Vincent, Nicholas, *The Holy Blood: King Henry III and the Westminster Blood Relic* (Cambridge, 2001)

Waddell, Helen, *The Wandering Scholars* (London, 1927)

Warren, W. L., *King John* (London, 1961)

Weir, Alison, *Eleanor of Aquitaine, by the Wrath of God, Queen of England* (London, 1999)

Wheatcroft, Andrew, *Infidel: The Conflict between Christendom and Islam 683–2002* (London, 2003)

Wiese, L., *Die Lieder des Blondel* (Dresden, 1904)

Wiesflecker, Hermann, *Die Regesten der Grafen von Görz und Tirol, Pfalzgrafen von Kärnten* (Innsbruck, 1949)

Wilhelm, James J. (ed.), *Lyrics of the Middle Ages: An Anthology* (New York, 1990)

Index